Discourse as Data

Discourse as Data: A Guide for Analysis

This book forms part of a 16-week module (D843 *Discourse Analysis*) which is offered by The Open University Masters in Social Sciences Programme.

The Open University Masters in Social Sciences

The Masters Programme enables students to select from a range of modules to create a programme to suit their own professional or personal development. Students can choose a programme of study leading to an MA in Social Sciences, or may specialize in a particular subject area.

There are study lines leading to:

MA in Cultural and Media Studies

MA in Environment, Policy and Society

MSc in Psychological Research Methods

MSc in Psychology

MA in Social Policy

MA in Social Policy and Criminology.

OU Supported Learning

The Open University's unique, supported open ('distance') learning Masters Programme in Social Sciences is designed to introduce the concepts, approaches, theories and techniques associated with a number of academic areas of study. The MA in Social Sciences programme provides great flexibility. Students study in their own environments, in their own time, anywhere in the European Union. They receive specially prepared course materials, benefit from structured tutorial support throughout all the coursework and assessment assignments, and have the chance to work with other students.

How to apply

If you would like to register for this programme, or simply find out more information, please write for the Masters in Social Sciences prospectus to the Call Centre, PO Box 724, The Open University, Milton Keynes MK7 6ZS, United Kingdom: tel. +44 (0)1908 653231, e-mail ces-gen@open.ac.uk

Alternatively, you may visit the Open University website at http://www.open.ac.uk where you can learn more about the wide range of courses and packs offered at all levels by The Open University.

Discourse as Data

A Guide for Analysis

MARGARET WETHERELL, STEPHANIE TAYLOR
AND SIMEON J. YATES

in association with

The Open University

The Open University, Walton Hall, Milton Keynes, MK7 6AA

© 2001 The Open University

First published in 2001

Sage Publications Ltd
6 Bonhill Street
London, EC2A 4PU

Sage Publications Inc
2455 Teller Road
Thousand Oaks, California 91320

Sage Publications India Pvt Ltd
32, M-Block Market
Greater Kailash – I
New Delhi 110 048

British Library Cataloguing in Publication data

A catalogue record for this book is available from The British Library.
ISBN 0 7619 7157 2 (hardback)
ISBN 0 7619 7158 0 (paperback)

Library of Congress catalog record available

Edited, designed and typeset by The Open University
Printed by Bath Press, Bath

Contents

Contributors

Jean Carabine is a Lecturer in Social Policy at the Open University. Her current research interests centre on the relationship between social policy and sexuality, and on changing forms of governance. She has written extensively on the intersection of welfare and sexuality discourses. She is also an editor of the journal *Critical Social Policy*.

Nigel Edley is a Senior Lecturer in Social Psychology at Nottingham Trent University. For some years now he has been interested in looking at the issues of ideology, identity and subjectivity from a social constructionist framework. He is the co-author (with Margaret Wetherell) of numerous publications including *Men in Perspective: Practice, Power and Identity* (1995, Prentice Hall/Harvester Wheatsheaf).

Norman Fairclough is Professor of Language in Social Life at Lancaster University. He has published widely in critical discourse analysis, and his current focus is on language in the contemporary restructuring of capitalism and in neo-liberalism. His books include: *Language and Power* (1989, Longman), *Discourse and Social Change* (1992, Polity Press), *Media Discourse* (1995, Arnold)*, Critical Discourse Analysis* (with Lilie Chouliaraki, 1995, Longman), *Discourse in Late Modernity* (1999, Edinburgh University Press) and *New Labour, New Language?* (2000, Routledge).

Mary Horton-Salway is an Associate Lecturer at the Open University. She completed her PhD research in the Department of Social Sciences at Loughborough University in 1998. Her research interests include illness narrative, medical case construction and the application of psychology in primary care settings.

Stephanie Taylor is a Lecturer in Social Psychology at the Open University. Her main teaching is in the area of research training and methods. She is the editor of *Ethnographic Research: A Reader* (in press, Sage). She has had considerable experience teaching adults in universities and other contexts. Her research interests are in discourse analysis and discursive constructions of identity, place and nation.

Margaret Wetherell is Professor of Social Psychology at the Open University. Her research interests include work on discourse and masculinity and discourse and racism. In recent years she has focused on developing theories and methods in discourse research for social psychology and has published a number of books and articles in this area. She is currently co-editor of the *British Journal of Social Psychology*.

Robin Wooffitt is a Senior Lecturer in the Department of Sociology at the University of Surrey. His research interests include conversation and discourse analysis, language and identity, and the sociology of anomalous human experiences. He is the author of *Telling Tales of the Unexpected* (1992, Harvester Wheatsheaf), *The Language of Youth Subcultures* (with Sue Widdicombe, 1995, Harvester Wheatsheaf), and *Conversation Analysis: Principles, Practices and Applications* (with Ian Hutchby, 1998, Polity).

Simeon J. Yates is a Senior Lecturer in Communications Studies at Sheffield Hallam University. He has conducted research into the social impacts of new communications media. He is currently researching the processes of science communication and the representation of science in the media.

Discourse as Data: A Guide for Analysis

Introduction

Margaret Wetherell, Stephanie Taylor and Simeon J. Yates

This book offers a practical guide to conducting discourse analysis. Discourse analysis is probably best described as the study of talk and texts. It is a set of methods and theories for investigating language in use and language in social contexts. Discourse research offers routes into the study of meanings, a way of investigating the back-and-forth dialogues which constitute social action, along with the patterns of signification and representation which constitute culture. Discourse analysis provides a range of approaches to data and, crucially, also a range of theorizations of that data.

On reflection, the study of discourse might seem a rather esoteric or specialized interest. Our book is intended for social scientists but surely language is the province of linguists. Why should social scientists pursue such methods and theories? One answer lies in changing research trends. Increasingly, researchers in the social sciences are turning to new forms of empirical research. A search through social science journals of the 1960s or 1970s, for example, would probably reveal that the most commonly used research method of that period was the survey or, in some disciplines, the experiment. Researchers worked with relatively large samples, attempting to quantify social action. Typical examples would be research in sociology on the demography of poverty and investigations in social psychology using attitude questionnaires. In contrast, a similar search through contemporary journals would show that many researchers now use qualitative approaches. In many (though not all) areas of social science, a typical piece of research now involves the analysis of text or interviews. This research is usually intensive rather than extensive and involves interpretation as the main analytic activity.

As Chapter One demonstrates, the development of discourse analysis as a method for doing social scientific research has to be seen in this changing context. Moreover, the development of discourse research reflects some very interesting transformations in social theory. These are discussed in detail in the companion volume to this text – M.Wetherell, S.Taylor and S.J.Yates (eds) *Discourse Theory and Practice: A Reader*, London, Sage in association with The Open University. As that Reader makes clear, discourse analysis emerges from profound changes in conceptualizations of communication, culture, language use and function, and the relationship between representation and reality. In this volume, in contrast, we will be concerned with methods and empirical work rather than large-scale theory development. The aim is to illustrate how to *do* discourse analysis. How do you actually proceed if you are interested in analysing people's talk in interviews or in other contexts? How do you begin if you want to work with texts such as historical documents or records of social events, or if you want to study social interaction as it happens on the streets, in clinics, in schools? How do you work with such material?

The main part of the book presents six step-by-step models. These come from five core traditions in discourse research – conversation analysis, sociolinguistics, discursive psychology, critical discourse analysis and Foucauldian analysis. They by no means exhaust the many kinds of discourse research in which social scientists are engaged but they present a good range which will be of particular relevance to social psychologists, sociologists, those working in culture and media studies, education researchers, social policy researchers and sociolinguists. The diversity of traditions also allows us to cover a useful range of discourse data including examples of natural conversation and institutional talk, computer-mediated communication such as e-mails, single interview and group interview data, policy documents and historical material.

The book begins and ends with two chapters by Stephanie Taylor which locate discourse analysis within social scientific research and review some common features that are characteristic of all discourse research. Chapter One considers the process of formulating research questions, the collection and transcription of data, common steps in analysis and the process of writing up research; Chapter Eight examines the task of critically evaluating and applying discourse analytic research.

Chapters Two to Seven, which illustrate the different models of analysis, are designed to act as a series of tutorials or mini workshops. The style is 'hands on', with activities for readers to engage in. Each author presents some discursive material, explicates the analytic concepts typical of a particular approach, such as conversation analysis or critical discourse analysis, then applies these concepts to some data. After this preparation, readers can attempt their own analyses of additional data.

A key advantage is that each author is presenting his or her own empirical work. These are experienced discourse analysts going behind the scenes of their published articles to show the reasoning and procedures which led to the finished product. This makes for interesting variety in the substantive topics presented. Thus in Chapter Two, the conversation analyst Robin Wooffitt works with a sample of instances of psychic practitioners, such as mediums and clairvoyants, interacting with their clients. In Chapter Three, Simeon Yates engages cyber-space and demonstrates what corpus sociolinguistics might offer someone who wants to find out what is going on in e-mails and chat rooms, and who wants to investigate the kind of talk and interaction found there.

Chapters Four and Five develop a psychological focus. Mary Horton-Salway and Nigel Edley are both concerned with questions of identity and self-construction but employ different styles of analysis within discursive psychology. Horton-Salway's approach is more fine-grained, based on participants' orientations. Her interest is in the construction of M.E. as an illness but also as an identity and an orientation to body and mind. In contrast, Edley uses his work on masculine identities to illustrate a more critical style of discursive psychological analysis focused on power, which anticipates the work on social relations and ideology in the two chapters which follow.

These next two chapters exemplify important strands in discursive work on culture and social relations. In Chapter Six, Norman Fairclough, well-known for his work on the language of New Labour, picks apart the discourse of a Green Paper and shows what critical discourse analysis can offer the sociologist or social policy researcher. The author of Chapter Seven, Jean Carabine, is similarly concerned with discourse and social policy but employs a Foucauldian approach. Her interest is in historical policy formation, specifically discourses of sexuality found in the Poor Laws from 1830 to 1990.

As this overview makes clear, *Discourse as Data* provides a vital introduction to contemporary discourse research. Method is meaningless without theory. Through the juxtaposition of the different approaches in these six chapters, with their very different definitions of discourse, their differing levels of engagement with discursive material from molecular to the more global patterns, contrasting aims, and theories of social action, subjectivity and social relations, this book demonstrates what is at stake in broader debates in discourse communities.

Note that for the student reader, the key concepts in each chapter have been highlighted in bold. We recommend that, as a way of summarizing the chapters, you might find it useful to formulate and collect together short definitions of each key concept as you proceed.

As a final point, we want to acknowledge that the production of this text has been a team effort. *Discourse as Data* is a component of the Open University Masters course in Discourse Analysis, D843. We received some very helpful advice from our External Assessor for D843, Professor David Silverman. Teams of critical readers, peer and student readers gave us feedback on early drafts. Among the peer readers, we want to thank most particularly Ann Phoenix, Janet Maybin, Gail Lewis, Troy Cooper and Sharon Gewirtz, and among the student readers Janet Ames, Sarah Seymour-Smith, Jill Reynolds, Jayne Artis and Anna Garleff. We especially want to acknowledge the magnificent level of support we received from our Course Manager, Jacqueline Eustace and our Course Secretary, Elaine Castle. The contribution of Jonathan Hunt (Open University Copublishing Depatment), D843's Editor, Penny Bennett, our commissioning Editors at Sage, Michael Carmichael and Naomi Meredith, Designer, Mandy Anton, and Compositor, Pam Berry, also went far beyond the call of duty.

CHAPTER ONE

Locating and Conducting Discourse Analytic Research

Stephanie Taylor

Introduction

The aim of this opening chapter, in conjunction with the final chapter of the book, Chapter Eight, is to provide a new researcher with a broad overview of discourse analytic research. In order to locate discourse analysis within the academic field, I will first venture a possible definition and discuss what *kind* of research it is. This will involve a brief discussion of language and a review of some of the premises underlying social research in general and discourse analysis in particular. I will also consider the role of the discourse analytic researcher. In the second half of the chapter I offer a brief guide to conducting a discourse analytic project, with sections on formulating research questions; data, including transcription; the process of analysis, and writing up a project into a research text. In Chapter Eight, I discuss the evaluation of discourse analytic research and its potential applications.

These opening and closing chapters are therefore intended as an introduction to a more complex academic area, rather than as self-contained guides to analysis. Whereas the intervening chapters, Two to Seven, consider specific forms of discourse analysis in detail, I will summarize some of the broader features of the field as a whole and discuss issues which are relevant to the work of most social researchers who would identify themselves as discourse analysts.

1 Locating discourse analytic research

The obvious starting point for this chapter is to define what discourse analysis *is*. You are probably already aware that the term has a wide reference (see Wetherell *et al.*, 2001). It can describe very different research activities with different kinds of data, as Chapters Two to Seven demonstrate. In order to cover this diversity, I will start with a loose definition, as follows: discourse analysis is the close study of language in use. To unpack this a little I will explore what is meant by 'language' and then present four possible approaches to discourse analysis. These are simplified descriptions and will not work as a definitive categorization system for any particular research project because the approaches are necessarily interconnected, as I will show. Discourse analysis is best understood as a field of research rather than a single practice but the four approaches provide a useful introduction.

The common starting point, then, is that discourse analysts are looking closely at **language in use** and, furthermore, they are looking for **patterns**. But what exactly is 'language'? One possible answer is illustrated in the way that most people attempt to learn a new foreign language, beginning with a few basic words and expressions. This common-sense strategy rests on a particular model of language, as a static system which can be broken down to its component parts. The student learns the parts, such as items of vocabulary, grammatical forms like plurals and tenses, and fixed expressions such as greetings, and then tries to connect them together again. In this way, hopefully, the student eventually learns to communicate with other users of the same language, by analysing what they say into its component parts, then building up appropriate messages back.

On this model, the system of language works for communication because it is a vehicle for meaning; in other words, it can be used to convey meaning from one person to another, provided that both are familiar with the elements of the language. It is as if speakers or writers encode meanings into the language and then hearers or readers decode them. Wertsch (1990, reproduced as Reading Sixteen in Wetherell *et al.*, 2001) calls this "the transmission model of communication": meaning is transmitted, or conveyed, through language, like signals through a telephone wire. However, two problems with this straightforward view of language quickly become apparent. These are especially interesting for the purposes of this chapter, because they highlight some of the concerns of the discourse analyst and distinguish certain approaches to discourse analytic research.

One problem with the model of language as a system is, of course, that the system is not static but is constantly changing. Because the elements change, the language which is in use is never the same as that in the grammar book or dictionary, however up-to-date and complete these may be. Change occurs over time (think of how quickly idiomatic expressions go out of date) and also within a single interaction. New meanings are created through the to-and-fro and the combined contributions of both (or all) parties. As a simple example, a term like 'this' or 'here' changes meaning as it refers to something different. Because these new meanings are being created, and also because the language is being used to do things, it is not sufficient to understand language as **transparent** or **reflective**. It is not a neutral information-carrying vehicle, as the transmission model of communication would imply. Rather, language is **constitutive**: it is the site where meanings are created and changed.

A small digression: the notion that language is not transparent is one of the fundamental assumptions of discourse analysis but it does create (constitute?) a problem for the analyst, as will be discussed further in Section 1.3. On the one hand, language is assumed to be constitutive, as I have just explained. On the other, in academia as elsewhere, no one entirely abandons the premise that talk and texts convey information about something else. So language is also assumed to be **referential**. (This is, of course, taken for granted as a feature of any academic text in which analyses are presented or issues are discussed, including the one you are reading now!) One issue becomes the extent to which data should be treated as referential or as constitutive. For example, when a researcher interviews someone, how far can their talk be treated as a reflection of something else, such as established memories and ready-formed opinions? Should it instead be analysed as the place and process in which memories and opinions are constituted?

These questions are addressed in more detail in Chapters Four and Five (see also Section 1.3).

Another problem with the static system model relates to the uses of language. Language is an important means for *doing* things: greeting, snubbing, claiming, persuading, denying or sowing doubts (see Potter, 2001). To understand what exactly is being done, it is often necessary, again, to know what occurred at an earlier point in a situation or interaction. This applies to both the immediate interaction of a conversation and the more protracted sequence which is implied in, say, a reader's letter in response to a newspaper article, or one academic text criticizing another. In other words, to understand what is being done with language, it is necessary to consider its **situated** use, within the process of an ongoing interaction.

Both of these problems show that the model of language as a static system is over-simplified. More importantly, for the purposes of this chapter they serve to introduce the four approaches to discourse analysis. In the first approach to discourse analysis, it is precisely the variation and imperfection of language as a system which is the focus. Discourse analysts study language in use to discover how it varies and relate this variation to different social situations and environments, or different users. In contrast, the second approach to discourse analysis focuses on the *activity* of language use, rather than the language itself. Here the analyst studies language use as a process, investigating the to-and-fro of interactions (usually talk) between at least two parties and looking for patterns in what the language users (speakers) do.

A third approach to discourse analysis is rather different. The analyst looks for patterns in the language associated with a particular topic or activity, such as the family of special terms and meanings around it: a study might focus on the language associated with a particular occupation, such as social work or nursing. And a fourth possible approach to discourse analysis is to look for patterns within much larger contexts, such as those referred to as 'society' or 'culture'. Here the interest is in how language is important as part of wider processes and activities. For example, the analyst might investigate patterns in the labelling and classification of people or activities within a society. The language of categorization will be implicated with, on the one hand, the values underlying it (for example, beliefs that certain people are 'good' or 'bad') and associated philosophies or logics (such as when an activity is evaluated negatively because it is believed to have negative consequences), and on the other, the consequences and social effects of the classification. The analyst's interests will therefore extend beyond language in use, that is, from the 'discursive' to the 'extra-discursive', probably blurring any distinction between them.

You have probably noticed that although I describe four approaches to discourse analysis, I have avoided giving a separate definition or definitions of 'discourse'. One reason is that that term is itself wide-ranging and slippery. More importantly, defining it still leaves the separate task of explaining 'discourse analysis' as a research activity. So for the remainder of this chapter I will focus on the latter, although this will sometimes involve introducing certain definitions of discourse.

My next task is to elaborate the four approaches I have outlined above. In the first approach, as I have said, the discourse analyst focuses primarily on the language itself. The patterns which are identified in the language in use may be similar to those which have conventionally interested linguists. For instance, they may be described in terms of vocabulary, structure or functions. Concepts like 'genre' or 'code'. may be employed to characterize an interrelationship between language and social situation. (See Maybin, 2001; Hodge and Kress, 1988, reproduced as Reading Twenty-one in Wetherell *et al.*, 2001.) The analyst's interest is, broadly, in regularities within an imperfect and unstable system.

In the second approach to discourse analysis, the analyst is more interested in the 'use' than the 'language' and interaction becomes the major focus. Patterns may be identified in terms of a sequence of contributions to an interaction, or a regular 'shape' like a script. This focus on use implies a particular view of the language user. She or he is not seen as a free agent using language to encode or decode a meaning in order to communicate it. To a great extent, any one person's contribution must follow on from that of the previous contribution and is inevitably shaped by what has gone before. Furthermore, meaning will be created within the interaction. The language user is therefore understood as **constrained** by the interactive context.

In the third approach to discourse analysis, the pattern within language in use which interests the analyst is the set or family of terms which are related to a particular topic or activity. This approach draws attention to how new terms enable people to talk about different things; for example, a student generally learns new vocabulary as part of the process of becoming familiar with a new field of work. This is not simply a matter of attaching different labels to already existing objects. As I have already described, there is also a sense in which language is constitutive; that is, it creates what it refers to. Of course this is not a once-and-for-all situation. Think about how meanings are created and eroded as part of ongoing social change. Technological change creates new *things* to be talked about and also new activities. For instance, the internet has given us alternative meanings for 'surfing' and 'browsing'. A language pattern of this kind (sometimes referred to as '*a* discourse' – note the article – or an 'interpretative repertoire': see Chapter Five) is therefore specific to particular circumstances. This approach would understand language as situated, but within a particular social and cultural context rather than a particular interaction (as in the second approach). In this respect, it blurs into the fourth approach to discourse analysis.

The aim of the analyst following the fourth approach is, broadly, to identify patterns of language and related practices and to show how these constitute aspects of society and the people within it. Ultimately such an analysis draws attention to the social nature and historical origins of the world 'out there' which is generally taken for granted. Controversy is basic to this form of discourse analysis because it involves the study of power and resistance, contests and struggles. The basic assumption here is that the language available to people enables and constrains not only their expression of certain ideas but also what they do.

To take a simple but well-known example, this assumption underlies the promotion of anti-racist and anti-sexist language. This is part of the equal opportunities policies of many organizations (such as universities) but is often disparaged as 'political correctness' (or 'pc'). In its simplest form, the aim is to reduce discriminatory practices in an institution by discouraging the use of discriminatory language. The proponents of this policy have criticized established images, for example in children's books, and taken-for-granted terms and expressions which contain negative stereotypes. Its opponents usually claim that such material is innocuous. Its proponents use a rationale which corresponds loosely to the notion that language is constitutive and that it blurs into practices. They argue that the way in which something, or, more likely, someone, is talked about does make a difference to the larger workings of society. It is through language, for example, that certain things or people are either categorized together or separated out as different, and through language that value is attributed or denied. This is particularly evident when language is used to classify and categorize for official purposes. For example, Rose (1985) describes how, as schooling became widespread in Britain, children began to be classified as good and bad learners. The requirements of the new education system created new categories of children, such as the 'feebleminded' child who had no obvious physical problem yet did not learn or progress through the school system.

This approach has given rise to historical studies, known as **genealogies**, which trace back the development of discourses (these are discussed more fully in Chapter Seven, which presents an example of a genealogical study). A famous example is Foucault's (1961) study of the development of the concept of madness. Rose's work, described above, also belongs in this tradition. A study of these practices explores their wider implications, such as the identities which they make available and the constraints which they set up. In general, a study based on either the third or fourth approach to discourse analysis is often on a larger scale than a study of interaction and may involve public contexts. It could be conducted, for example, through the study of official documents (see Chapter Seven: also, Helleiner, 1998; Stenson and Watt, 1999).

This fourth approach to discourse analysis draws attention to the all-enveloping nature of discourse as a fluid, shifting medium in which meaning is created and contested. The language user is not a detached communicator, sending out and receiving information, but is always **located,** immersed in this medium and struggling to take her or his own social and cultural positioning into account. Even more than with the second approach, this fourth approach to discourse analysis understands the language user not as a free agent but as one who is heavily constrained in her or his choice of language and action, even if these are not fully determined. And of course the discourse analyst is not outside these struggles and constraints but is one such user within them.

Although I have presented these four approaches to discourse analysis as distinct, it will already be apparent that they are implicated in one another and shade together. The outline of four separate approaches works as a useful but oversimplified introduction to the field of discourse analytic work. It does not make clear the controversies within the field, and the criticisms which different practitioners would level at each other's work. As a way into these, I will now approach discourse analysis from a different direction and ask: what kind of research is this and what kind of knowledge does it produce?

1.1 What kind of research?

So far I have offered a loose definition of discourse analysis (as the search for patterns within language in use) and discussed what it involves, elaborating the definition to cover research activities with four different foci. In this section I want to step back a little and consider a broader question: what *kind* of research is discourse analysis?

One way to answer this would be to locate discourse analysis within disciplines. Unfortunately, as anyone who has consulted a university library catalogue will be aware, the enormous range of academic work which is referred to as discourse analysis spans many disciplines. For example, as the focus on 'language' would suggest, discourse analysis is used in linguistics and sociolinguistics, and also in literary studies (though this last area is not covered in this book). The focus on 'use' or on society gives it a place in different fields of social research including sociolinguistics, sociology and social psychology as well as more 'applied' areas, such as social policy and education. More recently, it has also been used by students of politics and human geography.

Another answer to the question 'what kind of research is discourse analysis?' would be in terms of the classic dichotomy between qualitative and quantitative research methods. Certainly, researchers often become interested in discourse analysis because they want to find a form of qualitative analysis for interviews or documentary material (see Chapters Six and Seven). However, discourse analysis can also use quantitative methods (some examples are discussed in Chapter Three). Moreover, the qualitative/quantitative distinction is extremely broad.

In other words, attempts to locate discourse analysis by categorizing it as qualitative rather than quantitative are not much more useful than locating it within a particular discipline. To answer the question 'What kind of research is this?', the discourse analyst will have to return to the broad premises underlying social research and locate her or his own project with reference to these and to certain established debates. The next two sections will discuss discourse analytic research in these terms (for a much fuller discussion of these debates, see Wetherell, 2001a).

1.2 Locating social research in general

Epistemological issues

I have asked, 'what is discourse analysis?' and then 'what kind of research is it?' Another question would be about what we can use discourse analysis to find out. In other words, 'what kind of knowledge does discourse analysis produce?' This is a question about **epistemology**, meaning that it is concerned with the status of knowledge.

I have said that discourse analytic researchers are looking for patterns in language in use and I have suggested that these might be patterns within language or patterns of activity. In addition to identifying such patterns, the researcher will be making some kind of epistemological claim about them. There is a range of possibilities here but I will discuss them in terms of two broad traditions.

The first tradition is associated with the physical sciences and embraces **positivism** and **postpositivism**. These are themselves broad and varied traditions (see Smith, 1998, for a fuller discussion) but they share several assumptions. One is that through the use of appropriate methods, which have become well established, the researcher can obtain knowledge of the world and its workings, particularly of the causal relationships which operate within it. Identifying such relationships enables the researcher to apply the research to real-world problems by making accurate predictions, and possibly interventions. The knowledge obtained through the research is generalizable to other contexts because it is universal.

Another claim made in these traditions is that research produces knowledge which is value-free and objective, unaffected by any personal bias or world-view of the researcher. Good research is considered to produce neutral information and contribute to a cumulative process which aspires towards finding universal truths. The whole or final truth about the world may not be attainable, but successive researchers attempt to approach it, testing hypotheses and taking a fallibilistic approach in which previous findings are treated as provisional and open to further testing (see Seale, 1999). Each researcher's procedures and findings are, ideally, published, scrutinized and rigorously evaluated in terms of validity, reliability and replicability (see Chapter Eight; also Sapsford, 1999: 107 and 139). So here is one set of related claims, that research produces knowledge which is universal, in that it holds across different situations and different times, and is value-free. In ordinary terms, this is knowledge with the status of truth: it is enduring and it is separate from the opinions and values of the researcher.

A contrasting tradition (or more precisely, again, a composite of different traditions) is more strongly associated with the social than the physical sciences and with work around critical theory, postmodernism and poststructuralism. Underlying it are quite different epistemological claims. Researchers in this tradition do not usually aim or claim to capture the truth of reality but to offer an interpretation or version which is inevitably partial. This is not simply because they have more limited ambitions but is a consequence of various assumptions or premises! The first of these is that the complexity and also the dynamic nature of the social world mean that a researcher can seldom make confident predictions about it. There are too many factors operating in any situation and the relationships which operated in the past will not necessarily be those that prevail in the future. As a result, the researcher's aim is to investigate meaning and significance, rather than to predict and control (Banister *et al.*, 1994: 3).

A second premise is that no neutral single truth is possible in the social sciences because these involve the study of other people who have their own viewpoints. Any account of a social phenomenon or situation inevitably reflects the observer/researcher's partial understanding and special interest. To claim it as pure knowledge or truth would therefore be to deny the diversity of viewpoints and experiences of the other people who are involved (Said, 1978). A third and more complex premise is that no single truth is possible because reality is neither single nor regular: there are multiple realities and therefore multiple truths (this is not just an epistemological position, about the status of knowledge, but an **ontological** one, about the nature of the world itself). Furthermore, truth claims cannot be checked because accounts of the world are not simply reflections or records of what already exists. They themselves constitute and change what they purport to describe (this point relates to the discussion of language as constitutive in Section 1.1).

The epistemological claims being made in this second broad tradition are that the knowledge obtained by research is **partial**, **situated** (i.e. specific to particular situations and periods rather than universally applicable) and **relative** (i.e. related to the researcher's world view and value system). Such claims are particularly associated with qualitative research, including forms of discourse analysis such as those presented by Edley in Chapter Five and Carabine in Chapter Seven. Some other forms of discourse analysis, most notably conversation analysis (see Chapter Two) are closer to the first epistemological tradition.

To understand what kind of research discourse analysis is, it is not enough to study what the researcher *does* (like following a recipe!). We also need to refer back to these epistemological debates and their wider implications. It has been suggested that these debates have created for researchers a "double crisis of representation and legitimation" (Denzin and Lincoln, 1998: 21). The crisis of **representation** is that the researcher cannot claim to offer 'objective' knowledge of reality and of the world out there, but only a biased 'subjective' account. Indeed, since objectivity is impossible, the terms 'objective' and subjective' cease to be applicable. The most extreme interpretation of this position would be that research cannot tell us about the world but only about the world-view of the researcher! The crisis of **legitimation** is that there are no well-established procedures for evaluating the knowledge obtained. The main reason for this is that there is no assumption that the researcher's findings or claims can be checked against objective reality. Reality remains inaccessible so any attempt to verify results, for example, by duplicating the research, simply produces another unreliable version. It is as if the researcher is forever trapped inside a building in which all the windows contain distorting glass. It is impossible to go outside to get an open view of the world. The view from one window can only be checked against the view from another, which is also limited and distorted by the glass, but in a slightly different way.

I will return to the implications of this double crisis in Chapter Eight. It is worth noting, however, that the first issue, the problem of representation, is of particular interest to discourse analysts because representation is also the topic or focus of their research. We can imagine a potential (perhaps irritating!) spiral in which such a researcher conducts an analysis, then analyses her or his own representation of the analysis, then analyses the representation of the analysis of the representation of the original analysis, and so on! (For an example of a piece of work in this spirit, see Ashmore, 1989.)

The second issue, the problem of legitimation, might suggest that research can never be assessed or evaluated by anyone but the original researcher. This would create a situation in academia which Seale and Silverman have described as "methodological anarchy" (1997: 380). Aside from other problems, it would lead to professional difficulties for researchers whose future employment depends on others' assessment of the quality of their work! Fortunately, such anarchy does not, in practice, prevail, for reasons which will be discussed later in this chapter and also in Chapter Eight. The double crisis therefore needs to be understood by prospective researchers but it should not be exaggerated: a wide variety of research, including discourse analytic research, continues to be conducted, written up (for example, in academic journals), evaluated and widely debated.

Generalization

Another related point to consider is the claim that a researcher is making about **generalization**. I have said that discourse analysis involves the search for patterns within language in use. How general are these patterns and what form do they take? The answers to these questions again relate back to the analyst's premises or assumptions.

I have suggested that an analysis which focuses on the language itself is likely to approach language as a system, albeit one which is imperfect and fairly fluid. Consequently, the claims made are likely to be generalized. The analyst identifies features which occur across a range of contexts, or in a particular category of context (such as a type of interaction). The component elements might be defined structurally. Another possibility (not the only alternative) would be to analyse them in terms of functions. The analyst might identify them as part of an investigation of their wider effects, such as how they assist in the creation or reinforcement of groups and difference. In this form of analysis the body of data is sometimes very large (often referred to as a **corpus**) and the analysis might involve electronic sorting methods, such as concordancing (this is explained in Chapter Three), and possibly also some quantitative analysis. This broad description applies to much discourse analytic work in sociolinguistics and critical discourse analysis (see Chapters Three and Six).

If the discourse analysis focuses on interaction, it is still possible to generalize but the *basis* for doing so will be different. As I explained in Section 1.1, the analyst is likely to approach every interaction as unique, unfolding in a way which cannot be predicted and involving the development of new and context-specific meanings. So how can it be possible to generalize, to claim that the *particular* features which are identified in one interaction have a wider existence and relevance? One possibility is for the analyst to identify patterns or features which are common to many different interactions, such as sequences of 'turns' taken by speakers. This is demonstrated in the analysis by Wooffitt in Chapter Two. Like other conversation analysts, Wooffitt does not argue that such a pattern is inevitable or automatic; rather, it is an example of how speakers co-ordinate their talk/action by drawing on common knowledge. Such knowledge is sometimes referred to as 'members' methods' because it is shared by the members of a society. A somewhat different approach would be to generalize about interactions on the basis of the roles which speakers take up (such as doctor and patient). Commonalities could again be explained in terms of shared social knowledge (by arguing, for example, that people know how they 'should' speak in these roles and generally comply) or commonly held ideas and beliefs, perhaps discussed in terms of culture, or, at a deeper level, as related to cognitive processing, or enduring category memberships, such as gender.

A somewhat different approach is to consider interaction on a larger scale. It can be argued that *all* language use is interactive, addressed to others and responding to what has gone before. The interaction may address a party who is not present, as in the case of a letter. It may be directed towards someone who is imagined rather than known, such as a hypothetical political opponent or potential critic. Billig (1987) has described this form of language use as **rhetorical**. The analyst interested in rhetorical work may aim to identify the positions and arguments being addressed or countered, as a general feature of talk or other language use around a certain issue (this is one aspect of the analysis presented by Edley in Chapter Five).

An alternative to generalizing is to study something which has a *particular* significance in itself. This is the approach taken in studies using material from people or events which seem uniquely important. Examples include political or public figures like Lech Walesa (see Jaworski and Galasinski, 1998) or Diana, Princess of Wales (see Wetherell, 2001b); or historic events, like the Iran-Contra hearings in the USA (Lynch and Bogen, 1996). Similarly, a study could focus on features which exist only in one context, making the claim that they are not ephemeral, even if not completely stable, and also that their ramifications are fairly widespread. The claim would not be that the feature recurs but that it is significant and persistent. An example would be a study of racial categories employed within a *particular* society. Similarly, a researcher might look at practices which are unique to one society or historical period but (probably) relevant to a large area of that society. Historical (genealogical) analysis adds to the explanatory power of such analyses (see Chapter Seven). In these cases, the researcher would not be attempting to generalize up from component elements or particular instances but rather to describe some aspect of a whole.

To locate the research undertaken by a particular discourse analyst and understand what kind of research it is, it is necessary to look at the position she or he takes on these issues. The issues described in this section are common to much social research. The following section discusses others which are more specific to discourse analytic research.

1.3 Issues in discourse analytic research

I have said that discourse analysis is the close study of language in use. One debate around it involves the status of language as **topic** or **resource** (see also Chapter Five). The issue here is whether the analyst is studying talk or language *itself* or using the language as a resource for studying something else. Take the example of a psychologist who wants to study an emotion, like anger, and sets out to do so by collecting examples of people talking about their anger. How should this talk be analysed? Treating it as a resource, the psychologist might try to generalize about the causes of people's anger, how long it lasts, the physical experiences associated with it, and so on. However, an alternative approach would be to view this 'talk about anger' as the topic of the study. In this case, the aim would be to find patterns within the talk, for example, in how references to anger are located within interactions and how other speakers respond (see Edwards, 1997, reproduced as Reading Seventeen in Wetherell *et al.*, 2001, for a detailed example of this approach to the study of emotion).

Of course, it is a general feature of discourse analysis that language is not treated as information about something else but is somehow problematized. That is, the analyst approaches language as a topic. Nonetheless, the topic/resource question does arise, particularly in the fourth approach to discourse analysis which I have outlined in which the focus is on patterns across wider social or cultural contexts (see Section 1.1). For example, du Gay (1996: 148), investigating "the powerful discourse of enterprise", quotes workers in retail organizations who talk about the uniforms they have to wear. His interest is in their feelings about wearing a uniform and the conflicts they have with the company around how the uniform *should* be worn, as issues which relate to conformity and resistance. In this case, du Gay is using the talk about these issues as a resource in his analysis of identities and practices within the workplace, as part of the larger study of the discourse of enterprise.

Another debate concerns whether the analyst should investigate **process** or **content**. I have suggested that some discourse analysts are concerned with an ongoing, probably spoken, interaction, and with how speakers talk and what they do through talk. Other analysts may focus more on the content than the process of interaction. In this case, language use may be analysed as a completed whole, as if it were a finished performance. In practice, this amounts to a focus on, in the one case, the connections between consecutive utterances, and in the other, recurring elements in the body of talk (whether words, images, ideas or whatever) which are considered out of sequence. The focus, in turn, affects the way data are presented in the writing up of the project, as either a complete interactional sequence or as isolated extracts or a summary of features. This distinction between talk as an ongoing process and the content of talk is important in ethnomethodology and conversation analysis, described below (see Chapter Two and also ten Have, 1999 for a more detailed account).

A third major dispute is between '**etic**' and '**emic**' analyses. This has been described as the difference between "using an imposed frame of reference" (etic) and "working within the conceptual framework of those studied" (emic) (Silverman, 1993: 24). At the widest level, the issue here is who determines what language, especially talk, is 'about'. Should more weight be given to the interpretation of an outsider (the analyst) or an insider (the participant in the interaction)? An emic approach is particularly associated with conversation analysis, also known as **talk-in-interaction** (this is presented more fully in Chapter Two). Conversation analysis assumes that within an interaction, such as a conversation, the speakers jointly create meaning. The talk is about what all parties make it about as the interaction proceeds, in the way they 'orient' to the previous utterances. Talk therefore becomes 'about' what speakers make it about, employing their shared members' knowledge of how to do things and how to move forward, step-by-step. In an example quoted by Schegloff (1997), a dinner-table request to pass the butter, made by a woman to a man, becomes 'about' gender as he teasingly answers 'Ladies first' but helps himself. Conversation analysts have, therefore, criticized researchers who approach a body of talk with preconceptions of what it contains (see ten Have, 1999: 102). This also has implications for the collection of data, suggesting that a researcher who sets up interviews on a certain topic and subsequently analyses them as data on that topic may be imposing an incorrect interpretation on the interactions which took place.

1.4 The discourse analytic researcher

The previous sections have outlined theoretical issues which are common to all social research and also some which are specific to discourse analytic research. I have said that in order to locate an example of discourse analysis and understand what kind of research it is, we need to consider these issues. In addition, they have implications for the **role** of the discourse analytic researcher. A major question here is how far the researcher can be separate from the research. This section outlines the concept of **reflexivity** which suggests that separation is impossible, and then considers the implications of the identity of the researcher for data collection and analysis. Finally, it relates the role of the researcher to ethical issues in social research.

I suggested in Section 1.2 that in one research tradition associated with positivism and postpositivism, the researcher aims to be neutral, conducting the research efficiently but exerting no bias on the processes of data collection and analysis. This neutrality is essential to one of the conventional criteria for evaluating such research, **replicability** (see Chapter Eight). According to this criterion, a different researcher (or researchers) should be able repeat a research project and obtain the same or similar results. It is based on the ideal of a detached researcher who does not influence the data or the participants, that is, a researcher who does not cause **reactivity**.

However most researchers, particularly those in the second, more social scientific tradition outlined in Section 1.2, would consider that such neutrality is impossible because the researcher and the research cannot be meaningfully separated. The argument here is that a basic feature of social research is its reflexivity, namely, the way that the researcher acts on the world and the world acts on the researcher, in a loop. If this is accepted, the researcher moves from the 'service' role of a faceless technician – which is implied in the first tradition – to a central and visible position. Detachment is impossible so the researcher's influence must be taken into account and even utilized (Hammersley and Atkinson, 1995: 19). Doing this requires the researcher to be self-aware. It involves the imagined act of stepping back to observe oneself as an actor within a particular context. The researcher attempts to understand how her or his own presence and actions influence the situation. This includes considering the relevance of the researcher's identity to the research, an important area for discourse analytic research, particularly for studies which involve interviewing.

The **identity of the researcher** becomes relevant to discourse analytic research in several ways. First, it influences the selection of the topic or research area. The researcher is likely to conduct a project which chimes with her or his personal interests, sympathies and political beliefs. This is usual in all research but is perhaps particularly true when projects are relatively small and involve only one or two researchers, as in most discourse analytic projects. The researcher's special interests and, possibly, personal links to the topic are not in themselves a sufficient basis for research, but they are a probable starting point for the project. They are not seen negatively as bias but as a position to be acknowledged. (For an interesting example of a researcher setting out her own relationship to the research topic and the participants, see the first chapter of Frankenberg, 1993.)

The researcher's identity is also relevant to data collection. For instance, it can affect an interview in several ways. The gender of the interviewer may act as a constraint on certain topics or areas of talk. Sometimes different interviewers are used in a project so that male participants are interviewed by a male researcher, female participants by a female researcher. Nonetheless, it is important not to exaggerate the common ground provided by gender. A participant may feel ill at ease with an interviewer who appears older, younger, more confident, or richer, or because of numerous differences other than gender, many of which may be conveyed in a first impression by the interviewer's appearance and accent. (Conversely, in some circumstances it may be easier for a participant to talk to someone who is different than someone who appears similar to themselves.) It can be argued, therefore, that the interviewer should not try to approach participants as an insider who shares their situation or interests, but simply as an outsider. This may also be a more honest acknowledgement of the power differences between them. (The issue of power differences is discussed in more detail in the next sub-section on ethics. Also see Croghan and Miell, 1998, for an account of a project in which the differences between interviewer and participants are noted and the interview is acknowledged to be an unequal and apparently high-risk situation for the participants, women who are clients of welfare agencies.)

In an interview situation, taking account of reflexivity includes considering how the interviewer's questions influence the answers given. The questions may raise topics and problems which the participants would not otherwise have considered and, alternatively, discourage other topics as unsuitable. The general style of the interview is relevant here. Atkinson and Silverman (1997: 309) suggest that we live in an interview society. One consequence of this may well be that participants bring 'wrong' expectations to the interview. A researcher needs to be aware that the interviewer's manner, the questions asked and even the setting of the interview may invite different kinds of talk, such as the confession of personal feelings associated with a therapy interview or the expert knowledge given by interviewees on the television news. Participants may feel uncomfortable because the interview seems to ask them for a kind of talk which they do not want or feel able to provide (see Shakespeare, 1998: 41–59 for a discussion of different kinds of interviews and the talk which they may seem to invite or expect).

It can be argued that the identity of the researcher also influences interpretation and analysis, through the knowledge and general world view which she or he brings to the data. At the most basic level, the researcher needs to understand the language and references used by the interview participants or the writers of documents. (Some discourse analytic projects do translate material e.g. de Cillia *et al.*, 1999, but this is usually for the writing up of the project; the analysis is generally conducted on the untranslated material.) Even when the researcher and participants speak the same language, there may be barriers to understanding. For instance, if the project analyses material from another locality or time, the researcher may be unfamiliar with local idioms which are used and also with references to people and events (see Chapter Seven).

This practical point shades into the more theoretical issue of the boundary between content and relevant **context**. Some researchers, especially those working in the conversation analysis tradition, consider that contextual information is only relevant as speakers orient to it in their talk, that is, when it ceases to be background. Analysts may use material which they had no role in collecting and know only as audio-recordings of interactions which they did not witness. In this case, clearly, the analyst cannot depend on local knowledge or a similar background or experience to that of the participants. In contrast, other analysts include background information, especially about interview participants (see Mehan, 1996, reproduced as Reading Twenty-five in Wetherell *et al.*, 2001). Certain analysts would consider it important to have the double role of interviewer/ analyst, in order to bring the experience of the original interaction to the interpretation (see Edley in Chapter Five, for example). They would discuss their feelings during the interaction and their own connection to the topic and participants (e.g. Hollway, 1984, reproduced as Reading Twenty in Wetherell *et al.*, 2001).

Again, at the analytic level, taking account of reflexivity can change the interpretation of the data. In an analysis of talk, for instance, rather than looking 'through' what is said to the topic, as if it were transparent, the analyst would be looking *at* the talk itself, as a form of interaction. To give a more specific example, imagine the talk includes discussion of racial conflict. If the talk is analysed as information about racial conflict, this assumes that the talk is transparent and the speaker is a fairly truthful, neutral source of information, including information about her or his own views and attitudes. (An analysis which takes this approach unproblematically would not usually be considered to be discourse analysis.) Alternatively, the analyst can focus on what is happening in the interview where the participant is interacting with the interviewer and doing work to present herself or himself in a certain way. The focus of the analysis is now racism as a practice that is maintained and reproduced through talk. The analyst will look, for example, at how people talk about racial conflict, what they respond to, what rhetorical moves they make. (For an example of such an analysis, see Wetherell and Potter, 1992, Chapter 7.)

Altogether, a strong argument can be made for the claim that the identity of the researcher influences the project, especially the collection of data. However, as with the collection of data through interviews, it is important to acknowledge the limits to the closeness and understanding which can be achieved between analyst and participants. I have outlined arguments that language constitutes reality and that there is no single social truth to be discovered by the researcher. The same arguments would suggest that discourse analytic projects cannot reveal the 'true' inner states of language users. As a general rule, this means that the analysis should be confined to the discourse rather than to the people who produced the talk or documents. The researcher should not aim, for example, to reveal the intentions and meaning or beliefs of speakers or writers, or to see through their words to some underlying meaning, or to uncover attitudes or beliefs of which the speakers themselves are unaware. These are all large and dangerous claims for discourse analysts to make.

The extent of the researcher's influence is inevitably difficult to assess. Reflexivity extends to the writing up of the research (see Atkinson, 1990: 6–7). At the simplest level, this is shown by the researcher adopting a policy of openness with the aim of showing her or his place within the research process. The aim is to position her or himself within the project, as part of the social world in which the research is being conducted. In practical terms this means including some self-description and accounts of her or his own relation to the topic, participants and data. Other influences and constraints can similarly be acknowledged and discussed in the written account of the project (see Section 2.5). Self-awareness is incorporated in the writing up of the research, with the researcher assessing and qualifying claims as they are made, rather than presenting them as statements of truth.

The final point to note here is that if the identity of the researcher is relevant to a project, there may be cases in which that identity is problematic. In other words, a researcher may need to accept that she or he is not the appropriate person to conduct a particular project. This can be a difficult and controversial issue. De la Rey (1997) describes a South

African conference at which black women complained about being made the object of study of white women academics. In the prevailing political and social circumstances, sympathy and goodwill could not make such projects acceptable to the category of people that they focused on and were probably intended to help. This suggests that a researcher's identity is relevant not only to the way that a project is conducted but also, at an earlier stage, to the design of the project and even to the decision to conduct it.

Ethics

Reflecting on the project should also involve attention to the **ethics** of the research. Any researcher has ethical obligations, but these are highlighted when the researcher acknowledges her or his own presence within the research process and also abandons the claim to be discovering truth. Ethical concerns are always relevant because of the power relations between a researcher/analyst and the participants in a project. Throughout this chapter, reference has been made to 'participants' rather than 'subjects' in order to emphasize that the researcher has no rights over the other people who contribute to a research project. (This follows the recommendations of the British Psychological Society.) However, it would be an exaggeration to suggest that the researcher and participants meet as equals. In general, the researcher has more power than the participant and must be careful not to abuse it. Power can come from holding the status associated with being an academic and, supposedly, an expert. This status is particularly strong for researchers in certain disciplines; for example, it is important not to exploit the often unwarranted reverence which many lay people have for a 'psychologist'. (Mehan, 1996, reproduced as Reading Twenty-five in Wetherell *et al.*, 2001, is an account of a project in which this reverence is central to the analysis.) The researcher also has power because, as the person setting up the project, she or he has more information about it. Participants who agree to be interviewed, for example, may not anticipate the impact on themselves or others if their words are later published. Although most academic publications are not widely read outside the field, a few may be (newspapers often base articles on 'interesting' new research presented at academic conferences, for example). And, of course, non-academic participants may well have friends and relatives working within academia. For all these reasons, the responsibility is on the researcher to anticipate negative outcomes and take steps to protect participants.

Many projects will be designed to conform to the requirements of a university ethical committee or to the guidelines or codes of ethical practice issued by professional associations, such as the British Psychological Society or British Sociological Association. Researchers need to be generally guided by the obligation not to harm or distress participants. It should not be assumed that the end justifies the means: the interest or 'relevance' of a project cannot warrant dispensing with ethical requirements. As a first step, participants should be guaranteed anonymity: real names are not published and it may also be necessary to remove other information from transcripts (occupation, relationship to a public figure, and so on) which might identify a participant. (Notice, though, that there are limits to the confidentiality which can be guaranteed, for example, with relation to certain legal issues.) Particular problems arise when participants are drawn from a small community or narrow category of people whose defining feature makes them interesting to a researcher but also readily identifiable to others. This could be the case for people in an unusual occupation, especially if they are subject to media attention (e.g. professional sportspeople). It could also apply to people in a particular category, such as a profession, who are a minority within that category, perhaps because of race or sexual orientation (e.g. black lawyers; gay and lesbian police officers). In difficult cases, if confidentiality cannot be guaranteed to the participants, the proposed research project may have to be abandoned.

A second important ethical requirement is that the researcher should obtain **informed consent** from participants regarding their involvement in the project and also the use of the data they provide. In practice, making sure that the consent is informed, that is, that participants fully understand the implications of their involvement, can be difficult. There are limits to how much detail (for example, about the theoretical background and aims) most participants will want and also to how much the researcher may be able to provide (for example, about eventual findings and their publication). But there is still an obligation on the researcher to inform the participants as fully as is practicable and to obtain consent in advance. Also, it should be noted that obtaining such consent does not absolve the researcher from other obligations. (As a practical point, note that signed consent forms should not be included in any place, such as an appendix to a thesis or dissertation, where they may be accessible to others and so identify a participant.)

Thirdly, the researcher must observe the participants' legal rights. These can be complex, especially as they relate to protected documents, such as legal or medical records, or to participants who are legally minors. For example, a researcher planning to interview children about their lives would probably need to establish in advance whether full confidentiality could be promised if participants disclosed illegal behaviours, such as drug use and under-age sexual relationships, or situations which endangered them, such as abusive domestic relationships. More generally, there can be legal issues around the ownership and re-use of data, such as audio-recordings. Despite the fact that banks of qualitative data have been established to enable researchers to re-use recordings and transcripts collected in previous projects, the copyright of an audio-recorded interview is held by the interviewee. A researcher therefore has a legal obligation to obtain permission from a participant to use the material (see Bornat, 1994: 172, for a detailed account of the legal requirements and a sample consent form; also see ten Have, 1999, for a further discussion of confidentiality and consent issues).

This and the previous section have suggested some of the ways in which a social researcher, such as a discourse analyst, can influence the research which she or he is conducting. The notion of reflexivity has been introduced and the ethical responsibilities which the researcher has towards participants in the project have been outlined.

2   Conducting discourse analytic research

In the first part of this chapter I offered a brief definition of discourse analysis and outlined some (simplified) approaches to this form of research. I will now move on to the main concern of the book, conducting discourse analytic research. In contrast to the detailed presentations in Chapters Two to Seven, the remainder of this chapter is a more general guide to doing research, with sections on formulating research questions, choosing data, transcribing recorded talk, the process of analysis and writing up research.

2.1 The research question

Formulating research questions involves, as the term implies, narrowing the broad focus and wider theory of a project down to one or more questions which the research can be designed to answer. Although it might seem logical that the researcher will decide on a research question at the start of the research process, in practice she or he will probably need to conduct quite extensive background reading and library searches before formulating it. (Carabine gives a good account of this process in Chapter Seven.) A new researcher should also look for other studies in the broad area of the research topic. This can be initially disconcerting. Despite the apparently infinite range of possible research, it is usual to find that an original and exciting idea for a project has already been used by several other people! However, this does not mean that the proposal should be abandoned. Although it would be undesirable to duplicate another study exactly, these apparent duplicates will almost certainly differ from the new project in a number of important respects, possibly including the disciplinary area. With further work, a distinctive research question can be developed.

It is also possible for a new project to formulate its research questions in terms of a previous project, for example, by aiming to investigate the same topic or features in a different context. Seale (1999: 80) suggests that even those social researchers who do not accept the principle of replicability should design new studies to build cumulatively on previous findings. Of course, the accumulation of data cannot be equivalent to that associated with truth claims (see the discussion of comparison, below), but there is still a strong case for formulating a research question to refer back to previous research, either by building on it or challenging it.

The research question may be written as a question or alternatively as a **hypothesis**, that is, a statement which may or may not be supported by the findings of the research. In the positivist and postpositivist tradition, this would be related to a truth claim: the researcher's aim would be to establish or verify information about the world. The testing of a hypothesis is part of a **fallibilistic** approach, where the aim of establishing (provisional) truths is pursued negatively, by testing and challenging a point to see if it stands up (see Smith, 1998: 344, on falsification). However researchers outside this tradition may still formulate the research question as a hypothesis, with the difference that the final claims made in relation to it will be more provisional and, usually, confined to a more limited and specific context.

It is worth noting that extra care needs to be taken if the research question is formulated in terms of a comparison. Initial thinking about a problem will often lead a researcher to formulate a question which compares findings from different situations or participants. Another possible comparison is of the past with the present, usually to demonstrate change. However, a comparative design can raise special practical and theoretical problems. Practically, it can double the size of the project, which may make it unfeasible, especially for a researcher working alone. In the case of comparisons over time, there is often no available data for the 'past' which is to be compared with the 'present' or 'recent' situation. (Carabine, in Chapter Seven, discusses this problem.)

In addition, comparative designs raise the problem of whether like is being compared with like. The researcher may be drawing on several conflicting premises and traditions in the project design. First, there is the experimental tradition of positivist research in which researchers compare two situations which differ in only one feature, in order to measure the importance of that feature. However, even in this tradition, such minimal difference is only assumed to be attainable in a highly controlled and artificial situation. Second, and relatedly, there is the assumption that any difference resides in the phenomena under study rather than in the researcher: this is a return to the notion of the neutral researcher with unimpeded access to the meaningful world. A researcher who has rejected this assumption will have to present a reasoned justification for comparing different kinds of data or data from different situations. (Note that some discourse analysts would even challenge whether it is possible to make comparisons between two different interviews!)

A discourse analytic researcher planning a comparative project will therefore need to relate the project design to the assumed connections between language, meaning, context and interpretation. It is difficult to avoid theoretical confusion at an early stage of the project, so the researcher should not settle too quickly on the final form of the research question (or questions). The aim should be to refine and reword it a number of times, as the project design is developed. This will probably involve becoming more specific, incorporating terms from the theoretical background to the research, and referring specifically to the data for the project. It is possible in some cases that the final form of the question will not be decided on until the data have been collected.

The final wording of the research question needs to be very precise and will probably only emerge gradually. The researcher probably begins with rather general interests, for example in terms of topic area (such as race or gender) and material to be analysed (for example, from particular documents or interview participants). These interests are not in themselves research questions but will need to be refined. Silverman (1993: 2) draws a useful distinction between a problem that is discussed in the world around us, like homelessness, and a researchable topic. He points out that many new researchers make the mistake of attempting to research problems or answer questions which are impossibly large and wide-ranging. This is not, of course, a bad place to begin thinking: the mistake is to stop at this point instead of continuing to explore the possibilities and complexities before settling on the final form of the research question.

2.2 Discourse analytic data

It is likely that some prospective analysts, especially students, may have become interested in discourse analysis, and possibly turned directly to this section, because they already have access to a body of material, perhaps documents or recorded interviews, which they hope will provide the basis for some interesting research. This is a common situation and can lead to a successful project. However, it is important to consider exactly what constitute data, and not to approach the analysis with the assumption that whatever material is to hand somehow contains revelations, like gold within the dross, which can be extracted by a conscientious researcher working without preconceptions or any particular focus. Discourse analysis is not a neutral, technical form of processing but always involves theoretical backgrounding and decision making (see, for example, Potter, 1996: 130).

The above paragraph refers to a prospective researcher who already has a body of *material* rather than data. It is easy to assume that the data for discourse analysis already exist, and that new data are constantly being generated. In the world outside academia, newspapers are being printed and discarded, officialdom is producing documents, people are talking in a million contexts. Surely, it seems, all that needs to be done is to collect up the data and begin the analysis! However material only becomes data through certain considered processes, including selection. What count as data will depend on the researcher's theoretical assumptions, about discourse and also about the broad topic of the research.

I have said that one of the processes by which material becomes data is **selection**. There are several different criteria for selecting a **sample**. Most quantitative research, particularly surveys, uses a sample which is large enough to be representative of a population as a whole (that is, to include all the features which might be of interest) and which also permits generalization, based on assumptions about the frequency and regularity of features or phenomena. It is part of the special usefulness of quantitative work that large amounts (quantities!) of data can be analysed and summarized. Chapter Three presents some examples of quantitative discourse analyses, using computers.

In contrast, the analysis of qualitative data, including qualitative discourse data, is relatively inefficient and labour-intensive. It is often difficult to put the data into a succinct form for either analysis or presentation. The researcher is therefore likely to use a much smaller sample. This may, nonetheless, be designed to be as broad and inclusive as possible. For an interview study, participants may be selected to provide a balanced sample in terms of main population categories, such as gender. On the other hand, they may be selected *because* they belong to a particular limited category. For example, Wetherell and Potter (1992) sought participants who shared the same class and ethnicity. For a study of whiteness as a racial category, Frankenberg (1993) chose to interview white, female participants. These could be seen as examples of a sample selected to represent a 'specimen perspective' (ten Have, 1999: 50). The selection is not made to represent a population as a whole but a particular category within it: the aim is therefore to find participants who are 'typical' rather than exceptional.

A similar argument could be made for the selection of documents, and in both cases the claim that the selection are specimens could be supported by reference to statistics. Alternatively, the analyst might select documents because they are not broadly representative but highly specific, claiming that they are worthy of analysis because, for example, they are associated with powerful or well-known people. For example, Edwards and Potter (1992: Chapter 3) analyse newspaper articles and extracts from *Hansard* referring to the then-Chancellor of the Exchequer, Nigel Lawson; Stubbs (1996) analyses writings of the founder of the Boy Scout and Girl Guide movements, Baden-Powell; Jaworski and Galasinski (1998) analyse the talk of the former President of Poland, Lech Walesa. In these cases, there is an implied or stated argument that the origin or context of the material relates it to wider social practices. This can be similar to the argument of relevance as a criterion for evaluation (see Chapter Eight).

A somewhat different basis for selection could be justified in analyses which assume that language use reflects the knowledge or skills shared by members of the same culture. ('Culture' may be rather loosely defined here: it does not necessarily mean a distinctive national culture or any neatly bounded grouping.) For example, conversation analysts (see Chapter Two) assume that speakers hold in common a tacit knowledge of certain rules for conversational interaction and can recognize departures from these, such as when a conversational action does not receive an expected response. Discursive psychologists (see Chapters Four and Five) may assume that shared knowledge includes alternative understandings and constructions, for example, of the connection between mind and body (Chapter Four) or of what constitutes a 'good' couple relationship (Chapter Five). Following this, an analyst might select a relatively small sample of data with the justification that the patterns revealed in it indicate knowledge which is shared by other members of the culture.

Selection also extends to which **features** of material are relevant to the analysis and are, therefore, part of the data. For example, a study which focuses on language and assumes it is a (loose) system (as in the first approach to discourse analysis described in Section 1.1) might investigate patterns in its component parts, perhaps using computerized searching techniques such as concordancing (see Figure 2 in Chapter Three for an example). Following linguistics and sociolinguistics, Chapters Three and Six both select such features. (Another example is in Chapter 4 of Stubbs, 1996; a study which analyses language as part of an investigation of sexism.) The analyst might also be interested in features other than the words of the documents, such as the general appearance and layout. Again, Chapter Six provides an example of an analysis which considers these features. (Layout is also a feature in the analyses of local government documents by Stenson and Watt, 1999, and the analysis of a newspaper page by Kress, 1994.) In such cases, the data probably consist of original or photocopied documents rather than, say, a word-processed copy of the text.

In defining data, the discourse analyst must distinguish between the data themselves and **context** or **background information**. Some social researchers, such as ethnographers (see Hammersley and Atkinson, 1995, for an overview), do not make such a distinction: they attempt a form of total analysis in which it can be said that everything the researcher observes forms part of the data. Discourse analyses may be conducted as part of a larger ethnographic study (for example, du Gay, 1996; Back, 1996). Alternatively, some discourse analysts collect detailed background information to inform their analyses (see Mehan, 1996, reproduced as Reading Twenty-five in Wetherell *et al.*, 2001). Background information may also serve to define the data. For example, if the analyst's aim is to identify discourses within a certain class of official documents (see Chapters Six and Seven; see also Jagger, 1997, which analyses government talk and texts), those documents will only acquire their status as a result of their use within administrative systems, which may need to be established by the researcher.

Some analysts consider that the talk constitutes the data and no other information is needed. For a researcher interested in discourse as interaction, such as a conversation analyst (see Chapter Two), the focus is on what happens within the interaction. Background information is largely irrelevant and may even distort the interpretation. For example, it can be argued that including in the data the information that, say, one speaker is female and one is male amounts to a claim that gender is relevant to the interaction, when perhaps it is not. Is this necessary background information which should be provided, for example, about an interaction between a counsellor and a client or a doctor and a patient? (See below and Section 2.3 on transcription.) Similarly, there can be arguments for or against the relevance of other membership categories, such as age group, race, occupation and class. It could also be argued that the context and/or the physical location of the interaction are relevant to the data collection and analysis because they establish certain expectations for the kind of talk that is appropriate (see Shakespeare, 1998: 43–59). What counts as part of the data will depend, finally, on the particular project and the theory underpinning it.

Another process by which material becomes data is through **transcription**. This is discussed in more detail in the next section (see also Chapter Two) but some broad points can be made here. First, many (though not all) discourse analysts who study audio-recorded talk would not regard the talk itself as data without a process of further selection, through transcription. Furthermore, that basic material may provide different kinds of data, again depending on the focus of the analysis. For example, some social psychologists have investigated recurring patterns of word use, imagery and ideas within talk which have been defined as 'interpretative repertoires' (see Chapter Five). The exact definition is not necessary here (see Potter and Wetherell, 1987; Wetherell, 1998) but the approach is broadly similar to the third approach to discourse analysis outlined in Section 1.1. For a researcher interested in repertoires, the data are usually a body of interview material from different speakers. The researcher probably works from transcripts which record the words spoken by consecutive speakers but little further detail (see Gill, 1993; Marshall and Wetherell, 1989).

In contrast, for a conversation analyst who is interested in talk as interaction (like Wooffitt in Chapter Two), the data include not only the features of talk which are common to printed language (basically, the words) but also other aspects of the spoken interaction, such as the sequential organization of utterances from different speakers, including interruptions and pauses. Consequently, if the researcher works from transcripts, these will need to be much more detailed. The researcher will probably use a smaller quantity of data and will analyse each interaction separately. The analysis may require that the talk is 'naturally occurring' rather than collected through research interviews.

The description of language, usually talk, as **naturally occurring** has various possible meanings (see Chapter Four). In the most idealized form, it would probably refer to informal conversation which would have occurred even if it was not being observed or recorded, and which was unaffected by the presence of the observer and/or recording equipment. However, there are both technical and ethical problems with the covert recording necessary to obtain material of this kind (see Section 1.5 on ethics and informed consent). The closest satisfactory approximation is probably material which is obtained when the researcher has permission to record and the participants have become sufficiently accustomed to the presence of the recording equipment to act as if it was not operating (e.g. Goodwin, 1990). Of course, the researcher still has ethical obligations to the participants which may make some of the material unusable.

This approach assumes that naturally occurring talk is talk which is informal and occurs outside the context of situations with a declared purpose and particular venue. It can be argued that talk also occurs naturally in more structured situations such as courtrooms (Drew, quoted in Chapter Four), medical consultations (Coupland and Coupland, 1998), telephone calls to service providers (Sacks, quoted in Chapter Two), and even counselling sessions (Silverman, 2000; Edwards, 1997: 154). The naturalness here would not necessarily refer to whether the speakers were relaxed or unselfconscious, but to the talk being uninfluenced by the presence of the observer/recorder. (Again, the same ethical issues would apply.) One advantage for the researcher of using talk from these more structured situations might be that it is clearer in some ways what the talk is 'about'. However, this point is problematic. Medical consultation is not necessarily 'about' the medical problem under discussion or even about doctor/patient relations. But if the researcher is interested in interaction (as in my second approach to discourse analysis), talk from these situations might be taken as examples of a certain kind of interaction and could be analysed to show, for example, common features and patterns (e.g. Coupland and Coupland, 1998).

These various kinds of supposedly natural talk are usually contrasted with more conventional research interviews in which the researcher/ interviewer attempts to initiate talk which is 'about' something by conducting interviews specifically for the purpose of the research, usually working with a prepared list of questions or discussion topics. Discourse analysts who are interested in interaction may challenge the use of research interviews on two grounds. The first is that the interview is unnatural because the interviewer controls the interaction and influences the talk. The second is that the researcher incorrectly assumes that the talk is about the official topic of the interview, imposing her or his own interpretation on the talk (see the discussion of emic/etic in Section 1.3). Some researchers have attempted to avoid the first of these problems by setting up group discussions, usually in small groups, rather than one-to-one interviews (see Edley and Wetherell, 1997; Augoustinos *et al.*, 1999). Unfortunately, this can raise new problems of 'about'-ness: perhaps the interaction is now about group relations rather than the apparent topic of discussion? It can also raise new ethical problems related to confidentiality and respect for participants, especially if the topic of the research is a sensitive one. The researcher has an obligation to respect participants and avoid causing them distress, but one participant may feel no such obligation to another in the group and be careless of her or his feelings.

As this discussion has shown, discourse data vary widely. For every project, the researcher must establish the justification for the data being used, even if this is done cryptically through reference to a previous study. To conclude this section on discourse data, I will give some brief descriptions of published examples. In the first, as part of a study of nationalism, Billig (1995) analyses the main British newspapers on a single day. The data include the content of the news stories, the order and form of their presentation (for example, which pages they appear on), and also the language used. There is also some analysis at the level of the component parts of language, specifically of the deistic use of words like 'we' and 'our' (deixis means, loosely, that a word has no meaning except as it refers to another word: see Billig, 1995: 106). The nature of the data for this project follows from the ways in which both nationalism and discourse are theorized. Part of the researcher's task is to establish a connection between the broader topic or argument of the study and what are used as data, that is, between nationalism and particular features of newspapers. It is important to note here that this link is *not* created by treating language as transparent or reflective, and therefore as 'true' descriptions of phenomena. In this case, it would not be an adequate form of analysis to search the newspapers for all the references to 'nationalism' (although such a search might be a useful first step in coding material and choosing pieces for further analysis: see Section 2.4; also Potter and Wetherell, 1987: 167).

A second published example by Gill (1993) analyses interview transcripts in a study of equal opportunities for women in broadcasting, particularly radio. The interviews are conducted specifically for this study (in contrast to naturally occurring language, discussed above) and the researcher chooses to interview not women but men. The justification for this derives from a particular view of employment and of the factors which influence whether or not women are employed. A third study by Helleiner (1998) analyses documents rather than interviews. The data used here are parliamentary speeches and official reports on travellers and traveller children. In this study, part of the researcher's task is, again, to relate the data to the topic of concern. In both studies, the arguments which do this are subtle. This theorizing of the relationship between the general topic, the definition of discourse, and the data to be analysed cannot be taken for granted but needs to be established for each study.

This summary of issues around data and data collection, particularly as these relate to interviews, may seem frustrating, especially to a new researcher, since it raises many problems without offering firm solutions. It is always important to remember that no research is perfect, so every study must justify itself coherently and acknowledge (probably rather briefly!) the criticisms which can be made of it. This is particularly true about the selection of data. This will always be open to criticism and researchers working from very different premises may ultimately find each other's work and findings unacceptable. A project which is praised in one research tradition may be rejected by academics working in another discipline or theoretical area.

2.3 Transcription

An important aspect of data collection and selection in research involving talk is **transcription**. This is the process which, perhaps bizarrely, turns that talk into a document, a **transcript**. Doing transcription is a time-consuming process (estimates of how long it takes to transcribe an hour of recorded material range from about four hours for the simplest transcription of an audio-recording to perhaps more than twenty hours for detailed transcription of video). The best way to learn about it is probably to try doing it (see Chapter Two for a suggested activity). However, the following activity is intended to introduce some of the many issues around transcription.

Activity 1

Below are examples of transcript from five published discourse analytic projects. Look over them and try to answer the following questions for each transcript. The questions in Part A are concerned more with the practical process of transcription; those in Part B with the theoretical approach underlying it. You will probably want to read the discussion of Questions 1–4 before proceeding to Questions 5–6.

Part A

1 How many speakers are there?

2 How does the transcript differ from standard written text?

3 In addition to the words spoken, what details does the transcript include?

4 What extra information do you need to understand the transcript?

Part B

5 In what respects is the transcript a construction rather than a neutral record of talk?

6 What does the transcript show about the form of discourse analysis being used?

Extract 1

705:   *nie zauważyłem że hydra komunistyczna odrasta że pajęczyny*
706:   *tworzy że wlazło mi w całą gospodarkę i to to musi powodować*
707:   *niezadowolenie.*
705:   'I didn't notice that the communist hydra had been growing back
       that it spins webs
706:   that it has gone [me] into the entire economy and that must cause
707:   discontent.'

235:   *dzisiaj przymus wymaga przeciwstawić się (..) komunie która głowę*
236:   *podnosi*
235:   'today there is an obligation to oppose the commune which
236:   raises its head.'

Jaworski and Galinski, 1998, 'The last Romantic hero: Lech Walesa's
image-building in TV presidential debates', *Text*, vol.18, pp.524–44

Extract 2

Tony: W't's 'e g'nna do go down en pick it up later? er
                 something like (   ) [well that's aw]:ful
Marsha: [H i s friend]
Marsha: Yeh h[is friend Stee-]
Tony: [That really makes] me ma:d,

                          (0.2)
Marsha: ˙hhh Oh it's disgusti[ng ez a matter a'f]a:ct.
Tony: [P o o r J o e y,]
Marsha: I- I, I told my ki:ds. who do this: down et the Drug
                 Coalition ah want th'to:p back.h ˙hhhhhhhhh ((1.0))
                 SEND OUT the WO:RD.hhh hnh
                          (0.2)
Tony: Yeah.
Marsha: ˙hhh Bu:t u-hu:ghh his friend Steve en Brian er driving
                 up. Right after:: (0.2) school is out. En then hi'll
                 drive do:wn here with the:m.

Schegloff, 1997, 'Whose text, whose context?', *Discourse and Society*,
vol.8, pp.165–87

Extract 3

Shell: I'm quite, I'm certainly in favour of a bit of Māoritanga. It is
                 something uniquely New Zealand, and I guess I'm very
                 conservation minded (yes) and in the same way as I don't like
                 seeing a species go out of existence I don't like seeing (yes) a
                 culture and a language (yes) and everything else fade out.

Williamson: I think it's important they hang on to their culture (yeah) because
                 if I try to think about it, the Pākehā New Zealander hasn't got a
                 culture (yeah). I, as far as I know he hasn't got one (yeah) unless
                 it's rugby, racing and beer, that would be his lot! (yes) But the
                 Maoris have definitely got something, you know, some definite
                 things that they do and (yeah). No. I say hang onto their culture.

Wetherell and Potter, 1992, *Mapping the Language of Racism*

Extract 4

```
 1   D:  But er despite all of those things, in the majority
 2        of people the disease does come back
 3        (0.8)
 4   D:  even from the beginning.
 5   P:  Yes
 6   D:  And: (0.4) if it does come back we can try
 7        other drugs which may control it for a little while
 8   P:  mm um
 9   D:  but generally all that you can try and do is control
10        the symptoms.
11   P:  Yes mm.
12   D:  Uhm, the first time gives us the best chance
13        for a longer (0.5) survival hopefully long term
14   P:  hhm
15   D:  but the odds are generally against that.
16   P:  Yes um (0.4)
17   D:  But if we do nothing for these sorts of diseases it
18        kills you within a couple of months.
19   P:  Yes
```

Seale and Silverman, 1997, ensuring rigour in qualitative research',
European Journal of Health, vol.7, pp.379–84.

Extract 5

(nearing the end of the consultation)

```
 1   Doctor:     but er (.) I think things are OK and I think they'll
                 improve
     Patient:    yes
     Doctor:     OK?
 5   Patient:    well what the hell do I expect (.) I must be mad!
     Doctor:     (amused, reassuringly) I don't think you're mad
     Daughter:   chuckles
     Patient:    (laughs) I'm just a crabby old =

     Daughter:   =a thirty year old er brain inside an eighty year old
10              ⌈(laughs)
     Doctor:    ⌊that's right (.) it's frustrating isn't it?
     Patient:   (frustrated) I can't ⌈get on
     Daughter:                       ⌊oh but she's better than she says
     Doctor:    she is much better
15   Daughter:  yes
     Doctor:    OK
     Patient:   yes (warmly) thanks ⌈ever so much
     Doctor:                        ⌊that's alright (2.0) look after
                yourself
```

Coupland and Coupland, 1998, 'Reshaping lives, c9onstitutive identity
work in geriatric medical consultations, *Text* vol.18, pp.159–89.

Discussion of Questions 1–4

1   How many speakers are there?

In most transcripts the speaker is indicated on the left, like a playscript. So there are two speakers in Extract 2 (Tony and Marsha), two in Extract 4 (D and P) and three in Extract 5 (Doctor, Patient and Daughter). However in Extract 3 a different convention is used: the short comments of a different person, presumably the interviewer, are transcribed in brackets in the body of the talk of the main speakers. And in Extract 1 no interviewer or other person is included, although there was presumably at least one present (the title of the article indicates that the talk is from a television debate). It may be that no one else spoke during the stretches of talk which are transcribed here.

Other people may also have been present during the talk in other transcripts (for example, perhaps a researcher was in the consultation room in Extract 5). This raises the issue of whether the presence of other people is relevant: do they only count as part of an interaction and participants in the research if they speak?

2   How does the transcript differ from standard written text?

In these examples, Extract 1 is closest to standard written text, followed by Extract 3. Although a transcript is talk which has been in some way 'written down', it does not necessarily use standard sentences with punctuation such as commas and full stops, for the good reason that most of the time we do not speak in such sentences. (Notice, however, that elements of standard punctuation, like full stops and colons, may be used in a transcript to indicate other features of talk, as discussed in the answer to Question 3, below.) Extract 1 probably uses these conventions because the talk has been translated, and even here the sentences have been modified slightly, using layout and square brackets. Extract 3 organizes the talk into sentences but includes some of the irregularities typical of ordinary unscripted talk (for example, "I'm quite, I'm certainly" and "I, as far as I know he hasn't got one").

Notice that Extract 5 uses some conventions from a particular kind of writing, a dramatic script. Notes in brackets give information about the context ('nearing the end of the consultation'), sounds made ('laughs' and, not in brackets, 'chuckles') and also a speaker's feelings and speaking style ('amused, reassuringly', 'warmly') but whereas in a script, this information would be include as *instructions* to the director and actors, here it is included as description (see the discussion of Question 5 below).

As you are probably aware, it can be disconcerting to read a transcript for the first time, especially a transcript of your own talk, precisely because of the differences between spoken and written language. This may need to be discussed with participants if transcripts are to be returned to them for checking (see Chapter Eight): they may feel that the transcript gives a poor impression of them, as incoherent or poorly educated!

3   In addition to the words spoken, what details does the transcript include?

The most obvious extra detail is included in Extract 1 which presents the talk twice, in different languages, with the words in the original language (Polish) translated line by line.

Extracts 2, 4 and 5 attempt to differing degrees to record *how* the words were spoken, for example, by showing emphasis with italics, block capitals and underlining. Extract 3 does this to a lesser extent using spelling ('yeah' instead of 'yes', for example) and standard punctuation (an exclamation mark) and some phonetic conventions (the marks over some vowels, for example, in Māoritanga). All of the examples, except Extract 4, use spelling to indicate the contracted forms (didn't, it's, I'm) which are more commonly used, following complex conventions, in spoken than written English. Extract 5, as mentioned, also has additional notes similar to those used in a script to describe how something was said. Extract 2 and, to a lesser extent, Extract 1 use less obvious notations, like colons to indicate that a sound is drawn out. Notice that very detailed transcripts, like Extract 2, may borrow some conventions from phonetics, but they do not draw fully on any phonetic system, such as those used in dictionaries to indicate pronunciation; in other words, the attempt to indicate how participants speak is always partial and therefore selective.

Sounds other than words are indicated through the script-like directions in Extract 5 and spelled-out forms (oh, er, um, hhm) in Extracts 2, 4 and 5. In addition to the sounds made, Extracts 2, 4 and 5 indicate pauses and overlapping of talk. These are additional details about the sequence of the talk, which is recorded in all the transcripts using the left-to-right and top-down conventions of written English but notice that this is interrupted in two examples. In Extract 1, the talk in the original language (Polish) is followed directly by the English translation. In Extract 3, the speaker, Shell's, words do not follow from Williamson's but are taken from a different interview. In Extract 3, therefore, the top-down presentation indicates not sequence but *similarity*, a point I will return to.

There is other information which could be included in a transcript. The list of transcription symbols provided in Chapter Two indicates some possibilities, such as pace and intonation (the rising or falling tone noticeable, for example, in questions). There could be more information about the context or situation: for example, nothing in Extract 2 indicates that this is part of a telephone conversation. Some transcripts include details of actions, body language (such as smiles or grimaces) and gaze (see Swann and Graddol, 1994, for an example of the latter using notation and Suchman, 1997, for an example using words). West (1996) quotes from a transcript which distinguishes the different 'voices' used by a doctor who variously addresses a child patient and the parent and makes 'notes' into an audio-cassette recorder during a consultation.

These points raise the question of who the transcript is made *for*. A researcher working alone might include extra information in a transcript to assist her or his own analysis (this is similar to the 'metadata' described in Chapter Three). A professional transcriber or a researcher working as part of a team might add detail about context or speakers to help a different

analyst understand what was happening at a certain point in the talk.
(I recently returned to an audio-recording to help me understand its
transcript and, after some time listening and re-listening, realized that the
stilted quality of the interview, extended pauses and, on the recording,
occasional poor sound quality and strange background noises were all the
consequence of the participant having been interviewed while he was
eating lunch!) On the other hand, a transcript included within a publication
(like the five examples above) might have extra detail added or taken away
in order to improve the readability. An example is the line numbering
included in Extracts 1, 4 and 5. Similarly, arrows or other margin symbols
can be used to direct the reader's attention to key points.

In addition to what is included in the transcript itself, other information
about the talk is likely to be given in the text and elsewhere. Notice how
much information we are told about the talk in the titles of the publications
containing Extracts 1 and 5, for example. Footnotes could have been used
to explain local terms and references, such as Māoritanga, Pākehā and
Maori in Extract 3, if the analyst had judged that this was necessary.
Perhaps it would also be useful to know that 'rugby, racing and beer' is a
well-established expression with particular associations. And so on: the
decisions about what to include and explain blur the distinction between
transcription and interpretation.

4   What extra information do you need to understand the transcript?

The above discussion indicates some of the information which will have
to be supplied to enable a reader to understand a transcript: a list of
transcription symbols, if these are not obvious (see Chapter Two, Section 4,
for a list of the best known symbols, devised by Gail Jefferson);
supplementary information in the transcript itself or the accompanying text.
Some social researchers may present transcripts without an accompanying
analysis as a way of giving a voice to participants, but this is a different
research aim. Discourse analysis requires that even the most readable
transcript is presented only as part of a larger research text.

Discussion of Questions 5–6

*5   In what respects is the transcript a construction rather than a neutral
record of talk?*

I have already said that a transcript is a construction in so far as it cannot
be a total record of talk. Each of these examples therefore constructs the
talk through what is included or excluded.

As a brief summary, none of the extracts includes a record of actions and
body language, constructing the talk as more meaningful. They exclude
details about location which other analysts might consider relevant.
(Compare, for example, Suchman, 1997, and Goodwin, 1995, analysing talk
as part of workplace interactions). These transcripts also variously omit:
other participants in the talk (in Extract 1); information about how the
words are spoken (probably all to a greater or less extent, with Extract 2
least); details of the sequence, including pauses and overlap (Extracts 1, 3
and perhaps 4); contextual information, such as the date, occasion and

previous talk (though some of this is including in the accompanying texts for particular extracts); information about the speakers, such as gender and age, and so on. All the features discussed in answer to Question 3 are omitted from one or other of the transcripts. All of this selection works to construct certain features as meaningful.

The analyst's interpretation can also be reinforced by the inclusion of extra information in a transcript. For instance, all of these extracts, except Extract 1, give additional information within the transcript about the speakers and their relationships and roles. As a general point, notice that names, even when pseudonymous, can convey information about, for example, gender and, more subtly, class and ethnic background. The use of first names only may imply that the participants have an intimate relationship, family names only that they are speaking in a more formal role (see Billig, 1999). The identification of speakers as Doctor and Patient, or D and P as in Extract 4, not only reports these roles but suggests they are salient: in other words, the suggestion is that the identity of 'doctor' is more important here than the speaker's gender or any other identity. The role, therefore, constructs the talk as a certain kind of occasion and could be criticized for imposing this interpretation. We could ask: are the participants orienting to this?

In addition, more subtly, the transcript is a construction in that it *is* a transcript i.e. it is written rather than spoken; it selects a beginning and end point and it confers a special significance on *this* talk by discussing it in an academic research text. In other words, it is a selection from a much larger body of available material.

6   What does the transcript show about the form of discourse analysis being used?

As discussed above, a transcript emphasizes certain features of talk simply by recording them. By seeing what is included or excluded, we can draw some conclusions about the analyst's focus.

Transcripts which record in detail how people speak, or record sounds which are not words, suggest that these features are meaningful. In contrast, a transcript which presents talk as similar to writing, punctuating it as complete sentences, for example, suggests that the analyst is concerned with the meaning which resides in those features which talk shares with writing i.e. words. Whereas Extract 3 records the exact words used by speakers, Extract 1 suggests that meaning can be expressed in words, but the same meaning can be expressed in different ways, in slightly different words, or even in a different language. (Alternatively, it could be argued that Jaworski and Galasinski, from whom Extract 1 is taken, do not subscribe to the latter position but consider translation an inferior substitute, and this is the reason that the reader is not given just the translation but also the original talk, in Polish.)

A transcript which identifies participants in terms of roles (doctor and patient) is likely to focus on patterns in language in use associated with those roles and generalize accordingly. Transcripts which present the talk of different speakers in sequence suggest that the analyst is interested in meaning which is created through interaction, that is, jointly constructed.

Again, the focus could be mainly on the words used. This might require an extended sequence of talk (see Chapter Five). Alternatively, depending on the detail which is included, the focus could be on the conversational 'moves', such as interrupting, speaking over someone else, or failing to answer (Extracts 4 and 5 but particularly Extract 2) as part of social practices.

Transcripts which present parallel examples, such as Extracts 1 and 3, suggest that these contain patterns. From Extract 1, we can guess that the analysts are interested in patterns within the talk of a single speaker, whereas Extract 3 presents a pattern across the talk of different speakers, perhaps emphasizing the use of shared resources (see Chapter Five).

A final, and controversial, point to note is that an epistemological argument may be subtly conveyed by the sheer *quantity* of detail included in a transcript. On the one hand, an extremely detailed transcript may suggest that the analysis is derived directly from the data, downplaying the role and influence of the analyst, as in the positivist and postpositivist tradition outlined in Section 1.2. Relatedly, by making the transcript relatively difficult to understand, the detail may suggest that the analyst is a detached and objective technician rather than the involved interpreter implied by reflexivity (see Billig, 1999). On the other hand, an easily read transcript which uses standard writing conventions can work as a claim for the common-sense, uncontroversial nature of the interpretation presented.

Concluding comments

A transcript is a written-down version of what has been said, and in some cases done. The simplest form is probably a record of the words spoken. It can, in rare cases, be made from 'life' (West, 1996, quotes some examples). More usually, the transcript is made from an audio or video-recording which can be replayed and paused to allow the inclusion of more detail than an observer or participant could record, or even notice, in 'real time'. One advantage of the transcript is, therefore, the detail it contains. Another is its relative convenience and portability. Most analysts find they can work more quickly and efficiently from a transcript than by repeatedly listening to or watching recordings. However, it should be noted that working from recordings *is* a viable alternative, especially for preliminary analysis, such as coding (see Section 2.4 and Potter and Wetherell, 1987: 173). Furthermore, some researchers consider that transcripts should always be used in conjunction with the original recordings on which they are based, as a point of good practice. Others, more prosaically, may choose to work directly from recordings because the production of transcripts is, inevitably, extremely time-consuming. The ideal might seem to be to pay someone else to do the transcribing, but in practice this is expensive and often unsatisfactory.

Because, ultimately, transcription is a matter of selection and is therefore itself part of the analysis, not a separate stage (see Ochs, 1979: 44; also Riessman, 1993: 56–60), the researcher may need to refine transcripts made by someone else. (In Chapter Two, Wooffitt compares a transcript produced by a professional transcriber with the revised version he has produced for analysis.) A further use of transcripts is for the presentation of data to others. This has implications for the evaluation of research (see Chapter Eight). However, some researchers analyse from the recordings and then later transcribe short sections for presentation.

Transcripts involve selection, and precisely what is selected will depend on the theory and aims of the research project, as discussed above. It is important to emphasize, therefore, that there is no one way to do transcription, any more than there is one theoretical approach to discourse analysis. Correspondingly, there is not one set of transcription symbols. Although the best known are those devised by Gail Jefferson (a list of these is included in Chapter Two) most researchers using these will probably draw on a selection only. Other researchers will develop their own systems, perhaps based on standard written English. They may also use symbols to mark particular features which are important to their own projects. For a new analyst, the priority will be to decide which features of talk are significant and justify the decision, probably with reference to other published research.

This might suggest that transcripts are only usable for the particular project for which they are produced. However, in practice, researchers may conduct new analyses of transcripts produced for earlier projects. (Some research councils and other bodies compile archives of material for this purpose.) Researchers may also analyse transcripts produced for other purposes, such as the British parliamentary record, *Hansard* (see, for example, Activity 1 in Chapter Seven; also Edwards and Potter, 1992: 116). In these cases, there may be the problem that the transcript lacks details which the researcher would have wanted.

This might suggest that the ideal transcript is one which includes *everything*. However, as Activity 1 in this chapter has shown, this ideal is not attainable. First, there is the theoretical point which has been repeated throughout this chapter, that language is not assumed to be transparent or reflective. Logically, therefore, a transcript as a form of language cannot neutrally reflect the talk or interaction which it purports to record. It is itself a construction. Second, there are two practical objections to very full transcripts. As has already been mentioned, producing these involves unnecessary expenditure of time and money. In addition, excessive detail makes a transcript very large and extremely difficult to read and to work with.

The conclusion must be, therefore, that it is neither practical nor desirable to produce highly detailed transcripts as a substitute for identifying the focus of the study. Obviously it is reasonable and desirable to expect that the extended process of analysis will identify features which went unnoticed during transcription, itself an extremely useful first stage, especially if carried out by the analyst, but it is not feasible to treat transcription as a substitute for thinking and making decisions about the material. Approaches based in conversation analysis, also known as talk-in-interaction, do require the extremely detailed transcripts, but producing these may not be the first step in the analysis (see Chapter Two; also ten Have, 1999: 95).

There are other issues with transcription than those related to the level of detail. Ochs (1979: 46) points out that the convention by which consecutive utterances are placed below each other, like a play script, encourages the assumption that a particular utterance is a response to the one immediately preceding it. She suggests that this may not be the case when an interaction involves several people, or a child: "Young children frequently 'tune out' the utterances of their partner, because they are otherwise absorbed or because their attention span has been exhausted, or because they are bored, confused, or uncooperative". This comment may seem equally applicable to adults!

Decisions about the detail and the forms of notation used in the transcript are ultimately based in the theoretical approach. They can be challenged and disputed. An analyst may distort the meaning of the original talk by cutting an utterance short or extending it, in the same way that a news editor might change the import of a politician's comments by editing a film in a certain way. More subtly, an interpretation may be affected by the transcription (see the discussion in Chapter Eight of Seale and Silverman, 1997: 381–2, which includes Extract 4 above).

On the other hand, the elaborate notation of details which are not relevant to the analysis can make a transcript difficult to read. It can also reduce the amount of material which can practically be analysed and also reproduced in the writing up of the analysis (see Section 2.5). If the analyst's aim is to identify sets of related terms, such as discourses or interpretative repertoires (as in the third simplified form of discourse analysis described in Section 1.1), then she or he probably does not require the same level of detail as an analyst, like a conversation analyst, who is studying interaction (see Chapter Two).

A transcript therefore constructs a certain version of the talk or interaction which is to be analysed. This does not, of course, mean that it is false or misleading, but simply that it is not neutral. It selects out the features which the analyst has decided are relevant, that is, what the analyst counts as data.

2.4 The process of analysis

The title of this section is perhaps misleading in that it suggests that analysis is a distinct and separate activity. However, as I have already emphasized, the process of analysis includes transcription and to some extent also the definition and selection of data. Describing analysis in the abstract is necessarily inadequate, which is why the central chapters of the book, Chapters Two to Seven, work through examples from specific projects. However there are some useful general points which can be made for researchers new to discourse analysis.

The first of these is that most of the discourse analytic approaches presented in this book are qualitative. The nature of the analysis is therefore relatively open-ended and also circular, or **iterative**. The researcher is looking for patterns in the data but is not entirely sure what these will look like or what their significance will be. She or he must therefore approach the data with a certain blind faith, with a confidence that there is something there but no certainty about what. Conducting analysis involves going over data again and again, whether listening to recordings or reading transcripts or documents, noting features of interest but not settling on these. It involves working through the data over quite a long period, returning to them a number of times. Data analysis is not accomplished in one or two sessions. (These points are also made strongly in Chapter Seven, including in the useful guide to conducting one form of analysis, a Foucauldian genealogical discourse analysis.)

As possible patterns emerge, it is useful to note them but continue searching. Eventually there will be a range of possibilities to explore further. It will almost certainly be necessary to focus on some at the expense of others, leaving unfinished avenues for later exploration. Discourse data are 'rich', which means that it is probably impossible to reach a point where the data are exhausted, with nothing more to find in them because the analysis is complete.

Basic to this process is some kind of sorting and categorizing to identify patterns. The term '**coding**' has conventionally been used for the classification of research data into categories (Seale, 1999: 102–5). The common feature of software packages for data analysis is that they facilitate coding, for example, making it easy to underline or otherwise mark up sections of data (see Seale in Silverman, 2000, for a discussion of the use of computers to analyse qualitative data). Potter and Wetherell (1987) recommend broadly coding transcript as a starting point for discourse analysis in an approach similar to that presented by Edley in Chapter Five. This can be done using word-processor cut-and-paste functions. Notice, however, that they assume the use of broad and overlapping categories, whereas other approaches to data analysis have tended to set up exclusive coding categories, like those used in the analysis of survey data (Fielding, 1993). The principal difference, however, between discourse analyses and other data analyses is not this initial process of analysis but the analytic concepts involved. As has been discussed, these derive from how the research is located theoretically. Analytic concepts are given by the theoretical tradition, the research questions, and so on. The discourse analyst searches for patterns in language in use, building on and referring back to the assumptions she or he is making about the nature of language, interaction and society and the interrelationships between them. It is this theoretical underpinning rather than any sorting process which distinguishes discourse analyses.

Finally, with regard to writing up the analysis (see Section 2.5 below), notice that the final presentation of the analysis is not a record of the process but a summary of selected findings. Findings are presented for a reader so the most interesting or complete patterns are selected from others which are perhaps less complete. Writing up condenses a large amount of work. It is a common mistake on the part of researchers to allow too little time for data analysis compared to collection or the preliminary analytic task of transcription. The following section on writing up presents a fairly standard format for a research text in which the relative sizes of the sections do not in any way correspond to the time spent on any aspect of the research process.

2.5 Writing up the research

Several of the previous sections have emphasized that discourse analytic studies vary considerably, for example, in their data, foci and wider theoretical background. The design and conduct of a research project have been presented in terms of a series of decisions which confront the researcher, rather than through a straightforward model which can be followed. It would be an exaggeration to say that at the point of writing up, the decision making ceases. However, the positivist and postpositivist tradition has passed on a useful model for writing up research which continues to be relevant for many other researchers as well. Before introducing this, I should make a couple of points. It is, as I say, a loose model and, of course, has to be modified according to the discipline which the researcher is working in and also the purpose of the writing. For instance, a thesis is different from a journal article in several ways, apart from length, and a book chapter may be different again. Also, this model of the **research text** has been strongly challenged as a result of the double crisis of representation and legitimation discussed in Section 1.1 and some writers have rejected it completely. Nonetheless, it can provide a useful guide and starting point for producing a final research text, especially for a new researcher.

As a loose guide, the research text is divided into six parts. In practice, the number of these is not fixed, as I explain, but the text should be planned and written as several discrete sections. Students sometimes approach academic writing with a romantic image of a writer who, fired with inspiration, begins at the top of a blank page or screen and creates the text in a single creative flow, from the opening sentence to the ringing conclusion! This is over-optimistic and almost certainly inefficient. If the text is not planned, key points will probably be left out. Some sections, such as the account of how the project was conducted, can be prepared, at least in note form, while the research is being carried out. Others, like the introduction and conclusion, probably need to be written out of sequence. And, of course, the finished research text will not be read like a work of fiction, from start through to finish. Potential readers may skim the beginning and end first, and possibly the section headings and references, to see how the work connects to their own research interests. After that they may read the text as a single document. All of these points affect the process and final product of the writing up.

The **title** and the first **introductory section** of the research text present the research question or questions, the main claims which are being made, and an overview of the content of the whole text. The introduction should also be closely related to the closing section or paragraphs of the text, so that by looking at them both, as described above, an impatient prospective reader can obtain a fair understanding of what the text says. If the research is being written up for publication in an academic journal, there will also need to be an introductory **abstract**. This is an even more condensed summary of the text, usually in 100–200 words. One way to organize an abstract is to write a single-sentence summary for each section of the research text. The abstract will need further amendment and polishing before it is complete, but this is usually an effective way to begin.

The introduction will either flow into, or else be followed by as a separate section, the main **theoretical section** of the text. Following the conventions of good academic research practice (see Chapter Eight on evaluation), the broad task of this section is to locate the project in relation to an established tradition of academic work. The links may be positive or negative, in that the project may be presented as following on from or challenging previous research. This section explains where the current project is situated and also attempts to anticipate criticisms, justifying the approach being taken and possibly arguing against alternatives, particularly those that are best known or most recently published. For a discourse analytic researcher, there is likely to be a double task in locating the project theoretically. First, the text needs to present a position on the established theories and research-based publications related to the broad topic of the research: the most relevant will probably be those from the researcher's own discipline. The researcher may present the new project as following one particular theoretical tradition rather than another, or may argue for a modified or even new theoretical position. Second, this section presents the theory of discourse underpinning the research, perhaps through references to published research or perhaps as a more abstract discussion.

The next section of the research text is often referred to as the '**methods**' section (or chapter, in the case of dissertation or book). Conventionally, this consists of a full and detailed account of how the research was carried out. For a researcher who accepts the principle of replicability (see Chapter Eight), the aim is to enable a future researcher to replicate the project and, hopefully, confirm the findings. Other researchers, including most discourse analysts, may not expect that the research will, or even can, be replicated, but still use the section to describe the setting up of the project, and the collection and analysis of the data. The difference is that a researcher who accepts the concept of reflexivity (see Section 1.4) will not necessarily edit out problems and false starts: the aim is not to 'smooth' or idealize the research process. The researcher uses this account to acknowledge her or his own relationship to the research and discuss the constraints and limitations which operated. In addition, by describing exactly what was done, the researcher enables readers to assess the research. The detailed account can therefore work as a form of evaluation (see Chapter Eight). Finally, this openness has an ethical dimension: the researcher avoids concealment and accepts responsibility for the research and its outcomes (see Section 1.5).

Although the account of the research may assist others to evaluate it, this is not in itself sufficient. The evaluation of qualitative research is a complex and disputed area (see Chapter Eight). The methods section is therefore likely to include a discussion of the criteria which the researcher claims are relevant to the particular project, and arguments to support her or his claims that the research is of value.

The fourth section of the research text presents the **data analysis** and the **findings**. This is often a difficult section for the discourse analyst to structure because of the quantity of data used in the project. I will outline three possible ways to organize the section, each of which raises its own problems. The first is to present the data in full and work through the analysis to show the reader exactly how the data were interpreted and the conclusions were reached. This is the convention which is generally followed in conversation analysis for example (see Chapter Two). It operates as a form of reliability (see Chapter Eight), in that the analysis is open to scrutiny and criticism. The main problem, of course, is that only a limited quantity of data can be analysed. This is a practical difficulty, in that the analyst may have to leave out most of the material collected in larger-scale projects. It also has theoretical implications: either the claims which are made must be confined to the data presented, or there must be a theoretical justification for generalizing from that data to other cases (see Section 1.2).

A second structure for the analysis section is used in other traditions of social research which also use large quantities of qualitative data, such as ethnographic research (see Hammersley and Atkinson, 1995). The analysis and interpretation are conducted 'off-stage'. The analysis section presents only a summary of the data, perhaps with illustrative examples, and then explains the findings and conclusions and justifies them through argument. The process of analysis is not demonstrated completely because the reader is not presented with all of the data. An example of a discourse analytic research text which uses this structure is Brown (1999). The data for his study are twenty-two 'self-help' books, which obviously cannot be included in full. The research text presents summaries of the narratives, devices and the concept of self found in these, illustrated with brief quotations. The author's interpretation is written as a summary, without the data on which it is based. The general advantage of this second way of organizing the analysis section is clear: claims can be based on much larger quantities of data. A disadvantage is that the process of analysis is less open. Also, it can be difficult to find appropriate examples of data to illustrate the general claims being made: a feature which appears across a large sample may not be visible in a short extract. Finally, because discourse data tend to be rich, an extract offered as an example of a particular feature may be open to further analysis which distracts from the point it is intended to illustrate.

It should be noted, however, that the distinction between these two structures may blur. Even when the data for the analysis are presented in full, there has already been a process of selection and decision making, acknowledged or unacknowledged, about *which* data to use out of all that were gathered in the project. Interestingly, ten Have (1999: 24) analyses key papers in the conversation analytic tradition and shows how the authors do not limit the discussion and analysis to the data in the research text. He cites instances in which a claim is supported by reference to a larger body (or corpus) of material which is not presented to the reader. Reference is made to background or contextual information. In addition, reference is made to what might be described as general knowledge or common sense: "knowledge that any competent member (i.e. of society) is assumed to have on the basis of his or her own experience".

A third possible structure for an analysis section is only relevant if the theoretical approach permits language to be analysed out of the original context. One example of such a study is presented in Stubbs (1996). The focus of Stubbs' research is the means which are available within the

English language for indicating a speaker's or writer's point of view and attitude to a point being discussed (this is known as 'modality'). The data are examples from several very large corpora (a corpus, plural 'corpora', is a body of language data: the term is discussed more fully in Chapters Three and Eight). Particular short extracts, most of about four to ten words in length, are analysed in detail. In a few cases, a limited amount of background information is provided e.g. "A BBC radio news reader reported an explosion in a water-processing plant which had killed sixteen people" (Stubbs, 1996: 197). Claims are supported by references to the frequency with which a feature occurred, though this is not given in numbers e.g. "In my corpus data, the commonest surface form is ... " (p.212). The text is mainly written as a series of general statements, a style which is discussed in more detail below.

There may be other decisions around how to present data, such as how to make transcripts more readable (as was discussed in the previous section). At the stage of writing up the analysis, the original transcripts may be edited down and simplified or, alternatively, supplemented to make them more accessible to readers (for example, by indicating key utterances with an arrow, or with a label in an extra column on the right). In some instances the data may be translated (e.g. de Cillia *et al.*, 1999, see also ten Have, 1999: 93).

The fifth section of the research text is the **discussion** and/or **conclusion**. The divisions between sections will largely follow the conventions which operate in a particular discipline but also depend on how much data are included. One format would be for each piece of data to be analysed and the analysis to be discussed, in sequence. Another would be for all the data to be analysed and then the significance of the analysis discussed in a separate section (probably titled 'Discussion'). The conclusion may be very short, consisting mainly of a brief summary of the principal claims which refers back to the introduction. (The introduction and conclusion may well be written at the same time, to ensure that they 'tie together' well.) Alternatively, the conclusion may be a long section which contains the main discussion of the analysis. In either case, following again from the positivist and postpositivist tradition, the conclusion often addresses imagined researchers who would aim to replicate or build on the research as part of a cumulative tradition. It indicates directions for future research, perhaps to extend or clarify the findings of the current project or to fill gaps in a field. It may also discuss the applications of the findings of the project (see Chapter Eight).

The final two sections of the research text are the **references** and the **appendices**. These are, of course, differently formatted and do not continue the 'flow' of the account of the main text. However, I describe them here as sections to indicate their importance. The list of references contains all the works which are cited in the other sections. Some research texts require a fuller **bibliography** which also includes key works which have informed the project, even if these aren't referred to directly in the text. It therefore gives some indication of the traditions in which the analyst is working (though, of course, it will also include publications which are challenged and argued against, especially in the theoretical section). In a discourse analytic project, the appendices often contain extra data or information about data collection. For example, they may present samples of official documents if these are the data for the analysis. They may include extracts from transcripts which are too large to be included in the main text. However, it is not usually practical (for reasons of length), or desirable (for reasons of confidentiality) to include full interview transcripts as appendices. For an interview-based study, particularly for a larger research text such as a thesis, the appendices may include the question schedule (the list of questions or topic areas followed) and an example of the consent form used (note that this should not be an example which contains the name or signature of any participant). Appendices may also be used to present summarized information about participants (age, occupation etc.) in table form, if this is relevant to the selection of the data.

As well as offering a model for the structure of a research text, the positivist and postpositivist tradition originally established a certain writing style. In the same way that the researcher was not acknowledged as a presence in the research process, she or he was not referred to in the research text. Most obviously, the writing style avoided the use of the first person (references to 'I' or 'me') or expressions used in talk to indicate uncertainty or opinion (such as 'might', 'perhaps', 'seemed'). Also, as discussed above, the text, including the methods section, was written in grammatical forms which generalized the research procedures and findings and so suggested their universal nature. (An example from an early psychological study presents the findings as a 'law': "Of several responses to the same situation, those which are accompanied or closely followed by satisfaction to the animal will ... be more likely to recur", Thorndike, 1911: 244.) These features became conventions of academic writing, although they have broken down more recently in most social science disciplines. Particularly in social research such as discourse analysis, it is now more usual for the writer to 'appear' in a text through the use of 'I'. Alternatively, there may be references to 'we', though this is more ambiguous in tone: it may seem to refer to the research team, but it can also evoke the royal use of 'we' by a single person, and so return to the formality and the authority claims of the older style. Another change of style is that accounts of research are commonly written in the past tense as descriptions of particular events and situations rather than generalized procedures.

The conventional text model and writing style have been described because they offer a useful guide for new researchers. However, as the description also aims to show, there are theoretical associations and issues of power and authority attached to them. By using 'I' the writer introduces the voice of the author/researcher and hence brings her or him into the text. This can work against the impersonal authority of the conventional 'truth' text described above. Ideally, it can draw attention to the contribution of others to the research. Beckett (1996) is an example of an ethnographic/oral history study which attempts to give equal weight to the participants' and the researcher/analyst's voices. However, in other hands, this introduction of the researcher's voice can, less desirably, elevate the researcher to a position associated with a different kind of authority, the authority of charisma and celebrity associated with journalism and autobiographical writing. There is no neat answer to this problem but it is an example of the ongoing debates about the writing up of research. Some researchers have abandoned the conventional model in favour of more innovative, loosely structured pieces of writing, sometimes referred to as 'messy texts', which aim to move from a single voice to multiple voices. These issues also relate directly to the ultimate purpose of any research, which is discussed further in Section 3 in Chapter Eight

Conclusion

In this opening chapter, I have covered a very large amount of ground, albeit mostly in summary form. I have indicated some of the premises of discourse analytic research and the range of approaches which it encompasses. I have discussed some of the issues which the analyst must consider and offered an introductory guide to conducting discourse analytic research. The next six chapters present elaborated and detailed examples of the work of particular researchers, as a practical guide for readers who want to conduct their own discourse analytic projects. In the final chapter of the book, Chapter Eight, I resume my more general account and complete this overview with a discussion of the evaluation of discourse analytic research and its potential applications.

References

Ashmore, N. (1989) *The Reflexive Thesis: Wrighting Sociology of Scientific Knowledge*, Chicago, University of Chicago Press.

Atkinson, P. (1990) *The Ethnographic Imagination*, London, Routledge.

Atkinson, P. and Silverman, D. (1997) 'Kundera's *Immortality*: The interview society and the invention of the self', *Qualitative Inquiry* vol.3 pp.304–25.

Augoustinos, M., Tuffin, K. and Rapley, M. (1999) 'Genocide or failure to gel? Racism, history and nationalism in Australian talk', *Discourse and Society*, vol.10, pp.351–78.

Back, L. (1996) *New Ethnicities and Urban Culture: Racism and Multiculture in Young Lives*, London, UCL Press.

Banister, P., Burman, E., Parker, I., Taylor, M. and Tindall, C. (1994) *Qualitative Methods in Psychology: A Research Guide*, Buckingham, Open University Press.

Beckett, J. (1996) 'Against nostalgia: Place and memory in Myles Lalor's "oral History"', *Oceania*, vol.66, pp.312–22.

Billig, M. (1987/1996) *Arguing and Thinking: A Rhetorical Approach to Social Psychology*, Cambridge, Cambridge University Press.

Billig, M. (1995) *Banal Nationalism*, London, Sage.

Billig, M. (1999) 'Whose terms? Whose ordinariness? Rhetoric and ideology in conversation analysis', *Discourse and Society*, vol.10, pp.543–58.

Bornat, J. (1994) 'Recording oral history' in Drake, M. and Finnegan, R. (eds) *Sources and Methods for Family and Community Historians: A Handbook*, Cambridge, Cambridge University Press in association with the Open University.

Brown, S. (1999) 'Stress as regimen' in Willig, C., (ed.) *Applied Discourse Analysis: Social and Psychological Interventions*, Buckingham, Open University Press.

Coupland, N. and Coupland, J. (1998) 'Reshaping lives: Constitutive identity work in geriatric medical consultations', *Text*, vol.18, pp.159–89.

Croghan, R. and Miell, D. (1998) 'Strategies of resistance: 'Bad' mothers dispute the evidence', *Feminism and Psychology*, vol.8, pp.445–65.

de Cillia, R., Reisigl, M. and Wodak, R. (1999) 'The discursive construction of national identities', *Discourse and Society*, vol.10, pp.149–73.

de la Rey, C. (1997) 'On political activism and discourse analysis in South Africa' in Levett, A., Kottler, A., Burman, E. and Parker, I. (eds) *Culture, Power and Difference: Discourse Analysis in South Africa*, London, Zed Books.

Denzin, N. and Lincoln, Y. (1998) 'Introduction: Entering the field of qualitative research', in Denzin, N. and Lincoln, Y. (eds) *The Landscape of Qualitative Research*, Thousand Oaks, Sage.

Drew, P.(1990) 'Strategies in the contest between lawyers and witnesses' in Levi, J.N., and Walker, A.G. (eds) *Language in the Judicial Process*, London, Sage.

du Gay, P. (1996) *Consumption and Identity at Work*, London, Sage.

Edley, N. and Wetherell, M. (1997) 'Jockeying for position: The construction of masculine identities', *Discourse and Society*, vol.8, pp.203–17.

Edwards, D. (1997) *Discourse and Cognition*, London, Sage.

Edwards, D. and Potter, J. (1992) *Discursive Psychology*, London, Sage.

Fielding, J. (1993) 'Coding and managing data' in Gilbert, N. (ed.) *Researching Social Life*, London, Sage.

Foucault, M. (1961/1997) *Madness and Civilisation: A History of Insanity in the Age of Reason*, London, Routledge.

Frankenberg, R. (1993) *White Women, Race Matters: The Social Construction of Whiteness*, London, Routledge.

Gill, R. (1993) 'Justifying injustice: broadcasters' accounts of inequality in radio' in Burman, E. and Parker, I. (eds) *Discourse Analytic Research*, London, Routledge.

Goodwin, C. (1995) 'Seeing in depth', *Social Studies of Science*, vol.25, pp.237–74.

Goodwin, M.H. (1990) *He-Said-She-Said: Talk as Social Organisation Among Black Children*, Bloomington, Indiana University Press.

Hammersley, M. and Atkinson, P. (1995) *Ethnography: Principles in Practice*, London and New York, Routledge.

Helleiner, J. (1998) 'Contested childhood: The discourse and politics of traveller childhood in Ireland', *Childhood*, vol.5, no.3, pp.303–24.

Hodge, R. and Kress, G. (1988) *Social Semiotics*, Cambridge, Polity.

Hollway, W. (1984) 'Gender difference and the production of subjectivity' in Henriques, H. *et al.*, *Changing the Subject*, London, Methuen.

Jagger, E. (1997) 'The production of official discourse on "glue-sniffing" ', *Journal of Social Policy*, vol.26, pp.445–65.

Jaworski, A. and Galasinski, D. (1998) 'The last Romantic hero: Lech Walesa's image-building in TV presidential debates', *Text*, vol.18, pp.525–44.

Kress, G. (1994) 'Text and grammar as explanation' in Meinhof, U. and Richardson, K. (eds) *Text, Discourse and Context: Representations of Poverty in Britain*, Harlow, Longman.

Lynch, M and Bogen, D. (1996) *The Spectacle of History: Speech, Text and Memory at the Iran-Contra Hearings*, Durham: NC and London, Duke University Press.

Marshall, H. and Wetherell, M. (1989) 'Talking about career and gender identities: A discourse analysis perspective' in Skevington, S. and Baker, D. (eds) *The Social Identity of Women*, London, Sage.

Maybin, J. (2001) 'Language, struggle and voice: The Bakhtin/Voloshinov writings' in Wetherell, M., Taylor, S. and Yates, S.J., *Discourse Theory and Practice: A Reader*, London, Sage in association with The Open University.

Mehan, H. (1996) 'The construction of an LD student: a case study in the politics of representation' in Silverstein, M. and Urban, G. (eds) *Natural Histories of Discourse*, Chicago, University of Chicago Press.

Ochs, E. (1979) 'Transcription as theory' in Ochs, E. and Schiefflin, B. (eds) *Developmental Pragmatics*, New York, Academic Press.

Potter, J. (1996) 'Discourse analysis and constructionist approaches: Theoretical background' in Richardson, J. (ed.) *Handbook of Qualitative Research Methods for Psychology and the Social Sciences*, Leicester, BPS.

Potter, J. (2001) 'Wittgenstein and Austin: Developments in linguistic philosophy' in Wetherell, M., Taylor, S. and Yates, S.J., *Discourse Theory and Practice: A Reader*, London, Sage in association with The Open University.

Potter, J. and Wetherell, M. (1987) *Discourse and Social Psychology: Beyond Attitudes and Behaviour*, London, Sage.

Riessman, C. (1993) *Narrative Analysis*, Newbury Park, Sage.

Rose, N. (1985) *The Psychological Complex: Psychology, Politics and Society in England 1869–1939*, London, Routledge and Kegan Paul.

Said, E. (1978) *Orientalism*, London, Penguin.

Sapsford, R. (1999) *Survey Research*, London, Sage.

Schegloff, E. (1997) 'Whose text? Whose context? *Discourse and Society*, vol.8, pp.165–87.

Seale, C. (1999) *The Quality of Qualitative Research*, London, Sage.

Seale, C. and Silverman, D. (1997) 'Ensuring rigour in qualitative research', *European Journal of Public Health*, vol.7, pp.379–84.

Shakespeare, P. (1998) *Aspects of Confused Speech: A Study of Verbal Interaction Between Confused and Normal Speakers*, Mahwah: NJ, Lawrence Erlbaum Associates.

Silverman, D. (1993) *Interpreting Qualitative Data: Methods for Analysing Talk, Text and Interaction,* London, Sage.

Silverman, D. (2000) *Doing Qualitative Research: A Practical Handbook,* London, Sage.

Smith, M. (1998) *Social Science in Question*, London, Sage.

Stenson, K. and Watt, P. (1999) 'Governmentality and "the death of the social"?: A discourse analysis of local government texts in South-east England', *Urban Studies*, vol.36, no.1, pp.189–201.

Stubbs, M. (1996) *Text and Corpus Analysis: Computer Assisted Studies of Language and Culture*, Oxford, Blackwell.

Suchman, L. (1997) 'Centers of co-ordination: A case and some themes' in Resnick, L., Saljo, R., Pontecorvo, C. and Burge, B. (eds) *Discourse, Tools, and Reasoning: Essays on Situated Cognition*, NATO ASI Series F: Computer and Systems Sciences, vol.160, Berlin, Springer

Swann, J. and Graddol, D. (1994) 'Gender inequalities in classroom talk' in Graddol, D., Maybin, J. and Stierer, B., (eds) *Researching Language and Literacy in Social Context: A Reader*, Clevedon, Multilingual Matters in association with The Open University.

ten Have, P. (1999) *Doing Conversation Analysis: A Practical Guide*, London, Sage.

Thorndike, E.L. (1911) *Animal intelligence,* New York, Macmillan: cited in Roth, I. (1990) *Introduction to Psychology*, Hove, Lawrence Erlbaum and Associates Ltd in association with The Open University.

Wertsch, J. (1990) 'The multivoicedness of meaning' in Wertsch, J., *Voices of the Mind*, London, Harvester Wheatsheaf.

West, C. (1996) 'Ethnography and orthography: a (modest) methodological proposal', *Journal of Contemporary Ethnography*, vol.25, October, pp.327–52

Wetherell, M. (1998) 'Positioning and interpretative repertoires: Conversation analysis and post-structuralism in dialogue', *Discourse and Society*, vol.9, pp.387–412.

Wetherell, M. (2001a) 'Debates in discourse research' in Wetherell, M., Taylor, S. and Yates, S.J., *Discourse Theory and Practice: A Reader*, London, Sage in association with The Open University.

Wetherell, M. (2001b) 'Themes in discourse research: The case of Diana' in Wetherell, M., Taylor, S. and Yates, S.J., *Discourse Theory and Practice: A Reader*, London, Sage in association with The Open University.

Wetherell, M. and Potter, J. (1992) *Mapping the Language of Racism*: *Discourse and the Legitimation of Exploitation*, Hemel Hempstead, Harvester Wheatsheaf.

Wetherell, M., Taylor, S. and Yates, S.J. (eds) (2001) *Discourse Theory and Practice: A Reader*, London, Sage in association with The Open University.

CHAPTER TWO

Researching Psychic Practitioners: Conversation Analysis

Robin Wooffitt

Introduction

Conversation analysis (or CA) is a method for the analysis of naturally occurring interaction. Its key assumption is that language use is a site for social action: people do things to each other when they talk. Moreover, the way in which utterances are designed will be informed by, and thereby display the relevance of, the speakers' **communicative competencies**: procedures, methods, maxims and practices for producing mutually intelligible interaction which are available to them by virtue of their membership of a natural language speaking community. Finally, and perhaps most important, it is assumed that these tacit communicative resources are manifest in robust and oriented-to patterns in interaction, which can be identified and explored as the sites in which particular kinds of interpersonal activities are accomplished.

What I want to do in this chapter is to unpack this paragraph. Consequently, the early parts of this chapter will focus on the methodology of CA, and some of the assumptions which inform that method. (Unfortunately, then, there will not be much space devoted to a review of the findings from conversation analytic studies. However, a list of introductory accounts and seminal papers is provided at the end of the chapter.) To illustrate many points in the discussion, I will be using data from a corpus of recordings of members of the public having consultations with psychic practitioners, such as mediums, clairvoyants, astrologers, tarot card readers, and so on. This kind of material has been selected for several reasons. First, interaction between psychic practitioners and their clients exhibits some clear and recurrent patterns; this facilitates attempts to illustrate aspects of the focus of a conversation analytic approach. Second, psychic-sitter interaction allows me to raise some of the key issues in the study of what is known as **institutional interaction**. As will become apparent, CA does not only study conversational interaction, but can be used to investigate talk which happens in workplace settings, in which participants orient to the relevance of a limited set of work-related discursive tasks. Finally, psychic practitioners claim to have paranormal powers. This is a controversial claim, and considerable effort has been expended in trying to discover whether or not their claimed powers are genuine. However, CA's approach is markedly different in that it is agnostic as to the truth or falsity of what people are saying. By looking at the kind of data in which most people would be initially interested in *what* was said we are in a better position to appreciate CA's distinctive concern with *how* talk is produced.

1   What is conversation analysis?

What is now known as conversation analysis emerged from Harvey Sacks' utterly distinctive analyses of the organization of everyday language use, which were then developed in collaboration with his colleagues, Emmanuel Schegloff and Gail Jefferson in the 1960s.

What Sacks was trying to do was develop a new method of sociology in which the analytic observations were grounded in detailed analysis of actual instances of human behaviour; not idealizations of behaviour, or laboratory-produced exemplars of human conduct, nor introspectively-grounded intuition about social action, nor ethnographic field notes of events, and so on. It was this concern that led him to study language use. His concern to develop a sociology based on analysis of real life events meant he needed to have data which were some kind of record of those real life events, and which would facilitate repeated inspection. And the availability of recording technology ensured that it was easy to record talk. Moreover, recordings of real life interaction allow the analyst to transcribe in whatever detail he or she requires, and permit repeated listening and analysis.

In one of his lectures Sacks said:

> It was not from any large interest or from some theoretical formulation of what should be studied that I started with tape recorded conversation, but simply because I could get my hands on it and I could study it again and again, and also, consequentially, because others could look at what I had studied and make of it what they could, if, for example, they wanted to be able to disagree with me.
>
> (Sacks, cited in Atkinson and Heritage, 1984: 26)

So Sacks started to examine conversation because it was the most convenient form of human behaviour with the recordings of which he could try to develop his new method of doing sociology.

There is another benefit from studying actual instances of human behaviour. If a native speaker of English had to sit down and try to describe what happens in conversational interaction, they would certainly not be able to capture its complexity, or its orderliness: the importance of silences of less then a third of a second; the way speakers are able to exchange turns at talk with minimal gaps or overlap between consecutive speakers; the range of exquisitely subtle methods participants use to identify and deal with troubles or errors in interaction; the significance of false starts to words, restarts, minor corrections and the other range of odd noises and non-lexical sounds people produce in conversational interaction. But whereas intuition fails the analyst, recordings of actual events, and detailed transcripts of them, permits capture of the detail of participants' conduct. The analyst is relieved of the near impossible task of trying to imagine what goes on during the interaction: the analyst can actually find out by careful listening to the tape, and investigation of the subsequent transcript. (Transcription will be discussed in Section 2.)

Conversation analysis began with a question. Sacks had been working on a corpus of recorded telephone calls to the Los Angeles Suicide Prevention Center. He had observed that, in the majority of cases, if the Center's personnel gave their names at the beginning of the conversation, the callers would give their names in reply. Sacks came to notice, however, that in one call the caller (B) seemed to be having trouble with the agent's name.

Extract 1

A: this is Mr. Smith, may I help you

B: I can't hear you

A: This is Mr <u>Smith</u>

B: Sm<u>i</u>th

(Sacks, 1992, vol.1: 3)

Sacks also observed that for the rest of the conversation the caller remained reluctant to disclose his identity. This was not unusual, as the Center's staff frequently experienced difficulties in getting callers to identify themselves. The issue Sacks began to explore was 'where, in the course of the conversation could you tell that somebody would not give their name?' (1992, vol. 1: 3). It was this problem, and this sequence, which led to Sacks' unique approach to the study of conversation. In a memoir of Sacks, Schegloff recalls that:

> It was during a long talking walk during the late winter of 1964 that Sacks mentioned to me a 'wild' possibility that had occurred to him. He had previously told me about a recurrent and much discussed practical problem faced by those who answered phone calls to the Suicide Prevention Center – the problem of getting the caller to give their names ... On the one hand, Sacks noted, it appears that if the name is not forthcoming at the start it may prove problematic to get. On the other hand, overt requests for it may be resisted. Then he remarked: is it possible that the caller's declared problem in hearing is a methodical way of avoiding giving one's name in response to the other's having done so. *Could talk be organized at that level of detail? And in so designed a manner?*

> (Schegloff, 1992: xvi–xvii, emphasis added)

With this question, Sacks raised the possibility of investigating utterances as objects which speakers use to get things done in the course of their interactions with others. That is, an utterance as simple as 'I can't hear you' might be analysed to reveal how it is being employed to achieve a specific task in the course of the conversation. Sacks' subsequent analysis reveals that by 'not hearing', the caller is able to establish a series of turns in the conversation which ensures that it is increasingly unlikely that the member of the Center's staff will be able to obtain the caller's name without actually requesting it. In this case, then, the caller's expression of an apparent hearing difficulty is a method by which he could accomplish the activity of 'not giving a name' without explicitly refusing to do so.

Sacks' subsequent detailed inspection of transcripts of recorded conversations began with the assumption that lengthy utterances, phrases, clauses, or even single words were used methodically in everyday interaction. They were studied as objects that were being used to do things. The goal of analysis, then, was to investigate the nature of these objects – how they were designed, where in interaction they occurred – and to describe the underlying organization of the way they were used: in short, to investigate how a speaker came to use these words, in this way and on this occasion.

This leads us to a key assumption of conversation analysis. Sacks' interest in the methodic properties of speakers' utterances should not be taken to imply that he wanted to describe *psychological* reasoning processes. Neither does it imply that this form of analysis proposes that speakers *intentionally* use these words to achieve certain effects. Sacks' work, and subsequent CA research, has focused on **talk-in-interaction** as a domain of social activity that is inherently ordered and not reducible to the personality, character, mood, and so on, of the people doing the talking. While not denying that people have intentions, motives or interests, CA does not treat interaction as a mere externalization of these inner cognitive processes. However, Sacks was aware that his mode of analysis could be taken to imply that he was engaged in an attempt to model or describe the psychological processes which underpinned competence in language use. At the end of his first lecture on conversational organization, he observed that when confronted with a detailed analysis of the social organization of interaction, one might:

> ... figure that they [the speakers] couldn't have thought that fast. I want to suggest to you that you have to forget that completely. Don't worry about how fast they're thinking. First of all, don't worry about whether they're 'thinking'. Just come to terms with how it is that [the detail of talk] comes off. Because you'll find that they can do these things ... Look to see how it is that persons go about producing what they do produce.
>
> (Sack, 1992, vol.1: 11)

Interaction, then, is viewed as a domain of activity in its own right, and not as an expression of psychological idiosyncrasies and dispositions. Moreover, there has been a rejection of *a priori* theorizing about the significance of conversation *per se*, or particular activities in interaction. That is, the analyst does not begin analysis with a series of pre-established and theory-led questions or issues to be explored in the data. So conversation analysts won't approach data to examine, for example, how power is mobilized in interaction; or how gender differences influence conduct. One argument for this is, broadly, that the world is already interpreted by the participants themselves. It is important to investigate *their* interpretations of what is happening in the interaction rather than to impose somewhat arbitrarily a set of assumptions and relevancies, which might in fact, have no bearing on the details of participants' actual conduct. This is an issue we will return to later in this section.

In the following section we will explore further Sacks' recommendation to 'Look to see how it is that persons go about producing what they do produce'.

In his earliest lectures Sacks was interested in the way that certain conversational actions seemed to go together: for example, greetings, such as 'hello' – 'hello' seem to form a 'natural' pair. And there seems something equally right about the way that questions will be followed by answers, and the way that invitations will be followed by acceptances (or rejections), and so on. To account for the recurrent structural properties of the organization of these kinds of paired units, Sacks proposed the concept of the **adjacency pair**. Heritage (1984: 246) provides the following formulation.

An adjacency pair is a sequence of two utterances which are:

- adjacent

- produced by different speakers

- ordered as a first part and second part

- typed, so that a first part requires a particular second (or range of second parts).

So, for example, an invitation would be the first part of an invitation–response pair.

This may seem to be an overly complex account of fairly trivial everyday events. However, the concept is important because it points to the **normative** character of paired actions: a first speaker's production of the first part of a pair projects a slot into which the second speaker *should* produce the appropriate second part. That is, the second part of a pair is made **conditionally relevant** by the production of a first part (Schegloff, 1972).

There are various kinds of evidence for this. For example, if a first part has been produced, and the appropriate next has not been produced, first speakers will pursue the second part, thus demonstrating their tacit understanding that it is accountably missing. In the following extract, the child has asked her mother a question. After a gap of over a second, the mother has not answered, and the child speaks again.

Extract 2

Child:	Have to cut the:se Mummy
	(1.3)
Child:	Won't we Mummy
	(1.5)
Child:	Won't we
Mother:	Yes

(Atkinson and Drew, 1979: 52)

Note how the child provides increasingly truncated versions of the initial question. This indicates that the child is not proceeding on the understanding that her mother did not hear her (for that would entail a repeat of the whole question), but on the assumption that Mother has heard but has not answered. The child's next two utterances thus constitute increasingly focused prompts to her mother to produce the now conditionally relevant appropriate second part. In this sense, the child's understanding of the normative properties of paired actions informs her (tacit) analysis of the absence of her mother's response and her subsequent utterances. The normative properties of paired action sequences thus provide a valuable resource for speakers by which to make sense of what is happening in interaction, and what would be an appropriate turn to produce next. (See Heritage, 1984: 247–53, for a more detailed discussion of the evidence for the normative basis of paired actions.)

The discussion of adjacency pairs illustrates CA's fundamental concern with **sequential analysis**. It is not interested in single utterances, but it is centrally concerned to explore how utterances are designed to tie with, or 'fit' to, prior utterances, and how an utterance has significant implications for what kinds of utterances should come next. In short, CA explores how utterances cohere together to become identifiable sequences of conversational actions which have regular properties. It is for this reason that we refer to paired action *sequences*.

However, there is something quite interesting about certain kinds of paired action sequences. If a question is asked, it is apparent that what should come next should be an answer, or some reason why an answer can't be provided. Some first parts of pairs, however, could be followed by one of two second parts: for example, an invitation can be followed by an acceptance or a refusal. Similarly, offers can be accepted or declined. It is noticeable, however, that these kinds of possible second parts are not equivalent in that they are produced in very different ways. Consider the following extracts.

Extract 3

1   **Jo**: T's- tsuh a beautiful day out isn't it?

2   **Lee**: Yeh it's jus' gorgeous.

(Pomerantz, 1984: 59)

Extract 4

1   **A**:   Why don't you come up and see

2   me some ⌜times

3   **B**:   ⌞I would like to

(Atkinson and Drew, 1979: 58)

In Extract 3 the first speaker offers an assessment, which could be met either by agreement or disagreement. Here the speaker agrees and does so quickly, without any delay after the end of the first speaker's turn. And in Extract 4, the first speaker produces an invitation which is accepted before the first turn is completed. However, consider the following extract in which an offer is declined.

Extract 5

1	**B**:	Uh if you'd care to come over and
2		visit a little while this morning
3		I'll give you a cup of coffee
4	**A**:	hehh Well that's awfully sweet of you,
5		I don't think I can make it this morning
6		hh uhm I'm running an ad in the paper and and uh I
7		have to stay near the phone.

(Atkinson and Drew, 1979: 58)

Even from an initial glance it is obvious that the action of declining an invitation is accomplished in a markedly different way to acceptance. First, in contrast to the immediate or even 'early' agreement or acceptance in the previous extracts, the refusal is not produced immediately, but delayed slightly by the out breath "(hehh)", which is in Line 4. The speaker then says "well" (a word which is routinely used at the beginning of refusals) followed by an appreciation of the offer: 'that's awfully sweet of you'. The rejection itself is very different from the agreement and acceptance, which were unequivocally positive. The rejection "I don't think I can make it this morning" is not as definite: the "I don't think" somehow qualifies and thereby softens the force of the rejection. Finally, in Lines 6 and 7 there is a clear account as to why the speaker can't accept the offer: the fact that she has to stay by the phone is offered as the excuse for the refusal.

These different ways of accomplishing acceptances and rejections are not specific to these two cases, nor to these two sets of speakers. In fact, Extract 5 illustrates a very consistent pattern which occurs when invitations or offers are declined or rejected. The same components appear in the declining turn in the following extract, and in the same order.

Extract 6

(S's wife has just slipped a disc.)

H: And we were wondering if there's anything we can do to help

S: ⌈Well at's

H: ⌊I mean can we do any shopping for her or

something like tha:t?

(0.7)   **Delay**

S:	Well	**Preface**
	that's most kind Heatherton	**Appreciation**
	At the moment no:.	**Mitigated rejection**
	because we've still got	**Account**
	the boys at home.	

(Heritage corpus data, ref. Her: 0II:2:4:ST)

In CA the terms **preferred** and **dispreferred** are used to capture the systematic differences in the ways that alternative second parts are designed. The format of agreements, acceptance, and so on is called the preferred action turn shape and the term for the format of disagreements, rejections and refusals is called the dispreferred action turn shape (Pomerantz, 1984: 64).

It is important to note, however, that the concept of preference, as it is used in CA, does not refer to the psychological motives or intentions of individuals. Rather, the terms preferred and dispreferred allow the characterization of the different structural features of the ways in which alternative but non-equivalent second parts may be produced.

At first, it may appear that conversation analysis aims to produce no more than a rather gross kind of subjective interpretation of the materials being examined. For example, in Extract 2, there may be other ways of interpreting why the child said what she did. On what basis, then, can conversation analysts claim any priority for their analyses? Does the reader have to take the analyst's interpretations on trust? No, because analytic claims are always grounded in detailed explication of the details of interaction; moreover, they are warranted by reference to the participants' tacit understanding of, or orientation to, the normative underpinning which demonstrably informs their conduct. The phrase '**demonstrably informs**' is crucial to conversation analysis research, and leads to a discussion of another central methodological point.

It is important to emphasize that the goal of conversation analysis is not to furnish an academic or 'outsider's' reading of some conversational sequence, but to describe the organized interpretations that *people themselves* employ in the moment-by-moment course of conversation. Thus the analytic claims about the child's utterances in Extract 2 were based upon her understanding of what was happening at that moment *as it was revealed in the kind of turn she went on to produce.* That is, if she had analysed the situation and concluded that the mother hadn't heard the question, there would have been little point in providing a shorter version, and she would have gone on to produce a different kind of utterance. That she provided a truncated version of the question demonstrates that she had interpreted the absence of talk after her question as a slot for which an appropriate action – in this case, an answer – should be produced.

The focus of analysis, then, is the understanding of 'what-is-going-on-right-here-right-now' which speakers themselves have, and which are revealed – and thereby, demonstrable – in the design of subsequent utterances.

To explain this key methodological principle, consider the following extract, which comes from an exchange between a mother and her son about a Parent Teachers Association meeting.

Extract 7

1 **Mother**: Do you know who's going to that meeting?

2 **Russ**:   Who?

3 **Mother**: I don't know!

4 **Russ**:   Oh, probably Mr Murphy and Dad said Mrs

5   Timpte an' some of the teachers

(Terasaki, 1976: 45)

In this extract Mother's question "Do you know who's going to that meeting?" can be interpreted in two ways: as a genuine *request* for information about who is attending the meeting, or as a *pre-announcement* of some news concerning the people who will be attending the meeting. In the examination of this exchange, the analyst can identify which of these interpretations Russ makes by looking at the next turn after Mother's question. He returns the floor to his mother with a question, thereby displaying that he treats her utterance as a pre-announcement. Mother's next turn displays that on this occasion Russ's inference was incorrect.

The kinds of interpretative and reasoning procedures that CA seeks to identify are thus displayed in the trajectory of language use, which is organized on a turn-by-turn basis. It is for this reason that conversation analysts place great emphasis upon the examination of *sequences* of interaction, rather than, say, the detailed analysis of utterances which have been extracted from the sequential context in which they occurred. The methodological import of this is stressed by Sacks *et al.*:

> ... while understandings of other turns' talk are displays to co-participants, they are available as well to professional analysts who are thereby afforded a proof criterion (and search procedure) for the analysis of what a turns' talk is occupied with. Since it is the parties' understandings of prior turns' talk that is relevant to their construction of next turns, it is *their* understandings that are wanted for analysis. The display of those understandings in the talk of subsequent turns afforded both a resource for the analysis of prior turns and a proof procedure for professional analysis of prior turns – resources that are intrinsic to the data themselves.
>
> (Sacks, Schegloff and Jefferson 1978: 45 [1974], original emphasis)

Summary

It would be useful to summarize the discussion so far.

- CA emerged from the pioneering work of Sacks and his colleagues Schegloff and Jefferson.
- CA is a method for analysing the way people talk which treats language as action: it is interested in the way utterances can be designed to do things.
- It sets out to identify and describe the properties of action sequences: patterns of interaction with robust and consistent properties.
- It examines how speakers' conduct displays a sensitivity to the normative dimensions of action sequences.
- Contributions to interaction are taken to be shaped by the immediate context of the preceding utterance; and insofar as an utterance is followed by another, it shapes the context for the subsequent turn(s).
- It focuses on people's own analysis as revealed in the turn-by-turn unfolding of conversation.
- Empirical work must be done on naturally occurring data: intuition will not reveal the details of talk, nor the significance of specific features.
- Interaction is viewed as a domain of activity in its own right: not an expression of psychological idiosyncrasies and dispositions.
- CA is data driven, not theory led.

Activity 1

So far we've talked about CA but we haven't discussed how to go about doing it. This is, in part, because it is hard to identify a specific set of procedures which can be followed: unlike the set methods for conducting certain kinds of statistical analyses, there is no 'recipe' for doing conversation analysis. Moreover, there are variations in the ways different analysts proceed. Paul ten Have's (1999) introduction to conversation analysis has a useful account of some of the techniques used by analysts. What is common to all CA research, however, is the application of what Schenkein (1978b: 1ff) has called a 'conversation analytic mentality': a way of looking at data in such a way as to begin to develop an appreciation of the organized practices which inform interaction. And the first step in developing an analytic mentality is to begin to look at data carefully, and to try to produce as formal a description as is possible of what is going on.

Below is a collection of data fragments. Work through each one, noting anything that seems interesting or significant. Make as many notes or observations as you can, but remember that you only have the data in front of you. Your observations cannot stray into speculation about the speaker's personality, what you think they intended or 'what they really meant'. Stick to what's there and describe it. Once you've done that, try to find things in common between the fragments. And also look to see what is different.

An analogy might be to imagine that you are a mechanic from an alien civilization, deposited on earth to study modes of personal motor transport. You are presented with several kinds of motorized vehicle (car, motorbike, jeep, coach, van, etc.), and your task is to find out how they are made, what parts they have, how those parts work and what parts the cars have in common. The first thing you're likely to do is strip down each one, getting a good idea of how it is put together, what part does what, and how. Once you've done that, you're in a position then to identify parts in common, and what parts are different, and why they may be different and how they will affect the running of the vehicle. Bear in mind that the personality of the owners, where they were born, how they voted, their gender, their sexual orientation, whether or not they like animals, and so on, is entirely irrelevant to the way the vehicle is put together, and what it is put together to do.

Ideally, to attempt this activity, you would have access to the transcript and the tape; unfortunately, due to the constraints imposed by the format of the written text, transcriptions will have to suffice.

Extract 8

Sydney: While you've been talking to me I mended two

nightshirts a pillow case enna pair'v pants

Extract 9

Maybelle: I think if you exercise it an' work at it

'n studied it you do become clairvoyant.

Extract 10

(The overlapping bracket indicates where the next speaker's utterance begins in relation to the ongoing turn.)

Matt: The good actors are all dyin' out.

Tony: They're all- they're all

dyin out ⌈yeah.

Matt: ⌊Tyrone Po:wuh. Clark Gable, Gary Cooper,

Tony: Now all of 'em are dyin.

Extract 11

(UK General Election, 1983)

Thatcher: There's no government anywhere that is tackling

the problem with more vigour, imagination and

determination than this Conservative government

Audience: Hear hear ((*begins to applaud*))

Extract 12

Heather: And they had like a concession stand at a fair

where you can buy coke and popcorn and that type of

thing.

Extract 13

Rudd: Oh they come from Jamaica en South Africa 'n,

all over the place

Discussion

Hopefully you will have noticed the following features (there may be other interesting properties but for the purposes of this exercise we'll focus the discussion on a limited range of features.)

In each case, the speaker makes a list of things, be they items of clothing being repaired, or famous-but-dead actors, or positive attributes of the (then) UK government.

- In Extracts 8 to 11 the speakers use three items with which to build the list. To give them a technical name, they are **three part lists**.

- Extracts 10 and 11 are different because they show some form of interaction between the respective parties to the interaction. In Extract 10 there are two people talking to each other; in Extract 11 we see some interaction between a platform speaker at a political party conference and the audience in the form of verbal expressions of approval 'Hear, hear' and clapping. What is interesting is that these responses seem very neatly co-ordinated to start right at the point where the prior turn ends. In Extract 10 Tony's utterance "Now all of 'em are dyin" is placed precisely at the point that Matt's prior utterance ends (we know it ends because there is no indication that he is going on to provide any further names). And in Extract 11 the audience's response, both vocal and physical, seems to be pitched right at the end of the point the politician was making. How did the audience and Tony know when to start? How did they know when the respective speakers were going to stop?

- Extracts 12 and 13 provide some clues here. Note that in both these cases, the speakers use only two items in their lists. They then produce "and that type of thing" and "'n all over the place" where an appropriate third item would come. Items like "and that type of thing", "'n all over the place", and so on, are ways of making sure the list in progress is realized as a list of three when, for whatever reason the speaker can't come up with an appropriate third item. They are 'generalized list completers'.

Extracts 12 and 13 are important because they tell us something very interesting about three part lists. By using general phrases such as 'and all that', these speakers seem to be displaying their tacit understanding that lists *should* have three parts, and are complete only upon the provision of the third part. It is as though there is a normative principle underlying people's actions which runs something like: 'if doing a list in conversation, try to do it in three parts'. This normative principle is a powerful organizing feature of interaction: it is noticeable that if a speaker is producing a list, and seems to be having difficulty finding a third item, co-participants may offer candidate third items, displaying their orientation that someone else's list should have three parts.

The upshot, then, is that when you hear someone building a list, you can draw on your culturally available tacit knowledge to project when it should end: at the end of the third item. This is a valuable resource in organizing turn taking: hearers monitor on-going utterances to anticipate those moments in interaction where a change of speaker might be legitimately initiated. Tacit knowledge that lists should have three components allows co-participants to anticipate when turn transfer may be attempted. This is what happens in Extract 10: Tony is able to anticipate precisely where Matt's list will end, and where turn transfer may occur. Similarly, in Extract 11 the audience can hear that the speaker is making a list and can thereby project when a collective display of affiliation will be appropriately positioned to ensure there is no collision of applause and the speaker still talking.

(The data used in this section come from Jefferson's, 1990, study of the interactional features of listing, with the exception of Extract 11, which comes from Atkinson's, 1984, study of political rhetoric.)

2   Transcription

Conversation analysis begins with the assumption that no interactional events can be simply dismissed as unimportant or irrelevant, however trivial they appear: false starts to words, minor gaps between words and turns, and even the simple act of drawing breath can have real consequences for the way in which interaction unfolds. Consequently, it is necessary to try to capture the detail of interaction in transcripts of data recordings; and this means not only transcribing what was said, but the way it was said, and making sure that things that might seem messy, 'accidental', or ungrammatical are recorded in the transcript and not filtered out in some form of tidying up process.

Gail Jefferson has devised a system of transcribing which uses symbols available on conventional typewriter and computer keyboards. It is particularly useful for capturing aspects of speech production and the temporal positioning of utterances relative to each other. Although initially used only by conversation analysts, it is now being adopted by some researchers in other fields, such as discourse analysis in social psychology (Potter and Wetherell, 1987). The main symbols are explained below and it would be sensible to familiarize yourself with these before going on further.

Transcription symbols

(.5)	The number in brackets indicates a time gap in tenths of a second.
(.)	A dot enclosed in a bracket indicates a pause in the talk of less than two tenths of a second.
.hh	A dot before an 'h' indicates speaker in-breath; the more 'h's, the longer the in-breath.
hh	An 'h' indicates an out-breath; the more 'h's, the longer the out-breath.
(( ))	A description enclosed in a double bracket indicates a non-verbal activity, for example *((banging sound))*.
-	A dash indicates the sharp cut-off of the prior word or sound.
:	Colons indicate that the speaker has stretched the preceding sound or letter. The more colons the greater the extent of the stretching.
( )	Empty parentheses indicate the presence of an unclear fragment on the tape.
(guess)	The words within a single bracket indicate the transcriber's best guess at an unclear fragment.
.	A full stop indicates a stopping fall in tone. It does not necessarily indicate the end of a sentence.
,	A comma indicates a continuing intonation.
?	A question mark indicates a rising inflection. It does not necessarily indicate a question.
Under	Underlined fragments indicate speaker emphasis.
↑↓	Pointed arrows indicate a marked falling or rising intonational shift. They are placed immediately before the onset of the shift.
CAPITALS	With the exception of proper nouns, capital letters indicate a section of speech noticeably louder than that surrounding it.
° °	Degree signs are used to indicate that the talk they encompass is spoken noticeably quieter than the surrounding talk.
> <	'More than' and 'less than' signs indicate that the talk they encompass was produced noticeably quicker than the surrounding talk.
=	The 'equals' sign indicates contiguous utterances.
[ ]	Square brackets between adjacent lines of concurrent speech indicate the onset and end of a spate of overlapping talk.
[[	A double left-hand bracket indicates that speakers start a turn simultaneously.

A more detailed description of these transcription symbols can be found in Atkinson and Heritage, 1984: ix–xvi.

To illustrate why a detailed transcript is so important, consider the two following extracts. They are two different transcriptions of the same section of a recording of a medium providing a sitting for a client. The first was done by a trained audio-typist using standard forms of punctuation. She provides this service to colleagues at the University of Surrey, and she is regarded as an accomplished and accurate typist. Consequently, the first version is probably similar in form and level of detail to the kinds of transcripts social scientists use in research which employs ethnographic or qualitative interviewing techniques.

Extract 14

('P' is the medium, 'S' is the client or sitter.)

1   **P**: So keep it, maybe you'll know it. Good. Trouble with

2   ankles. Your ankles have been bothering you or feet,

3   or someone's feet been bothering them please?

4   **S**: No

5   **P**: Who has had trouble with feet or ankles?

6   **S**: A friend of mine, but

7   **P**: Hang on. Did she talk to you about a sprained ankle or

8   some ankle problem or getting new shoes ... , or trouble

9   with her feet.

10   **S**: A friend of mine had some problem.

11   **P**: He's telling me this.

Now consider the same data transcribed using conversation analytic conventions.

Extract 15

1   **P**: so keep it, may ⌈be you (will) know it.=

2   **S**:   ⌊allright

3   **P**: =good.

4   (1.5)

5   **P**: mm hm, mm hm

6   (2)

7   **P**: ((blows air over lips))

8   (2.2)

9   **P**: mm hm mm

10   (2)   ((M whispering))

11   **P**: trouble with <u>ankles</u>. (.) Your <u>ankles</u> have been

```
12            bothering, you or feet,
13            (0.2)
14    P:   someone's feet been bothering them (.) please?
15    S:   n:o::,=
16    P:   =who's- who's had trouble with feet.
17            (0.2)
18    P:   or ankles.
19            (1)
20    S:   ah(m) friend of mi:ne but
21            (.)
22    P:   di⌈d she ⌉ (.) ⌈talk to yo⌉u about hh °hold on° h
23    S:        ⌊(but) ⌋      ⌊(na(r):h: ⌋
24    P:   did she talk >t'y'about< sp- (.) a sprained ankle
25            or some (s't've) ankle trouble or getting new
26            shoes for a
27            (.)
28    P:   (fw⌈( )⌉
29    S:        ⌊ a* ⌋(.) friend of mine had some problem,
30    P:   he's telling me this.
```

The revised transcript probably looks daunting and cluttered. This is a normal first reaction, but once you are used to the meaning of the symbols, transcripts do become easier to read.

But let's consider some of the differences. The medium claims to be receiving messages from the spirit world and relaying that information to the sitter. In this section his first utterance constitutes a closing remark to a discussion of the relevance of a message from the spirits offered prior to the start of this section. He then moves onto the topic of "someone having trouble with feet or ankles". Note that in Extract 15 it is apparent that prior to the production of this message, the medium does a variety of things: he produces utterances which are responses to the spirit voices he claims he can hear (for example the acknowledgement token 'mm hm' in Lines 5 and 9); he whispers something so quietly it is impossible to detect what he is saying; and he blows air over his lips, making a faint 'raspberry' noise, as if to demonstrate 'focusing' or 'concentrating'. All of this detail is lost in the standard transcript which simply provides the words that are said. Moreover, this detail could be significant: for example, the possibility of exploring the performative aspects of medium-sitter interaction would be severely hindered by a simple rendering of the words.

Conversation analysts take great care in transcribing sections of overlapping talk: moments when more than one participant is speaking at the same time. In the revised transcript, there are three instances of overlap, in Lines 1 and 2, 22 and 23, and 28 and 29. In the second case, the medium seems to be having some difficulty: he has offered a message from the spirits concerning a foot problem but the sitter seems less than enthusiastic about accepting this information. She has volunteered that a friend of hers has had some problem but in Lines 20 and 23 is clearly going on to register some doubt that this is what the spirits are referring to. Her second "but" comes in overlap with the medium's "did she". They both stop and then resume at the same moment. In overlap with the medium's "talk to you" the sitter produces an emphatic version of no: "na(r):h:". Her overlapping talk is not even recorded in the standard transcript. However, it may have some significance, because immediately afterwards the medium curtails the utterance he was making ("talk to you about ...") and then says, "hold on". So, we can begin to get a sense that his abandonment of that utterance happened fairly swiftly after the sitter's drawn out and definitive no, and this in turn suggests that it was generated out of his hearing a negative response from the sitter.

Moreover, the "hold on" (incorrectly reproduced in the standard transcript as 'hang on') is said very quietly, and almost whispered. This *sotto voce* production is consistent with other utterances in which the medium is apparently listening and responding to the spirits. This quietly spoken "hold on", then, marks the medium's temporary disengagement from the interaction with the sitter to attend to the spirits. Again, a simple rendering of the words would not capture the performative aspect of the medium's utterances.

By capturing the precise moments at which overlap occurred, we begin to raise some interesting analytic issues. For example, what can we say about the way in which the medium's invocation of the spirits, and thereby, momentary disengagement from the sitter, seems to happen in the immediate vicinity of the sitter's apparent rejection of an attempt to find the relevance of his message?

There are many other features of the revised transcript which could be discussed: the importance of timing periods of absence of talk; the significance of elongated or stressed words, and so on. However, this section has simply tried to demonstrate the kinds of information which are yielded by close attention to the detail of what actually happens in interaction.

It is important to stress that the comparison between the two transcripts should not be taken to imply inefficiency on the part of the audio typist. She was simply providing the kind of transcript which she has produced for social scientists, and researchers in other fields, on many previous occasions. The comparison was designed to highlight the level of detailed information (and features of possible analytic interest) lost in conventional transcription practices.

Finally, it is important to keep in mind that CA is not simply the study of transcripts: it seeks to make sense of those events of which the transcription is a representation. The transcript is merely an aid (albeit a valuable one) in the analysis of the events recorded on tape.

Activity 2

Record some naturally occurring interaction: a conversation between friends, or perhaps a radio or television news interview. Using the system developed by Gail Jefferson, try to transcribe a five-minute segment in as much detail as possible. One method would be, first, to produce a very rough transcript, consisting only of the words that were said, and then to go through the tape again, and on each successive listening, address different features of speech production: overlapping talk, then stress and emphasis, then sound stretching, and so on.

3   Getting started: developing analytic themes

In the rest of this chapter we will begin to see what kinds of lines of inquiry emerge from the application of a conversation analytic mentality to a particular set of data: recordings of one-to-one sittings between psychic practitioners, such as mediums, clairvoyants, psychics, palmists, tarot card readers, and so on, and their clients.

The data for this research come from various sources including 27 taped sessions of psychic practitioners conducting sittings with individual clients. The recordings were made by the psychics themselves as part of the fee for the sitting. The sittings were conducted either at 'psychic fayres' or at the psychics' homes, in various locations in the UK. The sitters were either students who volunteered to go to a medium and provide me with the tape, or people who have volunteered copies of tapes of sittings which occurred either prior to, or in the absence of any knowledge about, this research. In addition to these recordings, I recorded some data from a BBC documentary about mediums, and received video and cassette tapes from a private research foundation in the United States; a colleague also provided me with transcribed fragments taken from a tape of Doris Stokes, the famous English medium, performing at a theatre in London.

What is interesting about these kinds of interactions is that if psychic practitioners are to maintain their claim to have special powers, it is necessary that they produce a convincing demonstration when they are consulted by members of the public. Their status as authentic mediums and psychics rests upon some form of display of knowledge and its acceptance by the sitter as evidence of paranormal powers. However, any information, claim or description which is offered in a sitting or at a meeting as evidence of psychic powers, and the acceptance (or rejection) of that information, is negotiated verbally. What, then, is the nature of communication between psychic practitioners and their clients? And what is the organization of utterances in which evidential information is offered and accepted?

In order to develop some analytic themes consider the following extract. This is a transcript of part of a sitting between a clairvoyant and a young woman. During this sitting, the clairvoyant is using tarot cards to discern aspects of the sitter's present and future life. Immediately prior to this extract, she has just informed the sitter of an impending new relationship, and is describing some of the physical characteristics of the person with whom it is claimed the sitter will become involved. In this and subsequent extracts, the psychic practitioner is designated by the letter 'P', and the sitter by the letter 'S'. (All names have been changed to preserve the anonymity of the participants.)

Extract 16 (K/CC)

```
 1    P:   =y- I feel th't you go for eyes, you >know what I
 2         mean,<=you like people ⌈with nice eyes as well. .h and
 3    S:                           ⌊yea:h,
 4    P:   there's also travel, for you,
 5         (.)
 6    S:   m ⌈m hm⌉
 7    P:     ⌊.h  ⌋ and there's also ↑ money for you as we:ll:? .h
 8         an' are y' changing a ca:r,
 9         (0.4)
10    S:   No ⌈:.
11    P:      ⌊ and is your da:d, (0.2) 's your dad ehm, (0.8)
12         generous?
13         (1)
14    S:   ca:n be.=
15    P:   =okay, .h well I feel ja- your dad is showing you
16         generosity, h but I would say to you. (0.3) there's
17         going to be somebody else very generous
18         around' juh.h and I feel th't your job's to do with
19         communicating?
20         (0.2)
21    S:   I'm a s⌈tudent⌉ a⌈ctually  ⌉
22    P:          ⌊okay? ⌋  ⌊awright,⌋ so (.) >ehm< (0.3) there's
23         learning and studying? ⌈hh and are you going to be
24    S:                          ⌊ mm:.
25    P:   any sort of a communicator when you finished studying?,
26         (.)
27    S:   n::Not really I do(h-) ⌈ah do:n't reall⌉y know
28    P:                          ⌊an' and travel?⌋
29    S:   what I'm I'm go(n)- (.) (plan these)
```

30   travel ⌈s with- f' when've (.) ⌉

31   **P**:   ⌊okay well that will be:⌋eh ⌈:m:

32   **S**:   ⌊finished

33   **P**: that will be that then. ⌈travel? .h ahr: because

34   **S**:   ⌊yeah

35   **P**: feel that this country you've had en<u>ou</u>gh

36   of it fo⌈r a while   ⌉and the ⌉ studying and

37   **S**:   ⌊(k)hh hu ye(hh)ah⌋   ( ) ⌋

38   **P**: learning is saying that you haven't got the knowledge

39   at the moment, but you're go(n)- you're d<u>o</u>ing it.

40   **S**: y ⌈e:ah ⌉

41   **P**:   ⌊.h w⌋ho works at c<u>o</u>mputers sally.

42   (1)

43   **S**: Ehrm::

44   (0.6)

45   **S**: I can't think of <u>a</u>nybody actually

46   **P**: °mm°?

47   (0.2)

48   **P**: somebody could be gon' >on a course of< studying

49   with eh:m

50   (0.5)

51   **P**: ahr::(m)

52   (0.2)

53   **P**: comp<u>u</u>ters?

54   (0.3)

54   **S**: > Oh(r) ⌈we-well ah mean< we use computers

56   **P**:   ⌊y'know

57   **S**: on the cou⌈rse

58   **P**:   ⌊do you?

59   **S**: ⌈⌈yeah.

60   **P**: ⌊⌊OK<u>a</u>:y,(.) maybe that's what it be .h

It is apparent that this kind of exchange has some interesting and distinctive features which set it apart from what we might intuitively understand as routine conversational interaction. For example, one party seems to be able to direct the focus of the interaction: the sitter does not actually raise a topic herself in this exchange. Moreover, it seems that the psychic is able to decide when it is appropriate to initiate new topics. It is also important to remember that the psychic is consulting tarot cards laid out in front of her; and at various points in the sitting (although not in this extract), these are discussed, remarked upon, alluded to, invoked and so on. How can CA help us analyse interaction that so clearly departs from what we might understand ordinary conversation to be?

The first point to keep in mind is that, despite its name, CA is the study of talk-in-interaction *per se*, not some narrowly defined understanding of 'conversation'. More relevant, though, is the considerable body of research on the organization of talk-in-interaction in a variety of institutional or work related settings: in court rooms, in doctors' surgeries, in calls to emergency services, in talk-radio programmes and in television news interviews.

CA studies of these forms of interaction have proceeded on the assumption that what makes **institutional talk** distinctive is the way in which its organization departs from those recurrent practices found in mundane conversational interaction. In this sense, ordinary conversation is treated as having a foundational or 'bedrock' status with respect to forms of interaction in work settings.

Heritage (1997) has identified some of the key features which demarcate institutional talk from ordinary conversation.

- Participants in institutional interaction are normally concerned with specific sets of tasks and goals which are clearly connected to the 'business' of the institution; moreover, these goals are tied to identities relevant to that institution: for example, doctors provide information about medical problems, and teachers teach.

- It is understood that there are constraints on what kinds of participation are normatively appropriate: for example, it is not expected that a patient offers medical advice to the doctor, nor tell jokes, or engage in a lengthy monologue about local geography.

- The practical tasks or business of the institution will shape the kinds of inferences about and understanding of on-going interaction.

Collectively these features constitute what Heritage and Greatbatch call a 'fingerprint' of the patterns in interaction in each institutional setting (1991: 95–6). What properties might constitute part of the fingerprint of interaction between psychics and sitters?

In this relatively short extract, the clairvoyant introduces various topics: changing a car, travelling, the generosity of the sitter's father, and somebody working with computers. Some of these topics are hearably tied to, or potentially touched off from, issues raised in earlier sections of the exchange. For example, the possibility of travel raised in Line 28 seems transparently tied to the sitter's minimal acceptance of the clairvoyant's earlier statement that "there's also travel, for you" in Line 4. Other topics seem disjunctive to on-going topical threads. For example, "who works at computers sally" in Line 41 does not appear to be related to any prior topic in this extract, or indeed, to any topic introduced in the entire sitting prior to the section transcribed here. (Although there is no record of what was said prior to the onset of the recording of the session.)

A routine feature of this extract, and indeed, the discourse between psychic practitioners and sitters more generally, is the clairvoyant's use of questions to initiate topics which then become, even if only momentarily, the focus for both participants. Moreover, these questions refer to aspects of the sitter's current circumstances, or their future plans, information which should not be available to a stranger such as the psychic. And, in the extent to which they can establish that these references to ostensibly private matters are correct or accurate, psychic practitioners provide evidence for and, by implication, demonstrations of, their access to paranormal sources of information.

These topic initiating utterances, then, seem to be a routine feature of this sitting, and clearly connected to one of the key 'work' tasks of the psychic practitioner: convincing displays of parapsychological abilities. It would be appropriate to work through one instance, and the subsequent interaction, in some detail. The following exchanges occur later in the same sitting.

Extract 17 (K/CC)

(The psychic has just been saying how the sitter is restricted because she has to complete her course of academic study.)

```
1     S: yeah th ⌈at's true  ⌉
2     P:        ⌊and who's⌋ got debts,
3        (0.3)
4     P: somebody got=
5     S: =me: hh
6        (.)
7     S: huh huh ⌈hah ha .HHhh ⌈hih hih heh
8     P:        ⌊HA           ⌊I've got some debts
9        accumulat⌈ing so in other words you're
10    S:         ⌊hhh >(ch)hu yeah<
11    P: looking ⌈for pennies from heaven⌉ t'fall
12    S:         ⌊hhhh(.)ih yeah hih hi    ⌋
13    P: outta the sky::,
```

The following points come from my preliminary consideration of this extract. They are simply an example of the kind of analytic considerations or 'noticing' which might be produced on first inspection of a piece of data. Read through them while consulting the data extract.

- The psychic's utterance in Line 2 initiates a new topic.

- This utterance is designed as a question.

- There are no specific details: no names are mentioned, and there is no characterization of the kind of debt: accumulated non-payment of mortgage, bank loan, business loan, personal loan, etc. Moreover, this is to hear "debts" as a reference to financial obligations, but it could be interpreted to refer to an obligation to repay non-monetary favours: we could owe a debt to parents or friends for support or practical assistance. It is not clear to what exactly the utterance refers.

- It is designed in such a way as to imply or propose that the recipient does indeed know someone who has debts. This in turn implies that the psychic has some knowledge about the sitter's life.

- There is a short gap after the initial question.

- The next person to speak after the gap is the psychic. Her next utterance appears to be the initial part of a slight reformulation of the prior utterance.

- The difference between the first and projected second version is that there is a shift from "who's got debts" to "somebody got" (debts). The first version appears more confident because it implies there is somebody, known to the sitter, who fits that description, whereas the second version simply addresses the possibility that someone known to the sitter has got debts. There is, then, a scaling down of implied certainty.

- The psychic's 'weaker' version can be seen to be generated from her analysis of the significance of the 0.3 second gap. That she has revised her initial utterance suggests that she treats the gap not as something insignificant, but as indicating the absence of the sitter's next turn. The subtly revised second version displays her inference that the sitter's difficulty was connected to the stronger or more certain version of her initial turn.

- Before the psychic can complete the second version the sitter provides a short answer: "me", and then begins to laugh.

- The psychic participates with the laughter but only briefly: her "HA" (Line 8) has the character of recognition of the humour generated by the sitter's self-identification as the person with debts, and subsequent laughter, rather than her own spontaneous laughter.

- The sitter's bout of laughter has two phases. After the first four 'bubbles' of laughter she draws breath, as people do after such an expressive activity as laughing. At this point the psychic begins to speak, but ends up talking in overlap with the continued laughter of the sitter.

- The psychic's next turn is "I've got some debts accumulating so in other words you're looking for pennies from heaven t'fall". This accomplishes a number of things. First, it provides an account for how the psychic knew that someone had debts: "I've got" (that someone has debts) characterizes that information as being observable or 'read off' from the arrangement of the tarot cards. Second, this establishes a paranormal source for the information that the sitter knew someone with debts. Third, it extends the nature of the initial topic: someone with debts is now elaborated into got "some debts accumulating". Fourth, it extends the topic of debt but in a way which is fitted to the answer the sitter gave: it is the sitter, who by virtue of her financial circumstances, who is characterized as "looking for pennies from heaven t'fall". It is noticeable that in this turn the psychic is clear in her identification of the person who has the debts.

These observations range over a variety of features which could be pursued in more detail. They are by no means exhaustive, however, and we could investigate others: Why is the psychic's question prefaced by "and"? Why does the sitter delay her utterance which reveals she has debts? Is there any indication that the sitter demonstrates an understanding that the self-identification might be an inappropriate or unexpected action to fill that slot? What is the laughter doing here? Could it be fitted to her identification of herself as the referent of the psychic's question? And why does the psychic use a variant of the idiomatic phrase "pennies from heaven" in this slot? However, for the purposes of this chapter, we will focus on the broader structural features of the sequence.

The structure of Extract 17 can be characterized as:

1   A question from the medium which a) initiates a topic and b) can be heard as proposing that the sitter does indeed know someone with debts.

2   The sitter's utterance which, given that it reveals that she does indeed know someone with debts, stands as a confirmation.

3   The psychic's second turn a) demonstrates that the information alluded to in the first turn was derived from a paranormal source and b) addresses that topic in such a way as to take account of the information the sitter has just provided.

These are interesting observations insofar as they address one of the key 'tasks' related to psychic–sitter interaction: providing demonstrations of parapsychological abilities. Moreover, these turns seem to form a unit:

• question implying knowledge of sitter

• confirmation/acceptance

• attribution of now established knowledge of sitter from a paranormal source; this attribution is produced at the start of the psychic's second turn.

It is at this stage that it is necessary to return to the data corpus to search for other sequences which seem to have similar properties. It is only when such a collection is available that the analyst can begin to make stronger claims about the sequence being investigated. This does not mean, however, that conversation analytic claims rest on showing that an interactional phenomena has occurred ten, twenty or a hundred times in a corpus of data. It is not the case that CA seeks some form of statistical or numerical measures by which to validate its analytic claims. In this, CA differs significantly in its approach to that adopted in most social science disciplines, in which a corpus of data is collected and examined with a view to identifying trends and patterns in those data as a way of making statistical statements about a wider population. In CA, a collection of data is taken to be a series of (candidate) instances of a specific phenomenon, each of which is considered to be worthy of detailed analysis to discover how its features were interactionally produced by the participants. The objective is to identify the recurrent organizational properties exhibited by the instances in the collection. Consequently, it is useful to have a collection of instances taken from a range of sources and settings. In my study of the three turn sequence identified in Section 2, I used instances taken from face-to-face readings in the United Kingdom and the United States. For my work on mediums, as noted earlier, I have drawn from recordings taken from a televised documentary about mediums; and have also been able to consult transcripts of a famous British medium providing demonstrations of mediumship to an audience of several hundred in a theatre.

In building a collection of instances which may have the same properties as the target data, it is not necessary to look for identical matches: a loose criterion by which to select other sequences for closer study would suffice. In examining the corpus of psychic-sitter interactions, I looked for instances of psychic practitioner's questions which were followed by some form of positive response. As you work through your collection, it is highly likely that close inspection will reveal that many cases in fact exhibit markedly different organizational features. However – hopefully – you will be able to assemble a collection of cases which seem to share many key features. It is at this point that you should try to provide the most formal account of the sequential organization exhibited in these extracts.

While it is certainly the case that a collection of instances of a phenomenon does permit the analyst to demonstrate its recurrence over a series of interactional episodes, CA's key task is to show how participants' orientation to the properties of that sequence inform their conduct. One consequence of this analytic task is that it is extremely important to examine cases in which there seems to be clear deviation form the established pattern. This will be discussed in more detail in Section 4.

Activity 3

The purpose of this exercise is to sharpen your analytic and descriptive skills. Look at the three extracts which follow; work through each one in as much detail as possible, and focus on describing the structure of the interaction as it is built up over successive turns.

Extract 18 (JREF B)

```
1      P:  So spirit wants me to do a scan on your bo:dy, talk
2          about your health, so I'm going to do that okay? I'm
3          going to do this for your health (0.8) Let's see
4          what's going on with you. .hh number one thing is your
5          > mother in spirit please?<
6          (0.2)
7      S:  Yes
8      P:  > 'cause I have (n-m) y'r mother standing right over
9          here, hh and she said I WANna TAlk to HEr and I want
10         to speak to her because hh your mother has very
11         lou::d when she comes through. .h she speaks with a in
12         a very lou:d way a very uhm (.) y'understand
13         very ⌈she has to be
14     S:        ⌊ye:s:.
15     P:  heard, .h and like this would not happen today
16         without her coming through for you. D'y' ⌈un'erstand?
17     S:                                           ⌊'kay
18     S:  Ye:s.
```

Extract 19 (EV)

```
1      P:  >'ave you 'ad< (.) bit >(o')< trouble with your
2          back as well.
3          (0.2)
4      S:  yes a little bi⌈t
5      P:               ⌊he says ah'd best send
6          her a bit of sympathy down so you understand it,
7          hh⌈h
8      S:    ⌊ye⌈s
9      P:       ⌊coz y'know .h y'try to bottle things up and
10         you don't always let people get close to you in
11         that sense do you
12     S:  no.
13     P:  he says she can be quite stubborn at times y'know
14         (.)
```

15   **P**: is that true

16   **S**: °yes°

17   **P**: an' he knows cz .h you are <u>fussy</u> about the

18   bungalow aren't

19   you ⌈girl

20   **S**:   ⌊yes I am

21   **P**: bless her he says

Extract 20 (CD/DR)

1   **P**: .h ↑y'ever though(t) o(f) .h did you want to go

2   into a caring pro↓fession early on, when >y'w's uh(t)<

3   y'know when you were ch<u>oo</u>sing which way you were

4   gonna go.

5   (.)

6   **S**: yeah I wanted to: go into child care

7   actuall⌈y when I   ⌉

8   **P**:   ⌊MMMmm:::⌋::::.=

9   **S**: =when I left school

10´   **P**: That's right yeah >well< .h (.) 'm being shown

11   that>but (t)-< .h it's (0.2) it's not your way ye(t)

12   actually but i(t) y'y may be caring for (t-)ch- children

13   or whatever later on okay?

Discussion

We will consider each extract in order. Extract 18 begins with a section from a medium's description of how the sitting will proceed. After this initial preamble, he produces a question about the sitter's mother. This has an interesting design in that it could be heard as a genuine question about the sitter's mother; that is, it may be equivalent to "has your mother passed on or is she still living?"; or it could be heard as a question which seeks confirmation of information already known to the medium. The sitter's minimal response does not disambiguate the prior turn, in that a simple "yes" could be 'a telling' or 'a confirmation'. The medium's next turn, however, reveals that he is in contact with the spirit of the sitter's mother. This retrospectively characterizes his first turn as a 'question seeking confirmation of information already at hand'. Moreover, it can now be inferred that the knowledge that the sitter's mother has died is now revealed to have come from a paranormal source: the spirit of the mother in communication with the medium. There are then, strong similarities in the structure of this sequence to that derived from analysis of Extract 17.

Extract 19 provides three further examples of the sequential unit outlined above. There are three questions, each of which can be heard as displaying some kind of intimate knowledge about the sitter: that she has back trouble, that she can be withdrawn, and that she is house-proud. To each of these questions the sitter provides minimal positive responses. And in each occasion the medium then goes on to report what the spirit of the sitter's husband has said to him, thereby making it inferable that it was the spirit who provided the information about the sitter.

The sequence in Extract 20, however, shows a slight deviation in that although the sitter does respond positively to the psychic's question, she does not do so with a minimal response. After an initial "yeah" she goes on to elaborate upon what she infers the psychic to be referring to in his question about 'wanting to go into a caring profession'. The sitter thus treats this slot in the exchange as a place in which it is appropriate to provide an elaborated confirmation. Moreover, the psychic begins to produce an elongated and unusually loud agreement token while the sitter is talking. She cuts off her turn and then produces the completion latched on to the end of the psychic's "mm". Finally, in previous extracts the psychics have attributed the now confirmed knowledge to a paranormal source. The psychic does this in Extract 20 by saying that he is "being shown" (the information provided by the sitter). However, in the other cases of this sequence we have considered, it seems that psychics produce this attribution as early as possible in their second turn: in this case, that action is delayed, coming after "that's right year >well<.h". This means, then, that this extract does not match the structure found in previous extracts. However, it should not be discarded as analytically uninteresting, as deviations from the emerging pattern can be highly informative.

Having identified this sequence as potentially interesting, and certainly observable in a number of data extracts, a next analytic step is to produce a more formal description of its properties. We can say that it is a three turn series of utterances, in which a claim about the sitter is proposed, accepted by the sitter, and which is then characterized as originating from a paranormal source. This sequence can be described schematically as:

T1 Psychic: a question embodying a claim about, or knowledge of, the sitter, their circumstances, etc.

T2 Sitter: minimal confirmation/acceptance

T3 Psychic: demonstration that the information embodied in the question has come from a paranormal source

4   Methodological digression

Note that the characterization of the sequence shown above does not rely on the specific details of what was actually said, but the actions accomplished by turn design, and the organization of the ways in which people take turns talking together. This sets CA apart from many other social scientific studies which use recorded data, in which it is customary

for the analyst to focus on thematic issues which are revealed in the
content of peoples' talk. We can illustrate the importance of this by
considering the following extracts.

Extract 21 (LL/RC)

(Discussing holidays; tape unclear)

P: .hhh was your mum very short.

      (1)

S: she was ye⌈ah

P: ⌊mm yeah

S: °yeah°

P: she's giving you a lovely cuddle

      (.)

P: (k)H⌈Hh HUh HUh huh hah ha hh and (are they birthdaying)

S: ⌊(k)ohhh huh huh hu

P: in ma̲y

Extract 22

P: she's so: ha̲ppy,

      (0.7)

S: good.

P: and so happy to se̲e: (.) everybody, and she brings me the
beau:tiful colour of violets, (0.2) that lovely soft colour of violets,
(0.5) which is lovely (.) and it's beautifully peaceful (0.3) and uh
(1.2)

P: and then (.) she just said don't ↑e̲ver be afrai:d, (0.4) don't ↑e̲ver
be afrai:d, (0.2) there's nothing to be afraid of. (0.7) an(g)uh:,
(3.3)

P: (ptch) oh it's lo̲:vely, (0.2) she just leaned forward and put a scarf
round your neck and turned your collar up huh huH HUH HAH
HAH HAh(n) nn.HHH which is a wa(hh)y o(h)f sa(hu)ying, .hh (.)
.h I look after you((ch)huh) (ch)hih huh=

S: =Yeah.

P: .h (ch)Hhu(n) sure she would've always been concerned ↑are
you wa̲rm enough,

     (w'y-) .hh hu(n)

In many conventional sociological studies these two extracts might be interpreted as showing two instances of the same phenomenon: the psychic practitioner's report of the spirit's displays of physical attention to the sitter. Moreover, it is likely this feature would be interpreted in terms of conventional sociological concerns: for example, it might be deemed significant that in both cases it is a female spirit being physically affectionate, and this in turn might be taken to show how expectations of gendered patterns of caring behaviour are transposed upon or reflected in depictions of the spirit world. However reasonable such interpretations might be, there is a danger that they obscure investigation of the details of the ways in which such descriptions are produced, and the interactional or inferential significance they may have for the participants themselves. For example, it is clear that, at a sequential level, these two extracts display very different interactional phenomena. Extract 21 displays the success sequence outlined earlier; and the medium's depiction of the spirit's activity constitutes the third turn. And we have an understanding of the kind of action the medium's description of the spirit is doing: insofar as it displays that the spirit is visible to the medium, it is both an account for how she knew about the physical characteristics of the sitter's mother and a demonstration of paranormal abilities. However, the depiction of the spirit's caring behaviour in Extract 22 is markedly different: it does not occupy the same kind of sequential position; its significance is then explicitly formulated by the medium as "a wa(hh)y o(h)f sa(hu)ying, .hh (.) .h I look after you"; and, most important, insofar as the sitters' next utterances differ, it may be the case that *they* are treating the prior turns as performing very different kinds of activities. And this is crucial, because in the first instance these utterances were produced by people for each other in real life situations. Analysis of the significance of these turns, or indeed, any naturally occurring interaction, should prioritize participants' own interpretations of the moment-by-moment unfolding of interaction by examining how those interpretations inform the design and placement of subsequent turns.

5   Demonstrating participants' orientation to a sequence

Having arrived at an account of the recurrent properties of a sequence, it is now important to demonstrate that this pattern is interactionally produced: to show how participants' orientation to the requirements of that sequence inform their activities, and in so doing, 'bring off' or realize that sequence collaboratively. There are two investigative strategies. First, we can inspect the corpus for instances in which the oriented-to **design of an utterance** is revealed in some aspect of the speaker's turn. Second, we can analyse how **deviations** from the sequence are addressed in subsequent turns.

5.1 Identifying the design features of an utterance

In the success sequence, the psychic's first turn is designed to embody a claim about, or propose some information relevant to, the sitter.

Overwhelmingly, this turn is produced as a question. But is there any evidence that participants actively work to make sure it comes off in a question format?

Consider the following two extracts.

Extract 23 (CD/DR)

P: .h ↑y'ever though(t) o(f) .h did you want to go into a caring pro↓fession

early <u>on</u>, when >y'w's uh(t)< y'know when you were ch<u>oo</u>sing which way

you were gonna go.

Extract 24 (GR/RC)

P: er:m: (0.2) I also think that uhm:(.) .h are there three of you th't're

very cl<u>o</u>se,

In both cases the speakers perform self repair on the design of their utterance while they are in production. In Extract 23 the psychic's ".h ↑y'ever though(t) o(f)" has the character of the start of a turn in which advice is given. This projected turn is terminated and the utterance then develops into a question about the sitter's early career aspirations. In Extract 24 we see the speaker produces another self-repair of the on-going utterance. The initial components of her turn project a 'telling' or a statement (albeit modulated by "I also think") which is discontinued and replaced by a question. While the object of repair is ambiguous, in that it could be a repair on the format of the utterance or the topic, the shape of the eventually completed turn provides evidence as to the psychic's orientation to the appropriateness of a question format.

So, in addition to the fact that the first turn in a success sequence is usually a question, or has a questioning character, these two extracts provide instances of the speakers terminating on-going utterances which do not have the character of questions, and then producing utterances which do. Why might psychics and mediums orient to the appropriateness of a question format for a turn in which they exhibit, for confirmation or disconfirmation, a knowledge claim about the sitter?

Consider this: the authority of the psychic's claim to have special powers would be compromised were he or she to endorse proposals about the sitter which subsequently transpire to be false. Any knowledge claim proposed by the psychic, therefore, cannot be confirmed as an instance of, for example, the agency of the spirit world, or the use of special parapsychological faculties, until it is accepted by the sitter.

What seems to be significant in Extracts 23 and 24 is that the projected turn formats which are abandoned may be heard as expressing the psychic's commitment to or endorsement of the knowledge of the sitter which is being proposed. A statement that X (a state of affairs) is relevant to Y (the sitter) implies that, at least, the medium believes it to be true. It is a positive proposal. A question which addresses the same relationship or set of relevancies, however, makes the same proposal in a modulated form. And perhaps most significantly, the information being proposed is not heard as being endorsed by the medium, an inference which is available from the statement format. Similarly, an utterance which advises a course of action may be deemed to reflect or express the speaker's endorsement of that advice. In both cases, then, we find that self-repair is carried out on utterances whose projected shape might, if completed, facilitate the recipient's inference that the psychic is endorsing the accuracy or validity of the proposed knowledge claim prior to its confirmation by the sitter.

We can locate further evidence of an orientation to the features of the sequence in the design of the sitter's acceptance/confirmation turn. As we have already noted, these tend to have two features. They are produced quickly after the psychic's question, and they take a minimal form.

Extract 25 (K/CC)

P: and are you going to the states,

       (.)

S: yeah.

Extract 26 (29/EV)

P: can you understand a g<u>en</u>tleman with cancer,

S: yes

Extract 27 (J/BJ)

P: is your brother quite s<u>en</u>sitive?

S: yes

Extract 28 (VP RS 13)

P: was this cancer that he passe⌈d with⌉ please?

S: ⌊y:es, ⌋

Although it is hard to make a case that turns have a distinct design procedure from the absence of certain turn components, there is a sense in which sitters' minimal turns withhold any further comment. For example, apparently accurate claims by the psychics are not treated by sitters as the basis of puzzlement, nor as a warrant for displays of surprise. But there is another feature: minimal turns allow the sitters to return the floor to the psychic as soon as possible. Thus minimal positive responses facilitate the speedy onset of that place in the sequence where psychics can demonstrate that the now-accepted claim about the sitter came from a paranormal source. Minimal acceptance/confirmation turns are thus not only constitutive of the sequence, but they also display the sitter's understanding of the turn-by-turn progression of the sequence, and a sensitivity to the significance of the kinds of action undertaken in the third turn.

5.2 Analysing deviant cases

An important step in building a conversation analytic account of an interactional phenomena is to examine cases in which there seems to have been some departure from the established pattern, and investigating how participants' utterances display their understanding of the significance of that departure. 'If someone displays in their conduct that they are "noticing" the absence of a certain type of turn from a co-participant, then that demonstrates their own orientation to the relevance of the sequence that the analyst is aiming to describe' (Hutchby and Wooffitt, 1998: 98).

   To illustrate this, look at this fragment again, in which a question is not followed by an answer.

Extract 29

Child:	Have to cut the:se Mummy
	(1.3)
Child:	Won't we Mummy
	(1.5)
Child:	Won't we
Mother:	Yes

It is clear that the child's second and third versions of the initial question display that she has 'noticed' the absence of the mother's answer. Moreover, her repeated attempts to solicit an answer display her orientation to the normative expectation that an answer should follow a question. Thus what seems on first inspection to provide evidence which undermines claims about the properties of paired action sequences (for example, that second parts should follow first parts), actually displays the participant's orientation to the normative relevance of those properties.

   Let's consider a form of deviant case from the psychic-sitter corpus: occasions in which a sitter accepts or confirms the claim made in the prior turn, but does not use a minimal turn format.

Extract 30 ((B)H/RC)

P:	are you fi:nding that >y'got to have< check ups and it's getting you down
	(1.8)
S:	yea:h ah've got my ⌈( )⌉
P:	⌊yeah.⌋ yeah >we(ll) ah know<
	'cos I've got the medical: (0.2) feel arou:nd
	you .hhh erhm:

In this extract the psychic's question displays that she knows something
about the sitter's ill health. The sitter's next turn begins with a simple
"yeah" but it is apparent that she is departing from the established pattern
in that with "ah've got my" she embarks on what appears to be some kind
of report of medical or health related events. It is noticeable, however, that
the psychic does not wait for an appropriate place at which to start her
next turn, but cuts across the sitter's on-going turn, which is then
terminated before reaching any recognizable completion. The psychic's turn
is initially composed of "yeah" repeated, and it is only when she is clear of
co-occurring talk from the sitter does she, first, explicitly claim already to
be in receipt knowledge of the sitter's problems, and second, attribute that
knowledge to a paranormal source: "cos I've got the medical: (0.2) feel
arou:nd you". It may appear that P's second turn in this sequence is an
interruption. However, to describe this turn as interruptive would be to
implicitly ascribe some significance or meaning to the participants' conduct
prior to detailed examination, a practice which is strenuously resisted in
CA. Moreover, in a series of studies, Gail Jefferson has shown that many
forms of overlapping talk, which may intuitively seem like a violation of
turn taking conventions, display a number of orderly interactional
properties which mitigate against the use of term 'interruption' (Jefferson,
1983; 1986).

In the following case the psychic proposes that earlier in her life the
sitter may have considered a career in what is characterized broadly as a
caring profession. The sitter treats this as correct, but instead of a minimal
acceptance, she states specifically which kind of caring profession she had
intended to enter.

Extract 31

P: .h ↑y'ever though(t) o(f) .h did you want to go

        into a caring pro↓fession early on, when >y'w's uh(t)<

        y'know when you were ch<u>oo</u>sing which way you were

        gonna go.

        (.)

S: yeah I wanted to: go into child care actuall⌈y when I ⌉

P: ⌊MMMmm:::⌋::·.=

S: =when I left school

P: That's right yeah >well< .h (.) 'm being shown

        that>but (t)-< .h it's (0.2) it's not your w<u>ay</u> ye(t)

        actually but i(t) y'y may be caring for (t-)ch- children

        or whatever later on okay?

Something intriguingly similar seems to be happening in this extract. The sitter does not provide a one-word acceptance/confirmation, but embarks on an extended turn in which it is apparent that she is disclosing factual information. And while the psychic's long agreement marker in Extract 31 anticipates the onset of a place where turn transfer could legitimately occur (at the end of "actually"), it has the same consequence in that the sitter terminates her utterance (albeit temporarily in this case), and the end of the psychic's overlapping agreement marker occurs in the clear. The main difference here is that the sitter completes her turn exactly at the point where psychic's "mmm" finishes. And, as in the previous extract, when the psychic eventually gets the chance to produce the third turn in this sequence, the demonstration of knowledge obtained from a paranormal source is delayed by the inclusion of "That's right yeah", an item designed to underline that the psychic was already in receipt of the information the sitter has just revealed.

In both cases, then, the sitters' departure from the established pattern of second turns is followed by the psychics' departure from the established pattern of third turns: instead of moving immediately to attribute the now accepted information to a paranormal source, the sitter's disclosure (or projected disclosure) of information is met with an item that is produced while the sitter is speaking, and not necessarily in the vicinity of places where turn transfer may legitimately be initiated. Thus there is good evidence that the overlapping utterances initiated by the psychics demonstrate an orientation to a requirement to start the third turn as soon as possible.

But why should this be? We can suggest an answer to this if we consider what kind of deviant second turns the sitters were producing. In both cases they were providing factual information. This can be a delicate issue for a psychic. In Extract 31, for example, in his next turn, the psychic is placed in the position of having to claim that information which has just been explicitly disclosed by the sitter has also been revealed to him through a paranormal source. Moreover, insofar as the sitter has elaborated upon the kinds of work indexed by "caring profession", it is now apparent that the paranormal source has provided less detailed information than the sitter. This diminishes the potential effectiveness of the third turn as a site in which a psychic can build a claim to possess powers of extra-sensory perception. Indeed, the psychic's next turn begins with agreement with information which has just been made publicly available in the sitting; this constitutes, at best, a weak demonstration of his claimed powers. And his subsequent prediction about the sitter's *future* involvement with child care – "it's not your way ye(t) actually but i(t) y'y may be caring for (t-)ch- children or whatever later on" – seems transparently to originate from her disclosure that she had *wanted* to work in this area, a formulation from which it can be inferred that she had not yet done so.

The psychics' post-acceptance turn is crucial in the production of valid demonstrations of special powers, as it is here that they establish the paranormal source of their claim about the sitter. There is, then, a premium on arriving at the third turn in the sequence as soon as

possible (an understanding displayed also in the minimal form of the
established second turn); and, moreover, to ensure that a very human
source (the sitter) does not explicitly offer detailed information prior to the
psychic's attribution of his or her knowledge to a paranormal source.
The ways in which psychics may address precisely this kind of
departure from the established sequence display their sensitivity to the
significance of the third turn. Moreover, the inferential significance of the
third turn thus provides a motivation, intrinsic to the properties of the
sequence itself, for psychics' attempts to curtail those sitters' turns which
can be heard to depart from the established pattern to provide factual
information.

So far we have only considered extracts in which the 'deviance' of the
case rests in the extension of one turn in a success sequence. In this final
section we will make some remarks on activities which follow the
occurrence of much more marked deviation: occasions when the sitter
simply does not accept or confirm the relevance or accuracy of the
information proposed in the psychic's question.

One strategy available to the psychic is to abandon that topic, and
produce another question which proposes new information about the
sitter.

Extract 32 (K/CC)

8	**P**:	an' are y' changing a ca̲:r,
9		(0.4)
10	**S**:	No⌈ :.
11	**P**:	⌊ and is your da̲:d, (0.2) 's your dad ehm, (0.8)
12		generous?
13		(1)
14	**S**:	ca̲:n be.=
15	**P**:	=okay, .h we̲ll I feel ja- your dad is sho̲wing you
16		generosity,

The psychic's embodied proposal in Line 8 is unequivocally rejected by the
sitter in Line 10. However, even as the sitter is saying "no" the psychic asks
another question on an entirely unrelated topic. The success sequence
projected by the turn initiating the topic of "changing a car" is abandoned,
and the psychic produces another candidate first turn. Thus the opportunity
to realize a successful sequence is recycled.

Alternatively, psychics can maintain the validity of the original proposal
by broadening or extending some parameter(s) of the information
displayed in the question, thereby increasing the likelihood that the sitter
will be able to accept the now revised claim.

Extract 33 (K/CC)

```
41      P:  - .h w-ho works at computers sally.

42          (1)

43      S:  Ehrm::

44          (0.6)

45      S:  I can't think of anybody actually

46      P:  °mm° ?

47          (0.2)

48      P:  somebody could be gon' >on a course of< studying

49          with eh:m

50          (0.5)

51      P:  ahr::(m)

52          (0.2)

53      P:  computers?

54          (0.3)

54      S:  >Oh(r) ⌈we-well ah mean< we use computers

56      P:         ⌊y'know

57      S:  on the cou⌈rse

58      P:            ⌊do you?

59      S:  ⌈⌈yeah.

60      P:  ⌊⌊OKa:y,(.) maybe that's what it be .h
```

In Extract 33 it is proposed that the sitter knows someone who works with computers. When the sitter does not accept this, the psychic revises the proposal to include people who might be going on a course studying with computers, a reformulation which, given the prevalence of computers in schools and in further and higher education, is clearly designed to facilitate a positive response while at the same time maintaining the relevance of the proposal. And indeed, this expansion does generate some form of recognition in that the sitter announces that she has contact with computers on her own course. And while this turn is not as positive as other forms of sitter acceptance, the sitter's disclosure that she has dealings with computers is then characterized by the psychic as what the tarot cards were referring to.

If a sitter rejects or disconfirms a proposal by the psychic, there is no rationale for even attempting to establish that the information contained in that proposal was obtained from a paranormal source: the sequential basis of a claim to possess special powers of cognition cannot be developed. The psychic's activities in Extracts 32 and 33 reveal two methods by which psychics can respond to an initial negative response, both of which demonstrate an understanding of the significance of the third turn. In

Extract 32 the psychic simply abandoned the topical line proposed in the first turn, and initiates the first turn of another sequence with a different topic, thus recycling the possibility of a successful sequence. In Extract 33 the psychic expands the parameters of the initial claim thus providing the sitter with a wider field of possibilities in which to locate the relevance of the psychic's proposal. While this strategy may not result in the kind of 'ideal' third turn as we have seen in many other extracts, it does mean that the sequence concerned with this topic can be completed with some form of success.

Activity 4

Recall that earlier in the chapter, we discussed how sitters' positive acceptance/confirmation turns are produced immediately after the initial question or with little delay. Now examine the following extracts. Focus on what happens after the psychic's question, and the design of the sitter's subsequent turns.

Extract 34 (K/CC)

P: -.h w-ho works at computers sally.

       (1)

S: Ehrm::

       (0.6)

S: I can't think of anybody actually

Extract 35 (JREF 1)

P: is there a wedding coming up?

       (1.0)

S: not- not to my knowledge

Extract 36 (DS 14)

P: And who lived at number seventeen?

       (1.5)

S: I don't know Doris.

Extract 37 (DS)

P: Who's Peter?

       (0.8)

P: Peter living.

Extract 38 (DS)

P: Who's Bill?

         (1.0)

P: Spirit side?

Extract 39 (DS)

P: Erm, there's a Sarah also, yes?

         (0.7)

P: Going back?

Discussion

The first thing to note is that after the psychic's initial utterance, the sitter does not produce a minimal acceptance; instead, there is a gap. In every case the gap is around one second in length. In her study of gaps and silences in everyday interaction, Jefferson (1989) suggests there is a standard metric of approximately one second. Her analysis of instances of silences falling within a 0.8 to 1.2 second boundary reveals that speakers orient to this critical period as a 'tolerance interval' which marks the acceptable length of absence of talk in conversational interaction. After silences of duration between approximately 0.8 to 1.2 seconds, speakers can be observed to begin talking so as to terminate the silence. This suggests that silences which extend to nearly a second are likely to be treated as a sign of 'trouble' in the conversation.

That norm for conversational interaction seems to be in operation in these data. In Extracts 34, 35 and 36, after the gap threatens to extend into or indeed beyond the tolerance boundary, the sitters eventually disclose that they can not accept the psychic's implied claim. You might also want to look at the way in which these rejections are designed: note the way in which the rejection is modulated or softened by reference to the sitter's 'lack of knowledge'. This preserves the possibility that the psychic may be correct, in that the sitters portray themselves as not (yet) aware of the information proposed in the prior turn.

So, there is a tacit convention that the absence of the sitter's response which extends to approximately one second after the initial question may indicate that the sitter is having trouble accepting the proposed claim. This provides psychics with a resource to anticipate and even address what that problem might be. In Extracts 37, 38 and 39 there is a gap after the psychics' questions. But the next person to speak is the psychic; and in each case, an amendment to the original claim is offered, thus addressing what the source of the trouble might be, and thereby increasing the chance of a positive sitter response.

Conclusion

In this chapter I have tried to illustrate CA's central focus on the discovery and explication of sequences of utterances: patterned ways of talking together in which participants engage in a circumscribed set of interactional and inferential activities.

This entails close examination of the ways turns in sequences are designed; and, relatedly, how the design features of utterances can reveal the participants' understanding of the normative properties of sequences: that certain activities are appropriately placed in specific positions – expectations which are further exposed for analysis in the design of activities which address marked departures from established sequential patterns.

But what does a CA approach offer us with respect to understanding psychic-sitter interaction? To answer that, it is useful to consider alternative perspectives on the language used by psychic practitioners. Sceptics have claimed that the apparent success of psychics can be explained by reference to what are called 'cold reading' strategies (Hyman, 1981). Cold reading is simply a set of techniques of character assessment by which we may gain information about someone: subtle inspection of the sitter's appearance, their tone of voice, observation of facial and other physical responses, and so on. A common theme in cold reading literature is that mediums will ask questions to obtain information which can then be recycled, in some suitably amended form, as evidence of spirit contact. According to this perspective, then, psychics use questions to get information. Intuitively, that seems a reasonable claim. But when we consider the sequential and interactional use of questions, a different answer emerges. In the data we have looked at, we have identified a sequence which is invariably initiated by a question; these questions, however, are not motivated by the need to elicit information, but are designed to initiate a short sequence of utterances which return the floor to the psychic with minimal sitter participation. And there is empirical evidence for this account: if sitters provide more than a minimal acceptance, psychics begin to talk in overlap with them, eventually curtailing that turn. We can understand this because of the significance of the third turn *in this interactional sequence*: it is in this sequential location that the psychics can attribute the now-accepted information as coming from a paranormal source. Yet this does not commit us to a sceptical position on the genuineness or otherwise of the powers claimed by psychics. Regardless of the origin of the proposed knowledge, the way in which such claims are presented to the sitters, accepted and subsequently ratified as emanating from a paranormal source, is socially organized and collaboratively produced. It is this level of organization and interactional collaboration which CA can disclose.

Harvey Sacks, the founder of CA, was tragically killed in a car accident in 1975, but the discipline he established has flourished. Conversation analysts have gone on to provide detailed accounts of a range of interactional phenomena; for example, the ways in which turn taking is organized; how overlapping talk is managed; how difficulties and errors in conversation are identified and addressed; the relationship of posture and body movement to verbal activities; how an understanding of grammar is relevant to the interactions between speakers; and how talk in work or institutional settings embodies or instantiates aspects of that institution's 'character', 'culture', 'goals', and so on. Running right through these studies is a concern to identify the sequential and normative basis of verbal activities.

Moreover, the findings and methods of CA are beginning to have impacts in related social science disciplines. For example, the emergence of discursive psychology in the United Kingdom in the 1990s has been strongly influenced by conversation analytic studies of interaction; researchers in artificial intelligence concerned with the design of interactive, speech-based computer systems have tried to draw from the findings of conversation analytic studies of ordinary interaction; and speech therapists have found that CA's focus on the detail of interaction can be a valuable resource in understanding the ways in which speech disorders impact upon everyday conversational activity.

But perhaps CA's primary contribution is to identify that talk-in-interaction is a domain of activity in its own right. In its systematic focus on the detail of actual verbal interaction, it stands in stark contrast to conventional sociological approaches, which tend to treat language use simply as a screen onto which more traditional sociological concerns can be inscribed: gender, status, power, and so on. Moreover, conversation analysts do not assume that the procedures which are displayed in naturally occurring talk have to answer to, and are thereby less significant than, underlying and supposedly determinant cognitive realities.

CA has not only generated a substantial and cumulative body of findings about the nature of interaction, but it has developed as a distinctive sociological method for the analysis of social activities. This may have far reaching consequences. Insofar as language use infuses all those aspects of society that may be regarded as the key concerns of sociology, the scope of CA's analytic remit may be immense. It is the medium through which parents socialize their children; institutional norms are transmitted through a variety of forms of discourse; family life is resonant with jokes, complaints, and arguments; face-to-face or telephone interaction drives the smooth running of business institutions and other places of work; the education of young people is, in part, dependent upon the ability of teachers to enthuse, discipline, persuade, or cajole their students; ordinary language use is perhaps *the* site in which our social identities may be established, negotiated and warranted; and legal declarations are administered in courtroom trials which involve the verbal interrogation of witnesses and defendants for the benefit of an overhearing jury. Conversation analysts have already begun to investigate the use of language in interaction in various kinds of specialized or institutional settings, and in so doing have generated a new range of empirical questions. In this, CA has the potential to transform and invigorate the traditional concerns of a range of social science disciplines.

Further Reading

It is important to note that this chapter has not attempted to provide a full account of the basic findings from conversation analytic studies of everyday interaction. There is, then, no account of the turn-taking system in mundane conversation; nor has there been a report of the various methods to identify and deal with various troubles or problems in conversation, such as misunderstandings, mis-hearings, slips of the tongue, and so on. Introductory discussion of these (and other) key aspects of the organization of conversational interaction can be found in Hutchby and Wooffitt (1998), ten Have (1999) and Levinson (1983). The seminal paper in turn-taking was written by Sacks, Schegloff and Jefferson (1974) (which is reproduced in Schenkein, 1978a). Key papers on repair are Schegloff, Jefferson and Sacks (1977), and Schegloff (1979; 1992b).

General introduction to CA can be found in Heritage (1984), Hutchby and Wooffitt (1998), ten Have (1999), or Psathas (1995). While all these texts provide good introductions to key conversation analytic findings (among other things), it is important to stress that there is no substitute for reading primary sources. In this respect, ten Have provides a useful list of classic or key studies at the end of each chapter.

Collections of key CA studies can be found in Atkinson and Heritage (1984), Button, Drew and Heritage (1986), Boden and Zimmerman (1991), Button and Lee (1987), Drew and Heritage (1992), Psathas (1979), Schenkein (1978a) and Sudnow (1972).

However, the first port of call for anyone interested in conversation analysis should be the lectures of Harvey Sacks (published as Sacks, 1992). Schegloff's (1992a) introductions to the lectures are a fascinating account of the intellectual context in which Sacks' ideas and work began to take shape. Silverman (1998) provides an accessible introduction to Sacks' work.

Acknowledgements

I would like to thank the team of assessors who made valuable comments about an earlier draft of this chapter. I would also like to thank the Departments of Sociology at the Universities of Surrey and York who provided me, respectively, with a sabbatical and the environment in which to write this chapter.

References

Atkinson, J.M. (1984) *Our Master's Voices: the Language and Body Language of Politics*, London, Methuen.

Atkinson, J.M. and Drew, P. (1979) *Order in Court: the Organisation of Verbal Interaction in Judicial Settings*, London, Macmillan.

Atkinson, J.M. and Heritage, J. (eds) (1984) *Structures of Social Action: Studies in Conversation Analysis*, Cambridge, Cambridge University Press.

Boden, D. and Zimmerman, D. (1991) *Talk and Social Structure*, Cambridge, Polity Press.

Button. G., Drew, P. and Heritage, J. (eds) (1986) *Human Studies*, vol.9, (Special Edition on Interaction and Language Use.)

Button, G. and Lee, J. (eds) (1987) *Talk and Social Organisation*, Clevedon and Philadelphia, Multilingual Matters.

Drew, P. and Heritage, J. (1992) *Talk At Work: Interaction in Institutional Settings*, Cambridge, Cambridge University Press.

Heritage, J. (1984) *Garfinkel and Ethnomethodology*, Cambridge, Polity Press.

Heritage, J. (1997) 'Conversation analysis and institutional talk: analysing data' in Silverman, D. (ed.) *Qualitative Research: Theory, Method and Practice*, London and Thousand Oaks, Sage.

Heritage, J. and Greatbatch, D. (1986) 'Generating applause: a study of rhetoric and response at party political conferences', *American Journal of Sociology*, vol.92, pp.110–57.

Heritage, J and Greatbatch, D. (1991) 'On the institutional character of institutional talk: the case of news interviews' in Boden, D. and Zimmerman, D.H. (eds) *Talk and Social Structure: Studies in Ethnomethodology and Conversation Analysis*, Berkely, University of California Press.

Hutchby, I. and Wooffitt, R. (1998) *Conversation Analysis: Principles, Practices and Applications*, Oxford, Polity Press.

Hyman, R. (1981) '"Cold reading": how to convince strangers that you know all about them' in Frazier, K. (ed.) *Paranormal Borderlands of Science*, Prometheus Books, New York.

Jefferson, G. (1983) 'Notes on some orderlinesses of overlap onset', *Tilburg Papers in Language and Literature No. 28*, Department of Linguistics, Tilburg University.

Jefferson, G. (1986) 'Notes on 'latency' in overlap', *Human Studies*, vol.9, pp.153–83.

Jefferson, G. (1989) 'Notes on a possible metric for a standard maximum silence of approximately one second in conversation' in Roger, D. and Bull, P. (eds) *Conversation: an Interdisciplinary Perspective*, Clevedon and Philadelphia, Multilingual Matters.

Jefferson, G. (1990) 'List construction as a task and resource' in Psathas, G. (ed.) *Interaction Competence*, Washington D.C., University Press of America.

Levinson, S. (1983) *Pragmatics*, Cambridge, Cambridge University Press.

Pomerantz, A. (1984) 'Agreeing and disagreeing with assessments: some features of preferred/dispreferred turn-shapes' in Atkinson, J.M. and Heritage, J. (eds) *Structures of Social Action: Studies in Conversation Analysis*, Cambridge, Cambridge University Press.

Potter, J. and Wetherell, M. (1987) *Discourse and Social Psychology: Beyond Attitudes and Behaviour*, London, Sage.

Psathas, G. (ed.) (1979) 'Everyday Language: Studies' in *Ethnomethodolology*, New York, Irvington.

Psathas, G. (1995) *Conversation Analysis: the Study of Talk in Interaction*, Thousand Oaks and London, Sage.

Sacks, H. (1984) 'Notes on methodology' in Atkinson, J.M. and Heritage. J. (eds) *Structures of Social Action: Studies in Conversation Analysis*, Cambridge, Cambridge University Press.

Sacks, H. (1992) *Lectures on Conversation* (2 Volumes, edited by G. Jefferson) Oxford, Basil Blackwell.

Sacks, H., Schegloff, E.A. and Jefferson, G. (1974) 'A simplest systematics for the organisation of turn-taking for conversation' in Schenkein, J., (ed.) *Studies in the Organization of Conversational Interaction*, New York, Academic Press (originally published in *Language*, vol.50, pp.696–735).

Schegloff, E.A. (1972) 'Sequencing in conversational openings' in Gumperz, J.J. and Hymes, D. (eds) *Directions in Sociolinguistics: the Ethnography of Communication*, New York, Holt, Rinehart and Winston.

Schegloff, E.A. (1979) 'The relevance of repair to syntax-for-conversation' in Givon, T. (ed.) *Syntax and Semantics, Volume 12: Discourse and Syntax*, New York, Academic Press.

Schegloff, E.A. (1992a) 'Introduction to volume 1' in Sacks, H. (1992), *Lectures on Conversation* (volume 1, edited by G. Jefferson) Oxford, Basil Blackwell.

Schegloff, E.A. (1992b) 'Repair after next turn: The last structurally provided defense of intersubjectivity in conversation', *American Journal of Sociology*, vol.97, pp.1295–345.

Schegloff, E.A., Jefferson, G. and Sacks, H. (1977) 'The preference for self-correction in the organisation of repair in conversation', *Language*, vol.53, pp.361–82.

Schenkein, J. (ed.) (1978a) *Studies in the Organisation of Conversational Interaction*, New York, Academic Press.

Schenkein, J. (1978b) 'Sketch of the analytic mentality for the study of conversational interaction' in Schenkein, J. (ed.) *Studies in the Organisation of Conversational Interaction*, New York: Academic Press.

Silverman, D. (1998) *Harvey Sacks: Social Science and Conversation Analysis*, Oxford, Polity Press.

Sudnow, D. (ed.) (1972) *Studies in Social Interaction*, New York, Free Press.

ten Have, P. (1999) *Doing Conversation Analysis: a Practical Guide*, London and Thousand Oaks, Sage.

Terasaki, A. (1976) 'Pre-announcement sequences in conversation', *Social Science Working Paper 99*, University of California at Irvine.

CHAPTER THREE

Researching Internet Interaction: Sociolinguistics and Corpus Analysis

Simeon J. Yates

Introduction

Extract 1: Electronic mail message

```
Date: Mon, 21 Jul 1997 12:38:48 +0100
To: t.sumner@open.ac.uk
From: s.j.yates@open.ac.uk
Subject: Interviews
Cc:
Bcc:
X-Attachments:


Tried to get you all day but your phone is always
engaged! I have the examples of written work. I'll look
at them tonight and then pass them on. Are you free for
a drink tonight? We could do an evening drink in the
sun and swap papers.


S.
```

Extract 2: Internet relay chat

```
<zed> i like this channel
<mouse> Why are all us American's in the Ireland group
<mike> likes GA
<frd3> Really you came here, why!? :)
<GA> I lived in North Carolina!
<zed> we are drawn toghrther
```

The above examples come from one of the fastest growing new
communications media – namely the internet. (Other examples of electronic
mail messages given in the chapter are anonymous contributions to Open
University on-line conferences.) The first being an electronic mail (e-mail)
message, the second being a 'transcript' from an internet-relay-chat (IRC)

interaction. In fact they are both examples of a wider range of media that go under the title of '**computer-mediated communication**' (CMC). In this chapter CMC will be used in two ways. First, CMC technologies raise a number of questions and problems for researchers interested in discourse. Second, CMC provides data that can readily be employed by those discourse researchers using more 'linguistic' or '**corpus**'-based methods. Both of these points will be discussed in greater depth later. The broad aims of this chapter are therefore:

- to introduce you to the 'linguistic' or 'corpus' methods employed by some discourse analysts

- to introduce you to the types and forms of data that can be explored using such methods

- to introduce you to some of the issues raised by these kinds of data and methods

- to make use of CMC data and research as an example of this work.

The methods presented in this chapter do not follow a specific methodological framework, such as that employed by conversation analysis, or a specific theoretical position, for example that employed in Foucauldian analysis. This chapter brings together a set of methods that can be broadly described as linguistic and reflect some of the approaches to discourse taken by those working within an '**interactional linguistics**' framework (see Wetherell *et al.*, 2001). The methods employed range from corpus linguistics (see McEnery and Wilson, 1996), sociolinguistics (see Stubbs, 1996), as well as linguistic approaches to discourse structure and development (see Coulthard, 1992; 1994). There are two major differences between the analyses presented here and those in some of the other chapters in this volume. First, corpus work tends to be more **quantitative** and general. It is based on large samples of language use that the researchers hope are representative of general **language practices** across a group, culture or even a society. It therefore often involves the counting or **measuring** of linguistic features. Having said this, not all work in this tradition is purely quantitative and more qualitative methods, akin to those used in the rest of this volume, are also employed. Second, the analyses tend to be comparative across groups, cultures and contexts, etc. The hope being that the relationship between language practices and other variables such as context or culture can be identified. In the examples given in this chapter, comparisons are made across different modes of communication (e.g. speech, writing and CMC), as well as across cultural variables (e.g. gender). The assessment of variations across different examples of discourse can involve the use of statistics.

The chapter begins in Section 1 with an exploration of one of the questions that CMC researchers have focused upon – is CMC spoken-like or written-like? The section also introduces the basic ideas and methods to be explored further in the rest of the chapter. Section 2 discusses the broad range of methods used in corpus work. The section also explores some of the reasons why CMC data has been approached in this way. Section 3 explores the question of identity on-line. Section 4 provides you with the opportunity to conduct your own analysis of a CMC interaction based on data provided in the Appendix to the chapter. The focus of the activity in this section is the exploration of gender and CMC issues. Before jumping straight into these discussions, let's begin by exploring the two examples of CMC that were given at the start of the chapter.

Activity 1

Look again at Extracts 1 and 2 and try to answer the following questions:

1 Do they look like any other forms of communication or records of that communication?

2 Looking at Extract 1, can you work out any of the following:

– Was it written by a man or a woman?

– Where was it written?

– Is it happy, sad, ironic, factual, friendly, or aggressive?

3 Looking at Extract 2, can you work out any of the following:

– Are the speakers men or women?

– Do the turns make sense?

– Is this one conversation or several?

Discussion

I'm not sure there are clear answers to these questions. Taking Question 1 first, you could argue that Extract 1 looks like a letter or a memo. There has been quite a bit of research conducted on the history of the e-mail message and how it connects to the history of the letter and the memo (Yates and Orlikowski, 1992; Yates, 2000). Extract 2 looks like the transcript of spoken interaction. In fact it is the record of a typed exchange.

You might be able to make a guess as to the gender of the author of Extract 1, but it would have to be a guess. I actually know that the person's gender is male but it is hard to tell from the message itself. There are some indicators as to where the message was written. The '@open.ac.uk' element of the writer's e-mail address lets you know that they are part of the 'Open University' (the 'open' part), which is part of the UK's (the 'uk' part) academic (the 'ac' part) internet network. You still can't tell (though you might be able to guess from the content of the message) whether this was written at work, at home, even abroad, as this address only tells you where the 'mailbox' of the user is, not the actual location where they read and write their e-mails. As to the tone of the e-mail message, it seems quite friendly to me but all I have to go on is the text. The answers to Question 3 are even less clear. Extract 2 looks like a transcript but the turns do not seem in order. There is, in fact, an order but this can only be seen if we view this as a set of multiple conversation threads involving several overlapping sets of speakers. As for the gender of the speakers, all we have are the usernames to go on, and anything they might say in the interaction.

The issues highlighted in Activity 1 have formed the basis of a large amount of CMC research. These issues can be expressed in three simple questions:

1   How is the medium of CMC related to other communications media?

2   How do users interact on-line?

3   How do users construct identities on-line?

These three general questions will follow us through this chapter. Section 1 will present an analysis that explores specific aspects of the questions 'How is the medium of CMC related to other communications media?' and 'How do users interact on-line?' Section 3 will present an analysis of the question 'How do users construct identities on-line?' Section 4 takes a closer look at how gender functions on-line.

1   What is CMC?

CMC technologies come in a wide range of forms. Each of these technologies supports a range of interactions. In order to make sense of this range, CMC researchers tend to categorize CMC systems across two dimensions. First, there is the extent to which the interactions are **synchronous**. Synchronous communication, as exemplified by speech, requires both parties to be present for the interaction to take place. An example of synchronous CMC is IRC. Other CMC systems such as e-mail do not require participants to both be present. E-mail messages are sent asynchronously, that is, in delayed time, in the same manner as letters. We expect a delay between sending a letter and receiving a reply. Second, CMC can be categorized by the nature of the interaction. This can be one-to-one, one-to-many or group communication.

By using these criteria we can categorize the various types of CMC. At the synchronous end of the scale are 'chat' systems where the interacting parties must be '**co-present**' at their respective computers at the same time. Given this direct virtual co-presence, the interactions tend to consist of short single-line turns. At the other end of the scale are technologies such as e-mail and computer-conferencing. In this case the medium is designed to be asynchronous with users sending and receiving messages under the assumption that the others are not virtually co-present. In between these extremes are CMC media that support varying degrees of synchronicity/asynchronicity, these include such things as Multi-User-Domains/Multi-User-Domains-Object-Orientated (MUDs/MOOs) and Usenet. Figure 1 is an idealized representation of the types of synchronicity/asynchronicity that CMC systems support. Each technology supports a mixture of one-to-one,

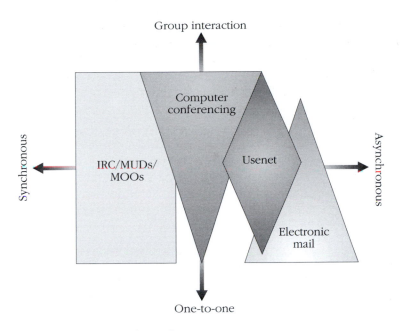

Figure 1   CMC and synchronicity

one-to-many and group communication (see Yates, 2000, for a full discussion).

One of the first questions CMC researchers asked was: 'Is CMC written-like or spoken-like?' This question arises from the fact that CMC consists of typed texts, but, as Figure 1 implies, CMC is used in contexts such as synchronous group communication where we would normally expect a spoken interaction. This is, of course, a specific version of one of the three questions highlighted above – namely 'How is the medium of CMC related to other communications media?'

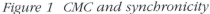

Activity 2

The following are some more examples of CMC texts. This time the elements of the text that mark them out as being from an e-mail or 'chat' interaction have been removed and they are presented as though they are 'turns' as they occurred 'next' to each other in an interaction. Read these two extracts and try to decide which of the 'turns' are 'more spoken-like' or 'more written-like' – note down why you decided they were more written-like or spoken-like.

Extract 3

It is fairly obvious that managing information technology change is an area which can be expected to be of importance to more or less every organisation. Every organisation has an information system and every information system is susceptible to the use of new technology.

Sorry, not been around for a couple of days. What I
meant was, we should examine all the processes
involved in our operation, not just the way in which we
write or deliver our courses.

Extract 4

A: 13 was very special for me, B. But it went downhill a
bit at 18, then brightened up at 19 when I threw my ex
out.

B: Your teen years were obviously a lot more eventful
than mine. Then again everybodys teen years were more
eventful than mine!

A: Life is what you make it, kid ... though I could have
done without some of my events!

B: I know that now. It just took me a long time to work
that out.

Discussion

Extract 4 seems obviously spoken-like to me. Not only does it look like the
transcript of a spoken interaction but also the topic and tone of the content
reminds me of a quite personal face-to-face interaction. Having said this we
must be careful. In Chapter One, Taylor pointed out that the way in which
language data is transcribed is directly linked to the analysis. Transcription
is not a neutral activity. In the case of Extract 4, the fact that I presented
this as a transcript can be seen to have had two possible effects. First, it
may have made it easier to see the spoken-like nature of the interaction.
Second, it may have hidden some of the written-like aspects of the
interaction. What do you think? Here is how the interaction would have
appeared on screen:

Extract 5: Computer-conferencing chat

```
============================
dt200-chat #209, [A]
This is a comment to message 208
There is/are comment(s) on this message
There are additional comments to message 208
--------------------------
13 was very special for me, B. But it went downhill a
bit at 18, then brightened up at 19 when I threw my ex
out.

A
```

```
============================
dt200-chat #210, [B]
This is a comment to message 209
There is/are comment(s) on this message
----------------------------
Your teen years were obviously a lot more eventful than
mine. Then again everybodys teen years were more
eventful than mine!

B


============================
dt200-chat #211, [A]
This is a comment to message 210
There is/are comment(s) on this message
----------------------------
Life is what you make it, kid ... though I could have
done without some of my events!

A


============================
dt200-chat #212, [B]
This is a comment to message 211
There is/are comment(s) on this message
----------------------------
I know that now. It just took me a long time to work
that out.
```

Looking at the version of the interaction in Extract 5, I find that the 'spokenness' is less clear. The message headers provide a 'memo'-like feel to the interaction.

Extract 3 in Activity 2 is less clear. First, though it is laid out as a transcript, the turns don't seem to follow from one another. Once again it is an example of the ways in which many CMC interactions involve multiple threads running concurrently and where the specific 'temporal' sequence of messages does not fit exactly the turns of the interaction – as it does in speech. Turn one seems more written-like not only because of the content and tone but also because of the grammatical structure (I come back to this point later when we analyse data in Example Analysis 1). You could argue that turn two is also written-like – though more like a chatty letter than the turns in Extract 4. I might argue that turn two of Extract 3 is, in fact, spoken-like because of its the grammatical structure.

Once again we could ask if the form of transcription is getting in the way of a fuller understanding/analysis? Here is the 'on-screen' form.

Extract 6: Computer-conferencing discussion

```
===========================
dt200-forum/IT Management #40, [1]
This is a comment to message 25
There is/are comment(s) on this message
There are additional comments to message 25
---------------------------
It is fairly obvious that managing information
technology change is an area which can be expected to
be of importance to more or less every organisation.
Every organisation has an information system and every
information system is susceptible to the use of new
technology.


[1]


===========================
dt200-forum/IT Management #41, [1]
This is a comment to message 28
There is/are comment(s) on this message
---------------------------
Sorry, not been around for a couple of days. What I
meant was, we should examine all the processes
involved in our operation, not just the way in which we
write or deliver our courses.
```

You might have noticed that in both cases the turns are marked in the headers of the messages 'This is a comment to message XX'. Users have to follow these threads rather than the temporal sequence of messages in order to understand the turns. But also note that in both Extract 5 and Extract 6, some messages have multiple responses so even the threads don't follow 'normal' face-to-face turn-taking conventions (such as 'There are additional comments to message XX'). The problems of defining CMC as being spoken-like or written-like, and the problems of understanding turn-taking in CMC, have quite important implications for how CMC researchers have gone about their work.

1.1 Example Analysis 1: Exploring the medium of CMC

In the rest of this section I will walk you though an analysis designed to answer the question 'Is CMC spoken-like or written-like'. First, I will discuss some of the reasons for choosing the data and the methods. Second, I will describe the collection and analysis of the data. Third, I will present and discuss the results. The purpose of this walk through is to explore the implications of Activity 2 and to introduce you to some of the ideas and concepts that will be examined in more depth later in the chapter.

Taylor, in Chapter One, outlined four approaches to discourse work. In many respects the analyses that follow can be placed in the first two of these approaches. Wetherell *et al.* (2001) separate discourse work into the study of three broad areas.

- social interaction

- minds, selves and sense-making

- culture and social relations.

In this typology, the following analyses fall into the area of social interaction and the 'interactional sociolinguistic' method of analysing such interactions. It therefore draws upon ideas and methods from linguistics more than from conversation analysis, psychology or sociology.

Activity 3

As you read through Example Analysis 1, make some notes on the following issues:

- How was the data collected?

- How was the data analysed?

- How did the analysis link data, theory and methods?

I'll discuss my responses to these questions once you have finished reading this Example Analysis.

Background

In general, the analysis that follows is based in a 'cultural' or 'critical linguistic' understanding of the difference between speaking and writing (see Hodge and Kress, 1988, reproduced as Reading Twenty-one in Wetherell *et al.*, 2001). It is based on the assertion that CMC, as a typed 'text-based' medium, must draw upon users understandings of 'doing writing'. It assumes that CMC communication is a new kind of '**literacy practice**'. Barton (1991) claims that the definition of literacy practices comes from various sources, the main two being Scribner and Cole (1981) and Street (1984). Scribner and Cole define practice in the following manner:

> By a practice we mean a recurrent, goal-directed sequence of activities using a particular technology and particular systems of knowledge. ... Practice always refers to socially developed and patterned ways of using technology and knowledge to accomplish tasks. Conversely, tasks that individuals engage in constitute a social practice when they are directed to socially recognized goals and make use of a shared technology and knowledge system.
>
> (Scribner and Cole, 1981: 236)

So we can begin the analysis by assuming that the way people 'write' CMC messages is probably defined by the ways in which 'doing speaking', 'doing writing' and 'doing CMC' have been socially and culturally organized. This in turn will leave its mark in the actual discourse produced through CMC interactions. In order to explore this we will need CMC data as well as spoken and written data for comparison.

Collecting the data

As the first part of this section made clear, there are very many kinds of CMC. What we want to know is the range of spoken-like to written-like forms in CMC. One form of CMC that tends to display a whole range of message types, levels of synchronicity (virtual co-presence) and one-to-one to group interaction is computer conferencing. This analysis therefore collected data from one computer conferencing system. There are a number of technical reasons (to do with how messages are stored) and ethical reasons (to do with access to 'private' messages) why computer conferencing is an easier option than other media. Cherny (1999) provides a full discussion of the ethical concerns raised by the study of CMC.

The data for this analysis were collected from an Open University computer conferencing system (CoSy). The examples of computer conferencing interactions you have seen so far (Extracts 1, 5 and 6) come from this system. Given that corpus work tries to be general in scope, the CoSy interactions provided useful data for a number of reasons. First the user base was spread across the whole of the United Kingdom and there were, on average, 2,000 registered members of the CoSy system at any one time. It therefore provided a large social sample, including both novice and experienced users. Second the system supported a range of **genres** of interaction including both formal educational interactions and more informal 'chat' interactions. The data can therefore be seen as representative of a range of users and types of interaction. As Taylor noted in Chapter One of this volume, selecting the respondents and data for discourse studies is a key part of the process. Here we have gone for a very 'quantitative' approach – collecting a lot of data from a range of sources to produce a 'generally representative' sample.

While one obvious method for collecting the CMC material would be to download all that was available, this would produce a very large set of data! One also needs to consider the corpora against which comparisons will be made, as well as taking seriously the ethical issues about access. The first selection therefore consisted of a sample of 50 messages from 152 publicly open conference discussions. This provided a total of some 648,550 words and an average of 4,267 words per conference discussion. This set of data will be referred to as the CoSy:50 corpus.

Given that the above selection consisted of only partial discussions, and given some of the possible methodological problems this raises, a corpus of full conferencing interactions was also collected. Rather than randomly sample a set of conferences, it seemed more useful to purposefully sample from specific sources. The sources once again included a range of 'chat' and formal interactions. In total 66 conference discussions were collected totalling some 1,573,499 words. I will refer to this as the CoSy:Full corpus. In the end, most analyses used a combination of the CoSy:50 and the CoSy:Full corpus. This provided a total of 218 texts and 2,222,049 words.

The two sets of data have been described as '**corpora**'. So what is a corpus? A corpus is collection of linguistic data, nowadays stored on computer, which is seen to be representative of a certain type of text, interaction or discourse. It is interesting to note that the development of interest in corpus work has coincided with the availability of personal computers capable of storing and manipulating very large amounts of text-based data. There are now a large number of corpora available for use by language and discourse researchers. In the UK, the British National Corpus contains about 100 million words. 20 million of these are transcribed from 'naturally occurring speech' recorded on 'Walkman' tape recorders by a representative sample of the UK population. The other 80 million words were sampled from printed and written materials.

Another possible reason why CMC researchers have tended to use corpus or content analysis methods derives directly from the fact that CMC is **digital text**. It is, in fact, far easier to build a CMC corpus than any other. As the data is already digital it requires no transcription or copying from another form such as tape recording or the printed page. As one of the earlier corpus researchers noted:

> The computer revolution has brought with it new forms of discourse which also deserve systematic study. One of these is electronic mail ... Electronic mail reveals features of both speech and writing. Like other forms of discourse, new as well as old, it deserves the attention of future corpus workers.
>
> (Johansson, 1991: 307–8)

The main idea behind collecting a corpus is the exploring of general features of a language or a specific kind of text or interaction.

In order to conduct our analysis we will need to compare our CMC corpus with spoken and written corpora. The analysis presented here used the Lancaster-Oslo/Bergen corpus of written British English and the London-Lund corpus of spoken British English. The Lancaster-Oslo/Bergen (LOB) corpus of written texts consists of 500 individual texts of approximately 2,000 words each. These texts are distributed across 15 separate text categories.

Table 1 Number of texts per category in the LOB corpus

Code	Category	Number of texts
LOB:A	Press: Reportage	44
LOB:B	Press: Editorial	27
LOB:C	Press: Reviews	17
LOB:D	Religion	17
LOB:E	Skills, Trades and Hobbies	38
LOB:F	Popular Lore	44
LOB:G	Belles lettres, Biography, Essays	77
LOB:H	Miscellaneous (government documents, foundation reports, industry reports, college catalogue, industry house organ)	30
LOB:J	Learned and Scientific Writing	80
LOB:K	General Fiction	29
LOB:L	Mystery and Detective Fiction	24
LOB:M	Science Fiction	6
LOB:N	Adventure and Western Fiction	29
LOB:P	Romance and Love Story	29
LOB:R	Humor	9
	Total Texts:	500

An example of the data in this corpus is presented in Corpus Example 1. This is a 'transcription' of a newspaper report. As you can see it contains markers designed to indicate such things as headings and sentence breaks. This is in fact from the 'untagged' version of the corpus. The 'tagged' version gives information on the 'part-of-speech' or grammatical function of each of the words.

Corpus Example 1: Extract from 'untagged' LOB corpus text

```
A01 2 *<*'*7STOP ELECTING LIFE PEERS**'*>
A01 3 *<*4By TREVOR WILLIAMS*>
A01 4 |^A *0MOVE to stop \0Mr. Gaitskell from nominating any more Labour
A01 5 life Peers is to be made at a meeting of Labour {0M P}s tomorrow.
A01 6 |^\0Mr. Michael Foot has put down a resolution on the subject and
A01 7 he is to be backed by \0Mr. Will Griffiths, {0M P} for Manchester
A01 8 Exchange.
```

```
A01 9 |^Though they may gather some Left-wing support, a large majority
A01 10 of Labour {OM P}s are likely to turn down the Foot-Griffiths
A01 11 resolution.
A01 12 *<*7*'ABOLISH LORDS**'*>
A01 13 |^*0\0Mr. Foot's line will be that as Labour {OM P}s opposed the
A01 14 Government Bill which brought life peers into existence, they should
A01 15 not now put forward nominees.
A01 16 |^He believes that the House of Lords should be abolished and that
A01 17 Labour should not take any steps which would appear to *''prop up**'' an
A01 18 out-dated institution.
A01 19 |^Since 1958, 13 Labour life Peers and Peeresses have been created.
A01 20 |^Most Labour sentiment would still favour the abolition of the
A01 21 House of Lords, but while it remains Labour has to have an adequate
A01 22 number of members.
```

The London-Lund corpus of spoken English consists of 100 spoken texts. The full corpus consists of some 500,000 words. Each individual text therefore contains some 5000 words (see Greenbaum and Svartvic, 1990) and is therefore comparable to our CoSy:50 corpus.

Table 2 Categories of spoken texts in the London-Lund corpus

Code	Category	Number of texts
LLc:1	Conversations between equals	14
LLc:2	Conversations between equals	14
LLc:3	Conversations between disparates	7
LLc:4	Conversations or discussions between equals	7
LLc:5	Radio discussions and conversations between equals	13
LLc:6	Interviews and discussions between disparates	9
LLc:7	Telephone conversations between equals	3
LLc:8	Telephone conversations between equals	4
LLc:9:1–2	Telephone conversations between disparates	2
LLc:9:3–5	Telephone, dictaphone and answerphone	3
LLc:10	Spontaneous commentary, mainly radio	11
LLc:11	Spontaneous oration	6
LLc:12	Prepared oration	7

Much of the data in the London-Lund corpus consists of academics in discussion, indicating that the main source for much of the data was the researchers' own social environment.

Corpus Example 2: Extract from London-Lund corpus

```
1 1 1     20 1 1 A    11   ^w=ell# . /
1 1 1     30 1 1 A    11 ((if)) did ^y/ou _set _that#   /
1 1 1     40 1 1 B    11 ^well !J\oe and _I# /
1 1 1     50 1 1 B    11 ^set it betw\een _us# /
1 1 1     60 1 1 B    11 ^actually !Joe 'set the :p\aper# /
1 1 1     70 1 1 B    20 and *((3 to 4 sylls))* /
1 1 1     80 1 1 A    11 *^w=ell# . /
1 1 1     90 1 1 A    11 ''^m/\ay* I _ask# /
1 1 1    100 1 1 A    11 ^what goes !\into that paper n/ow# /
1 1 1    110 1 1 A    11 be^cause I !have to adv=ise# . /
1 1 1    120 1 1 A    21 ((a)) ^couple of people who are !d\oing [dhi: @] /
1 1 1    130 1 1 B    11 well ^what you :d\/o# /
1 1 1    140 1 2 B    12 ^is to - - ^this is sort of be:tween the :tw\/o of /
1 1 1    140 1 1 B    12 _us# /
1 1 1    150 1 1 B    11 ^what *you* :d\/o# /
1 1 1    160 2 1 B    23 is to ^make sure that your 'own . !c\andidate /
1 1 1    170 1 1 A    11 *^[\m]#* /
1 1 1    160 1 2 (B   13 is . *.* ^that your . there`s ^something that your /
1 1 1    160 1 1 (B   13 :own candidate can :h\/andle# - - /
1 1 1    180 2 1 B    21 ((I ^won`t)) /
1 1 2    190 1 1 A    11 *((^y\eah#))* /
1 1 2    180 1 1 (B   11 ((be a m/inute# - - /
1 1 2    200 1 1 B    20 3 to 4 sylls)) - - - /
```

Analysing the data

One difference between speech and writing that many researchers have commented upon is that of the differing modes of production and **consumption**. Speech is produced 'on the fly' and is intended to be consumed – heard – in the same rapid and dynamic manner. Writing on the other hand is static; it is produced at the pace set by the writer alone and can be consumed at any speed that the reader chooses. The effects of such differences in production are likely, it is claimed, to generate differences in the language used. One aspect of this concerns vocabulary use. Chafe and Danielewicz claim that:

> As a consequence of these differences, speakers tend to operate with a narrower range of **lexical choices** than writers. Producing language on the fly, they hardly have time to sift through all of the possible choices they might make, and may typically settle on the first words that occur to them. The result is that the vocabulary of spoken language is more limited in variety.
>
> (Chafe and Danielewicz, 1987: 88 my emphasis)

In order to examine the differing use of vocabulary more empirically Chafe and Danielewicz make use of the **type/token ratio**. The type/token ratio used by Chafe and Danielewicz is that of the number of different words (**types**) divided by the total number of words (**tokens**). In this calculation all words of all types were counted (Chafe and Danielewicz, 1987: 88).

Activity 4

What is the type/token ratio of this sentence?

The answer is 1.0 or 100%. There are 9 words, all different.

What about the following utterance? 'I would like to agree, but I would not be able to take that position, I would not agree.'

The type/token ration here is 0.58 or 58% as there are 11 different words (types) and a total of 19 words (tokens). Now try to calculate the type/token ratio for Extract 1 at the start of this chapter – ignore the 'header' part of the message.

I calculate the type/token ratio to be 0.875. You probably found this quite a boring and possibly tedious process. You will not be surprised to hear, then, that computers normally carry out such analyses. In fact most corpus work involves the use of computers, as even simple analyses such as this would take excessive amounts of time if conducted 'by hand'.

There are some problems with the above method that are too detailed to discuss at this point. A more rigorous measure of vocabulary use is to remove the words that are essentially **grammatical** (e.g. and, if, it, the, etc.) and to focus on lexical words (content words). One then calculates the ratio of the number of different lexical items (**lexical types**) to the total number of lexical items (**lexical tokens**). Computer software did this analysis across the three corpora. The general result is presented in Table 3. If a statistical analysis is conducted on the data in this table the differences prove to be statistically significant. In other words, the differences are not the product of simple chance.

Table 3 Mean type/token ratios for three corpora

Corpus	*CoSy (CMC)*	*LOB (writing)*	*London-Lund (speech)*
Mean type/token ratio	0.590	0.624	0.395

This result would seem to indicate that CMC is more akin to writing than speech in terms of vocabulary use. The most obvious conclusion is to follow Chafe and Danielewicz and see this as a product of the medium itself, and the opportunity it allows for longer gestation over the content of utterances. Careful thought about this point, though, raises a complication. The texts contained within the LOB corpus were mostly produced prior to the advent of the word processor or the electronic text. The CMC corpus contains only word-processed electronic texts. What the electronic text brings is an even greater set of opportunities to correct, change, restructure and review utterances. Following Chafe and Danielewicz, one would expect to see even higher levels of vocabulary use – therefore higher type/token ratios. Even more interestingly, it is writing that demonstrates the greatest variation in vocabulary use (type/token ratios) as compared to speech and CMC which have comparable variances. The implication of this result is that factors other than simply the mechanical aspects of the medium are at work in producing utterances. Vocabulary use covers a large number of social and cultural issues and, despite having a clear relationship to the production and consumption of a text, it is not the only measure of the textuality of an utterance.

One measure that attempts to incorporate these social and cultural issues is '**lexical density**'. Halliday (1985) begins his explanation of lexical density with the following examples:

- If you invest in a rail facility, this implies that you are going to be committed for a long time. (*Lexical density = 0.35*)

- Investment in a rail facility implies a long-term commitment. (*Lexical density = 0.7*)

Halliday argues that the first of these sentences appears much more like the record of spoken communication than written. The first of these sentences has 7 lexical items and 13 grammatical ones. The lexical items are: *invest; rail; facility; implies; committed; long* and *time*. In the second sentence there are 7 lexical items and 3 grammatical ones. The lexical items are: *investment; rail; facility; implies; long; term* and *commitment*. Halliday attributes this difference to the different cultural and contextual uses to which we put speech and writing and the social roles our linguistic practices have to support. It is not the medium but society and culture that motivates differences in speech and writing.

In the above examples the ratio of lexical items to grammatical ones (the lexical density) is lower for spoken language than it is for written. Lexical density therefore provides a quantitative difference between spoken and written utterances. In the above example the first sentence has a ratio of 7 to 13 whilst the second sentence has a ratio of 7 to 3. These can be better represented as a ratio or percentage of the number of lexical items to the number of total items within an utterance. On this measure the first sentence would score 7 out of 20 or 0.35 (35%). The second sentence would score 7 out of 10 or 0.7 (70%). These types of score are *lexical density* scores (Halliday, 1985). Such a test was conducted using our three corpora and the results are given in Table 4. Once again the differences in the results were statistically significant.

Table 4 Mean unweighted lexical densities for three corpora

Corpus	CoSy (CMC)	LOB (writing)	London-Lund (speech)
Mean lexical density (unweighted) (%)	49.258	50.316	42.292

The interpretation of these results is not straightforward. On one level it implies that some texts in the corpus are more written-like and some more spoken-like – thus making an average result in between. On the other hand a more detailed study indicates that there are styles – genres – of CMC that are themselves between the oral and the literate. In fact these genres are often used by experienced users who have developed their own 'CMC' practices (in contrast to oral and literate practices) and their use is very dependent on social context (see Yates, 1996).

1.2 Comment on Example Analysis 1

Example Analysis 1 is very quantitative and very different from nearly all the analyses you will find elsewhere in this volume. It does, though, highlight some of the key issues faced by corpus-based research. Let's review the three questions that were set out in Activity 3.

How was the data collected?

The only data that was collected by the researcher was the CMC data. This was simply 'downloaded' from a CMC system (CoSy) and used as given. Unlike both the written and spoken corpora, this data did not need to be transcribed. On one level this might seem to be a benefit of CMC data. The practical problem it raises is that of having too much data. In fact one could argue that the ease with which large amounts of CMC data can be collected leads researchers towards corpus methods. Being pushed into a methodology by the nature of your data is something that all discourse analysis workers need to take note of. It is also something that should not be done 'blindly'.

The spoken and written data were gained from existing corpora. In Chapter One, Taylor notes that large amounts of qualitative data are now being archived for use by future researchers. She notes that for qualitative researchers, re-using others' data has a number of problems that derive from the separation between the data collection and the analysis processes. In the case of corpora, most linguists do not see this problem, all they are concerned about is the representativeness of the corpus. As you will see in the analyses that follow in this chapter, this may, in fact, be a difficult position to maintain.

How was the data analysed?

It could be argued that the data was 'analysed' by computer. The three corpora were processed by software to provide the relevant type/token ratios and lexical density scores. In fact the setting up of these measures was theory driven and they represent the 'operationalization' of these theories into a specific form of quantitative analysis. These results were then subjected to statistical analyses. This represents a very quantitative approach informed by essentially positivist models of the research process. In the analyses to follow you will see how CMC researchers have moved away from such methods as they begin to address more social and cultural questions, though they continue to make use of the opportunities provided by computer software tools.

How did the analysis link data, theory and methods?

We have already begun to answer this question above. The link between theory and methods is based on the following logic. Oral and literate practices leave their mark in the structure and content of utterances. This must also be true of CMC. We can theorize what these marks might be – for instance vocabulary variations. We can use these ideas to construct empirical quantitative measures – for instance type/token ratios or lexical density. By applying these measures we can make statements about the nature of CMC as a medium. This model of the process is based in a 'positivist' framework in that it follows the model of the natural sciences. In this model, research follows the stages of: theory; hypothesis; operationalization; measurement; results; analysis and theory.

Summary

What have we learnt from Section 1? It introduced a number of important methodological issues and the analysis made use of corpora. Corpora are large sets of linguistic data, often in the order of several million words. For linguists interested in discourse analysis, corpora provide readily available data. Section 1 also introduced the idea that a key aspect of discourse – the very manner in which the interaction is grammatically and linguistically constructed – can be studied in a very quantitative manner. This approach drew upon a range of linguistic ideas and methods and made the assumption that the record of linguistic interactions can be taken as evidence of discursive processes.

2   Methods

Section 1 briefly mentioned the use of computer software to conduct data analyses. Computer software allows the researcher to access or analyse the millions of words in a corpus which would simply be extraordinarily difficult and time-consuming otherwise (though not impossible, see Zipf, 1935). Before looking at another example analysis let's reconsider these three issues:

- the development of a corpus of data
- the range of corpus methods
- using computers.

2.1 The selecting corpora and corpus methods

As McEnery and Wilson (1996) note, corpus methods have been used in everything from formal linguistic studies of lexis and grammar through to cultural studies, social psychology and discourse analysis. At the same time, those linguists interested in the sociological, cultural and social-psychological aspects of language use often employ much more qualitative methods than those presented in Section 1. To say that this range of methods follow a well-defined set of rules, or that methods are coherent across disciplines would be untrue. Corpus methods, especially in the area of discourse analysis, are still 'under development' and there are few full and detailed discussions of the practical and methodological implications of such an approach to the study of language and communication. One of the few discussions of the use of corpus-type methods in the study of discourse and culture is provided by Stubbs (1996). In this work, Stubbs makes use of varying methods and corpora. Table 5 lists the data and the methods Stubbs employs.

Table 5 Corpus methods employed by Stubbs

Topic/Data	Methods	Analysis
Institutional language use: spoken and written texts.	Lexical density	Differences in language use in context
Sexist language: speeches by Baden-Powell to Boy Scouts and Girl Guides	Content analysis – word frequency and use	Exploration of lexical choices in a text
Language in courtrooms: transcript of a judge's summing up	Content analysis – word frequency and use, discourse markers, modal verbs and syntactic complexity, concordance	Exploration of interpretation of 'complex' language and the production of 'facts'
Language in teaching texts: geography text books	Content analysis – word frequency and use; Key-words-in-context	Exploration of the role of agency in pedagogic explanations
Cultural connotations of words: 130 million words of written English from the *Cobuild* corpus	Collocations of words	Exploring the connotations and contexts of word use
Positioning and framing of utterances: various selections from corpora	Content analysis – word frequency and use; collocations	Exploration of the use of modal auxiliaries to position speakers in relation to utterances

Elements of all of these methods will be employed in the examples in the following sections. Word frequency lists allow you to see the terms and topics that are most frequently used in a text. Some software also provides graphical displays of the position and frequency of target words throughout texts. **Key-words-in-context (KWIC)** analyses provide lists of all the occurrences of a word and the context (e.g. sentence etc.) around it. Concordancers do a similar job. **Collocations** are frequency lists of the words that occur in the context around a key word. For example if one were to study the use of racist language in political debates, one could explore the words that occur near to a key word such as 'immigration'. Other software provides 'part-of-speech' analyses. These allow you to explore the forms of grammar and syntax in use. The use of word frequencies, key-words-in-context, and qualitative content analyses will be used in this chapter.

2.2 Using computers

All of these methods can and often have to employ computers. In order to search corpora for specific key words, or to count and display occurrences of words and phrases in a corpus of several million words, requires the use

of computers and specialist software. In the following sections two types of
computer software were employed. The first can best be described as
'linguistic tools'. The second type are **computer assisted qualitative data
analysis software** (CAQDAS) designed for use by qualitative researchers.
Both of these types of software are usable by anyone working with
'linguistic' data. In fact they represent a spectrum of tools from quantitative
word counters to tools specifically designed to help those working within
some form of qualitative data analysis framework.

Corpus linguistic tools include concordances, key-word-in-context
(KWIC) systems, and word counting and sorting tools. Various forms of these
are available on nearly all major computing platforms, though classic
examples include the Oxford Concordance Program for UNIX, or
WordSmith[TM] for the PC which brings a suite of such tools together in one
piece of software. Though such tools do not allow coding of the text they
can easily make considerable use of 'part-of-speech' as well as any other
annotations and transcription markers included within the text. Some of
these systems are designed to be interactive, allowing the researcher to
dynamically explore large bodies of text at a detailed linguistic level.
Figures 2, 3 and 4 show a corpus linguistic tool in action on some CMC data.

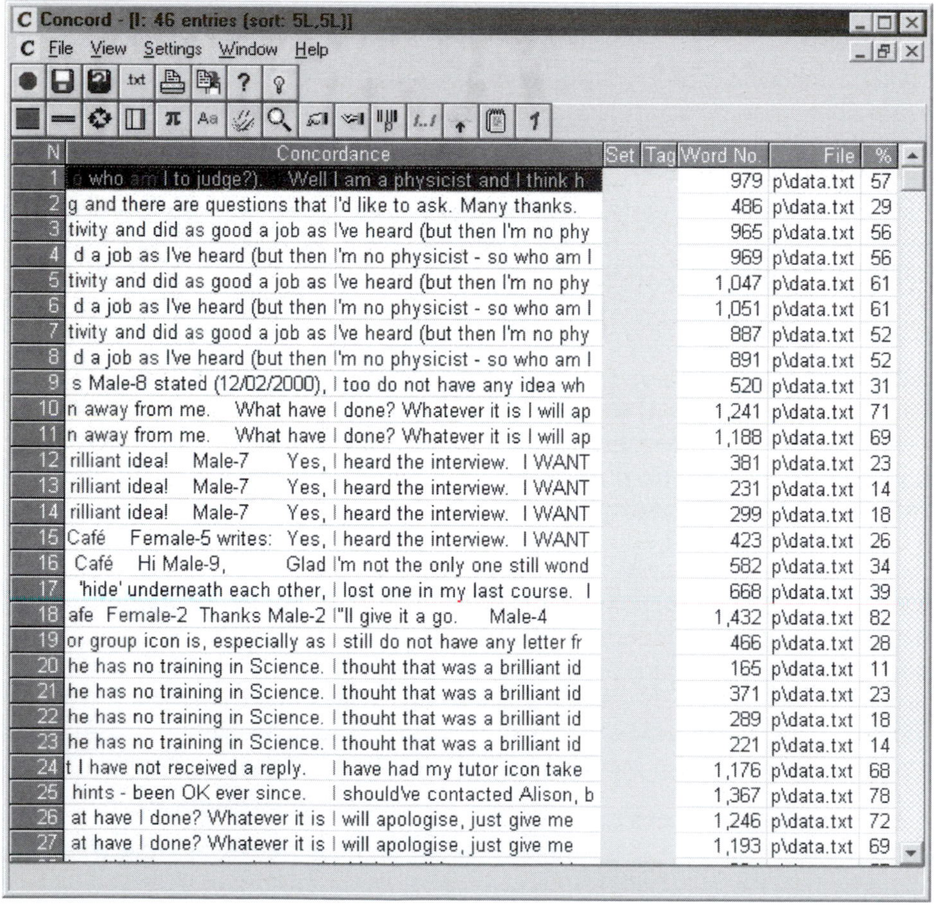

Figure 2 Concordance (KWIC) of the use of 'I' in the data from the Appendix

WordList

File   Settings   Comparison   Index   Window   Help

new wordlist (A)

N	Word	Freq	%
1	A	24	1.30
2	ABOUT	5	0.27
3	AC	5	0.27
4	ACCESSED	2	0.11
5	ACID	1	0.05
6	ADVISE	1	0.05
7	AFTER	4	0.22
8	AGREED	2	0.11
9	ALAN	1	0.05
10	ALISON	1	0.05
11	ALL	1	0.05
12	ALLOCATED	1	0.05
13	AM	4	0.22
14	AN	9	0.49
15	ANALYSE	1	0.05
16	AND	18	0.98
17	ANY	4	0.22
18	ANYONE	3	0.16
19	ANYWAY	3	0.16

new wordlist (F)

N	Word	Freq	%
1	THE	55	2.99
2	MALE	51	2.77
3	TO	41	2.23
4	I	38	2.07
5	CAFE	33	1.79
6	FEMALE	31	1.68
7	FROM	29	1.58
8	ITEM	26	1.41
9	SUBJECT	26	1.41
10	FOR	25	1.36
11	A	24	1.30
12	WAS	22	1.20
13	ON	21	1.14
14	CAFÉ	19	1.03
15	OF	19	1.03
16	RE	19	1.03
17	THAT	19	1.03
18	AND	18	0.98
19	FEBRUARY	18	0.98

new wordlist (S)

N	
Text File	DATA.TXT
Bytes	10,256
Tokens	1,840
Types	398
Type/Token Ratio	21.63
Standardised Type/Token	26.60
Ave. Word Length	4.03
Sentences	40
Sent.length	16.27
sd. Sent. Length	11.43
Paragraphs	100
Para. length	18.40
sd. Para. length	17.68
Headings	0
Heading length	
sd. Heading length	
1-letter words	168
2-letter words	369
3-letter words	267
4-letter words	472
5-letter words	153
6-letter words	128
7-letter words	128
8-letter words	59
9-letter words	51
10-letter words	28
11-letter words	10

Figure 3   Word frequencies and other statistics from data in the Appendix

Figure 4   Frequency plot of the use of 'I' in the data from the Appendix.

CAQDAS tools are particularly designed to support the process of coding and analysis. Such tools do not do the coding or analysis for you but allow you to work interactively with the data and often allow more varied representations of your data and codings. The specific features of these systems and their uses have been detailed extensively elsewhere (Fielding and Lee, 1994; Weitzman and Miles, 1995). Some of the main key advantages provided by such software include:

- coding of large bodies of qualitative data

- coding of digitized media clips

- powerful search tools

- powerful indexing and querying tools

- complex comparative reporting

- visualization of relations between data and codes.

One way of viewing such systems is as tools for adding **metadata** – to borrow a phrase from computing – to the transcribed data. Metadata is a structured set of comments, annotations and mark-ups that provide information about the data to which it is linked. The addition of the metadata makes it possible to find, sort and restructure your data at a more abstracted level. The addition (coding) and manipulation (analysis) of meta-level data is, of course, part and parcel of written/printed text-based qualitative data analysis. Figure 5 shows the Atlas/ti^{TM} CAQDAS tool in use. This system allows the researcher to see their data and the coding of that data side-by-side on the screen. Such systems provide a large range of output, including reorganizations of data by codes, or graphical representations of inputted relationships between codes, as well as numerical tables of types and amounts of coding.

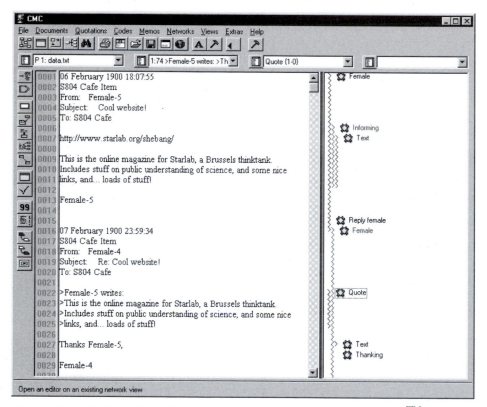

Figure 5   Initial coding of data from the Appendix using Atlas/ti^{TM}

Summary

What can we conclude from this short section on methods? First, it is clear that corpora and corpus methods provide and opportunity for those linguists interested in discourse analysis issues. Second, that there are a number of 'costs' that are incurred in taking up this opportunity: Some of these are:

- There is no 'text-book' that lays out the use of corpus methods in discourse analysis. Corpus methods employ a range of activities from quantitative word counting to more complex and qualitative content analyses.
- Corpus methods take on board some epistemological baggage. In particular they take linguistic data as direct evidence of discursive processes and practices. This contrasts with the other approaches in this book, especially Chapters Two, Four and Five.
- Corpus methods rely upon the use of computer software that ranges from 'linguistic' tools, such as word counters and concordances, to CAQDAS tools.

Section 3 will now take you through another example analysis. This time the main question to be addressed is 'How do users construct identities on-line?'.

3   Doing identity in CMC

As with the Example Analysis 1, we will begin with a review of the available theoretical literature. Example Analysis 2 will consider two theoretical approaches to the question 'How do users construct identities on-line?' and will then discuss the data to be used in addressing this question. Subsequently, 'corpus' methods and more qualitative content analysis methods will be used to explore the issues to hand. The section concludes with a discussion of the methods and data that have been used in Example Analysis 2.

3.1 Example Analysis 2: Constructing identities on-line

Activity 5

As you did with the previous example read through Example Analysis 2 and make some notes on the following issues

- How was the data collected? (In particular focus on the amount of data that was collected)
- How was the data analysed? (How quantitative was the analysis this time?)
- How did the analysis link data, theory and methods? (Was there such a clear link between theory and methods in this case?)

I'll discuss my responses to these questions once you have finished reading Example Analysis 2.

Background

To date there have been several models of 'identity on-line'. This analysis will focus on two of these. These can be described as the '**limited cues**' and the '**social presence**' models. The first model predominated early work on CMC and developed from social-psychological experiments designed to elicit the 'nature' of CMC interactions. These experiments were based on the 'social presence' model derived from the work of Short *et al.* (1976). Short compared face-to-face, video and telephone/intercom interactions and explored how users rated telecommunications media across a number of factors such as:

- unsociable–sociable

- insensitive–sensitive

- cold–warm

- impersonal–personal.

The crucial issue which Short found to influence use and perception of the communication was the level of 'social presence'. Media with less 'social presence' were viewed less favourably. The explanations of why users perceive such media as being 'asocial' or lacking in social presence focus on the lack of face-to-face cues. Interestingly, many analyses based on such 'cue-less' models have tended to set up dichotomies between task-orientated (un-emotional) and 'socio-emotional' forms of communication and interaction. Such approaches have been used in the study of CMC (see Rice and Love, 1987). One outcome of this research was a model of CMC interaction put forward by Kiesler (1986) and Kiesler *et al.* (1984). In this model the interplay of various factors (especially the lack of face-to-face cues) leads, according to the results of Kiesler *et al.*, to group polarization in CMC interactions. This in turn leads to aggressive forms of interaction (called 'flaming' in the CMC jargon). Interestingly, despite the focus on 'group polarization' these models leave out any discussion of how group membership and identities, both individual and group, are negotiated or produced on-line.

   The 'social presence' model develops from but criticizes the 'limited cues model'. Spears and Lea (1992) offer an alternative to that of Kiesler *et al.* which starts from the physical separation of CMC users. They claim that two important factors need to be reconsidered if a more rounded explanation of social processes in CMC interaction is to be developed. First, one must distinguish between *in situ* interpersonal cues normally derived visually in face-to-face interaction from general social context cues and markers of self-identity. The general social context can be defined by the subject matter of the interaction, the location of the interaction within a specific 'CyberSpace', the power relationships between members of the interaction, and so forth. Self-identity can be expressed in many ways from the use of 'signatures' at the end of e-mail messages to the choice of usernames in IRC or MUD interactions. A lack of *in situ* visual cues does not imply the lack of social context and self-identity markers. Nor does a lack of visual communication prevent the complex expression of identity.

Spears and Lea also distinguish between personal identity and social identity. Personal identity is a person's complex understanding of himself or herself as an individual. Social identity derives from people's presentation of identity as part of group membership or the taking on of a social role within the interaction. Using these factors, Spears and Lea argue firstly that the lack of an active visual feedback channel leads to greater, rather than less, self-awareness. Such extra self-awareness produces differing results dependent upon the social context. Coherence to group norms and the strong expression of group identity is only likely to take place in contexts where the maintenance of the group is more salient than individual personal expression. Visual anonymity in CMC does not directly lead to group polarization but, rather, sets up structures that under different contextual conditions lead to greater or lesser reliance on the expression of group identity.

We therefore have two models of CMC identity. The first implies that the lack of other channels than the typed text leads to simplified and polarized presentations of self and group identity. The second argues that CMC identities can be very complex and that CMC does provide a lot of contextual cues. How then can a 'interactional sociolinguistic' approach combined with 'corpus methods' help to explore these models? In the analysis that follows, 'linguistic markers', seen as indicators of identity-related behaviours, are used to measure and explore differences between media.

Methods and data

The analyses of CMC are based in corpus-based techniques and have relied upon several computer-based analysis tools. Much of the 'quantitative' work was conducted through the use of 'key-word-in-context' (KWIC) and 'concordance' software. The other system used in the analysis was a CAQDAS system. The analysis follows the advice of Stubbs (1996) who argues that useful and informative analyses need to be comparative. Stubbs claims that such comparisons provide the researcher with a handle on what are in most cases relative measures. Not only are many linguistic measures relative functions of the media, more importantly, they are also functions of social context. With this issue in mind, several corpora were used in the analyses.

The two corpora of spoken material used were the British National Corpus (BNC) and the London-Lund corpus. Two samples of face-to-face interaction material were used. In the case of the BNC this consisted of 350,000 words taken from the 20 million words of conversational data available in the British National Corpus. The second sample of conversational interaction was taken from the London-Lund corpus and consisted of 196,028 words collected from interactions between equals. Telephone data (46,084 words) was also taken from the London-Lund corpus.

Four types of CMC data were also collected. These included 'chat' logged from three publicly accessible internet relay chat-rooms (IRC) on the eu.undernet server. This data included a little more than 25,000 words representing 10 hours of interaction (2,500 words per hour). In all three rooms several nationalities met to discuss a very broad range of topics. This allowed comparison with data from computer-based video conferencing (CU-SeeMe) that comprised just over 14,000 words from 8 hours of interaction (1,750 words per hour). The CU-SeeMe data was collected from a European site where a broad range of nationalities met to discuss numerous issues. The CoSy computer conferencing data consists of over 300,000 words posted on the Open University's computer conference system – this is a sub set of the CoSy:50 corpus described in Example Analysis 1. The Usenet postings comprised over 2,000 postings made to alt.usage.english during May 1996. The software used for the analysis automatically removed all headers, signatures and – where conventionally marked – material quoted from earlier posts which formed a significant portion of most postings. This editing left just over 200,000 words of data.

Quantitative measures of identity

One of the first ways in which the importance of identity within each of the media can be measured is through an examination of the relative occurrence of **identity markers** within the overall data set. It is often claimed that the word 'the' is the highest frequency word in the English language but this is true only of the written genres that were conventionally included in such word counts. In the data being used here, the personal pronouns 'I' and 'you' appear with higher frequency in interactive genres (whether face-to-face or mediated) than the overall means for the full BNC. In other words, direct reference to self and others is higher in the data than in a very large sample of general spoken and written English. We can compare the CMC data with the conversational and telephone interaction data from our various corpora. We can collect data on the most frequent words (say the top 10) and use these frequency figures to establish an 'egocentric' index for the materials according to the frequency of self-referring pronouns. We can measure this by counting self-referential pronouns per thousand words. Table 6 shows the results.

Table 6 Egocentricity of various media

Media	Pronoun reference to self per thousand words
CU-SeeMe	52
Telephone	44
Conversation	42
IRC	40
CoSy	28
Usenet	21

On the other hand, the counts for 'you' perhaps indicate the degree of interactivity and concern for other. The results of this analysis are presented in Table 7.

Table 7 Reference to others in various media

Media	Pronoun reference to other per thousand words
Cu-SeeMe	42
Conversation	33
Telephone	33
IRC	28
CoSy	12
Usenet	11

It is interesting that CU-SeeMe scores highest on both counts, ahead of either IRC or face-to-face conversation. Computer conferencing and Usenet interactions score lowest and have the word 'the' as the highest ranking item. This can be seen as a marker of 'literate' communications practices being employed. An attempt might be made to explain such results using a 'limited social/visual cues' approach with the presence of cues leading to greater interactivity. Yet such an argument would ignore nearly all the complex aspects of the data.

There are three important findings in this data. First, all of these media have much higher levels of the use of self-reference and interpersonal reference than the mean scores derived from the full BNC. This makes it very hard to claim that CMC is a de-personalized medium. Though 'I' is not the highest ranked item in the CoSy and Usenet data, it occurs almost twice as often in these data sets as it does in the full BNC. On these measures, CMC is a highly personalized medium where individuals are making considerable use of identity markers. Second, the result must be viewed not in technological (media) terms but in relation to the genres of communication. The choice of textual features is as much (in most cases more) a product of perceived social context and the social function of the interaction, as it is of the technology of communication.

In order to look more closely at the ways in which individuals are expressing and defining their identity we need to look at specific points in the interaction where direct reference to self takes place. An obvious starting point is the use of the phrase 'I am' (or 'I'm') in the various interactions. Taking three sets of sub-corpora data matched for a size of around 14,000 words (the size of CU-SeeMe data) from the CU-SeeMe, BNC Spoken and IRC data sets, a key-word-in-context (KWIC) search was conducted. The results of the search are far too large to present here, though Table 8 overleaf provides an extract.

Table 8 An example of a KWIC result

IRC addict is what	I AM	
says the same things	I AM	.
sharOn>: well	I AM	a nice wee lassie
	I'M	a working girl
HUGO_BOSS>:	I'M	from Lisbon, POrtugal
whizz -- you're an op,	I'M	not, I'm just an ordinary user
Druidd>: yah	I AM	not really from Scotlands
turkydog>:	I AM	not sure Moo?
chaos>: loesie:	I AM	not talkin about things
	I AM	not mixing my academic
Beaker>:	I AM	not breaker I am a dude
alexarose>: Yes and	I'M	not a dude I'm cool
The rest of the time	I'M	there.
Beaker>:	I AM	tired.
	I'M	trying it now and I'll get back
Sheena>: yeah,	I'M	trying to get tby online
Beaker>:	I AM	trying to get geocities acess
ceili>:	I AM	trying Dixon
maybe it's cos	I'M	usually on in the morning

Overall, the IRC and CU-SeeMe data, despite being multilingual and therefore containing less English data, contain more 'I am' sequences than the conversation data. It is also interesting that 'not' is found to be the most frequent word following 'I am' in conversational interaction. One might want to argue that the 'too much information' of face-to-face interaction has to be controlled and mediated by the negative definition of an individual's identity. In this case possible interpretations of contextual or social cues are bracketed off or controlled through statements containing the phrase 'I am not'.

Qualitative measures of identity

A further analysis of the use of 'I am' within the corpora was conducted using a CAQDAS system. Following from the findings above, individual occurrences of 'I am' in four corpora were examined. These corpora were the CU-SeeMe data, the IRC data, the London-Lund telephone interactions between equals and the London-Lund spoken interactions between equals. One of the important initial findings concerned the repetition of the phrase 'I am' within spoken and telephone discourse. The following examples are taken from spoken and telephone corpora respectively:

A: I see ((I'm I'M I'm it's)) very kind of you Sam

A: I AM ((I'm)) going out too

This type of repetition does not occur in the CMC data. Nor does the following case which occurs often in spoken discourse where 'I am' forms part of an incomplete utterance:

A: but I put it on the wall quite often and [m] and then I did some portraits and that I find absolutely fascinating for a stupid reason which is that I'M [m] my eyes focus differently you know and I see quite differently from a distance

Such a finding indicates that the numbers of occurrences of 'I am' in the spoken and telephone data is not directly comparable with that of the CMC data. Table 9 presents the data differently pointing out the number of 'turns' in all four data sets where an 'I am' phrase was coded in the analysis that follows. It is important to note that this is also an over-count as several turns were double coded (see below) though this double coding occurred across all media to a similar degree. This provides an even more striking result with speech having the lowest occurrence of turns containing the phrase 'I am/I'm' than all the other media measured as the number of occurrences per 1000 words.

Table 9 Occurrences of 'I'm/I am' in six corpora

Text	Total words	Total occurrences of 'I am/I'm'	Mean per 1000 words	Coded turns containing 'I am'	Mean per 1000 words
CU-SeeMe	16717	106	6.34	126	7.54
IRC	37489	171	4.56	226	6.03
Telephone	46084	187	4.06	122	2.65
Speech	196028	498	2.54	302	1.54
CoSy	450000	1411	3.14	Not categorized	
BNC Speech	345000	1107	3.21	Not categorized	

Such a result cannot be simply fitted into the model of reduced social cues leading to limited self-presence. On the contrary, a large amount of self-expression is taking place in the CMC media – with or without the visual channel. It does, though, fit the argument of Spears and Lea that the structure and content of the interaction is tied to the social context and perceived social relations. Both the CU-SeeMe and IRC data were taken from open forums where people from a large number of nations and societies met. In both cases the social context was defined by this meeting of strangers. One would, therefore, expect a greater discussion of self. In order to assess how this is being done we need to explore the aspects of self that are referenced by the use of the phrase 'I am'.

Each of the turns in which 'I am/I'm' occurred in all the texts were qualitatively categorized. The categories were derived from a close reading of the interactions.

Coding Scheme

The complete set of categories were as follows:

- Being in action – statements for the general form 'I am doing X'
- Gender – statements of the general form 'I am female/male'
- Being in physical/geographic space – statements of the general forms 'I am in Scotland/I am in the office'
- Knowing and feeling about self and others – statements that express knowledge of self and others both objective and subjective (i.e. their emotional/personal state)
- Nationality – statements of the general form 'I am Scottish'
- Being in social relations (including social status) – statements that express social relations or status such as 'I am her tutor'
- Age – statements of the general form 'I am X years old'
- Appearance – statements about appearance such as 'I am thin/tall'
- Occupation – statements about occupation such as 'I am a programmer'
- Negativity – negative versions of the coded statements such as 'I am not an economist/I am not sure how he feels', etc.
- Futurity – statements about future events such as 'I am off to the shops later'
- Being in CyberSpace – statements about place in CyberSpace such as 'I'm off to another IRC room/I am usually at the Cornell reflector'
- Contextual and undefined expressions – statements of 'I am' that are difficult to disambiguate from context, often used as answers to questions, also statements of identity that do not readily fit above categories.

In some cases, turns were double coded where either two occurrences of 'I am/I'm' were present or where two categories were involved. In the case of the negativity category all cases here were examples of this double coding.

Table 10 gives the numerical results of this analysis and Table 11 ranks the categories for each medium.

Activity 6

Using the occurrences of 'I am' in Table 8, categorize these uses of 'I am/I'm' using the coding scheme described above. You will have to work out some criteria for each category – what is often described as 'operationalizing' your concepts. You might find that some statements fit into more than one category. Did they easily fit into these categories? Did you want to be able to explore the surrounding text to be sure of their role or purpose?

Table 10 Categorization of 'I am/I'm' in four media

Category	CU-SeeMe			IRC			Telephone			Speech		
	Number	Normalized per 1000 words	Percent of turns	Number	Normalized per 1000 words	Percent of turns	Number	Normalized per 1000 words	Percent of turns	Number	Normalized per 1000 words	Percent of turns
Being in action	22.00	1.32	17.46	38.00	1.01	16.81	29.00	0.63	23.77	71.00	0.36	23.51
Gender	0.00	0.00	0.00	5.00	0.13	2.21	0.00	0.00	0.00	0.00	0.00	0.00
Being in physical/geographic space	22.00	1.32	17.46	51.00	1.36	22.57	10.00	0.22	8.20	16.00	0.08	5.30
Knowing and feeling about self and others	42.00	2.51	33.33	25.00	0.67	11.06	34.00	0.74	27.87	92.00	0.47	30.46
Nationality	4.00	0.24	3.17	14.00	0.37	6.19	0.00	0.00	0.00	1.00	0.01	0.33
Being in social relations	1.00	0.06	0.79	3.00	0.08	1.33	5.00	0.11	4.10	18.00	0.09	5.96
Age	3.00	0.18	2.38	6.00	0.16	2.65	0.00	0.00	0.00	4.00	0.02	1.32
Appearance	10.00	0.60	7.94	4.00	0.11	1.77	1.00	0.02	0.82	1.00	0.01	0.33
Occupation	8.00	0.48	6.35	21.00	0.56	9.29	2.00	0.04	1.64	8.00	0.04	2.65
Negativity	2.00	0.12	1.59	2.00	0.05	0.88	21.00	0.46	17.21	41.00	0.21	13.58
Futurity	0.00	0.00	0.00	0.00	0.00	0.00	11.00	0.24	9.02	13.00	0.07	4.30
Being in CyberSpace	9.00	0.54	7.14	43.00	1.15	19.03	0.00	0.00	0.00	0.00	0.00	0.00
Contextual & undefined expressions	3.00	0.18	2.38	14.00	0.37	6.19	9.00	0.20	7.38	37.00	0.19	12.25
	126.00	7.54	100.00	226.00	6.03	100.00	122.00	2.65	100.00	302.00	1.54	100.00

Table 11 Ranking of top five categories for four media (excluding undefined category)

Rank position	CU-SeeMe	IRC	Telephone	Speech
1	Knowing and feeling	Being in physical/ geographic space	Knowing and feelings	Knowing and feelings
2	Being in action *and* Being in physical/ geographic space	Being in action	Being in action	Being in action
3	Appearance	Being in CyberSpace	Negativity	Negativity
4	Being in CyberSpace	Knowing and feeling	Futurity	Being in social relations (inc. social status)
5	Occupation	Appearance	Being in physical/ geographic space	Being in physical/ geographic space

Discussion

Table 12 shows how I coded the occurrences of 'I am/I'm'.

Table 12 Coding of I AM/I'M

Occurrence			coding
IRC addict is what	I AM		Knowing and feeling
She says the same things	I AM	.	Knowing and feeling
shar0n>: well	I AM	a nice wee lassie	Gender
	I'M	a working girl	Gender
HUGO_BOSS>:	I'M	from Lisbon, Portugal	Being in space/ Nationality
whizz – you're an op,	I'M	not, I'm just an ordinary user	Occupation
Druidd>: yah	I AM	not really from Scotlands	Negativity/ Nationality
turkydog>:	I AM	not sure Moo?	Knowing and feeling
chaos>: loesie:	I AM	not talkin about things	Contextual and undefined
	I AM	not mixing my academic ideas	Knowing and feeling
Beaker>:	I AM	not breaker I am a dude	Negativity/Knowing and feeling
alexarose>: Yes and	I'M	not a dude I'm cool	Negativity/Knowing and feeling
The rest of the time	I'M	there.	Being in space
Beaker>:	I AM	tired.	Knowing and feeling
	I'M	trying it now and I'll get back	Being in action
Sheena>: yeah,	I'M	trying to get tby online	Being in action/ Being in Cyberspace
Beaker>:	I AM	trying to get geocities acess	Being in action/ Being in Cyberspace
ceili>:	I AM	trying Dixon	Being in action
maybe it's cos	I'M	usually on in the morning	Being in action/ Being in Cyberspace

Discussion

From the results in Table 10 and Table 11 it is clear that important differences exist between the four media. In the case of the CMC media, it is hard to accept the claim that reduced social/visual cues lead to a loss of self-awareness. On the contrary, as Spears and Lea argue, it seems to lead to heightened self-awareness and self-reference. Knowledge of self and others is high for all media. This implies that in all the media, from video conferencing to speech, interpersonal knowledge and understanding is central. Also the extensive self-reference in relation to action implies that even in virtual space individuals perceive themselves as social and material actors. For the CMC media, self reference is direct, positive, concerned with location – be that physical or virtual – and with appearance. This contrasts with the spoken and telephone data that are more concerned with the social structural factors (social relations and social time) and the negotiation/control of contextual factors (negativity and use of negative forms).

Accepting that CMC identities can only be constructed via the communications medium would imply, as has been argued time and again, that it allows only a limited number of methods for their expression and interpretation. Yet the work of many CMC researchers has noted the importance of gender identity markers (see Graddol and Swann, 1989; Herring, 1992; 1993a; 1993b; Spender, 1996; Turkle, 1996). The results above also make clear that CMC users spend considerably more time presenting aspects of identity through the communicative text than do people interacting in other media. The construction of CMC identities is only limited by the user's ability to provide coherent textual descriptions. By exploring the use of phrases such as 'I am/I'm', we are examining one of the direct methods through which such textual identities are constructed.

3.2 Comment on Example Analysis 2

How was the data collected?

Once again two existing corpora were used: the London-Lund and the BNC. In each case, though, the analysis focused on only part of these corpora. The CMC data were once again downloaded although some of these were then 'processed', for example, the Usenet data had the 'quoted text' removed. As Usenet does not have information on a messages position in an interaction, as conferencing does, users often include material (quotes) from the original posting to which they are replying. The corpora, then, were not 'exact copies' of the original interaction as was the case of the IRC and CU-SeeMe data. The size of the data sets was much smaller as well. There are a number of reasons for this. First, the IRC and CU-SeeMe data represented a lot of hours of interaction but not so much text. Second, and this is an important point, the data were to be subjected to qualitative methods. Even though these were supported by the use of a CAQDAS system they still required the researcher to painstakingly go though the transcripts coding up the relevant utterances. This is something that would not be possible for a corpus of several million words.

How was the data analysed?

The analysis this time included both quantitative and qualitative methods. It began with the creation of some basic measures of the levels of reference to self and to others in the data. The analysis then moved on to conduct qualitative content analyses of the data. In this case the occurrences of self-reference were put into categories that seemed to reflect their role or purpose in the interaction. This involved the kind of close reading that is more indicative of other discourse analysis approaches in this volume.

How did the analysis link data, theory and methods?

Unlike the previous example, the analysis (which followed an essentially 'positivist' model of developing a hypotheses and then measuring this analysis) proceeded from two possible explanations to an analysis that was more exploratory. Though some quantitative measures were put forward and the results of the qualitative content analysis were tabulated, the overall approach was one of understanding identity construction in CMC. No statistical methods were used and no hypotheses were proposed. The results were used to indicate the communicative practices of CMC users and to argue against the simplistic 'cue-lessness' explanation of CMC behaviour.

4   Gender on-line

This section is designed to give you an opportunity to analyse a CMC interaction for yourself. The data, which comes from an Open University computer conferencing interaction, are provided in the Appendix at the end of this chapter. The interaction took place in a 'chat' conference attached to a course focused on 'science communication' issues. The identities of the posters has been removed and replaced by markers indicating their gender combined with a number to differentiate posters (e.g. Male-1; Female-3). The topic under scrutiny is that of gender differences in language use.

Before setting you off on this task there are some background issues to be covered. It is now commonly accepted that there are differences in men and women's use of language – though the source of these differences is hotly debated. A large amount of psychological, sociological and linguistic literature on this issue now exists (e.g. Coates, 1997; 1996; 1993; Coates and Cameron, 1989; Coates *et al.*, 1989; Tannen, 1994; 1993). This research raises three main interrelated issues. First, there are the inequalities in the structure of male/female interactions. Second, there are differences in the linguistic practices and strategies that the sexes use in interactions. These can include differences in turn taking conventions, means of gaining the conversational floor, and means of directing the flow of the interaction. Third, there are differences in the purposes for which people engage in linguistic interaction.

Susan Herring (1992; 1993a; 1993b) has written extensively upon the issue of gender, language and CMC. This section will follow her main arguments and make use of her research methods. Herring used data collected from a study of two educational/academic discussion lists to clearly demonstrate differences in gender use and access to CMC. The two e-mail lists which Herring explored were the LINGUIST electronic mail list which is devoted to the discussion of all aspects of language and linguistics, and Megabyte University (MBU) which is a list concerned with computers and writing. Both lists represent university-level interactions between academics and students; the LINGUIST list having over 1,000 members and the MBU list over 250 members at the time of Herring's research. Over a period of one year, Herring conducted an ethnographic observation of the interactions taking place. This involved collecting a full transcript of the interaction and from this collecting data on the participants, the issues raised and discussed, and other relevant information (for a full discussion of a linguistic ethnography of CMC see Cherny, 1999). During this time she subjected two extended discussions of specific subjects from each discussion list to detailed linguistic and sociolinguistic analysis (Herring, 1993a).

The first important finding that Herring uncovered was the disparity in participation. Both lists had reasonably high numbers of women members (36% on LINGUIST; 42% on MBU). Despite this, women contributed far less than the men and the levels of participation varied according to the topic under discussion. For example 30% of women on both lists participated in 'sexism'-related discussions compared to 16% of women who participated in 'theory'-related discussions. Herring also found that messages from women were shorter on average with only men posting messages ten screens or more in length. Finally, Herring notes that women's messages gain fewer replies in these mixed gendered interactions.

Herring also notes differences in the CMC practices of men and women. The first of these is topic selection. Looking at her data from the LINGUIST list, Herring notes that men were more likely to post messages on specific issues or to provide specific information whereas women were more likely to post on personal aspects of the discussion or to post queries to other list members (see Table 13, based on Herring, 1993a).

Table 13 Topic selection and gender in CMC interactions

Gender	Most postings	⟵————————————⟶		Least posting
Women	personal	queries	information	issues
Men	issues	information	queries	personal

Herring next noted differences in language style and content. Using a set of features defined in terms of their attribution to different genderlects – gender-based language styles – Herring discovered large differences in style (see Table 14 below, taken from Herring, 1993a). Of the 261 LINGUIST messages she analysed, 68% of women's postings contained women's genderlect compared to only 31% of male messages. On the other hand, 48% of male messages contained *only* male features. This contrasted with only 18% of women's messages solely containing male genderlects. Lastly whilst 46% of women's messages *combined* both male and female genderlects, only 14% of male messages did so (Herring, 1993a). This result indicates that women are engaging in 'male' strategies in order to remain in the interaction.

Table 14 Features of women's language and men's language

Women's Language	Men's Language
attenuated assertions	strong assertions
apologies	self-promotion
explicit justifications	presuppositions
questions	rhetorical questions
personal orientation	authoritative orientation
supports others	challenges others
	humour/sarcasm

There is, of course, much more to Herring's work but for now we have a number of measures of gender differences in CMC interactions. These are:

- disparity in postings – measured by the different number of messages posted, with men posting more messages

- disparity in message length – measured by the longer postings by men

- disparity in replies – measured by the lower response rate to women's messages – they get fewer replies

- differences in message topics – as measured by the types of topics in men and women's postings (see Table 13)

- differences in language styles (see Table 14).

Activity 7

Using the five measures developed by Herring that are listed above, conduct an analysis of the data in the Appendix at the end of this chapter. Data on the proportions of men and women involved in the conference was not available so you will not be able to tell definitively if men posted proportionally more messages to the conference as a whole. You will also have to decide your own criteria for the categories in Tables 13 and 14 – you will have to operationalize your concepts. It might be easier to do this if you read the data through first. This should be fairly straightforward for Table 13. Is the message personal, querying, information-providing or issue-based (or possibly a combination)? Table 14 may be more difficult and you will find that you have to make some subjective choices. To help you along, Table 15 overleaf provides some suggestions.

Table 15 Examples of gender-based differences in language styles

Women's Language		Men's Language	
Attenuated assertions	Assertions on a topic that are prefaced with some form of distanced modality. E.g. 'It might be true that...'	Strong assertions	Assertions made without or with involved modalities. E.g. 'It is true that...', 'I am very sure that...'
Apologies	Retractions of position or statements employing apologetic language	Self-promotion	Statements that stress the rightness, importance or social standing of the individual
Explicit justifications	Statements that provide the justification or basis for opinions	Presuppositions	Statements that assume certain facts or opinions
Questions	Genuine open questions seeking a response	Rhetorical questions	Questions set up for an answer from the speaker themselves
Personal orientation	Presentation of statements and ideas from a personal position	Authoritative orientation	Presentation of statements and ideas from a claimed, assumed or asserted position of authority
Supports others	Statements in support of others' ideas or opinions	Challenges others	Statements that challenge others' ideas or opinions
		Humour/ sarcasm	Jokes or statements used to belittle others or others opinions.

You may wish to present your data as tables that allow comparisons between the genders. Do you find the same patterns as Herring in this small data set?

You might also, if you have the time and inclination, conduct analyses of the types described in Sections 1 and 3, for example type/token or lexical density measures, or the categorization of all the occurrences of 'I' or 'I am'.

Discussion

I will not provide you with all the 'results' but there are a few things you might wish to consider. First, defining criteria by which to categorize data is not as straightforward as it seems and requires you to make use of your understandings of both language (in this case English) and possibly of British culture as well. You might also have noticed how posters copy bits from previous messages – this is one way that the 'thread' of a conversation is maintained. Second, once you have worked out some categorization scheme, the actual coding is a relatively easy, if repetitive, task. The use of computer tools might make the process simpler and may allow you to deal with a greater body of data but they do not get rid of the intellectual effort required to select criteria.

To give you some indication of the types of results that you may expect, I looked at two criteria: message length and number of replies. I counted the actual number of new lines in each message (I ignored quotes) and compared this across gender and got the results shown in Table 16. This analysis took me a couple of hours. I will admit that I used a CAQDAS tool and statistical software. Even at this rate, to look at several hundred messages as Herring did, or to look at thousands as in Example Analysis 1, would have taken about 20 to 40 hours.

Table 16 Analysis by gender of message length and number of replies

Gender	Number of messages	Mean number of messages	Maximum length in lines	Mean number of lines	Median number of lines
Female	11	1.57	11.00	3.45	2.00
Male	15	1.86	12.00	5.07	5.00

This table seems to show that, on average, the men posted more and posted longer messages; the mean and median lengths of messages, as measured by the number of lines, are longer. Having said this, the sample is very small and the result is not statistically significant. Is the use of 'lines' the best measure of message length? I might be tempted to re-do this analysis by counting words per message as a more accurate measure of message length. I also looked at the number of replies to men and women and found that there were eight replies to women's postings and 13 replies to men. This implies that women had a 73% chance of being replied to compared to 87% for men, though this difference cannot be easily statistically tested.

Appendix

Please note that many of the messages contain 'quoted material' from other messages, even quotes within quotes. This part of the messages is marked with the usual '>' convention at the start of lines.

```
06 February 1900 18:07:55
N900 Cafe Item
From:  Female-5
Subject:  Cool website!
To:  N900 Cafe


http://www.starlab.org/shebang/


This is the online magazine for Starlab, a Brussels
thinktank.
Includes stuff on public understanding of science, and
some nice
links, and... loads of stuff!


Female-5




07 February 1900 23:59:34
N900 Cafe Item
From:  Female-4
Subject:  Re: Cool website!
To:  N900 Cafe


>Female-5 writes:
>This is the online magazine for Starlab, a Brussels
thinktank.
>Includes stuff on public understanding of science,
and some nice
>links, and... loads of stuff!


Thanks Female-5,


Female-4
```

```
09 February 1900 15:46:15
N900 Cafe Item
From:  Male-3
Subject:  Re: Cool website!
To:  S804 Cafe


>http://www.starlab.org/shebang/


Brilliant web site Female-5!


Regards


Male-3




09 February 1900 20:02:09
N900 Cafe Item
From:  Male-7
Subject:  Re: Cool website!
To:  N900 Café


Thanks for posting that website.
The chairman of Starlab was on the radio the other day.
He was offer
job because he has no training in Science. I thouht
that was a
brilliant idea!


Male-7




10 February 1900 18:30:38
N900 Cafe Item
From:  Female-5
Subject:  Re(2): Cool website!
To:  N900 Café

>Male-7,oufcnt2.open.ac.uk writes:
>Thanks for posting that website.
>The chairman of Starlab was on the radio the other
day. He was offer
>job because he has no training in Science. I thouht
that was a
```

```
>brilliant idea!
>
>Male-7
Yes, I heard the interview. I WANT HIS JOB!!!!!
```

```
11 February 1900 16:42:15
N900 Cafe Item
From:  Male-7
Subject:  Re(3): Cool website!
To:  N900 Café
```

```
>Female-5 writes:
>Male-7,oufcnt2.open.ac.uk writes:
>Thanks for posting that website.
>The chairman of Starlab was on the radio the other
day. He was offer
>job because he has no training in Science. I thouht
that was a
>brilliant idea!
>
>Male-7
>
>
>Yes, I heard the interview. I WANT HIS JOB!!!!!
```

```
Sorry, you can't have it because it's going to be mine!
```

```
12 February 1900 10:51:40
N900 Cafe Item
From:  Female-5
Subject:  Re(4): Cool website!
To:  N900 Café
```

```
>Male-7,oufcnt2.open.ac.uk writes:
>Female-5 writes:
>Male-7,oufcnt2.open.ac.uk writes:
>Thanks for posting that website.
>The chairman of Starlab was on the radio the other
day. He was offer
>job because he has no training in Science. I thouht
that was a
```

```
>brilliant idea!
>
>Male-7
>
>
>Yes, I heard the interview. I WANT HIS JOB!!!!!
>
>Sorry, you can't have it because it's going to be
mine!

Job share??


12 February 1900 12:12:03
N900 Cafe Item
From:  Female-4
Subject:  Re(3): Cool website!
To:  N900 Café

>Female-5 writes:
>Yes, I heard the interview. I WANT HIS JOB!!!!!

Me too!

Female-4


12 February 1900 15:35:22
N900 Cafe Item
From: Male-8
Subject:  TUTOR ICON
To: N900 Café

Hi,
 Can someone fill me in on what this tutor group icon
is,
especially as I still do not have any letter from my
tutor and the
TMA is looming and there are questions that I'd like to
ask. Many
thanks.

Male-8
```

13 February 1900 11:53:42
N900 Cafe Item
From: Male-9
Subject: tutor icon
To: N900 Café

G'day to all fellow communicators,

As Male-8 stated (12/02/2000), I too do not have any
idea what this
tutor icon is or whom is allocated as my tutor for this
module. I
would appreciate any help (via this medium) or do I
need to contact
the helpdesk?

please advise asap

13 February 1900 15:22:46
N900 Cafe Item
From: Male-8
Subject: Re: tutor icon
To: N900 Café

Hi Male-9,
 Glad I'm not the only one still wondering what is
going on.
Thanks for that

Male-8

13 February 1900 17:15:29
N900 Cafe Item
From: Female-6
Subject: Re(2): tutor icon
To: N900 Café

Don't know if its any help, but mine was 'hiding'.
It was underneath the OU icon.............have a
look........it could
be there!
Female-6

```
13 February 1900 19:50:17
N900 Cafe Item
From:  Female-7
Subject:  Hidden icons
To:  N900 Cafe
Male-9/Male-8,
```

As Female-6 said, the icons can 'hide' underneath each other, I lost
one in my last course. If you drag and drop the existng icons around
for a bit you may find the hidden ones. Good luck!

Female-7

```
13 February 1900 19:53:52
N900 Cafe Item
From:  Female-3
Subject:  Missing Tutor icons
To:  N900 Café, Male-8, Male-9
```

If you look at my message on the Noticeboard about N900 Tutors for
2000, you will see it lists which tutors are looking after students
in particular regions.
Thus Male-8, you should be looking for an icon on your desktop that
says N900 Sue's Group, which is the icon for Sue Barker's group, and
Male-9, you should be looking for an icon for John Forrester's group,
N900 John's Group.
If you can't see them immediately, try viewing by name.
Female-3

```
Female-3
N900 Course Manager
MSc in Science
```

14 February 1900 18:09:04
N900 Cafe Item
From: Male-8
Subject: Re: Missing Tutor icons
To: N900 Café

Thanks Female-3,

 it magically appeared after my message but definietly
wasn't there
before, X-files stuff!! Thanks.

14 February 1900 19:58:54
N900 Cafe Item
From: Male-7
Subject: TV Prog worth watching
To: N900 Café

Did anyone see ''6 Experiments that Changed the
World'' last night?
Ken Campbell was explaining General Relativity and did
as good a job
as I've heard (but then I'm no physicist -- so who am I
to judge?).

He's reproducing a different experiment every week on
Sunday nights
at 7:00 on Channel 4 (just after Time Team).

16 February 1900 00:14:46
N900 Cafe Item
From: Female-4
Subject: Re: TV Prog worth watching
To: N900 Café

>Male-7 writes:
>Did anyone see ''6 Experiments that Changed the
World'' last night?
>Ken Campbell was explaining General Relativity and
did as good a job

>as I've heard (but then I'm no physicist -- so who am I
to judge?).
>
Well I am a physicist and I think he did a pretty good
job too. Excellent stuff!

Female-4

16 February 1900 17:04:50
N900 Cafe Item
From: Male-5
Subject: Re: TV Prog worth watching
To: N900 Café, N900NoticeBoard, N900Male-5's Group

>Male-7 writes:
>Did anyone see ''6 Experiments that Changed the
World'' last night?
>Ken Campbell was explaining General Relativity and
did as good a job
>as I've heard (but then I'm no physicist -- so who am I
to judge?).
>
>He's reproducing a different experiment every week on
Sunday nights >at 7:00 on Channel 4 (just after Time
Team).

Well spotted Nick (and Jacqui). This was indeed an
enjoyable programme and one which could provide an
example for those searching for an example of science
communication to analyse for question 1 of TMA 01.

The series ''6 Experiments that Changed the World''
continues next Sunday evening (7pm on Channel 4) with
an examination of the work of Marie Curie.

best wishes
Male-5

04 March 1900 18:13:00
N900 Cafe Item
From: Male-6
Subject: Tutor Icon
To: N900 Café

Hello,

I have tried a mail to the help desk but I have not
received a reply.

I have had my tutor icon taken away from me.

What have I done? Whatever it is I will apologise, just
give me my
tutor icon back!!!

Thanks
Male-6

04 March 1900 18:31:44
N900 Cafe Item
From: Female-3
Subject: Re: Tutor Icon
To: N900 Cafe
Cc: Male-5

>Male-6 writes:
>I have had my tutor icon taken away from me.

>What have I done? Whatever it is I will apologise,
just give me my
>tutor icon back!!!
Don't know what happened Stuart -- one of these FC
'glitches'!
Anyway, it should back now -- ok?
Female-3

Female-3
Programme Course Manager
MSc in Science

04 March 1900 19:06:09
N900 Cafe Item
From: Male-2
Subject: Re(2): Fwd(2): Re: Problems with Athens and
passwords
To: MSc Sci Library conf, Male-4, N900 Café, Female-2

Alan has had probs with sciencedirect logging on -- I
did too, [made
my initial reg --> accessed sd OK once, then failed] --
contacted John
Doe -- their helpline on e-mail John.Doe@somewhare.net
which is on the
sciencedirect initial page -- he sent back an e-mail
with user ID and
password + hints -- been OK ever since.

I should've contacted Alison, but confess I forgot
'til now -- sorry!

Does this help -- I find it works well, 'tho not been
there for a week
or so....................

Regards

Male-2

05 March 1900 10:56:34
N900 Cafe Item
From: Male-4
Subject: Re(3): Fwd(2): Re: Problems with Athens and
passwords
To: Male-2
Cc: MSc Sci Library conf, N900 Café, Female-2

Thanks Male-2 I''ll give it a go.

Male-4

09 March 1900 23:05:10
N900 Cafe Item
From: Female-1
Subject: GM Foods
To: N900 Cafe
Tonight's Horizon was about the GM food debate and can
be accessed
on: www.bbc.co.uk/horizon.

10 March 1900 08:49:26
N900 Cafe Item
From: Male-3
Subject: Greenpeace = Starvation
To: N900 Café

Last nights Horizon programme brought out the true
colours of
Greenpeace. That they were willing to see people in the
Third Worlds
die of starvation.

That may have been a slip by their UK rep but it does
reveal their
non-public attitude.

I hope their support dries up!

Male-3

10 March 1900 20:49:41
N900 Cafe Item
From: Male-2
Subject: Re: Greenpeace = Starvation
To: Male-3, N900 Café

Come on, Greenpeace don't make the situation in these
countries -
that's a political situation -- like the Iraq one that
I was talking
about yesterday [to an Iraqi consultant]. If the
regime there is

maintained, either for balance of power, or for the
desires of a

dictator, the way around it is not to keep punishing
the people,

agreed -- but then why keep the food stocks, medicines
etc. for the

elite anyway?

Male-2

10 March 1900 22:46:30

N900 Cafe Item

From: Male-1

Subject: Re(2): Greenpeace = Starvation

To: N900 Café

>Male-2,oufcnt2.open.ac.uk writes:

>Come on, Greenpeace don't make the situation in these
countries -

>that's a political situation -- like the Iraq one that
I was talking

>about yesterday [to an Iraqi consultant]. If the
regime there is

>maintained, either for balance of power, or for the
desires of a

>dictator, the way around it is not to keep punishing
the people,

>agreed -- but then why keep the food stocks, medicines
etc. for the

>elite anyway?

Perhaps Male-3 was talking about Mexico where the
ground is too acid for normal corn.

Male-1

Further Reading

CMC

Cherny, L. (1999) *Conversation and Community: Chat in a Virtual World*, Stanford, CSLI Publications.

Cherny, L. and Weise, B. (eds) (1996) *Wired Women: Gender and New Realities in Cyberspace*, Seattle, Seal.

Herring, S. (ed.) (1996) *Computer-Mediated Communication: Linguistic, Social and Cross-cultural Perspectives*, Amsterdam, John Benjamins.

Hiltz, S.R. and Turoff, M. (1978) *Network Nation: Human Communication via Computer*, Reading, MA.: Addison-Wesley.

Jones, S. (1998) *Cybersociety 2.0: Revisiting Computer-Mediated Communication and Community*, Thousand Oaks, CA: Sage.

Lea, M. (ed.) (1992) *Contexts of Computer-Mediated Communication*, New York, Harvester Wheatsheaf.

Rheingold, H. (1993) *The Virtual Community*, Reading, MA.: Addison-Wesley.

Turkle, S. (1996) *Life on the Screen: Identity in the Age of the Internet*, London, Orion.

Analysis

McEnery, T. and Wilson, A. (1996) *Corpus Linguistics*, Edinburgh, Edinburgh University Press.

Stubbs, M. (1996) *Text and Corpus Analysis: Computer Assisted Studies of Language and Culture*, Oxford, Blackwell.

Tannen, D. (1993) *Gender and Conversational Interaction*, New York, Oxford University Press.

References

Barton, D. (1991) 'The contribution of a social view of literacy to promoting literacy among adults', *Centre for Language in Social Life: Working Paper Series, No.30*, Lancaster University.

Chafe, W. and Danielewicz, J. (1987) 'Properties of spoken and written language' in Horowitz, R. and Samuels, S.J. (eds) *Comprehending Oral and Written Language,* San Diego, CA, Academic Press.

Cherny, L. (1999) *Conversation and Community: Chat in a Virtual World*, Stanford, CSLI Publications.

Coates, J. (ed.) (1997) *Language and Gender*, London, Blackwell Publishers.

Coates, J. (1993) *Women, Men and Language*, London, Longman Higher Education.

Coates, J. (1996) *Women Talk*, London, Blackwell Publishers.

Coates, J. and Cameron, D. (eds) (1989) *Women in Their Speech Communities*, London, Addison Wesley.

Coulthard, M. (ed.) (1992) *Advances in Spoken Discourse Analysis*, London, Routledge.

Coulthard, M. (ed.) (1994) *Advances in Written Text Analysis*, London, Routledge.

Fielding, R. and Lee, R. (1991) *Using Computers in Qualitative Analysis*, Thousand Oaks, Sage.

Graddol, D.J. and Swann, J. (1989) *Gender Voices*, London, Blackwell.

Greenbaum, S. and Svartvic, J. (1990) 'The London-Lund corpus of spoken English' in Svartvic, J. (ed.) *The London-Lund Corpus of Spoken English: Description and Research*, Lund, Lund University Press.

Halliday, M.A.K. (1985) *Spoken and Written Language*, Deakin, Deakin University.

Herring, S. (1992) 'Gender and participation in computer-mediated linguistic discourse' in *ERIC Clearing House on Languages and Linguistics*, October.

Herring, S. (1993a) 'Gender and democracy in computer-mediated communication', *Electronic Journal of Communication*, vol.3, file Herring V3N293.

Herring, S. (1993b) 'Culture vs. Technology, or Why Computer-Mediated Communication Is Still Sexist', Paper presented to the International Pragmatics Conference.

Hodge, R. and Kress, G. (1988) *Social Semiotics*, Cambridge, Polity, extracts reproduced in Wetherell, M., Taylor, S. and Yates, S.J. (eds) (2001) *Discourse Theory and Practice: A Reader*, London, Sage in association with The Open University.

Johansson, S. (1991) 'Times change, and so do corpora' in Aijmer, K. and Altenberg, B. (eds) *English Corpus Linguistics*, London, Longman.

Kiesler, S. (1986) 'The hidden messages in computer networks', *Harvard Business Review*, Jan-Feb, pp.46–58.

Kicsler, S., Siegel, J. and McGuire, T. (1984) 'Social psychological aspects of computer-mediated communications', *American Psychologist*, no.39, pp.1123–34

McEnery, T. and Wilson, A. (1996) *Corpus Linguistics*, Edinburgh, Edinburgh University Press.

Rice, R.E. and Love, G. (1987) 'Electric-emotion: socio-emotional content in a computer mediated communication network', *Communication Research*, no.14, pp.85–108

Scribner, S. and Cole, M. (1981) *The Psychology of Literacy*, Cambridge, MA, Harvard University Press.

Short, J., Williams, E. and Christie, B. (1976) *The Social Psychology of Telecommunications*, London, Wiley & Sons.

Spears, R. and Lea, M. (1992) 'Social influence and the influence of the "social" in computer-mediated communication' in Lea, M. (ed.) *Contexts of Computer-Mediated Communication*, Hemel Hempstead, Harvester Wheatsheaf.

Spender, D. (1996) *Nattering on the Net*, North Melbourne, Spinifex Press.

Street, B.V. (1984) *Literacy in Theory and Practice*, Cambridge, Cambridge University Press.

Stubbs, M. (1996) *Text and Corpus Analysis: Computer Assisted Studies of Language and Culture*, Oxford, Blackwell.

Tannen, D. (1993) *Gender and Conversational Interaction*, New York, Oxford University Press.

Tannen, D. (1994) *Gender and Discourse*, New York, Oxford University Press.

Turkle, S. (1996) *Life on the Screen: Identity in the Age of the Internet*, London, Orion

Weitzman, E.A. and Miles, M. B. (1995) *Computer Programs for Qualitative Data Analysis: A Software Source Book*, Thousand Oaks, Sage.

Wetherell, M., Taylor, S. and Yates, S.J. (eds) (2001) *Discourse Theory and Practice: A Reader*, London, Sage in association with The Open University.

Yates, J. and W. Orlikowski, (1992) 'Genres of organizational communication: A structurational approach to studying communication and media', *Academy of Management Review*, vol. 17, pp.299–326.

Yates, S.J. (1996) 'Oral and literate linguistic aspects of CMC discourse: A corpus based study' in Herring, S. (ed.) *Computer-Mediated Communication: Linguistic, Social, and Cross-Cultural Perspectives*, Amsterdam, John Benjamins.

Yates, S.J. (2000) 'Computer-Mediated Communication – The future of the letter?' in Barton, D. and Hall, N. (eds) *Letter Writing as a Social Practice*, Amsterdam, John Benjamins.

Zipf, G.K. (1935) *The Pscho-biology of Language: An Introduction to Dynamic Philology*, Boston, MIT Press.

CHAPTER FOUR

The Construction of M.E.: The Discursive Action Model

Mary Horton-Salway

Introduction

In this chapter I will use the example of a controversial illness in order to demonstrate a particular type of discursive psychology approach to the analysis of talk and text. The 'discursive construction of M.E.' (myalgic encephalomyelitis) provides an interesting example from everyday life to study how people talk about illness and its causes. Rather than taking up a position in the debate and offering my own explanations and definitions of M.E., my analysis of data will focus on how the *participants* (mostly doctors and sufferers) make sense of its causes and definitions. This process identifies contexts such as medicine, health psychology and self-help groups as settings for doing discourse analysis, and shows how identities, minds and selves are constructed by medical scientists, clinical practitioners, and their patients in the process of talking (and writing) about causes, diagnoses and illness experiences.

It is the business of this introduction to position my work in relation to the other theoretical approaches in this volume, and the wider academic literature. Later in the chapter I will discuss how such categorizations and positionings are, in themselves, discursive *practices* that are designed to order the world in one way rather than another. In any specific context, categorizations (Horton-Salway, 1998) and the construction of similarity and difference (Mushakoji, 1999) can be treated (and analysed) as *situated* 'boundary work'. The process of how such categories are worked up as distinct and separate or blurred together, in the context of academic debate, is itself a fascinating topic for analysis. Having said that, I shall work to position my approach as an application of Edwards and Potter's (1992) model of discursive psychology (see also Edwards, 1997; Potter, 1996). They describe their approach as a "viable perspective on psychological life rather than just a mode of empirical analysis" (1992: 153). Their version of discursive psychology is presented as a fundamental re-conceptualization of **cognitivist psychology**, rather than just another kind of analytic method. ('Cognitivism' is referred to as the mainstream approach in social psychology, where people's accounts are taken to reflect their mental representations of the social world.)

Edwards and Potter (1992: 27) have identified the main theoretical areas influencing the development of their approach as:

1   the study of the relationship between knowledge and language use in linguistic philosophy (Austin, 1962; Wittgenstein, 1953; see also Potter, Reading Three, Wetherell *et al.*, 2001)

2   the adoption of a functional approach to language in speech act
    theories (Grice, 1975; Searle, 1969)

3   the study of members' everyday sense-making practices in
    ethnomethodology (Garfinkel, 1967; Heritage, 1984)

4   the application of ethnomethodological principles to the analysis of
    mundane conversations in conversation analysis (Atkinson and
    Heritage, 1984; Button and Lee, 1987; Levinson, 1983; Sacks *et al.*, 1974;
    see also Heritage, Reading Four in Wetherell *et al.*, 2001)

5   the study of scientists' discursive practices in the sociology of scientific
    knowledge (Ashmore, 1989; Gilbert and Mulkay, 1984; Potter and
    Mulkay, 1985)

6   the post-structuralist focus on the reality constructing nature of text
    itself in cultural and literary theory (Barthes, 1974; Derrida, 1977;
    Shapiro, 1988; see also Hall, Reading Seven in Wetherell *et al.*, 2001).

This broad approach has been applied to the social psychological concept
of attitude (Potter and Wetherell, 1987) and more recently to the analysis of
'fact construction' (Potter, 1996) and to the systematic theoretical re-working
of cognitive psychology (Edwards, 1997). The following examples of this
fine-grained analytic approach are relevant to the type of analysis
undertaken in this chapter and also the topics: the discursive construction
of social identity (Antaki and Widdicombe, 1998; Widdicombe and Wooffitt,
1995), the discursive construction of identities in doctors' and sufferers'
narratives about M.E. and its causes (Horton-Salway, 1998), an analysis of
identity management and blame in the Princess Diana interview (Abell and
Stokoe, 1999), and a conversation analysis (CA) informed critique of the
concept of 'hegemonic masculinity' by Susan Speer (2001) which provides a
useful contrast with Nigel Edley's critical discursive psychology approach to
the topic of masculinity in Chapter Five.

   In the Edwards and Potter model of discursive psychology, social
construction is treated as **epistemic**, which means, "it is about the
constructive nature of *descriptions*, rather than of the entities that
(according to descriptions) exist beyond them" (Edwards, 1997: 47–8). This
kind of detailed study of participants' talk is concerned with "how events
are described and explained, how factual reports are constructed, how
cognitive states are attributed." (Edwards and Potter, 1992: 2). These
phenomena are analysed as **discursive practices** and constructions rather
than as cognitive-perceptual processes. Compare this with Bakhtin/
Voloshinov's account referred to in Billig, 1997, reproduced as Reading
Fifteen in Wetherell *et al.*, 2001, "There is … nothing 'inner' about it, it is
wholly on the outside, wholly brought out in exchanges …".

   In making such relativist claims about the constructive nature of
descriptions, the authors of social research texts (including the author of
this chapter) become implicated in **reflexive** consequences because they
cannot transcend their own constructive practices. This reflexive 'dilemma'
is discussed in Edwards and Potter (1992: 172) and there are an increasing
number of reflexive studies in social science that celebrate this inevitable

aspect of authorship through their use of different kinds of **textual practices** and literary forms (for example, Ashmore, 1989; Horton-Salway, 1998; MacMillan, 1996; Mushakoji, 1999; Woolgar, 1988).

To summarize, Edwards and Potter (1992: 154) have introduced their **discursive action model** as a "conceptual scheme that captures some of the key features of participants' discursive practices". This will be explicated in Section 2 where we will apply their approach to the analysis of illness talk. But first, it might be helpful to 'set the scene' by introducing the topic of my research – the 'M.E. debate'.

1   The 'M.E. debate': a context for discourse analysis

The 'M.E. debate' has generated a range of different and often competing explanations for a 'mystery illness' and its causes. It has been the focus of long-standing medical arguments that have debated the relative significance of psychological and physical factors as causes of the illness. In the summary that follows I will provide an outline of the key features of that debate.

Dialogue 1[1]

STUDENT   Wait a minute! Before you write your summary, I need to discuss an important point with you. In the first paragraph of this chapter, you said you didn't intend to offer your own explanation and definition of M.E.

MHS   That's right. I only meant to give you some background context to show how the M.E. controversy has been constructed through participants' discourse.

STUDENT   But whose *description* will that be?

MHS   Mine of course!

STUDENT   Hm

MHS   What if I call it "A possible version of the 'M.E.' controversy"?

STUDENT   ((*pause*)) I suppo:se that's okay. But if it's your version, then it must be *your* construction, rather than the participants' construction.

MHS   Hm...perhaps we should come back to that question later.

1.1 A possible version of the M.E. controversy

'Royal Free disease': a new clinical entity?

On August 13th 1955, an announcement in *The Lancet* (p.351) introduced an outbreak of an 'unusual infection' that was first mistaken for glandular fever at the Royal Free Hospital, London. Later, on the grounds that clinical testing had proved negative, this was attributed to 'a known virus or its variants' or a 'new virus'. Comparative links were made between this 'obscure infection' and similar-looking outbreaks in Britain and around the globe.

The question of hysteria

In many of the accounts that appeared in *The Lancet* and *The British Medical Journal* between 1955–1959, authors commented on the anomalous collection of clinical signs and symptoms associated with the new disease phenomenon. Combined with the lack of positive scientific evidence for the existence of a new virus, this had "aroused suspicions of hysteria" (Galpine and Brady, 1957: 757–8). In 1970, two young psychiatrists, McEvedy and Beard, re-examined the case notes of the patients from the Royal Free epidemic of 1955. They offered the following explanation: "it is concluded that there is little evidence of an organic disease affecting the central nervous system and that epidemic hysteria is a much more likely explanation" and justified this by referring to evidence from "a previous epidemic of hysterical overbreathing" (Moss and McEvedy, 1966: 1295).

McEvedy and Beard (1970: 7–11) went on to claim: "We believe that a lot of these epidemics were psychosocial phenomena caused by one of two mechanisms, either mass hysteria on the part of patients or altered medical perception of the community". In other words, doctors who knew about the 'new disease entity' and its collection of symptoms were more likely to diagnose it! McEvedy and Beard went on to suggest that the name 'benign myalgic encephalomyelitis' (M.E.) should therefore be discarded in favour of "... 'myalgia nervosa' on the analogy of 'anorexia nervosa'...".

A 'storm of protest'

McEvedy and Beard's articles 'elicited a storm of protest' (Jenkins and Mowbray, 1991: 20) in *The British Medical Journal* (January 17, 1970). This took the form of a number of 'eye-witnessed' reports from both victims and practitioners who had been involved in the Royal Free epidemic of 1955. McEvedy and Beard's findings were dismissed by these witnesses as being based on little or flimsy evidence, and they were accused of failing to do their homework, demonstrating a surprising lack of information about the principles of epidemiology and of psychiatry, and using a diagnosis of hysteria as a 'diagnosis of exclusion', that is, because the patients' symptoms could not be explained in any other way.

Reinstating myalgic encephalomyelitis

In 1978 a leading article in the *British Medical Journal* (pp.1436–7) reinstated the original claims for an organic explanation of the illness. This was legitimated as authoritative by a Royal Society of Medicine symposium which arrived at a 'clear agreement that myalgic encephalomyelitis is a distinct nosological[2] entity'. Furthermore, M.E. was cited as the preferred term and was referred to as 'a paralytic disease', 'an infection', 'an encephalomyelitis', and 'possibly a persistent virus infection'.

Over the next decade there was an explosion of articles on M.E. appearing in different journals all over the world. However, articles on M.E.

disappeared from the journals in the 1980s and were replaced by articles on Chronic Fatigue Syndrome (CFS). In fact, one of the main debates in this controversy has been the question of whether M.E. and CFS (among other labels, such as Post-Viral Fatigue Syndrome) are the same or different. The division of opinion between participants on the question of organic versus psychological explanations has manifested itself through the adoption of labels which lend greater emphasis to one version or another. For a long while this polarization of views about the causes of the illness was punctuated only by occasional appeals (e.g. Gill, 1970) for a less dualistic way of understanding the illness, and claims that "Present controversy rests on a false dualism and an outdated separation of mind and body..." (David et al., 1988: 696–9).

It would seem rather obvious to point out that in the case of a medical controversy, there is bound to be more than one kind of explanation being offered on the strength of different kinds of scientific research. This lack of consensus over definitions, categorizations and treatment has remained a central issue right up until the present day. Against this controversial background it is hardly surprising that both patients and doctors have experienced a great deal of confusion about the illness, its causes, and appropriate illness management and treatments.

Dialogue 2

STUDENT   So you can't tell me what M.E. is then?

MHS   No, that's not really the issue for discursive psychology, but the context of on-going controversy surrounding the M.E. debate does provide a context to look at how medical practitioners and research scientists set about defining and challenging the idea of a new disease entity. The interesting thing for us as discourse analysts is that they do this in the research literature and related correspondence. You could say that the context we need to understand, the issues involved in the M.E. debate, is right there in those argumentative exchanges. (I mean the participants' actual exchanges rather than my constructed summary of it!) What the M.E. controversy amounts to is the positioning of alternative versions or explanations for the 'mystery illness'. The participants themselves construct 'it' as they go along.

STUDENT   Okay, fine, so how is all this linked to the construction of identities, minds and selves?

MHS   Good question. First we need some transcribed data to work with.

1.2 Data and focus

In what follows, I shall draw on various different kinds of data. These have been taken from interviews I conducted with M.E. sufferers and GPs, an

M.E. group discussion, a TV talk show, academic literature and official
reports (Horton-Salway, 1998). Interview and conversational material was
tape-recorded, and transcribed mainly according to the conventions
suggested by Gail Jefferson, and which have been set out by Rob Wooffitt
in Chapter Two of this book.

The main focus of our analysis will be how identities, minds and selves
are constructed and made relevant by the participants in their talk about
M.E./CFS. In view of the controversial status of this illness and the lack of
medical consensus, a concern with mind and body has become a central
one for the participants, both doctors and patients alike. As one GP put it:

> ... it's something that (.) certainly (.) se:en by patients (.) and I think to
> some extent (.) would be (.) y'know (.) by doctors <u>as</u> <u>well</u> (.) is this
> business of whether physical and mental things equate with real and
> imagined (.) do you know what I mean?
>
> (Dr W.)

There are two kinds of issues for participants here: First, 'all in the mind'
explanations clearly question the very *legitimacy* of the illness, and
therefore also the health status of sufferers: second, our common
understanding and management of diseases takes place within a cultural
context that traditionally distinguishes between physical and psychological
illnesses. "We live in a society which is used to thinking of illness as
'physical' or 'psychological' and which harbours different attitudes towards
these." (Westcare, 1994: 18). Psychiatric illness is still associated with a
stigma which many patients would prefer to avoid (Wessely, 1990) so it is
hardly surprising that accounts of M.E. should attend to concerns about the
nature and definition of the illness as mental or physical and that this
should be related to the *identities* of its sufferers.

2   The discursive action model

Here is a summary of the discursive action model to show you how this
kind of analysis works.

The discursive action model

Action

1   The focus is on action, not cognition.

2   Remembering and attribution become, operationally, reportings (and
accounts, descriptions, formulations, versions, and so on) and the
inferences that they make available.

3   Reportings are situated in activity sequences such as those involving
invitation refusals, blamings and defences.

Fact and Interest

4   There is a dilemma of stake and interest, which is often managed by
doing attribution via reports.

5   Reports are therefore constructed/displayed *as* factual by way of a variety of discursive techniques.

6   Reports are rhetorically organized to undermine alternatives.

Accountability

7   Reports attend to the agency and accountability in the reported events.

8   Reports attend to the accountability of the current speaker's action, including those done in the reporting.

9   The latter two concerns are often related, such that 7 is deployed for 8, and 8 is deployed for 7.

(Taken from Edwards and Potter, 1992: 154)

The following description is based on features of the discursive action model and uses examples of data to clarify its main points.

2.1   Action

The focus of analysis for discursive psychology is on what people *do* with their talk, rather than using discourse as a way of accessing what goes on in their minds. **Remembering and attribution** (and other psychological phenomena) are recast as things that people *do* in their interactions with others: they produce versions of events, objects and people. From this view we would want to ask how remembering is *accomplished* as a practical activity, what it is used for, and what people are doing with their causal attributions in everyday interactions. In other words, how do people assign causes to events in their descriptions and accounts?

   Consider the following extract of data, taken from the beginning of an interview with a married couple (Joe and Angela), on the topic of Angela's chronic illness. While there are many interesting analytic points that could be made about this piece, I shall focus on the way that '**joint remembering**' is accomplished as a practical activity and how that also does attributional work with respect to Angela's illness and its cause. (Note that the line numbers appear as they occur in the sequence of the interview and pseudonyms have been used in all data extracts and analyses.)

Extract 1

21   **MHS** mm and how did it (.) can you remember much about how it started? =

22   **J**   = heh heh

23   (.)

24   **A**   it started off with =

25   **J**   = it started with a sore throat =

26   **A**   = I had a sore throat and I had the very worst headache I've ever had in

27   my life (.) it was one evening =

28   **J**   = go back to where we believe it was caught at the swimming baths in

29   (town) =

30   **A**   = yeah =

31   **J**   = we'd been going down in the evening (.) swimming once a week (.)

32   and er it was after one of our sessions =

33   **A**   =yeah we thought we'd picked it up =

34   **J**   = I went swimming one week (.) you didn't feel up to it (.) then the

35   following week =

36   **A**   = <u>you</u> were alright weren't you? =

37   **J**   = yeah and this ties in because it's now known that M.E. is caused by

38   er (.) an enterovirus which is – a prime place to pick up an enterovirus is

39   a swimming baths (.) it's also the classic(.) <u>used</u> to be the classic place

40   to catch polio in the old days (.) hot summers (.) and I think with

41   swimming (.) kids being in the bath all through the day (.) at the end of

42   the day the water wasn't getting through the cleansing plant quick

43   enough (.) I suspect if you'd gone first thing in the morning it would be

44   absolutely spot on clean (.) but er I suppose by the time we got there (.)

45   I suppose the enteroviruses were still there (.) yeah (.) just unfortunate

Firstly, Angela and Joe's account can be seen as a joint production (Edwards and Middleton, 1986; Sacks, 1992; Tannen, 1989) in which they interrupt and prompt one another to tell the story of how Angela's illness started. This is in response to the demands of my question (Line 21: 'can you remember?') which is treated as a *request* to *describe* what happened. However, descriptions are never neutral, they are versions of reality, constructed by speakers in a particular rhetorical context. As Edwards and Potter (1992: 51) point out: "Descriptions are marshalled and facts are produced in so far as they have, or can be seen to have, bearing on specific accounts and narratives". However, since we have no 'bottom-line' version of objective truth against which to compare such accounts, all we can do is examine what speakers *do* with what they say.

This brings us to the links between description and attribution in Angela and Joe's account. Joe's intervention (Line 28: "go back to where we believe it was caught") is more than a prompting that Angela should recall the events in the order that they happened. It is also the beginning of an attributional story, which traces the origin of her illness to a virus "caught at the swimming baths" (Line 28). This account is further elaborated by Joe (Lines 37–45) starting with the assertion "because it's now known that M.E. is caused by er (.) an enterovirus". Descriptions of events and causal attributions are inextricably linked together in this account, since the formulation of a particular description of events *necessarily* implies that we can make particular causal links. Joe's 'theory of M.E.' as a medically recognizable organic disease, and the sequence of events that link Angela's illness with possible exposure to a virus, are being constructed here as uncontroversial. However, later in the same interview, they introduce an alternative explanation describing how Angela's illness had been defined as psychosomatic by their GP (Horton-Salway, 1998). This brings us to the third point in the discursive action model; that reports are embedded in activity sequences such as blamings or defendings. As such, Angela and Joe's account at the start of the interview might be seen as positioned against a possible alternative account of the causes of her illness, for example, a psychological explanation, or even the spectre of 'all in the mind' accounts.

2.2 Fact and interest

The next section of the discursive action model (points 4, 5 and 6) deals with the question of how people construct accounts in a way that makes them appear solid and factual, how they attend to other people's accounts as motivated by self-interest, and how they manage the **dilemma of 'stake and interest'** in their own accounts. People treat each other's accounts/ versions as motivated by self-interest. In constructing a version of events, anyone risks having their version discounted on the grounds of stake or interest. Participants attend to such risk in their accounts. This point can be illustrated by reference to the following extract taken from the film, *Scandal,* which dramatizes the notorious court case of 1963, the 'Profumo Affair' (in Edwards and Potter, 1992: 117).

Extract 2

Counsel	are you aware that Lord Astor denies any impropriety in his relationship with you
	(0.8)
Mandy Rice-Davies	well he would wouldn't he
Jury	[prolonged laughter]

Mandy Rice-Davies was a witness for the prosecution in the court case, where John Profumo and other leading public figures were implicated in a scandal involving prostitution and espionage. The remark, "well he would wouldn't he", was made in response to having her own version of events denied by the defence witness, and points out that Lord Astor might have an 'axe to grind' in denying his relationship with her. This highlights a dilemma that is frequently faced by speakers. When they give an account, particularly a controversial one, there is always the possibility of having their version dismissed or discredited on the grounds of stake and interest. In ordinary conversations and interviews, participants manage such risk by means of a device that Jonathan Potter (1996: 125) has termed '**stake inoculation**'. The example overleaf, taken from an interview with a GP, shows how this works.

Extract 3 MHS and Dr Turner

69 **MHS** I mean what do you <u>make</u> of the whole M.E. thi:ng?

70   ...

71 **Dr**   I was very sceptical initially, I have to say, for a while it seemed to

72   be y'know this decade's thing, and went along the same sort of lines as

73   Total Allergy Syndrome and things like that, which ultimately became

74   pretty well discredited (.) er as diagnoses and so I think initially, I think

75   it was seen as this year's trendy illness to have (.) er and people that

76   read about it, <u>knew</u> about it, developed it, sort of thing, that was my

77   original scepticism (.) about ten years ago it received that sort of

78   treatment, however I think it probably <u>is</u> an entity, a diagnostic

79   entity, a disease entity (.) whether or not it's post viral (.) whether it's a

80   slow virus or whatever (.) er (.) er (.) is still under debate, but as I say I

81   tend to think of it now as a disease entity

The remark "I was very sceptical initially" (Line 71) signals to the listener that Dr Turner might at one time have had a prior motivation to categorize M.E. as a dubious kind of condition. At Lines 72–76, he lists some grounds for his "original scepticism" (Line 77), but later he makes a statement about his *current* approach, as a believer in M.E. The 'stake inoculation' of "original scepticism" works to counter the possible suggestion that Dr Turner is someone who had a prior personal interest in recognizing M.E. as a disease entity, even while others in the medical profession were unsure; or worse, that he was in the first place duped by "this year's trendy illness" (Line 75).

2.3 Fact construction

Reports are constructed and displayed as factual by a variety of **discursive devices**, such as vivid description, narrative, consensus, and corroboration.

Consider again the following exchange from Extract 1, where Angela and Joe work up a consensus account of what happened at the start of Angela's illness.

24   **A**   it started off with =

25   **J**   = it started with a sore throat =

26   **A**   = I had a sore throat ...

Consensus is built between Lines 24–26 through the repetition of phrases such as "It started", "it started with a sore throat", "I had a sore throat". See if you can spot a similar kind of sequencing in this next extract which constructs the factual details of Angela's relapse.

Extract 4

```
76  J   one of the problems which caused (.) we suspect which pushed the

77      M.E. (1.0) was (coughs) she had a friend in the village (.) the same

78      friend who's now got a grand-daughter with a funny name (.) and she

79      came round to see Angela (.) I think your mother had gone back (.) or

80      your mother had gone back because she'd begun to become very

81      slightly better but she was still ill when she arrived (.) but Janet came

82      round and said 'oh you wanna get out you wann fight it y'know'

83  A = 'push yourself (.) ⌈you push yours⌉elf you'll be alri⌈ght'⌉
84  J                    ⌊'push yourself' ⌋                  ⌊and⌋she did

85  A = and I did (.) and I got worse and worse and worse after that

86  J = and I'll always remember the time I came home from work (.) the

87      kids were out (.) the house (.) when I opened the back door the house

88      was dead silent y'know (.) and I knew she was back in bed again and

89      that really was the thing that pushed her ⌈into⌉
90  A                                           ⌊push⌋ed it over the top
```

Note particularly the repetition of the term "push yourself" at Lines 83–84. This echoes Joe's statement at Lines 76–77 where he begins to attribute Angela's deterioration to following the advice of a friend. This pattern is repeated again at Lines 89–90. These sequences of repetition and joint construction function to build **consensus and corroboration** into the account of events, and imbue them with greater factual significance. Joe's story about coming home from work (at Lines 86–89) is the dramatic consequence. This is supported by the provision of a detailed description of circumstances; "the kids were out", "the back door", and "dead silent". This, and Angela's description (below) of her struggle to manage her household chores, paints a vivid and convincing picture of the circumstances and events of her illness.

Extract 5

```
98  A   Joe was at work (.) cause I've got two children there's

99      a lot of washing isn't there? I used to crawl round the floor and hang

100     over the sink and the washing machine trying to do a bit of washing (.)

101     and of course now we know this is the last thing you must ever do is to

102     push yourself when you first go down with M.E. (.) and I was doing all

103     the wrong things (.) and I think that's why I've never ever recovered
```

Angela's story is, of course, extremely moving and perhaps you will feel that it gives you a clearer appreciation of the effects of her illness.

However, one common critique of qualitative research has been to question the objective value of such accounts: how far can Angela and Joe's description of events be treated as an accurate and reliable representation of events and people? This question of authenticity and accuracy in people's narrative accounts has often been used to undermine the validity and reliability of traditional qualitative analysis. As Robinson points out:

> On the one hand they provide a density of texture, a depth of personal meaning, and an insight into the experience of illness not readily available through other means. On the other hand these very qualities seem to make any systematic, valid and reliable attempts to create generalizable propositions difficult, if not impossible.

> (Robinson, 1990: 1173)

Discursive psychology does not, however, treat people's narratives as a way of finding out about an independently existing world of events, objects and people (see Gergen, 1994, reproduced in Wetherell *et al.,* 2001). Since versions of the world are seen as being actively constructed through talk, factuality and authenticity are not at issue in precisely the same way. Instead, factuality and authenticity are seen as **discursive accomplishments**, and might sometimes be an *issue* for the participants themselves. For example, Angela's vivid account of struggling to manage her chores (Lines 98–103), and Joe's provision of details about the day he came home from work to find her in bed (Lines 86–88) actually help to *constitute* the factual and authentic nature of their descriptions. The provision of such detail works to give us some assurance that their accounts are not inaccurate or fictional, but real and credible. Also, at the start of their story (Extract 1, Line 28) Joe makes an issue of the *accuracy* of Angela's account, prompting her to "go back to where we believe it was caught". Compare this with how factuality is a concern for the participants in this extract from Harvey Sacks' data (taken from Edwards, 1997: 264):

Extract 6

1	**B**	...well, she *((wife of B))* stepped between me and the child,
2		I got up to walk out the door. When she stepped between me
3		and the child, I went to move her out of the way. And then
4		about that time her sister had called the police. I don't know
5		how she...what she...
6	**A**	Didn't you smack her one?
7	**B**	No.
8	**A**	You're not telling me the story, Mr B.
9	**B**	Well, you see when you say smack you mean hit.
10	**A**	Yeah, you shoved her. Is that it?
11	**B**	Yeah, I shoved her.

(Sacks, 1992, vol.1: 113, line numbers added)

Consider the comment, "You're not telling me the story, Mr B" (Line 8): where participant A displays "a sensitivity to what might count as a proper, 'well-informed' instance of a story" (Edwards, 1997: 265). As Edwards points out "The point of A's remark is that there is something quite specific (Line 6) that is hearably wrong with, or missing from, B's story" (*ibid*). At Line 9, B takes issue with the term 'smack' used by A at Line 6; at Lines 10–11, A and B reformulate this as 'shove', which has less violent connotations. The missing element, 'smack' or 'shove', is thus being highlighted by A (at Lines 6 and 8) as an essential part of the story since it is related to the matter of someone having had adequate grounds for calling the police. In a similar way, Joe's "go back to where we believe it was caught" (Extract 1, Line 28) provides an occasion to trace the origin of Angela's illness to a specific time, place and cause. Without this vital piece of information, their story would fail in its **attributional business**.

Note how reports such as Angela and Joe's are rhetorically organized to undermine alternative versions. Consider again how their story is organized at the start, and how that works to construct a particular explanation of Angela's illness as factual. The 'scene-setting' prepares the ground for what comes later: everything is geared towards constructing a physical definition of the illness and explaining how Angela caught a virus. The point is that the account could have been constructed differently; say beginning six months earlier, with an account of some stressful life event that might be connected to a depressive illness. By starting the story at that particular point in time only certain events are made relevant to the onset of Angela's illness, and this works to counter a possible alternative psychological explanation.

2.4 Accountability

In their accounts of events people also routinely attend to issues of agency and **personal accountability** as a discursive *practice*. Accounts can therefore be analysed to see how people accomplish the action of blaming and exoneration. Courtroom talk is full of material like this. As Edwards and Potter have pointed out:

> Courtroom testimony is a special kind of talk, but it is developed from, and draws upon, the resources of mundane talk. It is a routine feature of conversation, and a special feature of courtroom dialogue, that establishing 'what happened' is done with regard to issues of personal responsibility, such that the psychological categories of memory and attribution have to be seen as intimately connected, even as mutually constitutive. Reportings of events carry their attributional implications with them, and are constructed precisely to do that.
>
> (Edwards and Potter, 1992: 53)

The following extract of dialogue from a rape trial (Drew, 1990) exemplifies these claims:

Extract 7

(C is the defence counsel, W is the victim of an alleged rape.)

C   [referring to a club where the defendant and the victim met] it's where girls and fellas meet isn't it?

W   People go there.

C   And during the evening, didn't Mr O [the defendant] come over to sit with you?

W   Sat at our table.

According to Edwards and Potter: " ... C and W produce different and competing, but not contradictory, versions of the two incidents, each of which is 'designed to make available certain inferences to the overhearing jury'" (Edwards and Potter, 1992: 53).

Counsel attempts to establish a particular kind of *relationship* between the defendant and the witness by the phrase "where girls and fellas meet", and by the phrase "come over to sit with you". This wording suggests the possibility that the witness might have been flirting with the defendant. In doing this, Counsel is clearly attempting to attribute some level of responsibility and consent to the witness, thereby refuting the allegations of rape. The *implications* of Counsel's comments are resisted by W's use of the gender neutral term "people" rather than "girls and fellas", and by her choice of the phrase "sat at our table" rather than "sit with", which could have implied an invitation. As Edwards and Potter point out:

> ... what is ostensibly mere 'description' of actions and events can be constructed to generate specific implications concerning the speaker/actor's involvement with regard to attributional issues of responsibility and blame. ... A verbal remembering of events is a description. Descriptions can vary in a range of significant ways without their being merely (objectively, obviously) true or false ... .

> (Edwards and Potter, 1992: 51)

Note also how Angela and Joe's account (Extract 4), and Mr B's version (Extract 6), are organized to manage personal accountability. Angela and Joe's mention of the friend's advice, Mr B's significant omission, and re-negotiation of the term 'smack' are all part of descriptions that generate implications about who is at fault.

Consider also how Dr Turner (Extract 3) works up his grounds for saying that M.E. is a disease entity. His initial *scepticism* about a dubious medical category manages the risks that might be associated with making any sort of claim about M.E. as a legitimate disease entity. As a doctor, he is accountable for making any such claim on the basis of rational, scientific, medical evidence, rather than on the strength of some ill-informed or prejudiced opinion. In the *current* interaction, the management of stake and interest serves to bolster the credibility of his diagnostic opinions about patient cases, which he goes on to talk about later in the same interview.

Point 9 of the discursive action model indicates that points 7 and 8 are often linked together. For example, when constructing a version that attributes blame (or implicates risk), this is likely to bear on the accountability of the current speaker: "The act of blaming could itself be inspected for its partial or motivated nature, for instance, or for its adequacy *vis-à-vis* some version of the facts" (Edwards and Potter, 1992: 166).

Dialogue 3

STUDENT   I can see how psychological phenomena such as memory and causal attribution can be reconceptualized as things that people *do* in their talk. The discursive action model also explains things like fact construction, personal accountability, and stake management. Perhaps you could get around to explaining how all this applies to people's identities?

MHS   Okay, in the next section there are some 'before and after' stories from interviews with M.E. sufferers. Illness stories often focus on the way that illness has changed the lives of sufferers. This involves comparing lives and selves *before* the illness with lives and selves *after* the illness. In the case of M.E. you will have gathered that sufferers have to manage some rather sensitive and controversial issues, such as the question of whether the illness is a form of depression (or even 'all in the mind') and whether sufferers should be encouraged to take more exercise or whether they ought to take symptoms of fatigue as a sign that they should rest. No one really seems to agree on exactly what causes M.E. and how the illness should be treated, and this uncertainty raises issues of blame and personal responsibility that people have to manage in their illness stories. They do this by 'talking up' their identities.

---

3   Identity work in illness narratives

There is a huge body of literature on the topic of **illness narratives** in medical sociology and health psychology, which I will not attempt to cover in this short space (see the Further Reading section for a suggested selection). Some of the research has focused on using people's narratives as a way to find out about their subjective experiences of illness; their personal worlds, and changes in self and identity. The following quotation is taken from an interview with a multiple sclerosis sufferer: "I used to enjoy dancing, gardening and general 'busyness'. I now sit in a chair, wheelchair or motor car and I am fed up with having to ask people to do things for me and pass things to me" (Robinson, 1990: 1183).

Some researchers have interpreted such stories to make inferences about how the illness has actually affected the identity of the sufferer. For example, Kathy Charmaz (1983) points out that: "over time, many debilitated persons become dependent and immobilized. As they suffer losses of self from the consequences of chronic illness and experience diminished control over their lives and their futures, affected individuals commonly lose not only self-esteem, but even self-identity" (Charmaz, 1983: 163).

From this perspective, the self and identity are treated as residing within the individual, whilst being affected by outside influences, life experiences, and one's own perception. On the other hand, the discursive action model takes quite a different approach to the analysis of identities. They are seen as discursive products that are 'talked up' and negotiated in the context of conversations and accounts for specific interactional purposes. This does not imply that discursive psychologists are less concerned about people's suffering than other analysts. On the contrary, it is rather that our analytic practices are informed by a particular theoretical position that does not assume an equivalence between people's accounts and their internal experience and processes. When analysing any account or description it is therefore important to consider the following key issues:

- construction

- action

- rhetoric.

First, versions of reality are *constructed* in and through people's accounts; second, talk performs *actions* (such as blamings, justifications, and the management of personal accountability); and third, versions are constructed and *positioned* against actual or potential alternative accounts and explanations.

3.1 Before and after stories

From this rationale, discursive psychology is interested in how identities are *constructed* in talk, and how people's actions can be **scripted** as being either in or out of character, and how this gives credibility to one kind of explanation rather than another. Going back to Robinson's (1990) data above and his quote from the multiple sclerosis sufferer, we can see how this works: "I *used* to enjoy dancing, gardening and general 'busyness' ... I *now* sit down all day". In the context of this illness narrative, the scripting up of a previous **norm** of activity (i.e. what the sufferer *used* to do as a matter of routine) is accomplished as a discursive activity. "I *used* to enjoy dancing" works to construct a particular kind of identity; an active outgoing person, and this performs some interesting **rhetorical business**: it works to counter any possible suggestion that the patient might have been somebody who was typically inactive prior to illness, or has 'given up'. The very circumstances of the illness, 'sitting down all day' could be challenged as an accountable issue of illness management. This is an example of one of the sensitive issues mentioned by MHS in Dialogue 3.

Activity 1

Consider this next extract of data which is taken from a television debate chaired by Esther Rantzen, entitled, *M.E.: A Modern Plague or a Malingerer's Charter?* Make some analytic notes on the following topics:

- What alternative versions are being constructed in the extract, and how would you use the data to support them?
- What kinds of discursive devices are used to construct the facts in each case?
- How is P1's identity being constructed in the talk?
- What action does this perform?

(ER: Esther Rantzen, TS: Dr Thomas Stuttaford – medical correspondent for *The Times*, P1: Participant 1 – a member of the invited audience.)

Extract 8 (The Esther Rantzen show)

```
1     ER   so you think its a kind of depre:ssion?((hostile audience response))

2          (.)

3     TS   I think it may well be a kind of depression

4          (.)

5     ER   RIght (.) right (.) finish what you're say(ing

6     TS      ⌈⌈I

7     ER      ⌊⌊ you think it may well ⌈be?⌉

8     TS                               ⌊eh–⌋er (.) m–may we:ll be >a form of

9          depression< because patients will not realise (.) that depressed

10         (.) patients become ill (.) and therefore they resent being described as

11         (.) >having depression< (.) ⌈listen to them (.) li::sten to them you see⌉

12    ER                               ⌊well clearly (.)  clearly some people do⌋do

13         you resent it?(.) being described ⌈as depression⌉

14    P1                                     ⌊well its not th⌋at I resent it but I mean

15         I don't really look very depressed do I ? (.) I mean I was a head

16         teacher (.) and I loved my job (.) and I played squash (.) and I produced

17         concerts with the children (.) and overni:ght I was like a vegetable (.)

18         suddenly (.) in the most terrible pains...I couldn't think properly and

19         I couldn't speak properly and I lost so much power in my muscles (.)
```

Discussion

The speaker P1 is an M.E. sufferer who is a member of an invited audience. In a prior turn at talk, a doctor from the audience, TS, has suggested that M.E. might be a form of depression. Positioned against a hostile response from the audience, his explanation of the illness as depression is constructed as the version that is resented by patients (Line 9).

Consider also the account constructed by P1 (at Lines 14–18) to dismiss TS's explanation of the illness she suffers. First she rejects the accusation that she is resentful of his suggestions (Line 14), and then she assembles a catalogue of evidence that works to dismiss his version. For example, there is some face value evidence which is there for anyone to see: "I don't really look very depressed". The use of face-value evidence is one form of fact-construction. Note how this device is being used by TS (at Line 11) where he says "listen to them". He uses the audience's hostile response to his comments (at Lines 10–11) as a confirmation of the claim he has just made.

P1 then tells a **'before and after' story** which gives us some detail of her active lifestyle and professional status prior to the onset of illness. This is followed by a detailed description of the physical circumstances of her illness such as loss of bodily function and painful muscles: "like a vegetable", "terrible pains", "couldn't think ... couldn't speak", "lost so much power in my muscles" (Lines 18–19). The important analytic question is what kind of business is being performed through the construction of this 'before and after' story. How is P1's identity being worked up here in the talk? From her comments in Lines 15–19, what can we know about her prior self?

1   She was a head teacher who loved her job.

2   She played sport.

3   She was fully involved with the day-to-day running of her school.

From this **'three part list'** (Jefferson, 1990; for a further discussion of this see Wooffitt's account in Chapter Two of this volume), P1 has constructed a factual impression of an active, competent, professional woman who was suddenly afflicted by a disabling physical illness. The identity work performed by P1 (active, professional, competent, socially involved) in this 'before and after' story works to counter a particular kind of attribution about the cause of the illness; that she might be suffering from a form of depression, or worse still, that she might simply be a malingerer (which had been suggested as an option by the title of the TV debate).

Activity 2

Consider the following extract from Angela and Joe's interview. Make some analytic notes on the following questions:

- How is Angela's identity being constructed in the talk?

- What fact-constructing device does Angela use to support her identity work in Extract 9?

- How are the 'before and after' stories similar to that of P1 in the last extract? What are the key features of such stories and what *actions* do they perform?

Immediately prior to this extract, Angela has just given an account of her GP's suggestion that she might be suffering from a psychosomatic illness. This has made an alternative version of the nature of Angela's illness available to the interviewer, and could possibly work to undermine Angela's preferred version that she is suffering from a physical disease.

Extract 9

```
1   A   I think my mother was around at one of these times when that was

2       mentioned too (.) my mother said 'I know my daughter'(.) I can always

3       remember my mother saying that (.) 'I know my daughter'(.) because I

4       was always so active heh heh hyperactive in some respects

5       actually (.) because my Mum used to say to me 'for goodness sake

6       Angela sit down' (.) this was before I went down with ME (.) I never

7       wanted to sit down (.) I wanted to be on the go all the while (.) I was

8       happy that way (.) but er (.) things change (.) you're forced to sit

9       down
```

Discussion

Angela's identity as an active person, who was always "on the go", is being constructed here in Lines 4–8. She describes her pre-M.E. self as "active", "hyperactive", "never wanted to sit down", "on the go all the while", "happy that way". This version of her self is being sharply contrasted with her post-M.E. condition (Lines 8–9) "things change (.) you're forced to sit down". Notice how Angela uses corroboration to accomplish a solid factual tone to her story: her claims are expressed using her mother's 'voice' rather than her own. She establishes her mother's credentials for making an objection to the GP's suggestion of psychosomatic illness: "I know my daughter". The 'before and after' story goes on to fill in the details of what her mother knew about her. As point 4 of the discursive action model noted, people treat each other's accounts as being motivated by self-interest. Angela is attending to this possibility by using her mother's critical 'voice' which is likely to carry more weight than a simple assertion on her own behalf.

Activity 3

Compare the 'before and after' stories of Angela and P1, constructed in Extracts 8 and 9, with Angela and Joe's account in Extract 10. Make some notes on how Angela's identity is discursively accomplished and consider what kind of *action* that performs.

Extract 10

```
1   A      because we did it together you see (.) we always used to go

2          fell-walking ⌈and hik⌉ing cycling heh heh heh heh heh =

3   J                   ⌊cyclists⌋

4   MHS   outdoor people =

5   A     = yeah (.) swimming (.) physical things 'cause I know some couples

6          aren't in to that sort of thing (.) they're quite happy to stop at home and

7          sit (.) aren't they? =

8   MHS   = yes =

9   A     = well we were never like that (.) but we've been forced to be like that

10         in a way (.) to be sedentary instead of active (.) so it affects the other

11         one as well

12  MHS   = quite disruptive then really

13  A     = and of course I'll tell you how it does affect you very badly (.) er

14         with me with having it (.) it's the grandchildren (.) now it's repeating

15         itself because I can't play with them and my arms at the moment are so

16         weak I can't even lift the baby d'you know?

17  J     = well we (.) the ⌈only ⌉

18  A                       ⌊which⌋ is awful
```

Discussion

Angela begins with an account of the active lifestyle she and Joe used to enjoy before she had M.E. (Lines 1–2). She continues to construct this account at Lines 5–7. Then at Lines 9–10 she begins the contrast account of her post-M.E. lifestyle. Finally at Lines 13–18 she provides an illustration of how badly she is affected by her M.E.

This 'before and after' story works up an identity in the narrative to manage the personal accountabilities of illness. In any kind of talk about illness one risks being construed as the type of person who is looking for **secondary gain**. Herzlich (1973) referred to this as 'illness as a liberator' from the burdens of the world. This must be even more pertinent in the case of M.E. where the very legitimacy of the illness is itself 'at stake' and 'all in the mind' explanations and accusations of malingering have often been an issue. Angela's account counters such explanations by **working up an identity** as a robust, active, go-ahead person who was neither vulnerable to psychological illness nor the type to enjoy or wish for a sedentary lifestyle. She describes the *consequences* of her illness as now being deprived of the things that would be most enjoyable to her; that is, her active leisure activities and her relationship with her grandchildren. Her account makes available the implicit rhetorical question: what possible motive could she have to give up all the things that would make her life more enjoyable?

Dialogue 4

STUDENT Now tell me if I have this right. I can see the *actions* that identity work performs in these 'before and after' stories. People construct pre-illness identities as part of accounts that support a particular version of events and causes (such as a physical explanation for M.E.), whilst also dismissing other versions (such as psychological explanations) that might be associated with other kinds of identities.

MHS That's right. If we treat illness talk as a potentially risky business, we can look at how people's versions are well designed to manage some of those sensitive issues. For example, people do not treat each other's accounts as disinterested, and they orient to the possibility that they will be heard as having an interest in constructing one kind of account rather than another. There is a lot at stake in illness talk, and identity construction is part of managing all that.

STUDENT But wouldn't I need to know what those sensitive issues were *before* I analyse the data?

MHS Not at all. The participants will do that work *for* you. As an analyst I'm interested in what categories and issues *they* construct and make relevant in their talk.

STUDENT So did we really *need* your scene-setting on the 'M.E. controversy' after all?

MHS Good question! But it's actually quite interesting to see how someone *constructs* that kind of summary. You could even treat my account as another piece of data to analyse. Don't forget that it is *my* construction, and I use all the same fact-constructing devices as everyone else. For example, I make my account credible by using the 'voices' of others, citing precise dates, and employing a standard scientific style of writing which gives lots of factual detail. If you look closely you might even be able to find some three part lists. (Compare this with the discursive action model, which is constructed as three sets of three part lists!). As for setting the context for analysis – well *that's* another issue. You might need to think about that one. Not all discourse analysts agree on the topic of how much context we need, or the question of how far analysts should go in making use of their cultural knowledge.

STUDENT H::m ((sound of rustling paper))

MHS While she's finding a reference for *context* [3], I'll start on the next section where we can unpack some ideas on participants' categories.

4   Participants' categories

As pointed out in Section 1, one way to theorize the 'mind' from a discursive psychology view is to re-conceptualize cognitive processes as discursive actions; for example, attributions, and memories are things that people *construct* in their talk rather than things that people *have* inside their heads. This **non-cognitivist approach** has been the central focus of previous sections. (Remember point 1 of the discursive action model.) Another approach would be to analyse 'the mind' as the *topic* of people's talk. In other words, how do *participants* construct the *category* 'mind' as part of their accounts, and what kinds of *actions* does this perform?

Before going on with this section of analysis, it might be useful to say something about how the term '**category**' is being used here. For discursive psychology (of the Edwards and Potter type), a category (such as 'mind') is a social construction. Categories are designed to be used in our talk, and they represent particular ways of ordering the world. (See also my introductory comments on the categorizing and positioning of academic work.) Thus, in Western cultures, it makes common sense for us to use the categories 'mind' and 'body' as if they were distinct and separate from one another. 'Mind' is thus taken to be a psychological category, whereas 'body' is taken to be a physical category. However, the *precise* meaning of these terms is **indexical** and can only be understood by reference to their context of use. For instance, the word 'mind' is useful because we can use it to say that something is not 'body', or to say that something is not 'real'. Mind-talk is therefore likely to be part of mind and body talk, embedded in a set of contrasts, its meaning worked up by the participants *in situ*. Following Wittgenstein's (1958) approach to analysing concepts, Harvey Sacks (1989: 280–1) has argued that "formulating in terms of two-class sets is a method of doing things". It is not just that there are two classes of things; for example, male and female, young and old, rich and poor, mind and body, etc.: the point is that these binary oppositions lend themselves to the situated work of making comparisons and contrasts. As Edwards (1997) comments, this kind of binary contrast structure is not:

> ... simply a built-in feature of cognitive sense-making, nor a reflection of how the world itself happens to fall naturally into two-set classes. Rather, it is a powerful, general-purpose discursive device for constructing the world *as* such. That makes it ideally suited to ideological, dilemmatic, and rhetorical discourse (Billig *et al.*, 1988), and to the mundane, situated production of contrasts and alternatives (Atkinson and Drew, 1979; Smith, 1978).

> (Edwards, 1997: 237)

4.1 Mind and body talk

As documented in Section 1 (and also later in the Angela and Joe data) one of the central bones of contention in the 'M.E. debate' has been the issue of **mind or body explanations** for the illness. Many contributors to this field of knowledge, including 'official' reports from Westcare (1994) and The

Royal Colleges of Physicians, Psychiatrists, and General Practitioners (1996), have recently attempted to take the theoretical 'high ground' by rejecting arguments based on such dualistic concepts of mind and body. They have suggested, instead, that we should be using a more complex and interrelated model of mind and body in order to explain illness of all kinds. However, in the following collection of extracts, I shall demonstrate how the mind and its relationship with the body has been categorized in various different ways by medical practitioners. Following the Wittgensteinian rationale, the separate terms 'mind' and 'body' can be seen as well-designed and discursively useful for the purpose of constructing medical explanations. The significant questions for our analysis of the following extracts of data are: how do these doctors define and use the category 'mind'; and what do those definitions accomplish in the context of specific interactions? Later in this section you will have a chance to do some further analysis yourself, along similar lines, on a couple of longer extracts of data.

Extract 11 The mind as a reflection of the body

(The first extract is taken from an M.E. self-help group discussion where the invited speaker, FM, a clinical psychologist, is working to introduce the idea that psychology might have something to offer in the treatment of chronic fatigue syndrome.)

FM   the mind comes from the brain (.) the mind isn't separate from the body the mind is just a reflection of what's happening in the <u>brain</u>

FM is working up a definition of what he, as a psychologist, understands the 'mind' to be. First, the brain is being given primacy, second, there is no separation of mind and body, and third, the processes of the brain are treated as the reality, whereas the mind is 'just' the reflection of those processes. This kind of formulation of the 'mind' works to make the category of psychological processes *equivalent* to bodily processes. Later in this section you will have an opportunity to place this extract in its rhetorical context to see how FM uses his definition of the 'mind' to avoid a possible confrontation with members of the M.E. self-help group.

Extract 12 The body as a reflection of the mind

(In this extract, Dr Brown, an invited GP, is talking to another M.E. self-help group on the topic of 'A GP's view of M.E.' Here he is working to explain the relevance of the mind in the production of patients' symptoms.)

Dr Brown   the other concept I'd like to put across to you is that you can only actually know what's happening in your <u>mind</u> because of what you can feel in your body (1.0) cause the only reason that I know that I'm anxious is perhaps because I'll feel myself sweating (1.0) so we rely on our bodies to tell us what's happening in our minds

Here Dr Brown explains the body as a kind of 'text' or 'barometer' of the processes of the mind. What you "feel in your body" is construed as the outward signs of something that is *really* going on somewhere else but is not directly accessible. In contrast to FM's formulation in Extract 11, mind processes are being given primacy by Dr Brown, but these are treated as outside of our realm of control. Significantly, this account of the mind does not provide for personal agency. (Remember points 7, 8 and 9 of the discursive action model which deal with issues of accountability.) In the context of Dr Brown's talk to the self-help group, his account of the mind works to place psychology on the agenda as a candidate explanation for M.E. sufferers' physical symptoms without implicating them as being personally accountable for their illness.

Extract 13 Mind over matter

(At a different point in the same talk to the self-help group, Dr Brown uses a specific example to construct his definition of the mind.)

Dr Brown a classic one, if you like, is the couple who go through
about ten years of fertility investigations (.) and <u>nothing</u>
found (.) and they adopt – this happened to one of our
friends er (.) they adopt and within three months the wife's
pregnant (.) an– an y'know there's this cruel trick of nature
that once you relax about it and stop having the pressure on
you then you conceive (.) and so it really <u>is</u> mind over
matter

As with his account in the previous extract, Dr Brown construes the mind and body as *separate*, with the mind taking *primacy* over the body. There are, however, some interesting ambiguities in his account, which constitute the events of the reported case as both *agentless*, yet, on the other hand, in some way *influenced* by personal willpower. His use of event descriptions such as "this cruel trick of nature" and "having the pressure on you" suggest a lack of agency, while the expression, "once you relax about it" coupled with the phrase "mind over matter" suggest that people can actively effect changes in their bodily responses. In the context of Dr Brown's talk to the M.E. group, where the suggestion of mental illness or 'all in the mind' explanations are a sensitive issue, this **inferential ambiguity** allows him to make suggestions about the role of the mind in their illnesses while managing the possibility of a hostile reception.

4.2 'All in the mind?': a dangerous category

The following two extracts are taken from an interview with Dr Walker on the topic of M.E.

Extract 14

Dr Walker y'know it's something that I think doctors are sometimes
more comfortable with (.) they can say 'well this is a bit like
glandular fever (.) it's the aftermath of an infection' (.) and

> it's a working model if you like (.) which gives some
> reassurance that it <u>isn't</u> in the mind (.) there <u>is</u> something (.)
> there's an explanation for it

The category of 'in the mind' is being constructed here, by implication, as
a contrast to the category in which "there <u>is</u> something" like "the aftermath
of an infection". This reality is constituted as comforting and reassuring,
but it necessarily implicates its opposite; an *absence* of such reality (cf.
Sacks, 1989). In a different part of the same interview, however (see
Extract 15), Dr Walker goes on to problematize this kind of explanation,
commenting on the consequences of making the category of physical
equivalent to real.

Extract 15

Dr Walker I think what <u>is</u> a difficulty (.) I think it's this (.) I think it's
something that (.) certainly (.) seen by patients (.) and I
think to some extent (.) would be seen by doctors <u>as well</u> (.)
is this business of whether physical and mental things equate
with real and imagined (.) do you know what I mean (.) and
I think that's the <u>danger</u> of it

Here Dr Walker works to distance himself from the implications of
categorizing the mind and body in this 'dangerous' manner (i.e. "physical
and mental things equate with real and imagined"). In Extract 14, the
equation of physical with real is described as a position that "doctors are
sometimes more comfortable with", whereas in *this* context he points out
"the <u>danger</u> of it". In this context he could be orienting to a concern that
mental illness might not be given serious attention. This is, however, merely
an **analytic inference** on my part and I am in danger of going beyond
what is made *precisely* available by the participants in this piece of data. On
the other hand, in the following piece of data (Extract 16) a concern with
dismissal is hearably the *topic* of the doctor's talk.

Extract 16 'Something nice and physical'

Dr Brown and there's still this in people's minds they link nerves with
the fact that somehow the doctor is gonna be dismissing it
(.) and that they're being fobbed off er and these sort of
things (.) so again something nice and physical like your
heart attack or your broken bone (.) you feel that your
doctor's going to give you more (.) you're higher up in his
importance scales

Dr Brown works up his explanation for why patients might *prefer* to
present their doctor with "something nice and physical". They believe that
"nerves" are not taken seriously, whereas physical things place you "higher
up in his importance scales". In the context of Dr Brown's talk to the M.E.

self-help group, this description mitigates the suggestion (made available in Extract 12) that M.E. sufferers might actually be somatisers i.e. people who express psychological distress in the form of physical symptoms. In other words, if patients present psychological distress as physical symptoms, that's understandable because "there's still this in people's minds" that "the doctor is gonna be dismissing" mental illness. Note also that, in Dr Brown's account, it is the *patients* who are projecting this kind of prejudice onto their doctors. Even the category "nice and physical" is construed as a *patients'* naive belief, which Dr Brown claims is "in people's minds". In this way, Dr Brown is able to distance himself, and the rest of the medical profession, from the patients' use of this category *and* their underlying beliefs about M.E.

Extract 17 'The devil's own job'

(Finally, Dr Brown talks about the relationship between the mind and the body in M.E.)

> **Dr Brown** there are both physical and emotional components (.) and trying to figure out which is which is the devil's own job at times (.) but I suppose what I would say is 'it really doesn't matter' because er (.) if you actually look I would say that it really isn't mind versus body it's mind and body and the two are completely intertwined

In this extract, Dr Brown's use of the phrase "the two are completely intertwined" itself constitutes the mind and body as separate but, like the threads of a cloth, they are woven together and difficult to disentangle. In the context of his talk to the M.E. group, Dr Brown has been working to suggest that M.E. might have a psychological component. In his construction of this explanation he works to manage two kinds of issues. First, there is no definitive medical knowledge he can draw on to support his claims, and second, the members of the audience are likely to be resistant to hearing a psychological explanation for their illnesses. His construction of two separate components that are "the devil's own job" to disentangle works to avoid having to make any precise or contentious claims about the role of the mind in the illness process, and also justifies the vagueness surrounding the whole area of explaining M.E. in the first place.

Summary

In the above section, I have analysed some of the ways that the mind has been categorized by medical practitioners. As predicted by the principles of discourse analysis (Potter and Wetherell, 1987), these categorizations are variable even when authored by the same speaker within the same piece of talk. This is because the category of 'mind', its precise meaning and its implication for personal accountability is constructed *in situ* and is well designed to perform a particular kind of action. Compare this with my 'scene-setting' of the 'M.E. controversy', which provides an analyst's summary of mind/body explanations of a mystery illness. In doing so, I have selected what research literature to treat as significant, what is important about each paper, and used the classification of mind and body to set up two adversarial schools of thought. This tells us little about the way that the writers (as participants) have *themselves* used the terms 'mind' and 'body' as part of their situated discursive business in authoring such texts.[4] In other words, my summary of mind/body issues is not *itself* an analysis of their discourse, although it is perfectly possible to perform such an analysis on scientists' talk (e.g. Gilbert and Mulkay, 1984).

5   Managing accountabilities: 'What I mean by the mind'

In the data we analysed in Section 4, the fine-tuning of the category 'mind' works in the different contexts to construct people's illnesses as either physical and real, psychological or imaginary. As we have seen, the precise meaning of the term 'mind' alters with its context of use, and such variability of meaning constitutes a rich resource for the management of personal accountability as a practical activity. Note how these issues of accountability relate to the third component of the discursive action model. In this section you have an opportunity to apply the same kind of analysis to a piece of 'naturally occurring' interaction, where speakers work to manage some sensitive issues in the context of a discussion on M.E.

Activity 4

Consider the following extracts of data taken from an M.E. self-help group meeting, where an invited speaker, FM, (a psychologist) leads a discussion on the topic of M.E. This '**naturally occurring**' discussion was recorded as part of the group's routine practice of tape-recording meetings, rather than having been set up and recorded especially for the purposes of research.

You have already seen part of the next extract in Extract 11. We can now set the quotation in its proper context, so that it can be analysed in greater detail. Use your knowledge of the discursive action model, together with previous worked examples, to inform your analysis. As you read through the extract, make some notes on the following questions:

- How does FM manage the potential for a confrontation between himself and members of the M.E. group?

- How does he establish his grounds for making knowledge claims about the mind?

- How do the examples he uses contribute to the force of his argument?

- What is the 'sensitive' issue here?

- How is FM's account designed to 'manage' this issue?

Extract 18 'What *I* mean by the mind'

1 **FM** I mean (.) I get the impression that er (.) not from <u>this</u> group (.) but

2   <u>gen</u>erally (.) there's unease about the application of the psychological

3   approach to Chronic Fatigue Syndrome (.) I mean (.) I suspect that's for

4   two reasons (.) one is the fact I– I think some people have difficulty with

5   the idea that the mind

6   (0.6)

7 **FM** they like to see the mind and the body as two separate things (.) we've got a

8   body that's physical (.) and we have a <u>mind</u> that's separate (.) and of course as

9   a psy<u>chol</u>ogist I mean that doesn't make any sense (.) the <u>mind</u> (.) and the

10   body are two halves of the same thing (.) the mind comes from the brain (.)

11   the mind isn't separate from the body the mind is just a reflection of what's

12   happening in your <u>brain</u> er if anything happens to your brain like a stroke or an

13   injury (.) then the mind changes (.) the personality changes (.) your way of

14   seeing the world changes (.) the mind is the bra:in and the brain is an organ of

15   the body like any other organ of the body (.) and your brain is linked to every

16   y'know every other organ in your body

17   (0.8)

18 **FM** <u>by</u> the <u>nerv</u>ous system (.) and by your hormonal system (.) the brain's got

19   hormone glands in it– the adrenal gland that releases hormones that control

20   various aspects of your bodily functioning (.) so I <u>person</u>ally don't have any

21   difficulty in understanding how the mi:nd and the body can affect each

22   other cause they aren't two separate things (.) the mind's the brain and the

23   brain's a part of the body so to me

24   (0.6)

25 **FM** y'know I (.) whatever the problem is I can quite easily understand how (.) the

26   mind and the body affect each other and I suppose you see that in illnesses

27   like (.) stomach ulcers (.) most people accept that stomach ulcer's (.) a real

28   physical <u>prob</u>lem caused often by stress (.)'cause the stress increases the

29   nervous activity, to the nerves to the stomach, the stomach produces more

30   acid, the acid burns holes in your stomach (.) and you've got a stomach ulcer

31   (.) so there's no suggestion that people <u>im</u>agine the pain of stomach ulcers– it's

32   <u>real</u> pain but it's <u>caused</u> by a psychological problem originally (.) in a lot of

33   cases– not in every case but in a lot of cases (.) so I mean it's quite easy to see

34   how the mind affects the body (.) er (.) and there's evidence in other areas as

35   well for instance heart– research into heart disease (.) that shows that type A

36   personalities have a much higher risk of heart disease than type B

37   personalities-type A's aheh y'know high achi:eving (.) people who are under

38   a lot of <u>time</u> pressure more than most people do– very high standards for what

39   they want to achieve

40   (0.6)

41 **FM** in your Type A's that are much higher risk it's something to do with (.) no

42   one really quite knows <u>how</u> that mechanism works whether it's affe:cting (.)

43   the blood vascular system directly or (.) quite how it wo:rks but it's a well (.)

44   it's a fairly world widely accepted finding (.) so ah– I personally don't have

45   any difficulty with the idea that the mind (.) affects the body and the body

46   affects the mind-how your body is affects how you <u>feel</u> mentally as well

Discussion

- Prior to this extract, FM has introduced himself as a clinical psychologist.
  He has already raised the contentious topic of what label the illness
  should be given. He has announced his intention to speak to the group
  about Chronic Fatigue Syndrome (CFS) and is unsure of the members'
  acceptance of this label and its equivalence with, or distinction from,
  M.E. There is also a tacit understanding that FM has been invited to talk
  to the group about the role of psychology, and in particular cognitive
  behavioural therapy,[5] in the treatment of Chronic Fatigue Syndrome. As
  such, FM's talk is oriented to managing the potential for confrontation
  between himself and the members of the group.

  At the start of the extract, FM attends to this risk by addressing his
  controversial comments towards a non-specific group of people,
  distinguishing between them and the present audience. The "unease
  about the application of the psychological approach to Chronic Fatigue
  Syndrome" (Lines 2–3) is construed as happening in a different place,
  and not right there in the specific context of the meeting. This manages
  the potential for FM's comments to be treated as directly oppositional to
  the concerns of this particular group, and also allows him considerable
  rhetorical space to present a case for the 'acceptable face of psychology'
  which is worked up through his own definition of the mind and its
  relevance for their illness.

- He establishes his grounds for making knowledge claims about the
  influence of the mind by speaking "as a psychologist" (Lines 8–9). As he
  works through his account, the factual status of his claims is
  consolidated by underlining the obvious and sensible nature of his
  explanation. For example, he points out that "I <u>personally</u> don't have
  any difficulty in understanding how the mi:nd and the body affect each
  other" (Lines 20–22) and "I can quite easily understand how (.) the mind

and the body affect each other" (Lines 25–26) and "it's quite easy to see how the mind affects the body" (Lines 33–34) and finally "so ah– I personally don't have any difficulty with the idea that the mind (.) affects the body and the body affects the mind" (Lines 44–46). The *repetition* of this statement together with the *evidence* FM assembles to support his argument are powerful fact-constructing devices, and they make available the implicit rhetorical question: 'If the concept is so obvious, easy to understand and supported by evidence, why would *any* member of the audience want to disagree with him?' Their dilemma would be similar to that of a crowd who had been told of the Emperor's new suit of clothes. To continue the analogy, there *was* in fact a dissenting voice who took up the challenge later in the discussion!

- FM assembles an impressive range of evidence to support his argument. First he explains how a stroke or injury that results in brain damage, can affect the mind, and the personality (Lines 12–14). Then (Lines 26–34) he gives an account of how stomach ulcers can be caused by stress. Finally (Lines 34–44) he cites research evidence linking personality type to heart disease. All of these examples contribute to the force and factuality of his argument about the link between mind and body. The examples he uses are all recognizable as physical injuries or diseases, and in all three cases FM is careful to document the details of the underlying physiological mechanisms; for example, "the brain's got hormone glands in it – the adrenal gland that releases hormones that control various aspects of your bodily functioning" (Lines 18–20), "the stress increases the nervous activity, to the nerves to the stomach, the stomach produces more acid, the acid burns holes in your stomach (.) and you've got a stomach ulcer" (Lines 28–30), and "whether it's affe:cting (.) the blood vascular system directly or (.) quite how it wo:rks" (Lines 42–43).

- In the context of talking to a group of M.E. sufferers about the causes of their illness, this kind of formulation lends itself conceptually and rhetorically to managing some sensitive issues, such as the spectre of 'all in the mind' explanations for the illness. FM attends to the risk that he could be heard in that way at Lines 31–32, where he says "there's no suggestion that people imagine the pain of stomach ulcers – it's real pain but it's caused by a psychological problem originally". It is interesting and significant that FM has chosen to work up his account by stressing the psychological (rather than bacterial) causes of ulcers. Thus, by analogy, he is able to construct his preferred explanation for M.E. and suggest that the physical symptoms' of M.E. might have a psychological origin. Although the term 'psychological' is itself being grounded in the language of bodily functions, such as brain processes, hormones and nervous activity, FM's account firmly positions M.E. as a psychological phenomenon (and one that might be related to stress), rather than a simple example of physical damage to the body. In other words, FM's ulcer analogy, and his selective construction of its causes, is a powerful fact-constructing device which works in this context to

consolidate his version of what causes M.E. This does not imply that FM
is unaware of the recent medical developments that have changed the
emphasis from stress-related to bacterial explanations of ulcers. The
significant point is that his choice of a psychological version of the ulcer
analogy bolsters the credibility of his argument in *this* particular context.
Compare this with the examples of fact construction mentioned earlier
in the discursive action model.

Activity 5

Consider the following extract taken from further on in the same
discussion.

- Compare FM's definition of the relationship between the mind and the
  body with that in the previous extract.

- What does this allow him to accomplish in the context of this
  interaction?

Extract 19 Managing the 'dangerous' category.

68 **JJ** I think that's what I was trying to <u>say</u> (.) this is what's upset <u>some</u> people with

69   M.E. the fact that they've been told (.) or they've <u>read</u> (.) that it's purely a

70   psychological illness (.) and they <u>know</u> very well it <u>isn't</u> =

71 **FM** =I suppose this is the other area that (.) I think gets very confused– what do you

72   <u>mean</u> when you say something's psychological? Are you're saying that (.)

73   people think there's nothing physically wrong with you at <u>all</u> (.) that you're

74   sort of in a way <u>imagining</u> it ? (.) Is <u>that</u> what they mean? (.) Or do they mean

75   that it's (.) like a <u>stomach</u> ulcer– nobody (.) you could say a stomach ulcer is a

76   psychologically caused problem but that doesn't mean you imagine the pain

77   do you? Because (.) if you look in your stomach you can see the <u>hole</u> there (.)

78   but that <u>is</u> psychosomatic as much as it's caused by the mind affecting the

79   body (.) so it's very confusing what you <u>mean</u> when something is– is

80   psycho<u>logical</u> are you saying that it's all imagined (.) there's nothing

81   physically wrong with the body it's <u>all</u> in the mind (.) are you saying that the

82   mind <u>affects</u> the body (.) and therefore things could be partly psychological (.)

83   y'know an– and <u>that</u> to <u>me</u> when I (>talk about it being psychological<) that's

84   how <u>I</u> think of it (.) that the mind and the body affect each <u>other</u>

85   (1.2)

86 **FM** I don't– I certainly wouldn't seriously suggest that people (.) ima:gine the

87   symptoms that they have and they are genuine physical symptoms

Discussion

In this extract, the "unease about the application of the psychological approach to Chronic Fatigue Syndrome" (which FM referred to in Lines 2–3 of Extract 18), is hearable in JJ's comments at Lines 68–70 of Extract 19. FM attends to this as he begins to formulate his second reason (Lines 71–72) "I suppose this is the other area that (.) I think gets very confused– what do you <u>mean</u> when you say something's psychological?". FM continues to address these issues by returning to his work on defining meanings in the realm of psychology and the 'mind' (Lines 72–84). He accomplishes this by elaborating the stomach ulcer example and emphasizing the physical reality of the condition; "if you look in your stomach you can see the <u>hole</u> there" (Line 77). He also distinguishes between two categories; the *imaginary* and *psychosomatic*, where the former implies that the illness is not real but 'all in the mind', but the latter is a cause and effect process with "the mind affecting the body" (Lines 78–79) such that there are observable bodily signs like a stomach ulcer. FM works to distance himself from those who might draw on the 'dangerous' category of 'all in the mind' explanations (Lines 86–87) and using the term "genuine physical symptoms" he works to re-align himself with the group by presenting his views as the 'acceptable face of psychology'. In other words, he is someone who is prepared to take their symptoms seriously as physical problems, albeit caused by the mind and body affecting each other.

Note how, in different parts of his talk, FM has worked up two different positions on the relationship between the mind and the body. In Extract 18, he has defined the mind as *equivalent* to the brain. In other words, essentially, it is the same thing. In Extract 19, however, he works up a slightly different kind of definition in which there is a causal relationship between the mind and body that is effective in either direction. The important thing to notice about such variability is that it allows FM to accomplish some important and sensitive interactional business. First, the definition of 'mind equals brain' allows him to present psychology as non-threatening and related to physiological processes; second, this allows him to define away people's potential grievances; and third, his definition of mind and body as separate but related, "the mind and the body affect each <u>other</u>" (Line 84), together with his ulcer analogy in the previous extract, allows him to suggest that in some cases, physical symptoms are *caused* by psychological problems. If the direction of causality then becomes a contentious issue for the audience, (for example, later in the same discussion, JJ points out; "I think what <u>has</u> upset some people with M.E. in the past (.) is that some <u>doctors</u> say M.E. is <u>caused</u> by mental problems") then FM has the option of returning to the 'mind equals brain' construction to re-define the problem away.

Dialogue 5

STUDENT That's rather neat! Instead of having to make inferences about what the 'mind' is and what role it plays in illnesses, we can look at how people *use* the term and what they *do* with it in their explanations and accounts.

MHS Yes, remember the references to Wittgenstein and meaning in Section 4 on 'participants' categories'? Obviously linguistic categories, such as 'mind', are already imbued with some cultural significance, otherwise we would have no basis to understand one another, but the *precise* meaning and significance is **indexical**.[6] In other words, it's being constructed right there in the context of the interaction, and that serves some kind of purpose.

STUDENT That reminds me of something else I wanted to ask you about the meaning of categories. You focus on M.E. as a case study, and yet it's clear that many researchers and clinicians prefer to use the term CFS.

MHS Yes they do – and I'm glad you raised this issue. The point is that *labels* are never neutral. I used the term 'M.E.' because much of my data was collected from members of an M.E. self help group. As you can see from Angela and Joe's account (Extracts 1, 4, 5 and 9) M.E. is a **participants' category**. Its meaning and equivalence with CFS has certainly been a participants' concern which is hearable in much of the data. But you should be aware that in *any* piece of discourse, speakers/writers will select one category rather than another. Remember Mr B (Extract 6) and the negotiation of the words 'smack' or 'shove'? Likewise, the terms M.E. and CFS carry different kinds of implications, which, in this case, relate to the definition and nature of an illness.

STUDENT But if that's the case, and context is so important in the definition of the illness, shouldn't we look at the wider social context and see how these terms are used as part of different discourses – in the Foucauldian sense? And what does all of this imply about power relations?

MHS Depends what you mean by the wider social context. The discursive action model is partly based on the principles of ethnomethodology which is interested in the **situated 'sense-making practices** of participants'. Show me some discourse and I'll analyse what the participants do in that specific context. For example, I could analyse the talk that goes on between doctors and their patients in the clinic. I could analyse the texts of the research literature on M.E. and show how that works as a kind of argument between scientists [see Horton-Salway, 1998]. I could even examine the texts of official reports to see how the meanings of the categories M.E. and CFS are constructed in different accounts. For example, take a look at the next two extracts, Extract 20 and Extract 21, which are taken from a report published by the Royal Colleges of Physicians, Psychiatrists and General Practitioners.

5.1 More participants' categories: M.E. or CFS?

Extract 20

> The joint working group's report firmly dismisses the term M.E. on three grounds. First 'encephalomyelitis' [inflammation of the brain and spinal cord] describes a distinct pathological process absent from the conditions included within the term M.E. Second, the term M.E. implies a single diagnostic entity, which is unlikely and unproved. Third, it ignores the psychological dimension.
>
> (RCP, 1996: 44)

Given that the whole topic area of M.E. is so controversial, it is interesting to see how this report has been constructed in order to *legitimate* a set of claims about the nature of the illness. Note also how the grounds for dismissing the term M.E. are authoritatively worked up as a three-part list. The first and second points dismiss the existence of a physical diagnostic entity and the third point constructs "*the* psychological dimension" of the illness as an accepted 'given' by means of the definite article. The packaging of a contentious claim as 'given' information is a common feature of discourse in such settings as law courts, advertising, journalism and propaganda, as well as in mundane conversation (Edwards, 1997). In this case, "the psychological dimension" is packaged as a taken-for-granted and legitimate definition of the illness. The following extract explains why CFS is the preferred term.

Extract 21

> The most appropriate term for this syndrome is chronic fatigue syndrome (CFS), which is accurate and free from unproven aetiological claims.
>
> (RCP, 1996: 5)

Here, the term CFS is claimed to represent the symptoms of the illness accurately and neutrally in a way that is "free from unproven aetiological claims". In other words, they are claiming that the term does not implicate causality. In other words CFS merely *describes* a 'syndrome' (collection of symptoms) and therefore performs no attributional work whatsoever. However, from earlier analyses we have established that *descriptions* are never neutral, although people might *claim* that they are. And indeed, on closer inspection of the literature one finds that it is the different disease definitions *themselves* that result in the categorization of collections of symptoms into CFS or M.E. The categories of M.E. or CFS have themselves been defined by reference to two different collections of core and optional 'pick and mix' symptoms. These alternative sets of criteria differ in certain ways from one another, notably in the extent to which they include, or exclude psychiatric symptomology (see Holmes *et al.*, 1988; Sharpe *et al.*, 1991). Neither category can, therefore, be seen as aetiologically neutral, they both do some constructive work, which in this case relates to the *in situ* authorship of the *meaning* of the illness.[7] Given the on-going controversial status of the illness and the lack of consensus between different factions, this should not come as any great surprise!

Dialogue 6

STUDENT   While we're on the subject of **authorship**, and *before* you sneak off and write the References section =

MHS   = A::h yes I ⌈er

STUDENT   ⌊about these dialogues and your *brazen* appropriation of my voice. You're *even* trying to make it look like a 'real' conversation now, with pauses, overlaps and everything!

MHS   ((*fake uncomfortable silence*)) er (.) well I wanted to ⌈er

STUDENT   ⌊And another thing! I'm just a *fact*-constructing device in sheep's clothing. I work to summarize all your main points and ask all the 'right' questions. By the end of the chapter I even *sound* like you! Edwards and Potter [1992: 172–3] might say I'm an example of the 'usual slightly embarrassing fake conversation like Mike's stuff and the Woolgar book' [Mulkay, 1985; Woolgar, 1988b]. Apparently these **fake dialogues** 'remind readers that formal scientific texts are a particular literary convention'.

MHS   Do you mean like my conventional summary of the M.E. literature?

STUDENT   That *sort* of thing yes, but I'm also referring to the way that most of your chapter is designed, using all the usual introductions, content sections with headings, data analyses and teaching points. According to Jonathan Potter, these fake dialogues are not just a reflexive way of drawing attention to the constructed nature of your own writing, "they can turn into mini essays – you just end up sneaking in some more of the main text by the back door".

MHS   I *thought* I detected a draft!

                 (.)

STUDENT   But *who* is the author?

Conclusion

The research goals for the version of discursive psychology worked up in this chapter are theoretical as well as analytical. In other words, the analysis of identities, minds and selves entails the re-working of 'psychological' concepts as discursive products, rather than being treated as cognitive entities or processes (Edwards, 1997). This means that we have been able to step outside the framework of cognitivism and ask different kinds of research questions, such as the ones I have addressed in this chapter. For example, how do people construct their own and other people's identities in talk, and how are these accounts of 'self' used to support their own constructions of events such as the causes of illness? This involves looking at how 'the mind' is talked up in people's accounts and how that is related to identity talk. Rather than asking questions like 'how does illness affect people's identities?' we can ask 'how are identities worked up for particular discursive purposes, for example, to justify or blame?'. Such practices can be seen as a part of mundane everyday talk, and also as a part of how patients construct illness stories in interviews, or part of how health professionals justify their explanations and make them credible.

Through the worked examples of this chapter and its accompanying dialogues, I have tried to show how one kind of discursive psychology, the discursive action model, can be applied to the analysis of all kinds of discourse. To this end, I have included extracts from interviews with GPs, the illness narratives of M.E. sufferers and carers, 'naturally occurring' discourse from a self-help group setting and from a TV talk show. I have also tried to draw attention to the constructive practices entailed in the production of texts, such as research literature, official reports, and my own writing of this chapter. The dialogues that represent MHS's discussions with the imaginary student are designed not only to allow you to pause and think more deeply about some of the issues raised in the analysis, but they also invite you into the process of authoring meaning, which is itself an on-goingly negotiated and constructive practice between writer and readers. The inclusion of these 'alternative literary forms' (MacMillan, 1996) is not so much a 'licence to invent dialogue', nor is it intended to undermine the status of my account by making it into a fiction. Rather, it is a way to draw the reader's attention to their own engagement in the processes of authorship (although the inclusion of the reader's 'voice' is itself reflexively contested in the final dialogue). More often than not, we encounter the traditional scientific text "with its authority fused to it" (Bakhtin, 1981, cited in Wertsch, 1990, reproduced in Wetherell *et al.*, 2001). The construction of invented dialogue not only invites the reader into the text, but also displays the dialogism inherent in one's writing. The text is the site of **dialogical reality construction**. Like any other discursive context, that is where it all happens. As Bakhtin pointed out, "the word in language is half someone else's" (1981: 293–4); and the utterance is always addressed to someone. Such constructive practices and dialogic processes can be less than apparent in traditional texts which are more likely to be in the business of constructing factuality and authority than de-constructing it. I appreciate, however, that many readers and authors will not have been persuaded by these arguments, and the inclusion of alternative forms of writing will appear to them somewhat contrived and irritating. I celebrate such disagreement as one kind of dialogic response.

Where, then, can we position this chapter in relation to other versions of discourse analysis? It is clear that different kinds of discursive psychology share **a constructionist theory of meaning** but they take that in different directions. For example in the chapter that follows, Nigel Edley says that he 'steps outside the boundaries' of the kind of discursive psychology that is influenced more by the epistemological and analytic commitments of ethnomethodology and conversation analysis (CA). As pointed out in the introduction, and discussed in Dialogues 1, 2 and 5, CA involves a more fine-grained analysis of discourse, in which 'social context' would be conceptualized as a situated, interactive and local matter, rather than looking to a wider cultural or historical context for analytic inspiration. Much of my analysis fits into that 'fine-grained' mould and resonates with Schegloff's claims about an "object of enquiry furnished internally with its own constitutive sense". He points out that "talk-in-interaction has an internally grounded reality of its own that we can aspire to get at analytically" (Schegloff, 1997: 171). It is not so much that the 'wider social context' is treated as an irrelevance but, rather, that the search for such context would lead us only to the analysis of yet more situated reality construction.

Further Reading

For a review of reflexivity and examples of research that use alternative literary forms in social science:

Ashmore, M. (1989) *The Reflexive Thesis: Wrighting Sociology of Scientific Knowledge*, Chicago, University of Chicago Press.

MacMillan, K. (1996) 'Trance scripts: the poetics of a reflexive guide to hypnosis and trance talk', *PhD Thesis*, Loughborough University.

Mushakoji, S. (1999) 'The process of knowledge construction: a triple parallel wrighting of science, sociology of scientific knowledge and a candidate PhD Thesis', *PhD Thesis*, Loughborough University.

Woolgar, S. (ed.) (1988a) *Knowledge and Reflexivity: New Frontiers in the Sociology of Science*, London and Beverly Hills, CA: Sage.

For a discourse analysis of scientists' talk:

Gilbert, N. G. and Mulkay, M. (1984) *Opening Pandora's Box: A Sociological Analysis of Scientists' Discourse*, Cambridge, Cambridge University Press.

For a useful review of narrative analysis in health psychology:

Murray, M. (1997) 'A narrative approach to health psychology', *Journal of Health Psychology,* vol.2, pp.9–20.

For a Foucauldian analysis of identity and illness talk:

Eccleston, C. De C., Williams, A. and Stainton-Rogers, W. (1997) 'Patients' and professionals' understandings of the causes of chronic pain: blame, responsibility and identity protection', *Social Science and Medicine,* vol.45, pp.699–709.

Compare this with an analysis of the dilemmatics of illness talk in:

Radley, A. and Billig, M. (1996) 'Accounts of health and illness: dilemmas and representations', *Sociology of Health and Illness,* vol.18, pp.220–40.

For a review of discourse analysis as applied to health research:

Yardley, L. (ed.) (1997) *Material Discourses of Health and Illness*, London, Routledge.

Acknowledgement

My interest in the use of fictional dialogue as an 'alternative literary form' has been inspired by the work of Katie MacMillan, and Sumiko Mushakoji. Both authors have produced creative and reflexive doctoral theses supervised by Malcolm Ashmore (author of *The Reflexive Thesis*). MacMillan's work provides an accomplished and poetic example of reflexive writing on the topic of hypnosis, while Mushakoji provides an example of the reflexive analysis of scientists' talk about discovery in which she deconstructs her own analytic practices.

References

Abell, J. and Stokoe, E. (1999) ' "I take full responsibility, I take some responsibility, I'll take half of it but no more than that": Princess Diana and the negotiation of blame in the Panorama interview, *Discourse and Society*, vol.10, pp.297–319.

Anderson, N. (correspondence) *British Medical Journal* (1994) May, p.1298.

Antaki, C. and Widdicombe, S. (eds) (1998) *Identities in Talk*, London, Sage.

Ashmore, M. (1989) *The Reflexive Thesis: Wrighting Sociology of Scientific Knowledge*, Chicago, University of Chicago Press.

Atkinson, J.M. and Drew, P. (1979) *Order in Court, the Organization of Verbal Interaction in Judicial Settings*, London, MacMillan.

Atkinson, J.M. and Heritage, J.C. (eds) (1984) *Structures of Social Action: Studies in Conversation Analysis*, Cambridge, Cambridge University Press.

Austin, J.L. (1962) *How to Do Things with Words*, Oxford, Clarendon Press.

Barthes, R. (1974) *S/Z*, London, Jonathan Cape.

Billig, M. (1997) 'Discursive, rhetorical and ideological messages' in McGarty, C. and Haslam. A. (eds) *The Message of Social Psychology*, Oxford, Blackwell.

Billig, M., Condor, S., Edwards, D., Gane, M., Middleton, D. and Radley, A.R. (1988) *Idealogical Dilemmas*, London, Sage.

British Medical Journal (1970) Correspondence, January.

British Medical Journal (1978) Leading Article, June, pp.1436–7.

Button, G. and Lee, J.R.E. (1987) *Talk and Social Organisation*, Clevedon, Multilingual Matters.

Charmaz, K. (1983) 'Loss of self: a fundamental form of suffering in the chronically ill', *Sociology of Health and Illness*, vol.5, pp.168–95.

David, A., Wessely, S. and Pelosi, A. (1988) 'Postviral fatigue: time for a new approach', *British Medical Journal,* vol.296, pp.696–9.

Derrida, J. (1977) 'Limited inc abc ....', *Glyph,* vol.2, pp.162–254.

Drew, P. (1990) 'Strategies in the contest between lawyers and witnesses' in Levi, J.N. and Walker, A.G. (eds) *Language in the Judicial Process*, New York, Plenum.

Edwards, D. (1997) *Discourse and Cognition*, London, Sage.

Edwards, D. and Middleton, D. (1986) 'Joint remembering: constructing an account of shared experience through conversational discourse', *Discourse Processes*, vol.9, pp.423–59.

Edwards, D. and Potter, J. (1992) *Discursive Psychology*, London, Sage.

Foucault, M. (1980) *Power/Knowledge: Selected Interviews and Other Writings 1972–77*, trans. C. Gordon, Hemel Hempstead, Wheatsheaf.

Galpine, J.F. and Brady, C. (1957) 'Benign Encephalomyelitis', *The Lancet*, April, pp.757–8.

Garfinkel, H. (1967) *Studies in Ethnomethodology*, Englewood Cliffs: NJ, Prentice-Hall.

Gergen, K.J. (1994) *Realities and Relationships, Soundings in Social Construction*, Cambridge, Mass:, Harvard University Press.

Gilbert, N.G. and Mulkay, M. (1984) *Opening Pandora's Box: A Sociological Analysis of Scientists' Discourse*, Cambridge, Cambridge University Press.

Gill, C.H. (1970) 'Epidemic medicine', *British Medical Journal*, vol.1, p.299.

Grice, H.P. (1975) 'Logic and conversation' in Cole, P. and Morgan, J. (eds) *Syntax and Semantics 3: Speech Acts*, New York, Academic Press.

Hall, S. (2001) 'Foucault: Power, Knowledge and Discourse' in Wetherell, M., Taylor, S. and Yates, S.J. (eds), *Discourse Theory and Practice: A Reader*, London, Sage in association with The Open University.

Heritage, J.C. (1984) *Garfinkel and Ethnomethodology*, Cambridge, Polity.

Heritage, J. (2001) 'Goffman, Garfinkel and Conversation Analysis' in Wetherell, M., Taylor, S. and Yates, S.J. (eds), *Discourse Theory and Practice: A Reader*, London, Sage in association with The Open University.

Herzlich, C. (1973) *Health and Illness: A Social Psychological Analysis*, trans. D. Graham. London, Academic Press.

Holmes, G.P., Kaplan, J.E., Gantz, N.M. and Komeroff, A.L. (1988) 'CFS: a working case definition', *Annals of Internal Medicine*, vol.108, pp.387–9, International Federation of M.E. Associations *et al.* (1993), London, Criteria.

Horton-Salway, M. (1998) 'Mind and body in the discursive construction of M.E.: a struggle for authorship of an illness', *PhD Thesis*, Loughborough University.

Jefferson, G. (1990) 'List construction as a task and resource' in Psathas, G. (ed.) *Interaction Competence*, Lanham: MD, University Press of America.

Jenkins, R. and Mowbray, J. (eds) (1991) *Post-Viral Syndrome*, Chichester, Wiley.

Lancet (1956) 'A new clinical entity?', vol.1, pp.789.

Levinson, S.C. (1983) *Pragmatics*, Cambridge, Cambridge University Press.

Maybin, J. (2001) 'Language, struggle and voice: the Bakhtinian/Voloshinov writings' in Wetherell, M., Taylor, S. and Yates, S.J. (eds) *Discourse Theory and Practice: A Reader*, London, Sage in association with the Open University.

MacMillan, K. (1995) 'Giving voice: the participant takes issue', *Feminism and Psychology,* vol.5, pp.547–52.

MacMillan, K. (1996) 'Trance scripts: the poetics of a reflexive guide to hypnosis and trance talk', *PhD Thesis*, Loughborough University.

MacMillan, K. and Edwards, D. (1999) 'Who killed the princess: Description and blame in the British press, *Discourse Studies*, vol.1, pp.191–214.

McEvedy, C.P. and Beard, A.W. (1970) 'Royal Free epidemic of 1955: a reconsideration, *British Medical Journal*, vol.1, pp.7–11.

Moss, P.D. and McEvedy, C.P. (1966) *British Medical Journal*, vol.2, p.1295.

Mulkay, M. (1985) *The Word and the World: Explorations in the Form of Sociological Analysis*, London, Allen and Unwin.

Mushakoji, S. (1999) 'The process of knowledge construction: a triple parallel wrighting of science, sociology of scientific knowledge and a candidate PhD Thesis', *PhD Thesis*, Loughborough University.

Potter, J. (1996) *Representing Reality: Discourse, Rhetoric and Social Construction*, London, Sage.

Potter, J. (2001) 'Wittgenstein and Austin: Developments in linguistic philosphy' in Wetherell, M., Taylor, S. and Yates, S.J. (eds), *Discourse Theory and Practice: A Reader*, London, Sage in association with The Open University.

Potter, J. and Mulkay, M. (1985) 'Scientists' interview talk: interviews as a technique for revealing participants' interpretative practices' in Brenner, M., Brown, J. and Canter, D. (eds) *The Research Interview: Uses and Approaches*, London, Academic Press.

Potter, J. and Wetherell, M. (1987) *Discourse and Social Psychology: Beyond Attitudes and Behaviour*, London, Sage,

Robinson, I. (1990) 'Personal narratives, social careers and medical courses: analysing life trajectories in autobiographies of people with multiple sclerosis', *Social Science and Medicine*, vol.30, pp.1173–86.

Royal Colleges of Physicians, Psychiatrists, and General Practitioners (RCP) (1996) *Chronic Fatigue Syndrome*, Report of a joint working group of the Royal Colleges of Physicians, Psychiatrists, and General Practitioners, CR54.

Sacks, H. (1989) 'Harvey Sacks – Lectures 1964–1965' (ed. G. Jefferson) *Special Issue of Human Studies,* vol.12, pp.183–404.

Sacks, H. (1992) *Lectures on Conversation*, vols. I and II, edited by G. Jefferson, Oxford, Basil Blackwell.

Sacks, H., Schegloff, E.A. and Jefferson, G. (1974) 'A simplest systematics for the organisation of turn-taking for conversation', *Language*, vol.50, pp.696–735.

Schegloff, E. (1997) 'Whose text? Whose context?', *Discourse and Society*, vol.8, pp.165–87.

Searle, J.R. (1969) *Speech Acts*, Cambridge, Cambridge University Press.

Shapiro, M. (1988) *The Politics of Representation: Writing Practices in Biography, Photography and Policy Analysis*, Madison: WI, University of Wisconsin Press.

Shapiro, M. (1989) 'Textualizing global politics' in Der Derian, J. and Shapiro, M. (eds) *International/Intertextual Relations*, Lexington, Mass.: Lexington Books.

Sharpe, M.C., Archard, L. and Banatvala, J. (1991) 'A report – chronic fatigue syndrome: guidelines for research', *Journal of the Royal Society of Medicine*, vol.84, pp.118–21.

Smith, D. (1978) 'K is mentally ill: The anatomy of a factual account', *Sociology*, vol.12, pp.23–53.

Speer, S. (in press 2001) 'Reconsidering the concept of "hegemonic masculinity": a discursive and conversation analytic approach', *Feminism and Psychology*, vol.11.

Tannen, D. (1989) *Talking Voices: Repetition, Dialogue and Imagery in Conversational Discourse*, Cambridge, Cambridge University Press.

Wertsch, J. (1990) *Voices of the Mind*, London, Harvester Wheatsheaf.

Wessely, S. (1990) 'Old wine in new bottles: neurasthenia and "ME" ', *Psychological Medicine*, vol.20, pp.35–53.

Westcare (1994) Report from The National Task Force on Chronic Fatigue Syndrome (CFS), Post-Viral Fatigue Syndrome (PVFS), Myalgic Encephalomyelitis (ME).

Wetherell, M. (2001) 'Themes in Discourse Research: The Case of Diana' in Wetherell, M., Taylor, S. and Yates, S.J. (eds), *Discourse Theory and Practice: A Reader*, London, Sage in association with The Open University.

Wetherell, M. and Potter, J. (1992) *Mapping the Language of Racism: Discourse and the Legitimation of Exploitation*, London, Harvester Wheatsheaf.

Wetherell, M., Taylor, S. and Yates, S.J. (eds) (2001) *Discourse Theory and Practice: A Reader*, London, Sage in association with the Open University.

Widdicombe, S. and Wooffitt, R. (1995) *The Language of Youth Subcultures: Social Identity in Action*, London, Harvester Wheatsheaf.

Wittgenstein, L. (1953/1958) *Philosophical Investigations*, Trans. G.E.M., Anscombe, Oxford, Blackwell (2nd edn) p.1958.

Woolgar, S. (1988) *Science: The Very Idea*, London, Tavistock.

Notes

[1] Fictional dialogues are part of a tradition of reflexive studies that deconstruct their own textual methods of knowledge construction. (For a further discussion of this, see Shapiro, 1989, reproduced as Reading Twenty-three in Wetherell *et al.* 2001; other examples are Ashmore, 1989; MacMillan, 1996; Woolgar and Ashmore, 1988.) Although discursive psychology employs a deconstructive approach to the analysis of data, and acknowledges its own text as part of knowledge construction (see Potter and Edwards, 1992: 172), my own approach in this chapter leans further towards the use of dialogue as a way of *engaging* the reader in the dialogic process of authorship itself. See Maybin's discussion of Bakhtinian dialogism and Wertsch's (1990) discussion of

multivoicedness in Wetherell *et al.*, 2001. Although Bakhtinian dialogism has been one of the influences on discursive psychology, my analysis does not buy into a 'theory of mind'.

[2]Nosology is a branch of medical science dealing with the classification of disease.

[3] Note also the discussion of 'the role of the analyst' and 'what counts as context?' in Wetherell (2001). Compare this with my references to Schegloff (1997) in the concluding section of this chapter.

[4] Compare this with my comments on the classification of versions of discursive psychology in this volume e.g. p.147 and pp.182–3.

[5] Cognitive behavioural therapy (as applied to illness) is based on the idea that people might have dysfunctional beliefs about the nature of their illness and how to manage its symptoms. In the case of M.E./CFS, this is clearly controversial since there have been different opinions on the relationship between activity and worsening of fatigue symptoms.

[6] Indexicality is one of the fundamental precepts of ethnomethodology, whereby descriptions "are to be understood by reference to where and when etc. they occur" (Heritage, 1984: 140).

[7] Consider the authorship issues raised by the analyses in this chapter. The ownership of meaning can also be discussed in relation to the writings of Bakhtin who stressed the processes of dialogue and unfinalizability of meaning (see Wertsch, 1990, reproduced as reading Sixteen in Wetherell *et al.*, 2001). Authorship and the problem of 'speaking for others' is also a central concern in all kinds of reflexive analyses (e.g. MacMillan, 1995), including the analyses in this chapter.

CHAPTER FIVE

Analysing Masculinity: Interpretative Repertoires, Ideological Dilemmas and Subject Positions

Nigel Edley

Introduction

As is clearly evidenced by this volume, there is no simple way of defining or understanding discourse analysis. It has become an ever-broadening church, an umbrella term for a wide variety of different analytic principles and practices. At first sight *discursive psychology* might be construed as one of those separate strands, thought of, perhaps, as the application of discourse theory to the classic questions of psychology. Yet in reality, discursive psychology is itself a complex field, underwritten by a multiplicity of different, sometimes even contradictory, ideas and arguments. The overall aim of this chapter is to introduce you to another of the approaches that competes within the arena of discursive psychology. In the sections that follow we will be looking at some of the tensions and contradictions that exist between different styles of discourse analysis and we will also be encountering some of the concepts that stand at the centre of what one might call *critical* discursive psychology. However, rather than trying to deal with these debates in the abstract, I intend to discuss them in relation to a particular body of data or, more specifically, in relation to an on-going research project which looks at the discursive reproduction of men and masculinity.

In the first part of this chapter, then, I want to talk about some of the theoretical tensions which characterize discursive psychology, paying particular attention to how the approach described below both borrows and departs from other forms of discourse analytical work (see Wetherell, 1998). Then I want to look at how this body of ideas and concepts can be applied in such a way as to provide a powerful and distinctive contribution to social scientists' understanding of men and masculinity (see also Edley and Wetherell, 1996; 1997; 1999; Wetherell and Edley, 1998; 1999). Following a brief introduction to the background to this research, my main task will be to look at how we can go about analysing some data from the project. In order to do this I will be introducing you to three of the concepts which lie at the heart of critical discursive psychology: interpretative repertoires, ideological dilemmas and subject positions. The chapter will then close with the presentation of some more empirical data with which you can practise your new-found analytical skills.

1   Mapping discursive psychology

As we have seen in the previous chapter, discursive psychology differs from more traditional psychological approaches in placing language, or discourse, centre stage. Whereas in the past, psychologists have typically seen language as a *resource*, providing clues as to what is going on inside people's minds or brains, discursive psychology takes language as its *topic*, examining the ways in which people talk about – or construct – things like attitudes, memories and emotions (Potter and Wetherell, 1987; Zimmerman and Pollner, 1971 – see also Taylor, Chapter One in this volume). Discursive psychologists have drawn attention to the fact that when people express an attitude or recount an episode from the past, they are usually doing a lot more than just retrieving a stock of information. They have demonstrated that the way these accounts are produced is highly context-specific and that speakers can be seen to accomplish a wide variety of social actions via these different forms of talk.

This concern with the **action orientation** (Heritage, 1984) of people's discourse is a feature common to the version of discursive psychology outlined within this chapter and the previous chapter. Like Mary Horton-Salway, I want to draw attention to the interactional business that is performed in and through the production of descriptions or accounts. However, the scope of this chapter will be broader, stepping outside the boundary-lines that Horton-Salway (and others in that mould – e.g. Antaki and Widdicombe, 1998; Edwards, 1997; Edwards and Potter, 1992; Widdicombe and Wooffitt, 1995) impose upon themselves. More specifically, it will 'violate' a central conversation analytic-inspired imperative; namely, that we must at all times restrict our analytic attention to what is going on, for the participants themselves, within any given interactional sequence.

Broadly speaking, the version of discursive psychology advanced within this chapter insists upon seeing all such sequences as embedded within some kind of historical context (Wetherell, 1998). It recognizes that when people talk, they do so using a lexicon or repertoire of terms which has been provided for them by history. A language culture may supply a whole range of ways of talking about or constructing an object or event, and speakers are therefore bound to make choices. However, the options aren't always equal. Some constructions or formulations will be more 'available' than others; they are easier to say. This is because some ways of understanding the world can become culturally dominant or **hegemonic** (Gramsci, 1971). That is, they can assume the status of facts, taken for granted as true or accurate descriptions of the world. One of the central aims of this more critical form of discursive psychology is to analyse this process of normalization/naturalization and to enquire about whose interests are best served by different discursive formulations (see also Foucault, 1980; Mouffe, 1992; Shapiro, 1992).

In summary, critical discursive psychology aims to capture the paradoxical relationship that exists between discourse and the speaking subject. It acknowledges that people are, at the same time, both the products and the producers of discourse (Billig, 1991), the masters and the slaves of language (Barthes, 1982). It aims to examine not only how identities are produced on and for particular occasions, but also how history or culture both impinge upon and are transformed by those performances. It draws attention to the productive capacities of discourse, showing how it comes to structure both subjective experience and our sense of who we are.

In the sections that follow I want to develop these arguments in relation to research on men and masculinity. I will begin by attempting to clarify what is meant by masculinity as discourse before moving on to look in some detail at the discursive reproduction of masculinity.

2   Masculinity as discourse

In recent years there has been a high and sustained level of interest in issues to do with men and masculinity. As well as television programmes, newspapers and magazine articles, each year has seen the publication of a string of academic titles, spanning a wide array of disciplinary fields including anthropology (Cornwall and Lindisfarne, 1994), psychology (Scher *et al.*, 1993), sociology (Connell, 1995), linguistics (Johnson and Meinhof, 1997) and cultural studies (Berger *et al.*, 1995). Yet in amongst this diversity there is a growing consensus that language lies at the heart of understanding men and masculinity, with many writers now insisting that masculinity (and gender more generally) is something constructed in and through discourse.

However, because there are a number of different definitions of discourse or the 'discursive' in current circulation (see Jaworski and Coupland, 1999; Macdonell, 1987; Potter *et al.*, 1990) it becomes necessary to specify what one means by these concepts. In this chapter I shall be using a broader definition than Mary Horton-Salway developed for Chapter Four, one which encompasses a whole range of different symbolic activities, including styles of dress, patterns of consumption, ways of moving, as well as talking. Within contemporary British culture, for example, I would see masculinity as being made up of things like watching football, drinking pints of beer at the pub and trying to get away from the traffic lights faster than the cars in the next lane. It is part and parcel of putting up shelves, fixing the toaster and digging over the vegetable patch. All of these things (and many more) are viewed as being typical of men within our culture. This does not mean, of course, that all men will do them or even that they are the sole preserve of men (after all, plenty of shelves are put up by women). Rather, they are understood as *normative* forms of behaviour, the sum total of the **practices** and characteristics which we conventionally associate with men.

Discursive psychology's challenge to more traditional understandings of men and masculinity lies in the *status* it accords activities such as beer drinking and brawling. In the past they have often been seen as *symptoms* of masculinity; the by-products of something that is both prior to and more fundamental than the activities themselves. Many people today remain convinced that gender is in some way rooted in biology, such that when men race off from the traffic lights, for example, it is often attributed to an aggressive and competitive *nature* inscribed at the level of genes or hormones. Of course, within the human and social sciences there is a long established challenge to this kind of biological reductionism (see Edley and Wetherell, 1995, for a review). Amongst others, psychoanalysts, sociologists and psychologists have argued that people are not born masculine or feminine,

Discourse versus practice

It has been traditional, within the social sciences, to make a distinction between words and deeds, or between discourse and social practice. In discursive psychology, however, this is often considered a false distinction (or dualism). In drawing upon the arguments of people like Wittgenstein and Austin, discursive psychologists point out that language is *itself* a form of practice. It is used to *do* things, like giving orders, making promises and sealing bets. Still, some constructionists want to draw a distinction between discursive and 'material' practices (e.g. Parker, 1992; 1998). For example, they would see the theft of a car as consisting of two different orders of 'reality'; the car (and its removal) belonging to the material realm and the act of 'theft' belonging to the symbolic (i.e. it would be seen as a *constructed* reality – a consequence of viewing the event through a particular moral-judicial framework – see Foucault, 1977). Yet once again this distinction breaks down when it is put under pressure. For instance, the fact that a perpetrator's status as a 'thief' is constructed via a set of texts or discourses (e.g. the magistrate's pronouncement and the resulting criminal 'record') does little to diminish the damaging material effects of being so described. Those texts alone could cost the offender a good deal of time and money. Likewise, a car is much more than just a physical hunk of machinery. For as Barthes (1973) has ably demonstrated, cars have a strong mythical quality; they are important symbols of status and power. Indeed, it is precisely this quality of cars, as objects of desire, that renders them so vulnerable to being stolen in the first place. We should see that discourse and practice are inextricably bound up with one another.

but *become* gendered as they grow up in society. They have suggested that, like the making of a jelly or blancmange, the characters of new-born infants are initially quite fluid such that they can take on the shape or form of whatever 'mould' they are poured into. Socialization theories imply that it is only gradually that people begin to solidify into particular sorts of personalities. Once formed, we might 'wobble' a bit if pushed but, generally speaking, it is assumed that we will resist attempts to alter what we have become.

In contrast, a discursive psychologist would insist that gender is neither something into which we are born nor something that we eventually become. In terms of the same metaphor, we would argue that the jelly never sets. We claim that people's gender identities remain relatively fluid, capable of adapting to the particular social settings or contexts in which people find themselves. At the heart of a discursive psychological analysis are the practices listed earlier (i.e. fixing the toaster, digging the vegetable patch, and so on), for here gender comes to be understood as something that is 'done' or **accomplished** in the course of social interaction. So where traditional psychological analyses have seen men's tinkering with cars and their repeated conversations about beer and football as *footprints* and set out to track the animal that produced them, the discursive psychologist insists that these words and deeds *are the beast itself*. Masculinity is viewed as a *consequence* rather than a cause of such activities.

3 The discursive reproduction of masculinity

There can be little doubt that the recent proliferation of discourse-based accounts of gender is due, in no small part, to the fact that it constitutes such a powerful challenge to the essentialism and reductionism of more traditional understandings. The fact that discursive psychologists see masculinity and femininity not as permanent or fixed, but as constantly remade on a moment-to-moment basis provides not just a radical destabilizing of the assumption that gender is something that is natural, inevitable or God-given, but also a much more positive sense of how change may be effected. Transforming the *status quo* becomes understood as a matter of challenging and changing discourses, encouraging people to tell different stories about themselves and others. No longer can people hide behind the defence that they are just 'doing what comes naturally'.

At the same time, however, we are wary of seeming to exaggerate the ease with which such changes can be made. Reconstructing identities is not a simple matter of voluntary action (Eagleton, 1991); being a man is not something that a person can accept one day and refuse the next. When it comes to telling stories about gender identity, it is *not* a case of anything goes.

Activity 1

© *Corbis/Bettman/UPI*

Look carefully at the photograph. How are we to understand the scene? More specifically, what are we to make of the statement on the placards? What are these people doing? Is this a graphic, even prototypical, example of the construction of masculinity? In other words, does it depict people in the very act of 'accomplishing' themselves as men?

Discussion

A detailed examination reveals this scene as depicting a complex discursive act. At the time the picture was taken (around the mid to late 1960s), the statement "I AM A MAN" could be interpreted not just as a claim to masculinity but also as either a claim to humanity or to the status of adulthood (see Hoch, 1979, and Franklin, 1984, on the representation of black men as sub-human and/or child-like). Nevertheless, the photograph certainly illustrates the point that identities are not secured merely by proclamation. The fact that the men are campaigning or protesting tells us immediately that the accomplishment of an identity is far from a solitary exercise. Identities have to be negotiated or won. The statement "I AM A MAN" is part of just such a **negotiation**; it is an attempt to get a matter of opinion or belief elevated to an incontrovertible matter of fact (see Woolgar, 1988). Establishing one's identity as a man is a messy and complicated co-production. It is fashioned through social interaction, subject to negotiation and (as indicated by the row of men with guns) inextricably bound up with the exercise of **power**.

Indeed the centrality of power in the social construction of masculinity comes even more clearly into focus if we think about *why* the men in this picture were campaigning. According to commentators such as Franklin (1984), Wallace (1979) and Clatterbaugh (1990), many black American men during the 1960s felt angered by the structural barriers which prevented them from fulfilling the traditional masculine role. In particular, they resented the fact that they were denied the kind of work that would allow them to become the major breadwinners and heads of their respective households. We should realize, therefore, that the demand to be recognized as a man is not a purely symbolic issue. It is not just that people want to be thought of as men. What is at stake are the social, political and economic privileges that are associated with that symbolic status. Indeed, insofar as the practices of working and bringing home a wage are themselves constituent elements of being a man within many Western cultures, these two claims are coextensive with one another. In other words, they are part and parcel of the same thing.

There are restrictions that apply to the construction of gender identities. As we have just seen, the free-play of possibilities is certainly limited by what others will agree to or allow. People may be able to experiment with new versions or definitions of masculinity, but there is no guarantee that these will be accepted. Instead, men may rely upon much more tried and tested constructions; those versions of masculinity which they know from experience work. For many years men have learned, for example, that it pays for them to be forthright and assertive. They have discovered that society treats them better if they put a brave face on their hurts and disappointments (Cohen, 1990; Jackson, 1990; Seidler, 1989). In a sense, therefore, the historical reproduction of certain forms of masculinity is not so much a matter of 'doing what comes naturally' as doing what works best.

Yet the reproduction of more conventional forms of masculinity is not just a reflection of their functionality. And neither are the limits on identity construction always imposed from 'outside'. For instance, it has often been noted that, within Western cultures, men tend to avoid constructing themselves as emotional beings. Without doubt this has often been in their own best interests (see Seidler, 1989; 1994), but there is also evidence to suggest that men might find some difficulty in constructing themselves as emotional even when the situation 'demands' it. For example, Tannen (1991) tells a story of a man, who, having been advised by a marriage guidance counsellor to be more expressive of his feelings for his wife, took to washing her car! From the point of view of discursive psychology, it appears that when it comes to expressing certain feelings and emotions, many men are literally *out of practice.* In other words, 'emotion talk' represents a form of discursive activity which is not a part of many men's everyday, practical routine.

A critical discursive psychology recognizes that, as a way of being in the world, masculinity becomes something of a routine or habit (see Bourdieu's concept of *habitus* – 1977). Masculinity may well exist as a set of discursive practices which inform the way men speak, feel and think, but it is important to understand that many of these practices become so utterly familiar, so thoroughly routinized and automatic, that most men (and women) mistake history for nature. Men don't typically have to think about looking and sounding like men. When they spread themselves out on the sofa, for example, they don't have to concentrate upon the careful placement of their limbs (see Henley, 1986; Wex, 1979). They just plonk themselves down and make themselves comfortable. For most of the time the vast majority of men remain completely oblivious to the ways in which masculinity has inscribed itself upon their bodies. They fail to see how it has infiltrated their muscles and moulded their bones. And yet, even if they were to see the connection, it would be no easy matter to transform these bodily habits (Bourdieu, 1977).

Discursive psychologists (e.g. Edley, 1993; Edwards and Potter, 1992; Potter and Wetherell, 1987; Shotter and Gergen, 1989) and cultural anthropologists (Geertz, 1973; 1993) have tried to demonstrate that identities are more fleeting, incoherent and fragmented than many of us would have believed. They have identified the assumption that people are unique, self-contained motivational and cognitive universes as part of an 'Enlightenment myth'. At the same time, however, they acknowledge the productive (or constructive) power of that myth. They recognize that most people in the Western world are invested in a philosophical tradition which values personal integrity and the consistency of identity over time. Westerners are very keen to be seen, by themselves as well as others, as some*one* in particular. This explains why, when people are encouraged or forced to see the contradictions in their own identity 'projects', they often feel defensive or embarrassed. The ideology of the Cartesian subject works, as Foucault (1972) would say, to construct the object of which it speaks. It has become a socially or discursively constructed reality.

Summary

- Masculinity is a discursive accomplishment rather than a natural fact.

- It is something that is done collectively or jointly with others.

- Gender identities are typically negotiated and involve the operation of power.

- Men are not free to construct themselves as they wish. To some extent, it is their cultural history which determines the kinds of identities they can assume.

- Masculinity may be a performance, but it is one that often becomes habitual or routinized.

Implications

There are a number of implications that follow from this summary in terms of how we should go about a discursive psychology of men and masculinity. Firstly, we should be in no doubt about where to start, for if masculinity is reproduced and transformed in and through discourse then, as in Chapter Four, we need to focus our analytic attention upon people's talk. Moreover, as in that chapter, we need an approach that is capable of analysing conversations or dialogue, for it is precisely here that masculinities should be constructed and negotiated. Secondly, our approach needs to be sensitive to the cultural history of masculinity. It needs to be able to identify the various resources that society makes available for the construction of masculine identities. The beauty of being able to do this is that, in seeing what forms of masculinity are 'on offer', we start to get an insight into the kinds of choices that are being made. The third and final requirement is for an approach which is sensitive to the operation of power. We need to look at whose interests are best served by prevailing definitions of masculinity and to examine how they are maintained, resisted and transformed.

   Discursive psychology meets these requirements via a number of key concepts; namely, **interpretative repertoires**, **ideological dilemmas** and **subject positions**. A good deal of the remainder of this chapter will be dedicated to explaining and illustrating how these concepts work. However, as mentioned in the Introduction, I do not want to do this in the abstract. Rather, I intend to show how they have been employed in an on-going research project which looks at the discursive construction of masculinity. Let me begin with some background information about this project.

4   Analytical materials

All the data that are presented and analysed below come from a relatively large-scale project on the construction of masculine identities (Edley and Wetherell, 1996; 1997; 1999; Wetherell and Edley, 1998; 1999) based upon a number of different sources of empirical data gathered during 1992 and 1993. One branch of research involved an extensive period of 'field work' conducted in and around the sixth form common room of a UK-based, independent boys' school. Here small groups of 17–18 year old male students were interviewed (by myself) around eight times over the course of two school terms with the aim of gaining an insight into the construction of middle-class masculinities in one institutional site. A second source of data comes from a series of 'one off' small group discussions with a more heterogeneous collection of men who were all, at that time, in their first year of studying at the Open University. The aim here was to obtain a more general picture of the discursive and ideological climate in which masculinities come to be negotiated. Of the 60 men who took part in this branch of the study, most were white, aged between 20 and 64 years and came from a wide variety of occupations and social class backgrounds. Everyone who took part in these studies was a volunteer, and their anonymity was guaranteed through the use of pseudonyms.

The interviews were designed to explore a range of different issues central to men's lives, including work and family life, sexuality and friendships, and images of men in popular culture (see Wetherell, 1994, for full details). At all times the aim of the interviewer was to create an informal atmosphere in which, to a large extent, the participants themselves directed the flow of conversation. The meetings, which usually lasted for between 60 and 90 minutes, were tape-recorded and later transcribed (see the end of this chapter for a brief note on transcription notation). They were also sorted into large files by topic (such as fatherhood, sexuality and relationships, and so on) in order to allow for greater ease of analysis. The analyses themselves, however, were reorganized around the following set of concepts.

5   Discursive psychology: three key concepts

5.1 Interpretative repertoires

The concept of interpretative repertoires first appeared in 1984 with the publication of Nigel Gilbert and Mike Mulkay's book *Opening Pandora's Box*. Gilbert and Mulkay were working within the sociology of scientific knowledge (or SSK for short) – a branch of sociology interested in examining the way that science itself gets done. Gilbert and Mulkay were particularly concerned to look at participants' own understandings of what was involved in scientific work. So they gathered together a wide variety of accounts, from laboratory reports and published articles through to recordings of both formal meetings and break-time conversations. When they analysed these different accounts they discovered that there was no single, consensual story about how science proceeded. Instead, there appeared to be two quite separate ways of talking about or constructing scientific activity. Gilbert and Mulkay called these different ways of talking, interpretative repertoires.

The concept was later imported into social psychology by Jonathan Potter and Margaret Wetherell. In their highly influential book, *Discourse and Social Psychology*, they defined interpretative repertoires as "basically a lexicon or register of terms and metaphors drawn upon to characterize and evaluate actions and events" (Potter and Wetherell, 1987: 138).

The main point about interpretative repertoires is that they are relatively coherent ways of talking about objects and events in the world. In discourse analytical terms, they are the 'building blocks of conversation', a range of linguistic resources that can be drawn upon and utilized in the course of everyday social interaction. Interpretative repertoires are part and parcel of any community's common sense, providing a basis for shared social understanding. They can be usefully thought of as books on the shelves of a public library, permanently available for borrowing. Indeed, this metaphor captures nicely the point made earlier, that when people talk (or think) about things, they invariably do so in terms already provided for them by history. Much of it is a rehearsal or recital. This is not to say, of course, that there can never be such a thing as an original or novel conversation. Indeed, there is often no telling how conversations will turn out. What it does mean, however, is that conversations are usually made up of a patchwork of 'quotations' from various interpretative repertoires. Or, in terms of a quite different metaphor, interpretative repertoires are like the pre-figured steps that can be flexibly and creatively strung together in the improvisation of a dance.

Whilst this might give us a reasonably good idea of what interpretative repertoires are in theoretical terms, it is possible that we are left with a somewhat vague sense of what they actually look like 'on the ground'. When it comes to doing some of our own analysis, how do we go about spotting them? How do we know which interpretative repertoires are being utilized and how do we decide where the boundaries lie between one interpretative repertoire and the next? Unfortunately, there are no easy answers to these questions. As Wetherell and Potter (1988: 177) themselves note: "Analysis is not a matter of following rules or recipes; it often involves following hunches and the development of tentative interpretative schemes which may need to be abandoned or revised".

Identifying interpretative repertoires turns out to be a 'craft skill' rather than being something that one can master from first principles. It is an ability that develops with practice. Of course, this makes it a daunting prospect for students new to discourse analysis. However, as a general rule, the trick to spotting interpretative repertoires is familiarity with one's data. From my own experience, I know that it helps to have been the person who collected the data in the first place. As an interviewer, for example, there usually comes a time when one begins to feel as though you've heard it all before. People seem to be taking similar lines or making the same kinds of arguments as others previously interviewed. The same kind of thing occurs with the repeated reading of transcripts.

Gradually, one comes to recognize patterns across different people's talk, particular images, metaphors or figures of speech. This is a sure sign, as an analyst, that one is getting a feel for the 'discursive terrain' that makes up a particular topic or issue. In a very real sense, it is an indication that one has captured or encountered most of what there is to say about a particular object or event.

In order to provide a clear sense of how this is done in practice, I would like to look at some data that emerged from the research project described above, where the general topic of discussion was feminism and social change (see also Edley and Wetherell, forthcoming). This issue was typically introduced using one of three standard questions:

1   What is a feminist (or feminism)?

2   What do you think of feminism?

3   What do feminists want?

As we might expect, these questions generated a variety of responses. However, as we will see, they also produced some highly regular patterns of talk.

Extract 1

NIGEL: What are feminists (.) what are they after

HARRY: Women (.) what do women want

NIGEL: What do feminists want (.) yeah

HARRY: Equality

NIGEL: Right (.) just that

HARRY: Just that (.) equality (.) they er (.) that's all they need

Extract 2

NIGEL: Give me an imaginary picture of a feminist

ADRIAN: I seem to think of a feminist woman as like ugly women (.) with like shaved hair (.) stuff like that you know (.) who can't get a chap and so they think "I'll become a feminist"

NIGEL: Right

ADRIAN: Lesbians (.) that sort of thing (.) I don't know

Extract 3

NIGEL: What do you think feminists want of men [laughter]

SIMON: Well (.) I think they want us all to jump in the river don't they really (.) kill ourselves (.) I dunno (.) slaves [...] I think at times they seem to have us under siege and always blaming us for some of the most ridiculous things and I think to myself "What the hell do these people want (.) do they want us dead or what" (.) I mean they don't want to find any common ground (.) they just hate men (.) regardless

Extract 4

NIGEL: What do you think feminism is

NATHAN: It depends what (.) we've got one teacher who's got very strong ideas on feminism [...]

NIGEL: Go on (.) tell me

NATHAN: He's (.) well seeing as we're (.) we're in my group doing a feminist novel in the French Lieutenant's Woman and he's giving us his opinions on feminism (.) how feminists (.) they don't want equality with men they want to be better than men and they want to destroy all tradition without having anything to put in it's place (.) and there's a kind of anarchy sort of thing but I don't know (.) personally I could take some of his arguments but I think it's more trying to be equal

Extract 5

NIGEL: What's your impression of feminists (.) have you got any sort of mental image of who they are and what they're like [...]

TIM: I used to think they were like (.) you know (.) used to wear men's clothes (.) boots and things (.) you know (.) I've met so many that (.) they come in all sorts of (.) (**NIGEL**: Hmm) I don't think they're easily recognisable (**NIGEL**: Right)

CHARLIE: I think er I think when feminism probably first came to the forefront er (.) I think the initial impressions would be (.) as you said that a lot are very strong minded women who hated men (.) who probably have short cropped hair erm (.)

TIM: Doctor Marten boots [laughs]

CHARLIE: Yeah (.) whose sexuality would probably relate to the sort of lesbians and things like that

TIM: Yeah the sort of Greenham Common type women

CHARLIE: Yeah (.) when it first came out I think the initial impressions of that would be there (**NIGEL**: Hmm) bearing in mind I was a lot younger then when it sort of first came to the foreground (.) but I think nowadays it's sort of erm (.) I think for me I probably look at it in a different light thinking it's (.) they're probably women that are just fighting for (.) to be looked on as being equal to their male counterparts

Extract 6

NIGEL: Okay (.) so what [...] do you think feminists are after

JASON: The way I see it is equality

GREG: I was gonna say in one word <u>equality</u> of opportunities put [inaudible] opportunities yes but equal rights in (.) in everything

When assembled in this way it becomes fairly clear that there is not just one but two quite different ways of talking about feminists. There are, in other words, two distinctive interpretative repertoires in common circulation. In one, the image of the feminist is very simple and straightforward. She is portrayed as a woman who just wants equality with men (most evident in Extracts 1 and 6). By comparison, the second interpretative repertoire is much more rich and complex. It typically includes details of the feminist's physical appearance (invariably ugly and/or manly), sexual orientation (nearly always lesbian) and general demeanour (often aggressive men-haters). If we look at these few examples (of which there were many more in our data), we can see that these two repertoires are drawn upon in a number of different ways – to indicate what feminists are really like or what others say they are like or what people used to think they were like. However, there remained a high degree of consistency in terms of the content of these two constructions.

Interpretative repertoires are an important concept within critical discursive psychology because, in the context of this project, it is here that we encounter what I have referred to as the cultural history of masculinity. By looking for the different ways that people can talk about men and masculinity, we begin to understand the kinds of limitations that exist for the construction of self and other. That is, we come to see what is possible to say about men and what, by implication, is not.

'Interpretative repertoires' versus 'discourses'

One issue that students often raise concerns the relationship between the concept of interpretative repertoires and that of **discourses**. They see the two terms being used in much the same way but feel unsure about whether they are, in fact, synonymous.

Perhaps the first thing to say is that the two concepts are, indeed, closely linked. Potter and Wetherell (1995) have stated, quite explicitly, that the concept of interpretative repertoires was developed in order to do some of the same explanatory work as the 'post-structuralist' concept of discourses. Both concepts invoke the idea of repositories of meaning; that is, distinctive ways of talking about objects and events in the world. What is more, both the concept of interpretative repertoires and that of discourses see this fact as having the same major implication; namely, that in becoming native speakers, people are enticed or encultured into particular, even partial, ways of understanding the world. In short, they are committed or tied to the concept of **ideology**.

If there is a major difference between the two concepts then it is predominantly a matter of disciplinary 'ring-fencing'. In other words, the two concepts are often used to signal or signpost different conceptual and methodological positions within discourse analytical work. On the one hand, the concept of discourse is often used in the context of research which adopts more of a Foucauldian perspective. Here discourses are seen to construct entire institutions, such as medicine, the judiciary and science. Work declaring itself under this banner is often centrally concerned with the operation of power, and tends, if anything, towards a view of people as *subjectified* (see Section 5.3). In contrast, the concept of interpretative repertoires is used by those who want to place more emphasis upon human *agency* within the flexible deployment of language. Compared to discourses, interpretative repertoires are seen as less monolithic. Indeed, they are viewed as much smaller and more fragmented, offering speakers a whole range of different rhetorical opportunities.

5.2 Ideological dilemmas

The second analytic concept for organizing data that I want to introduce is that of ideological dilemmas, which made its first appearance in a book of the same name by Billig *et al.* (1988). The book was written in order to make a contribution to a long and complex debate about the nature of ideology (see Eagleton, 1991; McLellan, 1986). In particular, it sought to question or problematize the prevailing (Marxist) notion that ideologies were integrated and coherent sets of ideas that served to represent the domination of the ruling sections of society as natural or inevitable. Billig and his colleagues did not attempt to deny that ideologies could take this form. What they claimed instead, however, was that there was an additional kind of ideology. They drew a conceptual distinction between 'intellectual' ideologies – those that conform to the classical Marxist definition – and 'lived' ideologies. Lived ideologies were said to be composed of the beliefs, values and practices of a given society or culture. They are its 'way of life' (Williams, 1965), its *common sense*. In this respect, the concept of lived ideology comes close to what many other social theorists understand by the term *culture*. Billig *et al.* argued that one of the most crucial features of lived ideologies is that, unlike their intellectual counter-parts, they are not at all coherent or integrated. Indeed, quite the reverse, they were said to be characterized by inconsistency, fragmentation and contradiction.

The book *Ideological Dilemmas* is full of illustrations of how there is no unitary meaning to common sense. Time and again they show how it does not 'hang together' to provide people with clear indications as to how they should think and act. Instead, we see that it contains many contrary or competing arguments. For example, it tells us that we must 'look before we leap' whilst at the same time warning us that 'he who hesitates is lost'; it informs us that 'many hands make light work' but also that 'too many cooks spoil the broth'; it advises us that 'absence makes the heart grow fonder' but that someone who is 'out of sight' is 'out of mind'. Billig *et al.* point out that the contrary – or **dilemmatic** – nature of lived ideologies has led many modern commentators to write them off as faulty and unreliable. However, they argue that this ignores one of the central features of common sense; namely, that the indeterminacy of lived ideologies makes them wonderfully rich and flexible resources for social interaction and everyday sense-making.

Activity 2

According to the seventeenth century philosopher, Francis Bacon, common sense can be organized into any number of these kinds of competing or contradictory pairings. See how many others you can think of.

As we have seen, Billig *et al.* view lived ideologies or common sense as the condensed wisdom of a given culture or society. Following Gramsci (1971), it can be viewed as a sedimentary rock, containing an assemblage of different arguments and ideas laid down over the course of many generations. Individual maxims – like 'too many cooks spoil the broth' – can be thought of as *winning arguments*, rhetorically robust claims or statements that have stood the test of time. However, because that stock of knowledge contains so many tensions and contradictions, it can seldom guarantee to provide a definitive answer to any given problem or issue. Indeed, because common sense so often contains the 'seeds of its own negation', as far as Billig *et al.* are concerned it does more to *generate* argument and deliberation than it does to resolve them.

> It is not haphazard that common sense contains its contrary themes [...] that it possesses its dilemmatic character. The very existence of these opposing images, words, evaluations, maxims and so on is crucial, in that they permit the possibility not just of social dilemmas but of social thinking itself. Without these oppositions there would be no way of arguing about

dilemmas or understanding how opposing values can come into collision. As Bacon noted, the contrary maxims provide the seeds of arguments.

(Billig *et al.*, 1988: 17)

We should see that there are some clear points of overlap between ideological dilemmas and interpretative repertoires. Both are viewed as language resources that are 'out there', circulating in society, providing the raw materials for social interaction and 'private' contemplation. Indeed, if we think about it, we should see that interpretative repertoires must be *part* of a culture's common sense, as widely available ways of talking about different objects and events. Moreover, the notion of ideological dilemmas carries a further implication in that it alerts us to the possibility that different interpretative repertoires of the 'same' social object (be it men, feminists or whatever) are themselves constructed **rhetorically**. In other words, it implies that the different ways of talking about an object or event do not necessarily arise spontaneously and independently, but develop together as opposing positions in an unfolding, historical, argumentative exchange.

Once again it makes sense for us to attempt to firm up our understanding of the nature of ideological dilemmas through the examination of some empirical data. The material that we will be looking at next all comes from the independent school part of the masculinity project and features a set of discussions about the participants' 'imagined futures' (for more detail see Edley and Wetherell, 1999). More specifically, it derives from conversations stimulated by the question: "What do you think you'll be doing in ten years time?" If Billig *et al.*'s thesis about ideological dilemmas is correct, then we should be able to trace the structuring effects of competing or contrary themes in all but the most platitudinous conversational exchanges. For they are claiming that it is the productive tensions that exist between different ideological themes which prompts conversation itself.

Extract 7

NIGEL: Okay (.) the first sort of question is erm (.) sort of speculation (.) but try and put yourself ten years ahead (.) in ten years time and imagine what you're gonna be doing (.) what sort of life situation you're gonna be in (.) erm particularly around sort of work and family okay (.) erm (.) Carl what do you think you're gonna be doing in ten years time

CARL: Well (.) hopefully I'll be an RAF pilot stationed somewhere like Cyprus (**NIGEL**: Hm m) erm (.) I'm not sure whether I'll be married or not (.) I suppose I could see myself as being married with a small kid (.) a couple of years old (.) I think I'll be enjoying life (.) I hope I will anyway (**NIGEL**: Sure) that's about it really

In this first extract we see a typical response to the interviewer's question – typical insofar as it imagines the man as eventually employed and with a family. As Adrian puts it later in the same interview, "I think it's just something everybody wants to do really isn't it (.) well most people (.) have a wife and kids and have a good job". Discussions usually turned at this point to the issue of how they would envisage combining work and parenthood, and once again a common theme emerged. Virtually all the young men interviewed suggested that they did not expect a traditional domestic arrangement where the father went out to work whilst the mother stayed at home. Indeed, on several occasions, this arrangement was vehemently criticized as out-dated or old-fashioned.

Extract 8

TIM: I just don't think it has to be like (.) like so many people have it (.) it's an outdated thing (.) I really think it is (.) because (.) why can't the father change the nappies and do all the cooking and stuff (.) or why can't they share it (.) I mean both my parents have always been out to work (.) for as long as I can remember and my dad's done most of the cooking and cleaning and stuff because he always used to get back before my mum (.) they were both teachers for quite a long time and (.) if I remember rightly it was my dad that did most of the stuff (.) because my mum used to work most of the day (.) and it hasn't really made any difference (.) it's just the same as it would be the other way round [...] I think it all depends on the situation (.) I don't think that the mother should be expected to do such and such and stay at home when the child's young and the father go out to work and work on the car and everything (.) but it could be that way (.) it depends on the situation that the family's in but it shouldn't be expected of everybody because then a few people feel pressured into roles and stuff

Implicit within this kind of argument is the assumption that fathers are equally capable of looking after children as mothers – a view that we see made much more explicitly in the following extract.

Extract 9

AARON: I think (.) that I thought one of the (.) either the male or female would have to be there for the kids (.) when they went to school someone should be at home perhaps (.) for when they come home (**NIGEL**: Hm m) at least up to a certain age (.) er (.) but what I'm saying is it doesn't matter whether it's the man or the woman

In addition to revealing the notion of the interchangability of mothers and fathers in the provision of childcare, Extract 9 contains the traces of yet another significant theme; namely, that whilst it may not matter whether a child is cared for by its mother or its father, it should be done by one of them at least. In other words, it is implied that parents ought to look after their own children. Once again this argument was made more explicitly at other points in our data. In Extracts 10 and 11 for example, we see it emerge within the context of discussions about how the participants would deal with a situation where the mother of their children was equally career-oriented.

Extract 10

NIGEL: Okay (.) erm (.) how would you feel if for instance you married someone who was equally ambitious as you erm (.) about family and looking after the children

PHIL: but you'd never bloody see em then (.) you'd all be at work

NIGEL: but how would you arrange it (.) would you pack up your job

PHIL: would you get a nanny

PAUL: a nanny

AARON: ugghhh

PHIL: crap forget it

NIGEL: you would

AARON: [bangs table] Jesus Paul

PAUL: or grandparents or whatever

AARON: (laughs) this will be

PHIL: rent a parent (.) here we go [laughter]

NIGEL: so you'd both sort of continue your erm (.) careers and then you'd get child care

PAUL: hm m

AARON: so someone else is gonna bring up your kid

PAUL: well (.) to a certain point

AARON: no (.) someone else is gonna bring up your kid

PHIL: for you (.) you're not gonna know the kid

AARON: you'd go like 'Oh (.) hello (.) you don't know'

PHIL: I've been there (.) you know (.) you don't know the kid at the end of it

AARON: and your kid's gonna resent it

Extract 11

TIM: I was just wondering if both parents could stay at work like and the children could be looked after

ADRIAN: but then you don't get any relationship between the child and the parents because if the parents go off and drop the kid off at the minder's at half eight in the morning and then come to pick it up at five or six o'clock at night (.) you've only got like (.) fourteen hours together which is shit really isn't it because

they don't get any relationship at all between them because
when they pick the kid up they go to sleep straight away and
they take it home and it just sleeps all night until the morning

Perhaps more than anywhere, it is in these last two extracts (Extracts 10
and 11) that we can most easily see the outlines of what appears to be a
very powerful ideological dilemma. For it is in these moments of argument
and deliberation that the contrary themes of contemporary common sense
make themselves most plain. In Extract 10, for example, Aaron and Phil are
clearly siding with each other against Paul. They jointly characterize Paul's
'imagined future' as unreasonable and improper. It would be wrong of him,
they suggest, to have children and then not be there for them. In response,
Paul defends himself against their criticism by suggesting that he would not
be totally absent. He would be there as a father, just not all of the time.

There are several things we should note about this exchange. First of all,
we should recognize that Paul does not attempt to deny the importance of
being there for one's family. In a sense, therefore, he can be seen to
acknowledge and so reproduce this as an aspect of our lived ideology.
However, the second point to note is that, in spite of that
acknowledgement, the argument does not cease. It rumbles on because,
although they might agree that fathers ought to play an active role in
childcare, they also recognize that they want to be somewhere else (i.e. at
work). Paul's proposed 'solution' to this ideological dilemma might not
have met with Phil and Aaron's approval, but what none of them could
deny is that such a dilemma exists. Indeed, it is this same dilemma that
drives the following conversation (Extract 12) in which we find Paul putting
forward a different kind of solution.

Extract 12

PAUL: I think that er (.) my idea [...] would be that the male would
work night shift or whatever (.) the female would work in the
day (.) that way you both would have your own share of a
career (.) if you like

PHIL: they'd never see each other

PAUL: er (.) who knows

PHIL: the man would be asleep all day

PAUL: no (.) but then in the day the male looked after the kids

PHIL: he'd be a physical <u>wreck</u> (.) <u>no way</u>

PAUL: he wouldn't be he wouldn't be (.) it's already happened

AARON: he would be (.) I mean (.) he's gotta work through the night

PHIL: I've seen people who work on the night shift and (.) you know
(.) a friend of mine's dad worked on the night shift and he was
an okay bloke but as soon as he started working in the night
he was like a bear with a sore head (.) if I ever came round
during the day and he was woken up (.) he was like (.) you

> know (.) he was working seven or eight hours at night time (.)
> he doesn't want to look after kids during the day

PAUL: it's like my grandad would work night shifts and then in the day
looked after the kids and that was it (**NIGEL**: Hm m) and then he
had a perfectly fine relationship (.) it depends which way you
want it to work (.) I mean that would be my idea (.) more that
way (.) it wasn't my grandad it was my great grandad (.) sorry
(**NIGEL**: Hm m) and erm (.) I think there'd be (.) the male would
take on half the responsibilities of the female and the female
would take on half the responsibilities of the male (.) any
pushing any further would be biased and but I don't (.) think (.)

NIGEL: would you like that arrangement (pause)

PAUL: I don't know

PHIL: no (.) your lives revolve around the child too much (.) I mean the
child is very important (.) especially in its early years until it gains
some sort of independence (.) but I think there's always got to be
scope for spending some time with your partner (.) erm away from
the child (.) you don't want it to dominate your life (.) erm (.) I
can't say I've seen it happen but I could quite easily see something
like that er (.) sort of causing a rift in the marriage or whatever
(**NIGEL**: Hm m) or the relationship (.) er (.) if you were to take
Paul's example of the bloke working at night (.) the woman
working in the day and the bloke looking after the kid (.) they're
never gonna spend any <u>time</u> together at this sort of rate (.) I mean
on the weekend the guy's gonna be absolutely shattered (**NIGEL**:
Hm m) erm (.) I don't think it's great (.) I don't think it's a really
good arrangement (.) <u>I</u> wouldn't want it (.) because (.) I mean (.)
you're in love with this woman so hence you have the kid (.) so I
think you're gonna want to spend some time with her besides (.)
you know (.) you're just totally cha (.) diverting all your time to
the child (**NIGEL**: Right) which I don't think is correct

If anything, it is even easier in this extract to see how Paul's talk is oriented
around the dilemma of work versus family. Whereas, in Extract 10, his
proposal was based upon compromise, here both the father and the mother
seem to get everything. They are able to fulfil both their career aspirations as
well as their obligations as parents. Yet once again we see that the argument
fails to subside. This time Paul's suggestion is rejected on two separate
grounds; firstly, it is glossed as impractical – people, Phil says, wouldn't be
physically capable of being parents by day and employees by night. They
would soon become exhausted. The second counter-argument is even more
analytically revealing. The problem with Paul's suggestion, claims Phil, is that
it would mean the parents would get little or no time to be together. Couples
need time on their own, he says, away from the demands of children. And so
yet another element of our lived ideology is thrown into the ring: they want
to lead successful careers but they feel that they should be at home; they
want to spend lots of time looking after their children but they need time

away to maintain their relationships. In a sense, these young men are a battleground upon which the struggle between these opposing ideals is played out. Moreover, the way that they conduct their own lives will depend upon how they position themselves within this ideological field.

5.3 Subject positions

The third analytic concept that I would like to introduce; that is, subject positions, has a relatively established history, but more within cultural studies than psychology. In 1971 Louis Althusser published a very influential paper on ideology and what he called 'ideological state apparatuses'. In it he talked about the way that ideology creates or constructs 'subjects' by drawing people into particular positions or identities. Subjectivity, he argued, is an ideological effect. The way that people experience and feel about themselves and the world around them is, in part at least he said, a by-product of particular ideological or discursive regimes. Althusser talked about a process of **subjectification** which entails a dual sense of people as being both produced by and subjected to ideology (Althusser was a Marxist). He also came up with the concept of **interpellation**, which refers to the process of being called or 'hailed' by a particular discourse. This famous First World War poster of Lord Kitchener provides a clear illustration of what Althusser had in mind.

Activity 3

Look at this poster of Lord Kitchener.

© *Imperial War Museum*

Clearly he is 'speaking' but precisely who is being addressed? Moreover, what does the poster presume about its target audience? What does it imply about them?

Discussion

The first thing that we might notice about this poster is that Kitchener is pointing at us; we are singled out as the target of his attentions. When he says "Your Country Needs You", it is 'us' he is referring to; it is us as individuals that he is calling. We are also **positioned** by his utterance. In other words, we are being hailed as particular kinds of individuals or **subjects**. The poster constructs us as members of a nation state. More specifically, we are being hailed as British. Of course, were a Frenchman or an American to look at this poster they would not be engaged in the same way. However, the point that Althusser was trying to make was that a poster like this only speaks to us as British. In other words, at the precise moment we perceive ourselves to have been addressed by Kitchener, we will have inevitably done so as a British subject.

Within social psychology, Holloway (1984, reproduced as Reading Twenty in Wetherell *et al.*, 2001) and Walkerdine (1990) make a very similar point. They argue that people don't encounter discourses pre-figured or pre-formed. Instead, we are re-constituted as subjects in the moment of their consumption. Who we are, claims Hall (1988), always stands in relation to the available text or narratives. Identity, he says, is formed 'at the unstable point where the 'unspeakable' stories of subjectivity meet the narratives of a culture' (p.44). In other more familiar words, whatever we might say (and think) about ourselves and others as people will always be in terms of a language provided for us by history.

By now it should be clear why the concept of subject positions is so central to discursive psychology. In a sense, it is this concept that connects the wider notions of discourses and interpretative repertoires to the social construction of particular selves. Subject positions can be defined quite simply as 'locations' within a conversation. They are the identities made relevant by specific ways of talking. And because those ways of talking can change both within and between conversations (i.e. as different discourses or interpretative repertoires are employed) then, in some sense at least, so too do the identities of the speakers. However, this is not to imply (as did Althusser) that identity simply follows in the wake of discourse. We must remember that people are also the masters of language, the creators of texts. The Kitchener poster did not materialize out of thin air. It was a text that was specifically designed to have certain ideological effects. In the same way, people are not always 'hailed' from afar. Indeed, as we shall see, it is quite possible to subjectify 'ourselves' within the contours of our own discourse.

When it comes to actually doing analysis, the question of how to spot subject positions in data turns out, yet again, to be largely a matter of experience and intensive (re)reading. The trick, if there is one, is to try to stay aware of *who* is implied by a particular discourse or interpretative repertoire. What does a given statement or set of statements say about the person who utters them? All of the following extracts come from the Open University branch of the masculinity project and feature a range of participants involved in the production of themselves as men (for a fuller analysis see Wetherell and Edley, 1999). In Extract 13, Michael, a

26-year-old computer software designer and keen amateur boxer, is seen responding to a question about his experiences of feeling gendered.

Extract 13

NIGEL: Okay some people say that (.) you know (.) there's moments in their everyday lives when they feel more masculine than at other times (.) is there anything that [...] you could think of (.) erm (.) a time in your life where (.) you know (.) there might have been a particular moment or it might be a regular occurring thing you know (.) erm when you have a sense of yourself as masculine
[...]

MICHAEL: erm (.) well related to the boxing there's got to be times erm (.) boxing and training that I feel high and confident in my ability (**NIGEL:** Hm m) and I feel generally wha (.) perhaps what you'd term as erm (.) masculine (.) erm (.) times at work as well (.) a stand-up presentation (**NIGEL:** Right) erm

NIGEL: what is it about that then that gives you that sense

MICHAEL: erm (.) the challenge (.) I mean (.) was it yesterday (.) I got up and did a presentation to er (.) 20 or 30 people (.) that was when I went up to [another town] (.) like a sales pitch (.) erm on a technical basis and there was a lot of erm unknown technical ability (**NIGEL:** hmm) within the (.) within the audience (.) you know the (.) you know on the floor (.) people who had no knowledge of what I was talking about and people that had knowledge that erm (.) in many cases (.) one particular case that equalled mine and I was trying to sell to them that know as much about it as I do (**NIGEL:** hmm) and you don't know if there's gonna be a question coming up that you can't answer (.) I mean (.) one or two who you feel <u>threatened</u> by (**NIGEL:** right) purely because he's got (.) I know that that guy over there's got as much knowledge of the subject as me (**NIGEL:** hm m) if he wanted to try and erm (.) knock me down a peg or two (**NIGEL:** right) if there's anyone in the room who can do it's that guy (.) so you feel threatened by it (.) you feel a bit vulnerable (.) and erm (.) like on the one hand (.) but on the other hand I'm getting up and dictating the flow and making sure the meeting and the presentation's going how I want (**NIGEL:** hm m) I'm (.) I've got <u>control</u> to an extent of the meeting (.) (**NIGEL:** okay) and like there's a bit of a buzz with that along with a risk

The next extract comes from an interview with Graham, a 24-year-old unemployed accountant and amateur rugby player. It follows a long conversation about the role of rugby in Graham's life and sees him being asked to explain how he could enjoy playing such a violent game.

Extract 14

NIGEL: but I imagine some people listening to you who don't play
                   the game [...] are gonna say erm (.) you know you're talking
                   about (.) you're talking about not only punching people (.)
                   not only head-butting (.) not only erm getting cuts and
                   <u>giving</u> them erm you're (.) you're experiencing that as a
                   matter of (.) of <u>course</u> every weekend (.) right (.) erm and (.)
                   and yet you sound (.) you know (.) as if you really love it
                   (**GRAHAM**: yeah) now for someone who doesn't play the
                   game (.) imagine someone coming over from another
                   country where they don't play rugby (.) they're gonna say
                   'How on earth can you enjoy that?' (**GRAHAM**: yeah) I mean
                   that's the most amazing thing that you could subject yourself
                   to that <u>and</u> subject someone else to it.

GRAHAM: but as you said it goes (.) you used the word sort of a trial
                   of (.) I can't think what you said (.) (**NIGEL**: courage) a
                   challenge (.) a trial of courage (.) and that's what it comes
                   <u>down</u> to (.) it comes down to you're pitting yourself against
                   (.) in the <u>scrum</u> situation which is where I'm saying a lot of
                   the stuff goes on (.) you're pitting yourself against one man
                   erm (.) albeit you've got (.) you know you've got the whole
                   pack behind you (.) pushing (.) but in sort of (.) in
                   technique and in sort of (.) as I say (.) the kidology of it and
                   whatever (.) you've got basically one against one there and
                   erm (.) in I mean to a certain extent (.) I mean (.) I <u>would</u>
                   say this but the props are a very important part of the ball-
                   winning process and you maybe think you've got a lot of
                   status in that (.) possibly a lot of people who watch the
                   game <u>don't</u> think that (.) they think that the game's won and
                   lost by (**NIGEL**: outside) yeah (.) the scrum half or whatever
                   (.) but erm (.) I know (.) I can say that I think props are
                   very important and my hooker'll say 'No, you're just there to
                   hold me up (.) I do the work' (**NIGEL**: sure) or whatever (.)
                   but you do in yourself (.) you <u>have</u> a sort of self importance
                   and you do (.) and you enjoy the challenge and (.) if you're
                   (.) excuse the term (.) <u>dicked</u> about in the front row erm by
                   the opposition (.) you aren't gonna stand for that

Although produced by different people at different times, these two extracts
both work to construct a very similar masculine identity or subject position.
In each one we see an account of a man who seeks out and enjoys the
challenge of risky situations, who has the courage or nerve to face his
enemies without losing his cool. Of course, in many respects, this is a very
familiar subject position; it is the traditional masculine hero as exemplified
in popular culture by the likes of Rambo, Rocky and James Bond. The
point is, however, that here it is donned as a private and authentic form of
identity. In a sense, therefore, it represents the (mis)taking of a **voice** from
without for a voice from within (see both Wertsch, 1990, reproduced as

Reading Sixteen in Wetherell *et al.*, 2001, and Maybin, Reading Six in Wetherell *et al.*, 2001, for further discussions on the concept of *voice*).

At other points within the interviews, a second, quite different subject position emerged. Here the notion of heroic or macho masculinity would often make an appearance, but as a contrast or counter-point to the identity being claimed. We can see an example of this in Extract 15, where Raj (a 37-year-old contract engineer) and John (a 37-year-old maintenance engineer) are being asked to compare themselves with various images of men taken from a glossy magazine.

Extract 15

NIGEL: okay (.) now is there any one of those six images who you would <u>most</u> erm identify with (.) is there anyone there that you would say (.) you know (.) <u>that's</u> most like me

JOHN: out of those I'd probably go for four

NIGEL: number four (.) Raj (.) what do you think

RAJ: <u>yes</u> number four it seems to be (.)

NIGEL: okay why him

JOHN: he looks the most normal (laughs)

RAJ: sorry

JOHN: he looks the most normal I suppose

RAJ: yes that's right

JOHN: in the dress and (.)

RAJ: yeah half way (.) he's middle of the road

JOHN: I suppose Mr Average you might say (.) yeah

RAJ: mm

NIGEL: okay (.) right so (.) is it true to say then that erm (.) you two both feel (.) or don't have a very strong sense of yourself as being masculine (.) you know (.) it's not a erm (.) a very prominent part of your identity

RAJ: I would say yeah (.) that's my understanding (.) yes (.) I'm not a masculine man

NIGEL: hm m (.) John (.) what do you think

JOHN: yeah probably the same (.) yeah

NIGEL: yeah

JOHN: I would (.) I would have said averagely so

NIGEL: hm m (.) okay yeah (.) I wasn't saying that you feel that you're <u>un</u>masculine (**JOHN**: yeah) but that it's not a very (.)

JOHN: what I'm saying is (.) it's not (.) if you took your (.) like your archetypal macho man (.) I'm not there (.) I'm just middle of the road (.) just er (.) average again I suppose

As we can see, both Raj and John present themselves as 'ordinary' men, as 'middle of the road', as 'Mr Average'. They do not position themselves as masculine heroes. Indeed, in John's last turn, this identity appears as an 'archetype' – repackaged as something that is now alien, artificial and extreme. Once again this was far from being an isolated incident. In Extract 16, for example, we have a conversation between Martin (a 35-year-old unemployed musician) and Phillip (a 26-year-old police officer) in which they are being asked to assess their own masculinity. What is perhaps most striking about this stretch of talk is that the very identity claimed by Graham and Michael (rugby playing and dare doing – see Extracts 13 and 14) is here explicitly disavowed. As in the previous extract, macho masculinity becomes transformed into something contrived and unreal.

Extract 16

NIGEL: The first thing I want to get at is this (.) this discussion is about men and masculinity (.) okay (.) erm <u>men</u> we'd all understand as just being a straight forward biological category (.) erm (.) but masculinity is something different and a bit more complex (.) er have you any ideas initially about what masculinity is [...]

PHILLIP: er (.) not as such (.) I presume it's obviously to do with more macho type of images (**NIGEL**: hmm) rather than you know <u>feminine</u> images

MARTIN: or <u>stereotypical</u> images

NIGEL: right (.) so okay (.) so you see it as a stereotype (.) yeah

MARTIN: well (.) playing rugby (.) you know (.) shooting (.) doing daring things and what have you

NIGEL: okay (.) do you see yourselves as masculine men then

MARTIN: no (.) not by that description no

NIGEL: so (.) what do you think you are (.) do you think you are unmasculine

MARTIN: no (.) not unmasculine (.) no

NIGEL: So then would you argue that there are different forms of masculinity

MARTIN: well (.) perhaps it's a question of terms like (.) there's <u>male</u> (.) erm there is <u>sex</u> isn't there? (**NIGEL**: hm m) male and female sex (**NIGEL**: hmm) erm I suppose (.) you could judge masculinity by (.) how closely to accepted stereotypes you adhered erm in your background (.) your up-bringing would have a strong bearing on that

NIGEL: okay (.) so the closer you are to Rambo (.) or Arnold Schwartzenegger then the more masculine you are (.) and you sort of (.) as you come away from that stereotype (.) then you sort of <u>shade</u> away towards the more (.) I don't know (.) the gender neutral (.) is that how you see it

PHILLIP: err (.)

MARTIN: well that's not how I see it (.) no (.) it depends through which eyes it's being <u>seen</u> (.) isn't it (.) I mean if somebody likes Rambo (.) they would see that as being ultra-masculine wouldn't they

A third subject position that emerged within our data can be seen in the next two extracts. In the first, Sam, a 42-year-old psychiatric nurse and Harry, a 53-year-old bricklayer, are responding to the same opening question. Harry's response is simple and to the point – he is a masculine man – whereas Sam, on the other hand, draws upon a similar distinction between masculine men and 'macho' men in order to elaborate his own position. He describes himself as having 'all sides' to his personality and claims to be quite comfortable doing things which are more conventionally associated with women.

Extract 17

NIGEL: erm do you feel yourselves to be masculine men

HARRY: I think so yeah

NIGEL: you you think you feel as though you <u>are</u>

HARRY: yeah

NIGEL: do you

SAM: I feel <u>secure</u> that I'm masculine but I'm not a macho man (**NIGEL**: hmm) I'm quite comfortable with where I fit in the spectrum of things yeah

NIGEL: okay (.) it's interesting that you talk about security (.) how (.) how might you be made <u>in</u>secure then

SAM: I think somebody (.) if you take my background of nursing (.) it's er a female orientated profession (.) but erm I <u>could</u> feel insecure if people felt that that implies something about me but I don't because it doesn't mean anything (.) it's erm (.) I know where I fit into things so I'm not anxious about that

NIGEL: right but er (.) have you come across a lot of people who erm see that as indicative of something that's less than masculine

SAM: yeah (.) plenty of people I think er (.) some of my interests er (.) people are quite surprised if I tell them I can knit for example (**NIGEL:** hmm) I can't knit very well but I know how to knit (.) and it doesn't embarrass me to say I can knit erm whereas a lot of people I know would (.) would deny it at all costs because they would feel that it implied there was something effeminate about them

NIGEL: right (.) so why doesn't it embarrass you

SAM: well I've no reason to be embarrassed by it (.) I can't knit as
          well as my wife can but I can cook as well as she can (.) and I
          can do other things as well as she can which are (.) more likely
          to be seen as female pursuits but er it (.) it doesn't make me
          feel insecure (.) but I <u>do</u> know some people deny those sort of
          things because it might make them feel that way (.) but erm
          (**NIGEL**: sure) I'm quite comfortable that I am male and have
          all sides to my er personality really

A strikingly similar example of this kind of positioning appears in Extract
18. Here Greg, a 30-year-old brewery manager, also portrays himself as
something of a gender non-conformist or rebel. Like Sam, he declares
himself as confident in his unconventionality. Against the 'stereotypes of
masculinity', Greg presents himself as comfortable in his emotional
expressivity.

Extract 18

NIGEL: okay (.) what I'd like to start with is erm a comment really
          about that these discussions are on men and masculinity (.) erm
          so I'm making a distinction between on the one hand a
          biological category (**GREG**: right) and on the other hand
          something that's a little more tricky or difficult to define (.) so
          I'd like to start with your ideas on what you think masculinity <u>is</u>

GREG: mm (.) difficult (.) I think masculinity is (.) is almost a (.) it's
          probably (.) to me what it means to me is it's something that is
          (.) is not presented as natural (.) it's something that's
          represented to (.) to me as an individual by a number of factors
          (.) starting from a kid through the family (.) through friends
          and (.) and er sort of peer groups as it were and through work
          (.) so you <u>pick</u> up ideas of what masculinity means (**NIGEL**:
          hmm) from let's say society in general (.) that's how I would
          see it (.) erm and if you look at what I would consider to be (.)
          I don't know what masculinity is (.) I know what it's
          represented as and if I looked at that I would see the strong
          erm man (.) very little emotion shown (.) erm really just a
          strong sort of security figure (.) somebody who's gonna look
          after the family and the wife erm but predominantly being
          almost hard to the point of no emotion (**NIGEL**: right) erm
          quite a cold description but that (.) that's what it means to me
          through my sort of socialisation process shall I say

NIGEL: hmm (.) okay (.) erm an interesting distinction between what
          you say masculinity <u>is</u> and what it is represented <u>as</u> (.) what are
          you trying to keep away from saying

GREG: Well if (.) what I believe (.) I think masculinity is represented to
          me or <u>has</u> been throughout my life as what I've just said
          (**NIGEL**: hmm) what I think it <u>is</u> (.) is (.) it's har (.) it's probably

very difficult to define (.) I think masculinity is dependent on the individual (.) if that's not a cop out (.) I think each individual could look at it differently (.) I believe masculinity is being myself erm not (.) I've got this non-conformist streak in me from my punk days but not conforming to those stereotypes of masculinity erm if I want a damn good cry I'll have a cry and if I want to be supportive of my wife I'll be supporting with my wife (.) if I was (.) you know if my wife had a good job for instance and we decided to have children I'd be quite happy to stay at home and look after the children (.) so I don't think masculinity is (.) is erm (.) is necessarily about being the secure figure (.) being the hard man (.) I don't see it as that way (.) I personally see it as er (.) as a softer sort of image (.) I think it's represented as a different thing totally (.) but my personal opinion is it's a much softer sort of approach

A critical discursive psychologist would be interested in these subject positions for a number of different reasons. First, in line with Horton-Salway's approach in Chapter Four, they would want to see what they accomplish within the local context of their production (for example, the 'Mr Average' subject position may lend itself particularly well to the presentation of oneself as modest). Second, the very availability of these positions, as routine ways of describing men, tells us something about the broader ideological context in which such talk is done. For example, on the face of it, one could argue that Mr Average and the gender rebel represent a challenge to the cultural dominance of the traditional macho hero. And yet a closer examination reveals that, in some respects at least, these two positions 'buy back' into the dominant ideal with their emphasis on autonomy and independence. Greg talks about having 'a damn good cry' in much the same way as Graham talks about rugby. Indeed, what is being celebrated in Greg's discourse is not so much knitting, cooking and crying *per se,* but his courage, strength and determination *as a man* to engage in these potentially demeaning activities.

A critical discursive psychologist takes a similarly two-sided interest in interpretative repertoires and ideological dilemmas. With interpretative repertoires we would look at both their local deployment and their broader social implications. For example, we would note how the two repertoires of the feminist (outlined in Section 5.1) allow speakers not only to present themselves as liberal or fair-minded, but also to dismiss feminism as extreme (see Edley and Wetherell, forthcoming). As for ideological dilemmas, we would look at how the dilemmatic nature of common sense is used for a wide variety of rhetorical purposes, but we would also look out for their wider cultural significance. For instance, the conflict of fatherhood versus a career is telling because it would appear to be relatively new. Not that long ago men belonged to the public realm and women stayed at home. The fact that many men feel torn today suggests that an important ideological shift has occurred.

6   Analytical exercise – 'four in one night'

In this final section of the chapter I would like to present you with some more data from the same research project in order for you to have a go at applying the various concepts that make up critical discursive psychology. The material comes from the independent school part of the study and features a conversation between Aaron, Phil, Paul and myself. As you will see, the conversation is mainly concerned with what Aaron got up to at the weekend. It is a story of sexual prowess – of four girls in one weekend – which is told on Aaron's behalf by his friend Phil. Indeed, it turns out to be one of those stories that are probably best left to one's mates to tell on your behalf (see Wetherell, 1998, for a more detailed analysis of this data).

Activity 4

Carefully read through Extract 19 in order, first of all, to get an overall sense of the data. Now go through it again (and again!) whilst thinking about the following issues.

- This conversation is all about Aaron's sexual activities. However, across the extract, male sexuality and sexual relations are talked about in a number of different ways. What are the different *interpretative repertoires* of sex and sexuality at play within this extract?

- What are the different identities or *subject positions* being taken up by the various participants (including the interviewer!)?

- Billig *et al.* (1988) would insist that this conversation, like any other, will be structured around particular *ideological dilemmas*. What evidence can you find of those kinds of tensions?

- What, if anything, are the political or ideological implications of your findings? Who is most empowered, for example, by the discursive structures you have identified?

Extract 19

NIGEL: Okay yeah tell me about going with four people in one night

PHIL: alright [bangs table]

AARON: oh no

PHIL: go on

PAUL: on the record

PHIL: was it was it this (.)

AARON: I don't know I was a bit drunk

PHIL: I I'll tell he was drunk I'll tell you what I know because I am never drunk (**NIGEL**:   Hm mm) because I'm dead smug erm

AARON: he's never drunk it's true

PHIL: <u>Fri</u>day you went with Janesy on Friday

AARON: I did yes

PHIL: out <u>down</u> the pub I I <u>mi</u>ssed this completely a <u>com</u>plete shock to
           me (Aaron laughs) erm (.) went out down the pub one night as
           we do (.) erm I went home because I like live out of town er
           these stopped later (.) I was not aware of anything following
           night <u>big</u> party I mean there was like two hundred people there I
           would have thought big field (.) you know disco and all that shit
           (.) erm Aaron got <u>absolutely</u> out of his face (.) I was going out
           with someone she didn't turn up she rang me and told me
           (**NIGEL**: Hmm) she might not be going (**NIGEL**: Hmm) um

AARON: it was Karen

PHIL: it was Karen erm something wrong with her mum wasn't it or
           something I can't remember what it was

AARON: ah that's a good excuse

PHIL: anyway (.) sorry <u>yes</u> Aaron (Aaron laughs) erm so Aaron got
           <u>really</u> drunk and he went with (Aaron laughs again) Jenny
           Baxter (.) <u>nice</u> girl <u>our</u> year (.) Cathy Br<u>ewin</u>

AARON: no it wasn't Cathy Brewin it was another Cathy

PHIL: Cathy Cathy someone

AARON: it wasn't Cathy Brewin

PHIL: and you don't know who the other one was do you

AARON: no

PHIL: you forgot her name

AARON: yeah

PHIL: or didn't even find out

AARON: right

PHIL: it was just you could see him at various points of the evening
           with this girl like on the floor in this field (.) and I knew it was
           Aaron but I didn't know who the girl was because she kept
           changing

NIGEL: hm mm

PHIL: and you lost someone's <u>purse</u> didn't you

AARON: yeah (.)

PHIL: and um (.) then we walked (.) we decided to walk back from
           this party it was like out past [small village] so we had to walk
           back to [local town]

NIGEL: hm mm

AARON: good idea Aaron

PHIL: yeah

AARON: we were very lucky that day

PHIL: we were erm and we were walking back and he says oh I went with Janesy on Friday and I went yeah you went with three birds last night you went with one on Friday this was in his good month

NIGEL: hm mm

PHIL: so that like took me aback somewhat (.) so that was a good weekend for you

NIGEL: is that g<u>oo</u>d

PHIL: well in his books <u>yes</u> you know

AARON: yeah

PHIL: the thing is you got so much stick for it

AARON: well yeah I could take the stick because it was almost like (.) a good ego trip when everyone was taking the stick 'oh you got off with her ah ha ha' '<u>yep</u> I did so what's your problem' 'oh (.) er (.) errr'

PHIL: none of them were particularly pikey so you were alright really

AARON: no (.) they weren't none of them were like majorly pikey (.) one or two perhaps could have like

PHIL: I don't know I don't know I think I know this Cathy bird I know Jenny I know Cathy thing I don't know who the other one was an neither do you so can't tell

NIGEL: yeah I mean I wasn't sort of saying is four in two days good I mean it's <u>impressive</u> you know (Aaron and Phil both laugh) but I mean like (.) it presumes that erm that's a creditable thing (.) yeah (.) is it

PHIL: no because you're on the moral low ground

AARON: but I don't mind being on the moral low ground

PHIL: oh no you don't mind I I it didn't fuss me at all you know and I wasn't I thought it was quite (.) it was quite impressive you know you're sort of thinking that's shocking because it never happens to me (Phil and Aaron both laugh) but he was (.) by some people in the group he was li (.) they were just taking the piss it wasn't serious no one it didn't really <u>bo</u>ther anyone at all (**NIGEL**: hm mm) it was like Aaron was on the moral low ground because he was like (.) gigolo Casanova whatever

NIGEL: right (.) okay (.) what do you think Paul

PAUL: did you

PHIL: are you ap<u>pa</u>lled

PAUL: when you (.) no (.) when you went out

NIGEL: not appalled

PAUL: I jus I'll tell you in a minute when you went out (laughter) when you went out on that Friday (.) evening you were out on the pull yeah

AARON: <u>no</u>

PAUL: this (.) you were not

AARON: just out as a group

PHIL: just out as a group of friends

PAUL: on the Saturday you were out on the pull

PHIL: no

AARON: er not really

PHIL: he was drunk

AARON: I <u>wasn't</u> drunk unconscious (.) I was <u>very</u> merry [**PHIL**: (inaudible)] was like all erm (.) all like social guards were down

PAUL: yeah (.) and (.) when (.) so and (.) when you got off with the first one did you (Aaron laughs)

PHIL: who was first (.) can you remember

PAUL: on the Friday

AARON: errm on the Friday that that was Janesy

PAUL: did you have any sort of like intonation [sic] of carrying the relationship further

AARON: no

PAUL: so so you basically went for as many pullings off as you could get in a weekend

PHIL: no

AARON: I didn't go for it it just (.)

PAUL: it just happened

AARON: well yeah (.) it's not so much I thought <u>right</u> [hits the desk] this weekend (.) keep your pecker up lad you're away it's not like that it's just that I

PAUL: with any of them did you feel

AARON: I get lucky very [inaudible]

PAUL: that they'd be like a follow on

PHIL: he didn't know who <u>half</u> of them <u>were</u> do you

AARON: ah er I didn't (.) I mean it wasn't (.) I mean it wasn't like a right gitty thing to do it was like the other half knew as well that it wasn't gonna be (.) (**PHIL**: mm) erm (.) no it's it's you're getting it all wrong it's it's (.) it wasn't (.) errr Aaron come up with the phrase you want to say (.) it wasn't alright this kid's gonna get off with me then we're gonna go out oh no we're not gonna go out what a git it was (.) I'm gonna get off with this lad and that's alright

PHIL: fancied a bit of rough you know

AARON: fancied a bit of rough

PHIL: and it was mutual I imagine

Discussion

Interpretative repertoires

I would argue that there are at least five different interpretative repertoires of sex and sexuality spread across Extract 19. First of all, there is clearly a notion of sex *as an achievement* such that it is an activity that a person might aspire towards and receive credit for doing. This repertoire is most apparent in Aaron's comments about the weekend being 'a good ego trip' as well as in the formulation of my own follow-up question ("I mean it's impressive..." etc.). However, it is also implicit within Aaron's account of drunkenness in that it functions to protect him from accusations of boastfulness (which is why it was better for Phil to tell Aaron's story). Drunkenness is also at the heart of a second interpretative repertoire. The idea, provided by Aaron, that alcohol removes all of one's 'social guards' implies that *sexuality is a more basic, instinctive mode of expression* – something, perhaps, that everyone feels 'deep-down'. A third interpretative repertoire evident within the extract constructs sex *as something of a scarce commodity* such that a person is 'lucky' to get it (it is possible that this is a thoroughly gendered account – that it is the male who 'gets lucky' when a female 'gives' him sex). A fourth interpretative repertoire to appear is one that corresponds closely to what Hollway (1984) has described in her work as the *'have and hold'* discourse of sexuality. This is where sexual relations are held to be the reserve of full and committed relationships. This one makes its main appearance towards the end of the extract, where Paul questions the ethical propriety of Aaron's being 'out on the pull'. Fifth and finally, right at the end, Aaron draws on a repertoire of *permissive sexuality* (which also appears in Hollway's analysis). Here sex is constructed as a form of play. It is something that is fun, healthy and enjoyed equally by both men and women.

Subject positions

Whilst it is by no means inevitable, each one of these interpretative repertoires affords a corresponding subject position. In other words, as a man it is possible, via these discourses, to construct oneself (or another) as a sexual predator, as a Casanova or Don Juan, as a responsible loving partner, and so on, and so forth. However, these are not the only subject positions that are in play. For example, it is possible to suggest that during the sequence presented, Paul positions himself as a kind of interrogator, steadily probing and testing Aaron's motives in an almost Socratic fashion. This in turn, of course, places Aaron in the position of the *interrogated*, and sends him scurrying to the defence of his own actions.

Ideological dilemmas

Insofar as there are a whole range of different interpretative repertoires of sex and sexuality contained within this extract, it would hardly be surprising to find the existence of various ideological dilemmas. For instance, there is bound to be some friction between the notion of sex as playfulness and froth and one that sees it as an almost solemn statement of romantic and personal commitment. However, as discourse analysts, we do not need to resort to mere hypothesizing as the very pattern and direction of the conversation is itself animated by particular ideological tensions. To take just one example, look at Phil's contribution to the discussion on p.220, around the middle part of the extract (from where he says, "so that like took me aback somewhat" down to "never happens to me "). Within this short sequence of turns Phil can be seen to oscillate between two different subject positions. At both the beginning and the end of the sequence Phil seems very much in alignment with Aaron in talking about sex *as an achievement.* However, on at least two occasions he appears to distance himself from this discourse (and its associated subject position), choosing instead a position from within the '*have and hold*' repertoire (e.g. it is from there that he describes Aaron as being "on the moral low ground"). Oscillations like this are a tell-tale sign of the presence of an ideological dilemma, as people switch back and forth between two or more equally balanced but contradictory aspects of a culture's common sense.

The politics of representation

The question of who is most empowered by these 'structures of intelligibility' (Shapiro, 1992) is a difficult one to answer. For whilst, at first sight, some of these interpretative repertoires of sex and sexuality would seem to carry different liberatory potentials (from, say, a feminist point of view), in the end it usually boils down to how they are actually deployed in social interaction. For example, the repertoire of sexuality *as a basic instinct* can easily be used in attempts to excuse or justify acts of male sexual violence. However, it is just as easy to imagine it being used in a courtroom to press for harsher sentences (i.e. on the basis that if the attacker cannot control himself, then he ought to be locked away). Similarly, whilst the '*have and hold*' repertoire has often been understood as a more woman-centred language of sex and sexuality (see Hollway, 1984), it could easily be used in ways that work against a woman's best interests. The key, therefore, is to study these structures *in situ.*

Conclusion

In this chapter I have attempted to trace the outlines of a more critical form of discursive psychology – one that is designed to highlight the way that speakers both exploit and are exploited by existing discursive formations. Through the delineation and explication of three key concepts, my aim has been to show how a discourse analyst can maintain this dual focus. For in order to fully understand the complex relationship that exists between discourse and the speaking subject, we not only need to study the way that people draw upon psychological concepts in the course of ordinary conversation, for example, but we also need to look at how particular discourses of the 'self' and 'mind' come to structure how we all think, feel and talk.

Further Reading

Billig, M. (1996) *Arguing and Thinking: A Rhetorical Approach to Social Psychology*, (Second edition) Cambridge, Cambridge University Press: one of the truly foundational texts in the development of discursive psychology.

Billig, M., Condor, S., Edwards, D., Gane, M., Middleton, D. and Radley, A. (1988) *Ideological Dilemmas: A Social Psychology of Everyday Thinking*, London, Sage: for the original exposition of the concept of ideological dilemmas.

Davies, B. and Harré, R. (1990) 'Positioning: the discursive production of selves', *Journal for the Theory of Social Behaviour*, vol.20, pp.43–65 reproduced in Wetherell *et al.*, 2001: offers a more detailed discussion of the concept of subject positions.

Edley, N. and Wetherell, M. (1997) 'Jockeying for position: the construction of masculine identities', *Discourse and Society*, vol.8, pp.203–17: for an analysis of how social relations are conducted in and through the construction of masculine identities.

Freeman, M. (1993) *Rewriting the Self: History, Memory, Narrative*, London, Routledge: offers a lucid account of how selves are both spoken and storied.

Potter, J. and Wetherell, M. (1987) *Discourse and Social Psychology: Beyond Attitudes and Behaviour*, London, Sage: another foundational text in the development of discursive psychology.

Sampson, E.E. (1993) *Celebrating the Other: A Dialogic Account of Human Nature*, Hemel Hempstead, Harvester Wheatsheaf: an accessible US-based account of the social or discursive production of selfhood.

Wetherell, M. (1998) 'Positioning and interpretative repertoires: conversation analysis and post-structuralism in dialogue', *Discourse and Society*, vol.9, pp.387–412: for a discussion of how critical discursive psychology differs from more conversation analytic forms of discourse analysis.

References

Althusser, L. (1971) *Lenin and Philosophy and Other Essays*, London, New Left Books.

Antaki, C. and Widdicombe, S. (1998) *Identities in Talk*, London, Sage.

Atkinson, J.M. and Heritage, J.C. (eds) (1984) *Structures of Social Action: Studies in Conversation Analysis*, Cambridge, Cambridge University Press.

Barthes, R. (1973) *Mythologies*, London, Paladin.

Barthes, R. (1982) 'Inaugural lecture, College de France', in Sontag, S. (ed.) *A Barthes Reader*, London, Jonathan Cape.

Berger, M., Wallis, B. and Watson, S. (eds) (1995) *Constructing Masculinity*, London, Routledge.

Billig, M. (1991) *Ideology and Opinions: Studies in Rhetorical Psychology*, London, Sage.

Billig, M., Condor, S., Edwards, D., Gane, M., Middleton, D. and Radley, A. (1988) *Ideological Dilemmas: A Social Psychology of Everyday Thinking*, London, Sage.

Bourdieu, P. (1977) *Outline of a Theory of Practice*, Cambridge, Cambridge University Press.

Clatterbaugh, K. (1990) *Contemporary Perspectives on Masculinity*, Boulder, Westview Press.

Cohen, D. (1990) *Being a Man*, London, Routledge.

Connell, R. W. (1995) *Masculinities*, Cambridge, Polity.

Cornwall, A. and Lindisfarne, N. (eds) (1994) *Dislocating Masculinity: Comparative Ethnographies*, London, Routledge.

Eagleton, T. (1991) *Ideology: An Introduction*, London, Verso.

Edley, N. (1993) 'Prince Charles – our flexible friend: accounting for variations in constructions of identity', *Text*, vol.13, pp.397–422.

Edley, N. and Wetherell, M. (1995) *Men in Perspective: Practice, Power and Identity*, Hemel Hempstead, Prentice Hall/Harvester Wheatsheaf.

Edley, N. and Wetherell, M. (1996) 'Masculinity, power and identity' in Mac An Ghaill, M. (ed.) *Understanding Masculinities: Social Relations and Cultural Arenas*, Buckingham, Open University Press.

Edley, N. and Wetherell, M. (1997) 'Jockeying for position: the construction of masculine identities', *Discourse and Society*, vol.8, pp.203–17.

Edley, N. and Wetherell, M. (1999) 'Imagined futures: young men's talk about fatherhood and domestic life', *British Journal of Social Psychology*, vol.38, pp.181–94.

Edley, N. and Wetherell, M. (forthcoming – 2001) 'Jekyll and Hyde: analysing constructions of the feminist', *Feminism and Psychology*, vol.11.

Edwards, D. (1997) *Discourse and Cognition*, London, Sage.

Edwards, D. and Potter, J. (1992) *Discursive Psychology*, London, Sage.

Foucault, M. (1972) *The Archaeology of Knowledge*, London, Tavistock.

Foucault, M. (1977) *Discipline and Punish*, London, Penguin.

Foucault, M. (1980) *Power/Knowledge*, New York, Pantheon.

Franklin, C.W. (1984) *The Changing Definition of Masculinity*, New York, Plenum.

Geertz, C. (1973) *The Interpretation of Cultures*, New York, Basic Books.

Geertz, C. (1993) *Local Knowledge: Further Essays in Interpretive Anthropology*, London, Fontana.

Gilbert, N. and Mulkay, M. (1984) *Opening Pandora's Box: a Sociological Analysis of Scientists' Discourse*, Cambridge, Cambridge University Press.

Gramsci, A. (1971) *Selections from Prison Notebooks*, London, Lawrence and Wishart.

Hall, S. (1988) 'Minimal selves' in ICA documents no. 6, *Identity: The Real Me*, London, Institute of the Contemporary Arts.

Henley, N.M. (1986*) Body Politics: Power, Sex and Nonverbal Communication*, New York, Simon and Schuster.

Heritage, J. (1984) *Garfinkel and Ethnomethodology*, Cambridge, Polity.

Hoch, P. (1979) *White Hero, Black Beast: Racism, Sexism and the Mask of Masculinity*, London, Pluto Press.

Hollway, W. (1984), 'Gender difference and the production of subjectivity' in Henriques, J., Holloway, W., Unwin, C., Venn, C. and Walkerdine, V. (eds) *Changing the Subject: Psychology, Social Regulation and Subjectivity*, London, Methuen.

Jackson, D. (1990) *Unmasking Masculinity: A Critical Autobiography*, London, Unwin Hyman.

Jaworski, A. and Coupland, N. (1999) *The Discourse Reader*, London, Routledge.

Johnson, S. and Meinhof, U.H. (eds) (1997) *Language and Masculinity*, Oxford, Blackwell.

Macdonell, D. (1987) *Theories of Discourse: An Introduction*, Oxford, Blackwell.

Maybin, J. (2001) 'The Bakhtin/Volosinov writings on heteroglossia, dialogism and reported speech' in Wetherell, M., Taylor, S. and Yates, S.J. (eds) (2001) *Discourse Theory and Practice: A Reader*, London, Sage in association with The Open University.

McLellan, D. (1986) *Ideology*, Buckingham, Open University Press.

Mouffe, C. (1992) 'Feminism, citizenship and radical democratic politics' in Butler, J. and Scott, J.W. (eds) *Feminists Theorize the Political*, New York, Routledge.

Parker, I. (1992) *Discourse Dynamics: Critical Analysis for Social and Individual Psychology*, London, Routledge.

Parker, I. (ed.) (1998) 'Social constructionism' in *Discourse and Realism*, London, Sage.

Potter, J. and Wetherell, M. (1987) *Discourse and Social Psychology: Beyond Attitudes and Behaviour*, London, Sage.

Potter, J. and Wetherell, M. (1995) 'Discourse analysis' in Smith, J., Harre, R. and van Langenhove, L. (eds) *Rethinking Methods in Psychology*, London, Sage.

Potter, J., Wetherell, M., Gill, R. and Edwards, D. (1990) 'Discourse: noun, verb or social practice?', *Philosophical Psychology*, vol.3, pp.205–17.

Sampson, E.E. (1993) *Celebrating the Other: A Dialogic Account of Human Nature*, Hemel Hempstead, Harvester Wheatsheaf.

Scher, M., Stevens, M., Good, G. and Eichenfield, G.A. (eds) (1993) *Handbook of Counselling and Psychotherapy with Men*, London, Sage.

Shapiro, M. (1992) *Reading the Postmodern Polity*, Minneapolis, University of Minnesota Press.

Shotter, J. and Gergen, K.J. (eds) (1989) *Texts of Identity*, London, Sage.

Seidler, V.J. (1989) *Rediscovering Masculinity: Reason, Language and Sexuality*, New York, Routledge.

Seidler, V.J. (1994) *Unreasonable Men: Masculinity and Social Theory*, New York, Routledge.

Tannen, D. (1991) *You Just Don't Understand: Women and Men in Conversation*, London, Virago.

Walkerdine, V. (1990) *Schoolgirl Fictions*, London, Verso.

Wallace, M. (1979) *Black Macho and the Myth of the Superwoman*, New York, Dial Press.

Wertsch, J.W. (1990) *Voices of the Mind: A Sociocultural Approach to Mediated Action*, London, Harvester Wheatsheaf.

Wetherell, M. (1994) 'Men and Masculinity: A socio-psychological analysis of discourse and gender identity', *ESRC grant No. R000233129.*

Wetherell, M. (1998) 'Positioning and interpretative repertoires: conversation analysis and post-structuralism in dialogue', *Discourse and Society*, vol.9, pp.387–412.

Wetherell, M. and Edley, N. (1998) 'Gender practices: steps in the analysis of men and masculinities' in Henwood, K., Griffin, C. and Phoenix, A. (eds.) *Standpoints and Differences: Essays in the Practice of Feminist Psychology*, London, Sage.

Wetherell, M. and Edley, N. (1999) 'Negotiating hegemonic masculinity: imaginary positions and psycho-discursive practices', *Feminism and Psychology*, vol.9, pp.335–56.

Wetherell, M. and Potter, J. (1988) 'Discourse analysis and the identification of interpretative repertoires' in Antaki, C. (ed.) *Analysing Everyday Explanation*, London, Sage.

Wetherell, M., Taylor, S. and Yates, S.J. (eds) (2001) *Discourse Theory and Practice: A Reader*, London, Sage in association with The Open University.

Wex, M. (1979) *Let's Take Back Our Space*, Hamburg and Longmead, Dorset, Element Books.

Widdicombe, S. and Wooffitt, R. (1995) *The Language of Youth Sub-Cultures: Social Identity in Action*, Hemel Hempstead, Harvester Wheatsheaf.

Williams, R. (1965) *The Long Revolution*, Harmondsworth, Pelican Books.

Woolgar, S. (ed.) (1988) *Knowledge and Reflexivity: New Frontiers in the Sociology of Science*, London, Sage.

Zimmerman, D. and Pollner, M. (1971) 'The everyday world as phenomenon' in Douglas, J. (ed.) *Understanding Everyday Life*, London, Routledge and Kegan Paul.

Transcription notation used in this chapter

The following transcription notation represents a simplified version of that developed by Gail Jefferson (see Atkinson and Heritage, 1984, for a more comprehensive account).

(.)	Short untimed pause
[...]	Material deliberately omitted
[text]	Clarificatory information
<u>text</u>	Word(s) emphasized

CHAPTER SIX

The Discourse of New Labour: Critical Discourse Analysis

Norman Fairclough

Introduction

What does critical discourse analysis (CDA) have to offer students of social science? How does it differ from other approaches to discourse analysis? CDA provides a way of moving between close analysis of texts and interactions, and social analyses of various types. Its objective is to show how language figures in social processes. It is critical in the sense that it aims to show non-obvious ways in which language is involved in social relations of power and domination, and in ideology. It is a resource which can be used in combination with others for researching change in contemporary social life – including current social scientific concerns such as globalization, social exclusion, shifts in governance, and so forth.

This chapter will begin by describing the objective of critical discourse analysis (CDA), the social context of its development, and its theoretical origins and intellectual background. I then set out an analytical framework for discourse analysis based upon a view of discourse as an element of social practices dialectically linked to other elements. The next section works through an example using that framework. The framework is applied to an example of the political discourse of New Labour in Britain – an extract from the Government Green Paper (a consultative document) on welfare reform. Finally there are guided exercises to help you to do your own CDA.

1 The aims and origins of CDA

1.1 What is critical discourse analysis?

Critical discourse analysis asks: how does language figure as an element in social processes? What is the relationship of language to other elements of social processes? (See Chouliaraki and Fairclough, 1999; Fairclough, 1992; 1995; Fairclough and Wodak, 1997; Wodak, 1996.) Although most CDA focuses on language, some analysts also consider visual images (photographs, diagrams, etc.) or 'body-language' (gestures, facial expressions, etc.). I therefore refer below to **semiosis** as well as language. Semiosis is meaning-making through language, body language, visual images, or any other way of signifying.

The starting point for CDA is social issues and problems. It analyses texts and interactions, and indeed any type of semiotic material (written texts, conversations, television programmes, advertisements on billboards, etc.)

but it does not begin with texts and interactions; it begins with the issues which preoccupy sociologists, or political scientists, or educationalists. For instance, there is a great deal of current debate and concern about democracy and the negative effects of 'globalization' on democracy. One focus is upon what is widely perceived as a crisis in the 'public sphere'. Spaces for citizens to debate issues of common concern are seen as under threat, or as compromised by commercial interests (e.g. in television). Major social theorists of the public sphere see it in linguistic terms – as a matter of the forms of public dialogue that are available, as well as the places available for public dialogue. CDA asks: what changes have taken place and are taking place in forms of interaction around political and social issues? Do these forms of interaction constitute 'dialogue' in any substantive sense? And how do they compare with ways in which politicians and others in public life represent 'dialogue', 'deliberation', or 'debate'?

CDA is therefore inherently interdisciplinary. It opens a dialogue between disciplines concerned with linguistic and semiotic analysis (including discourse analysis), and disciplines concerned with theorizing and researching social processes and social change. If the dialogue is to be fruitful, it has to be 'transdisciplinary' rather than just interdisciplinary – committed to producing new theories and new methods of analysis which cut across existing disciplines (Fairclough and Chouliaraki, 1999). For instance, when discourse analysts work on specifying analytical categories of discourse analysis, such as 'genre', or indeed 'discourse' itself, they can draw upon and incorporate thinking from other disciplines (Fairclough, 2000b).

But CDA is not just concerned with analysis. It is **critical,** first, in the sense that it seeks to discern connections between language and other elements in social life which are often opaque. These include: how language figures within social relations of power and domination; how language works ideologically; the negotiation of personal and social identities (pervasively problematized through changes in social life) in its linguistic and semiotic aspect. Second, it is critical in the sense that it is committed to progressive social change; it has an emancipatory 'knowledge interest' (Habermas, 1971). For instance, an analysis of language in the neo-liberal global order would include a focus on how language figures in resistance to the detrimental effects of the new order (such as widening the gap between rich and poor or causing huge environmental damage). And it would also include an assessment from a language perspective of possibilities and strategies for strengthening and broadening struggles against these effects.

1.2 Discourse in contemporary social life

Critical awareness of language is widespread in contemporary social life, and perhaps CDA is best seen as part of that general self-consciousness about language. For instance, people are often critical of the language used in advertising, or sexist and racist ways of using language. Feminist and anti-racist political movements see the critique and change of language as part of their objectives. This increasing critical consciousness reflects important shifts in the function of language in social life, some of which are longer-term and characterize modern societies, while others are more recent.

Language has become more important in a range of social processes. The emergence of a 'knowledge-based' economy means an economy is also 'discourse-based' in the sense that new knowledges are produced, circulated and applied in production as new discourses, for instance, the discourse of 'teamwork'. We can say that knowledge and, hence, language and other forms of semiosis become commodities (Lyotard, 1986–7). For example, knowledge of how to conduct appraisals at work, including the language to use, is produced and sold as a commodity by management consultants. New communication technologies have transformed the means of semiotic production, producing a new articulation between older and newer communication technologies (i.e. new ways of using them in combination). In so doing it has transformed the order of discourse, the relative salience of semiosis in relation to other elements within the network of social practices, and the relation between language and other forms of semiosis (e.g. the visual clues). This is how we can approach the apparent increasing importance of 'communication' in contemporary social life.

We can also talk of a process of 'globalization' with respect to language and semiosis, though that term needs to be used with caution, not only because the process is in some cases more of a 'regionalization', but also because 'globalization' is a keyword in what might be seen as an ideological discourse of change. This is partly a matter of the emergence of a global language – 'global English' – but it is also a matter of the globalization of particular ways of representing the world – 'discourses' – and of particular ways of interacting – 'genres'. (I shall give a more explicit definition of 'discourses' and 'genres' in Section 2.1.) That is, it is a matter not only of the restructuring of relationships between 'global English' and other languages, but also of the restructuring of relationships between the discourses and genres of particular societies (and between their 'orders of discourse' – see Section 2.1). For instance, one aspect of global processes is the globalization of discourses which constitute representations and narratives of contemporary processes of change. They involve key words such as 'globalization' itself, 'modernization', 'flexibility', 'transparency', etc. All these key terms both register real change, and represent real change in particular ways linked to particular perspectives and interests. Another aspect of global processes is the globalization of genres such as the appraisal interview referred to above, or the genre of television news. At the same time, the emergence of a global language and a global order of discourse are obviously connected; English is both the vehicle and source of much of the globalization of the order of discourse (see below).

The increased importance of language in social life has meant more conscious attempts to shape it and control it to meet institutional or organizational objectives. We might refer to this as a **technologization of discourse** (Fairclough, 1992), echoing Foucault's concern to specify the social technologies of modern society. Technologization of discourse involves the systematic institutional integration of research on language; design and redesign of language practices; and training of institutional personnel in these practices. Let us return to the example of the appraisal interview: such genres are constantly being evaluated and redesigned, with institutional personnel being 'updated' accordingly. Another example of the technologization of discourse is the language used by operators in telephone sales or 'telemarketing' (Cameron, 2000). Technologization of discourse is an aspect of the enhanced 'reflexivity' of contemporary social life. Contemporary social life is becoming more reflexive in the sense that people increasingly shape and reshape the ways in which they live their lives on the basis of knowledge and information about their social practices (Giddens, 1991). Technologization of discourse is the institutional side of modern reflexivity, but enhanced language reflexivity is also a feature of everyday life. We can also see critical awareness of language as a feature of contemporary social life, not just as critical academic analysis of language. Is CDA itself perhaps an academic pursuit rooted in the properties of contemporary life?

It is important for CDA to address these larger changes in the way language and semiosis figure in social life. We can argue that critical theory and research should seek to address the central problems and issues which face people at a particular point in time. The dramatic changes in economy and society, to which I have briefly referred here, lie, I would argue, at the root of the problems, insecurities and struggles of contemporary social life. If CDA wants to address the latter, it has to have a picture of how language and semiosis figure in the former.

1.3 The theoretical origins of CDA

Critical discourse analysis can be seen as an application of the sort of critical analysis which has developed within 'Western' Marxism to language in particular. Western Marxism highlights cultural aspects of social life, seeing domination and exploitation as established and maintained culturally and ideologically. It moves away from the 'economism' of classical Marxism. For instance, the Italian Marxist militant and theorist, Antonio Gramsci, saw the capitalism of his time (just after the First World War) in terms of a combination of 'political society' and 'civil society' – the former is the domain of coercion, the latter is the domain of what he called **'hegemony'**. 'Hegemony' is a term used by Gramsci (Forgacs, 1988) and others for talking about power and struggles over power. It emphasizes forms of power which depend upon consent rather than coercion. The hegemony of the dominant social class or class-alliance depends upon winning the consent (or at least acquiescence) of the majority to existing social arrangements. Hegemonic struggle penetrates all domains of social life, cultural as well as economic and political, and hegemonies are sustained ideologically, in the 'common sense' assumptions of everyday life (Forgacs, 1988).

The French Marxist philosopher Louis Althusser viewed ideologies not as a nebulous realm of 'ideas' but as material social practices in social institutions (for instance, the ways in which various categories of professionals, such as doctors, communicate with members of the public). He saw ideologies as positioning people in particular ways as social 'subjects' (Althusser, 1971). Pecheux (1982) gave a specifically Althusserian twist to the concept of 'discourse', which he understood as language from an ideological perspective, language in the ideological construction of subjects. For instance, women during pregnancy go through processes of institutionalization that include exposure to discourses which contribute to constructing them as mothers (or 'mums').

The idea of 'critical' social science and analysis is particularly associated with the Frankfurt School which originated in Germany in the 1920s, and was one the main elements in the formation of 'Western' Marxism. The Frankfurt School resisted the reduction of culture to an epiphenomenal reflection of economy; cultural processes have their own effects on social life, and constitute a domain of struggle. More recently, the German social theorist Jurgen Habermas has developed a communication-based version of critical theory which sees the potential for emancipation as lying in the hitherto unrealized or partly realized potential of communication, and provides a normative basis for the critique of 'systematically distorted' communication (Habermas, 1984).

Michel Foucault's work on discourse was explicitly directed against Marxism and theories of ideology. For Foucault, discourses are systems of knowledge (e.g. medicine, economics, linguistics) that inform the social and governmental 'technologies' which constitute power in modern society. Discourses are partly ways of using language, but partly other things (e.g. ways of designing prisons or schools). Foucault's work has given rise to a widely used form of 'discourse analysis' (see Chapter Seven) which has also been an important theoretical point of reference for CDA (Fairclough and Wodak, 1997).

Another important influence has been Mikhail Bakhtin (1986). Volosinov (1973, written 1928 – according to some by Bakhtin himself) proposed the first linguistic theory of ideology. This claims that linguistic signs (words and longer expressions) are the material of ideology, and that all language use is ideological. Linguistic signs are regarded as 'an arena of class struggle' – one focus of class struggle is over the meanings of words. Bakhtin's work emphasizes the dialogical properties of texts, their **intertextuality** as Kristeva (1986) puts it: the idea that any text is explicitly or implicitly 'in dialogue with' other texts (existing or anticipated) which constitute its 'intertexts'. Any text is a link in a chain of texts, reacting to, drawing in, and transforming other texts. Bakhtin also developed a theory of genre – a theorization of the different types of text available in a culture (e.g. casual conversations, interviews, formal speeches, newspaper articles, etc.). He claimed that while any text is necessarily shaped by the socially available repertoires of genres, it may also creatively mix genres. For example, interviews on television between journalists and politicians sometimes combine the genre of a conventional political interview with the genre of a television 'chat show' – which itself is a combination of the genres of everyday conversation and entertainment.

2   An analytical framework for CDA

2.1 Semiosis in social practices

CDA is based upon a view of semiosis as an irreducible part of material
social processes. Semiosis includes all forms of meaning-making – visual
images and body language as well as verbal language. We can see social
life as interconnected networks of **social practices** of diverse sorts
(economic, political, cultural, etc.). And every practice has a semiotic
element. By 'social practice' I mean a more or less stabilized form of social
activity. All practices are practices of production – they are the arenas
within which social life is produced, be it economic, political, cultural, or
everyday life. Let us say that every practice includes the following elements:

- productive activity

- means of production

- social relations

- social identities

- cultural values

- consciousness

- semiosis.

These elements are **dialectically** related (Harvey, 1996). That is to say they
are different elements but are not discrete, fully separate, elements. There is
a sense in which each 'internalizes' the others without being reducible to
them. So, for instance, social relations, social identities, cultural values and
consciousness are in part semiotic, but that does not mean that we theorize
and research social relations, for example, in the same way that we theorize
and research language – they have distinct properties, and researching them
gives rise to distinct disciplines (though it is possible and desirable to work
across disciplines in a 'transdisciplinary' way, as I said in Section 1.1).

   CDA is analysis of the dialectical relationships between semiosis
(including language) and other elements of social practices. Its particular
concern is with the radical changes that are taking place in contemporary
social life, with how semiosis figures within processes of change, and with
shifts in the relationship between semiosis and other social elements within
networks of practices. We cannot take the role of semiosis in social
practices for granted, it has to be established through analysis. And semiosis
may be more or less salient in one practice or set of practices than in
another, and may change in importance over time.

   Semiosis figures in broadly two ways in social practices. First, it figures as
a part of the **social activity** within a practice. For instance, part of doing a
job (being a shop assistant) is using language in a particular way; so, too, is
part of governing a country. Second, semiosis figures in **representations**.
Social actors within any practice produce representations of other practices,
as well as ('reflexive') representations of their own practice, in the course of
their activity within the practice. They **recontextualize** other practices

(Bernstein, 1990; Chouliaraki and Fairclough, 1999) – that is, they incorporate them into their own practice, and different social actors will represent them differently according to how they are positioned within the practice. Representation is a process of social construction of practices, including reflexive self-construction – representations enter and shape social processes and practices.

Semiosis as part of social activity constitutes genres. **Genres** are diverse ways of acting, of producing social life, in the semiotic mode. Examples are: everyday conversation, meetings in various types of organizations, political and other forms of interview, and book reviews. Semiosis in the representation and self-representation of social practices constitutes discourses. **Discourses** are diverse representations of social life which are inherently positioned – differently positioned social actors 'see' and represent social life in different ways, as different discourses. For instance, the lives of poor and disadvantaged people are represented *through* different discourses in the social practices of government, politics, medicine, and social science, and *within* each of these practices, through different discourses that correspond to the different positions of the social actors.

Social practices networked in a particular way constitute a **social order** – for instance, the emergent neo-liberal global order referred to above, or, at a more local level, the social order of education in a particular society at a particular time. The semiotic aspect of a social order is what we can call an **order of discourse**. It is the way in which diverse genres and discourses are networked together. An order of discourse is a social structuring of semiotic difference – a particular social ordering of relationships amongst different ways of making meaning, i.e. different discourse and genres. One aspect of this ordering is dominance: some ways of making meaning are dominant or mainstream in a particular order of discourse, others are marginal, oppositional or 'alternative'. For instance, there may be a dominant way to conduct a doctor/patient consultation in Britain, but there are also other ways which may be adopted or developed to a greater or lesser extent in opposition to the dominant way. The dominant way probably still maintains social distance between doctors and patients, and the authority of the doctor over the way the interaction proceeds; but there are others ways which are more 'democratic', in which doctors play down their authority. The political concept of 'hegemony' can usefully be used in analysing orders of discourse (Forgacs, 1988; Fairclough, 1992; Laclau and Mouffe, 1985). A particular social structuring of semiotic difference may become hegemonic and so become part of the legitimizing common sense which sustains relations of domination, but hegemony will always be contested to a greater or lesser extent, in hegemonic struggle. An order of discourse is not a closed or rigid system, but, rather, an open system, which is put at risk by what happens in actual interactions.

2.2 A proposed analytical framework

An analytical framework for CDA is represented schematically overleaf. It is modelled upon the critical theorist, Roy Bhaskar's, concept of **'explanatory critique'** (Bhaskar, 1986; Chouliaraki and Fairclough, 1999).

An analytical framework for CDA

Stage 1   Focus upon a social problem that has a semiotic aspect.
Beginning with a social problem rather than the more conventional
'research question' accords with the critical intent of this approach – the
production of knowledge which can lead to emancipatory change.

Stage 2   Identify obstacles to the social problem being tackled. You
can do this through analysis of:

a)   the network of practices it is located within

b)   the relationship of semiosis to other elements within the particular
     practice(s) concerned

c)   the discourse (the semiosis itself) by means of:
     – structural analysis: the order of discourse

     – interactional analysis

     – interdiscursive analysis

     – linguistic and semiotic analysis.

The objective here is to understand how the problem arises and how it is
rooted in the way social life is organized, by focusing on the obstacles to
its resolution – on what makes it more or less intractable.

**Stage 3   Consider whether the social order (network of practices)
'needs' the problem.** The point here is to ask whether those who benefit
most from the way social life is now organized have an interest in the
problem *not* being resolved.

Stage 4   Identify possible ways past the obstacles. This stage in the
framework is a crucial complement to Stage 2 – it looks for hitherto
unrealized possibilities for change in the way social life is currently
organized.

Stage 5   Reflect critically on the analysis (Stages 1–4). This is not
strictly part of Bhaskar's explanatory critique but it is an important
addition, requiring the analyst to reflect on where s/he is coming from,
and her/his own social positioning.

The analysis of discourse, as such, takes place in Stages 2c and 4 but if
CDA is to meet the objectives I discussed above, it is essential to 'frame' the
analysis of discourse in something similar to this framework.

Stage 1: A social problem in its semiotic aspect

CDA begins from some perception of a discourse-related problem in some
part of social life. Problems may be in the activities of a social practice – in
the social practice *per se,* or in the representation of a social practice. The
former are 'needs-based' – they relate to discursive facets of unmet needs
of one sort or another. An example might be the nature of interaction
between various categories of professionals or experts and members of the

public, such as my earlier example of doctor/patient communication. Certain forms of doctor/patient communication might prevent people from dealing with their health problems through the health service (for instance, if the doctor controls the interaction according to a diagnostic routine to the extent that patients do not have the space to explain their problems). An example of the second type of problem in the representation of social practices might be the ways in which the lives of particular groups or communities are represented in sections of the press – such as women, British Moslems or Russians. For example, Sarangi and Slembrouck (1996) use CDA to address problems arising from bureaucracy, Talbot (1998) looks at problems in the representation of women and in interaction between women and men, Fairclough (1993) addresses problems arising from the 'marketisation' of universities.

Stage 2: Identify obstacles to it being tackled

Obstacles to a problem being tackled can be identified in the networks of practices in which it is located, at different levels of generality. For example, in the case of doctor/patient communication, the network constituted within the process of patient care; the network which constitutes the medical system as a whole; or even the wider networks of public service on a global as well as societal level, might be seen as pervasively shaping such particular forms of communication. This raises the important question of how much 'context' is relevant for the critical analysis of documents like this. It is a matter of identifying the 'object of research' (Bourdieu and Wacquant, 1992): is it patient care, public service, or even the emergent neo-liberal global order? A critical discourse analyst needs to give some thought to the question of what the object of research is – what are the problems and where do the obstacles lie? A rule of thumb is to be open to the possibility that obstacles at a local level (such as the process of welfare reform) can be traced back to a more global level.

Obstacles to a problem being tackled are also partly attributable to the ways in which semiosis figures within the network of practices concerned. For instance, intense competition for readers means that some newspapers are prepared to do almost anything to keep or enlarge their share of the market. Damaging racist, sexist or chauvinist representations of social life, which are judged to be appealing to sections of the newspaper-buying public (for instance, unflattering representations of Britain's partners in the European Union, especially France and Germany), are closely linked into the economics of the newspaper industry and, correspondingly, are less likely to be changed in response to appeals for moral responsibility.

I have just begun to touch upon properties of the discourse itself as part of the obstacles. This involves getting a sense of how the 'order of discourse' is structured – how semiosis itself is structured within the network of practices. For instance, the media, from a semiotic perspective, are an order of discourse within which there are diverse recurrent representations of various areas of social life and various groups and communities. Thus British Moslems or French politicians are represented in different ways, some damaging and some not. Moreover, these representations do not carry equal weight. Certain discourses are dominant and so are particularly powerful and influential, others are relatively marginal. This depends not only on gross differences in the size of readerships, but also on which newspapers tend to set the agenda for the rest of the press. In semiotic terms, certain representations and discourses more readily 'flow' across different media outlets, i.e. they are more likely to be taken up in a variety of outlets. It also depends on how representations produced in particular parts of the media are taken up in other social practices (education, work, government, everyday life, etc.). For instance, governments sometimes fall in line with the agenda set and the discourses used by sections of the media (e.g. *The Sun* newspaper in Britain) which they regard as being particularly influential with voters. So we find politicians using journalistic terms like 'spongers' to refer to people accused of abusing welfare provision.

Looking at the discourse itself as part of the obstacle involves both structural and interactional perspectives; not only looking at how the order of discourse is structured, but also looking at what actually goes on in specific texts and interactions. It is at this point that we reach what many would see as the exclusive concern of discourse analysis – the actual analysis of the text. The approach I have taken, by contrast, delays this quite considerably, but I believe such a delay (or rather, framing) is essential if we are to use discourse analysis as a resource within critical social research. Nevertheless, what I call **interactional analysis** is a crucial and central part of CDA and, indeed, what makes it discourse analysis rather than some other form of social analysis. For that reason, I present an analytical framework specifically for 'interactional analysis' in a separate section below.

Stage 3: Does the social order 'need' the problem?

Does the social order 'need', for instance, the type of interactions between professionals or experts and the public which limit the capacity of the latter to meet their needs and set their own agendas? Does it 'need' racist, sexist or chauvinist representations? Such forms of interaction or representations could be seen as serving some wider social interest or purpose, for example sustaining relations of authority between elites or experts and the rest of society, or producing social divisions which might facilitate strategies of domination. The point of this stage of the analysis is to assess the degree to which problems in their semiotic aspect are an insuperable part of the social order as presently constituted, which therefore can be resolved only through radical social transformations. The question of ideology arises at this point. Let us assume that ideologies are representations which produce and sustain relations of domination between different groups in societies, through achieving a measure of hegemony (i.e. becoming the dominant representation). We can see that in these terms racist or sexist representations can work ideologically. But so, too, can dominant forms of interaction between doctors and patients, in the sense that they presuppose representations of knowledge, expertise and rightful authority.

Stage 4: Possible ways past the obstacles

So far the analysis has applied a relational logic to identify the basis of the problem and the way the obstacles to dealing with it in the network of practices, and the semiotic element within it, are structured. This stage is rather different – it shifts to a dialectical logic, focusing upon variation and difference within the network of practices, to discern hitherto unrealized potentials for change within the way things are. Rather than focusing upon how the network of practices holds together, it focuses on the gaps and contradictions that exist. This double logic is also applied in the interactional analysis, the analysis of texts and interactions that will be described more fully below. On the one hand, how does a text hold together to produce its own local network? On the other hand, what are the incompletions, gaps, paradoxes and contradictions in the text? It is, of course, within actual texts and interactions that unrealized potentials for dealing with the obstacles concretely manifest themselves. For instance, interactions between doctors and patients in contemporary social life often involve a mixture of conventional social distance and notions of authority, as well as 'democratic' notions of solidarity and egalitarianism – a contradictory mixture which can lead to problems and even breakdowns in communication.

Stage 5: Reflection on the analysis

If social life is, as I have suggested, a network of social practices within which semiosis is one element, any academic analysis of a domain of social life, such as government (and specifically welfare reform), needs to be seen as being located within a social practice networked in particular ways with other practices, including the practices which academics research. Semiosis figures in particular ways in academic practice and in the networking of academic practices with others, and critical social analysts (including analysts of discourse) are positioned, like other academics, within this order of discourse. All academics are under pressure to publish work which meets internal academic criteria of quality. The work of critical discourse analysts is published in specialist journals, just like the work of other academics. So one issue that arises is the general one of whether the specialist discourse of critical discourse analysts constitutes a barrier, that is, an obstacle to their work having any significance or value for people located in other social practices. How can critical analysis of texts and interactions contribute to emancipatory change? This requires critical reflection on how we are working, on how we write, on the meta-language we use for analysing semiosis, on where we publish, and so forth. For instance, as academics, when we identify and specify a problem, do we involve those whose problem it is? If we don't, are there ways that we could?

2.3 Interactional analysis

I need to complete my account of the analytical framework by going into some detail about interactional analysis which I mentioned in Stage 2c. I refer to the analysis of actual conversations, interviews, written texts, television programmes and other forms of semiotic activity as 'interactional analysis'. This means that even written texts are seen in interactional terms. Whereas in a conversation participants in the interaction are co-present in time and space, with written texts there is temporal and spatial distance between them, and the text acquires a degree of independence both from the writing process and the reading process (the same is true of television programmes). Nevertheless, texts are written with particular readerships in mind, and are oriented to (and anticipate) particular sorts of reception and responses, and are therefore also interactive (Bakhtin, 1986). I shall use the word **text** in a very broad way to include not only written texts but also all the forms of semiotic activity referred to above (so a conversation and a television programme can both be seen as 'texts').

Whereas analysis of orders of discourse tries to specify the semiotic resources available to people (the social structuring of semiotic diversity), interactional analysis is concerned with how those resources interact, that is, the active semiotic work that people are doing on specific occasions using those resources. It is in the process of being used and worked that these resources come to be transformed.

Interactional analysis within CDA can be represented as follows:

Linguistic/semiotic analysis of text

Interdiscursive analysis of interaction

Social analysis of interaction.

The aim of the analysis is to show how semiotic, including linguistic, properties of the text connect with what is going on socially in the interaction. What CDA claims is that this connection is **interdiscursively** mediated: that what is going on socially is, in part, what is going on interdiscursively in the text, i.e. how it brings together particular genres and discourses (recall the definitions of these terms above), and that the interdiscursive work of the text materializes in its linguistic and other semiotic features. The focus in this section is on linguistic features, though other semiotic features will be referred to.

Text

In accordance with the view of semiosis as an element in social practices, texts are seen as 'work', as part of productive activity and as part of the process of producing social life. Texts need to be analysed both **paradigmatically** and **syntagmatically**. The paradigmatic aspect of language, in accordance with the usual grammatical sense of 'paradigm', concerns the range of alternative possibilities available, and the choices that are made amongst them in particular texts. The syntagmatic aspect of language concerns the organization or 'chaining' of words together in structures (e.g. phrases or sentences). On the one hand, texts involve specific choices from available systems: choices from orders of discourse – choices of particular genres and discourses – and choices from linguistic and semiotic systems – choices of particular linguistic and semiotic forms (particular words, grammatical structures, visual forms, and so forth). On the other hand, they combine or 'chain' selected elements together in specific ways. Alternatively, we may say that texts give particular 'textures' to selected words, images, genres or discourses – they 'texture' them together in particular ways, in particular material forms. In so doing, they produce local social structurings of semiotic difference (in contrast to the more permanent social structurings of semiotic difference in orders of discourse) – they combine genres and discourses (and the linguistic and semiotic features which realize them) in particular ways that have the potential to be novel and creative.

The texturing work of texts has multiple facets. Texts simultaneously work on representations of the world (forms of consciousness), social relations, social identities, and cultural values. It is concretely and locally in texts that the dialectic between semiosis and these other elements of social practices is played out. Correspondingly, text analysis is analysis of the textual work of:

- representing

- relating

- identifying

- valuing.

Interdiscursive analysis

Interdiscursive analysis works both paradigmatically in identifying which genres and discourses are drawn upon in a text, and syntagmatically in analysing how they are worked together through the text. The working assumption is that texts mix both different genres and different discourses, though this is a matter of degree (see Bakhtin, 1986). Some texts are more 'hybrid' than others, and tendencies to greater or lesser hybridity depend on social and historical circumstances (for example on how stable networks of practices are, how strong the boundaries between practices are, and so forth). In being articulated in specific ways with others in a text, a particular genre or discourse is open to 'local' transformations. That is, the categories of 'genre' and 'discourse' are used at different levels of abstraction. So, on the one hand, genres and discourses acquire a degree of permanence and continuity as a (semiotic) part of the social order (social practices), while on the other, they undergo local transformations in texts. So we can talk about the 'genre' of a text in terms of its local distinctiveness, as well as recognizing it as being constituted in a specific articulation of maybe two or three relatively stable 'genres' (e.g. a television show whose genre mixes elements of political interview, everyday conversation and comedy routine – see Fairclough, 1995).

Linguistic analysis of texts

Analysing language is a complex and many-sided process. Linguistics is a subject area which specializes in language and language analysis, though language analysis also goes on in other areas. So the discussion of language analysis here has to be highly selective and schematic. Linguistic analysis of texts involves working on the language of a text at various levels. Here's an outline, in very broad terms, of what it can cover.

- **Whole-text language organization** – The narrative, argumentative etc. structure of a text; the way a dialogue is structured.

- **Clauses combination** – The linking of clauses in complex or compound sentences (i.e. with or without one being subordinated to another); other ways of linking sentences together.

- **Clauses** i.e. simple sentences – The grammar and semantics of clauses, including categories such as transitivity (transitive or intransitive verbs); verbs relating to action (thought, speech, being, having); voice (active, passive); mood (declarative, interrogative, imperative); modality (degrees of commitment to truth or necessity).

- **Words** – Choice of vocabulary; semantic relations between words (e.g. synonyms, hyponyms); denotative and connotative meaning; collocations (i.e. patterns of co-occurrence); metaphorical uses of words, etc.

Activity 1

As an example, let us look at the short text below, taken from the back of a cigar packet:

Extract 1

Hamlet

MILD CIGARS

Finest grade cigar tobaccos
from around the world are
selected for Hamlet. Choice leaves,
harvested by hand, are dried,
fermented and carefully conditioned.
Then the artistry of our blenders
creates this unique mild, cool,
smooth smoking cigar.

BENSON & HEDGES LTD

These cigars should reach you in perfect condition.
If you are not totally satisfied, return this pack and its contents to:
Hamlet PO Box 371 Weybridge KT13 0ZW

SMOKING DAMAGES THE HEALTH
OF THOSE AROUND YOU

I shall comment on the text below, but before looking at my comments, work on the text a little yourself. Look in turn at the whole-text organization (the narrative); how clauses are linked together; grammatical and semantic features of clauses; and words (vocabulary). Then consider:

a) what sort of image is constructed for this product?

b) how is the process of producing cigars represented?

Link your answers to these questions as far as you can to the details you noticed about the text.

Discussion

Whole-text organization

The whole-text organization is that of a narrative. The story of the production of the cigars is told, if briefly. Much of the narrative is compressed into the second sentence – "harvested", "dried", "fermented" and "conditioned" refer to processes which are sequentially ordered, though that is not made linguistically explicit (e.g. with 'and then'). The only explicit marker of temporal sequence is "Then" at the beginning of the third sentence.

Clause combination

In terms of clause combination, all the sentences are simple, though the second might be seen as an elliptical version of the compound sentence: 'Choice leaves, which are harvested by hand, are dried, and then they are fermented, and then they are carefully conditioned'. The first two sentences are linked through their vocabulary – we understand "leaves" to be leaves of "tobaccos", "selected" is semantically linked to "choice" and (as a stage in the production process) "harvested", "dried" etc. There are also vocabulary links between them and the third sentence, as well as the temporal conjunct "Then".

Grammatical and semantic features

Moving to the grammar and semantics of the clause, all of the clauses (simple sentences) are declarative (making statements, rather than, for instance, asking questions). In terms of **modality**, they are all statements using present tense verbs which make categorical assertions – there is no modulation of truth-claims through words like 'usually', for instance. The knowledge relations between writer and reader are clear-cut – those who know about the process are telling those who do not. In terms of **transitivity**, all of the clauses are transitive, i.e. they have verbs with objects. But the first two are passive – rather than, for instance, 'tobacco workers select (harvest, dry etc.)', we have "are selected (harvested, dried etc.)". The actors, the workers who do this work, are absent from the text. This strikes me as a significant absence: referring explicitly to the workers might remind readers of the exploitation of 'Third World' labour, which would not sit easily with the emphasis in the text on the fineness of the

product. The initial ('thematic') position in a clause is an informationally
prominent one; one effect of the passive verbs is to give this prominence to
"Finest grade cigar tobaccos" and "Choice leaves", foregrounding the
quality of the product. Similarly, the third sentence foregrounds "the artistry
of our blenders". The clauses are in the third-person except for "our" in the
third – the text producers have this explicit presence, though its addressees
do not (unlike many advertising texts, there is no 'you').

Words

The absence of direct addressees is linked to features of the vocabulary
(words) which connote distinction – restraint in not directly addressing
consumers fits in with the construction of these cigars as rather superior
products. "Finest" in collocation with "grade", "unique" and "artistry" have
this connotation, so also do "carefully conditioned" and "selected" (which
also implies care). Exclusivity is also suggested by the categorization of the
tobaccos as "cigar tobaccos" – many people (myself included) would
perhaps not be aware that cigars are made from a specific type of tobacco.
There are also other descriptors of the product which connote value:
"mild", "cool" and "smooth" are all assumed to be desirable qualities. The
vocabulary is also somewhat technical – the categorization of tobaccos as
"cigar tobaccos" is presumably done in the trade, and "fermented" and
"conditioned" are specialist terms (so too is "blenders", but that would
probably be more familiar to most readers).

The texturing work of the text

Let me briefly comment on the types of 'textual work' distinguished above
(representing, relating, identifying, and valuing). I have already commented
quite extensively on *valuing*: the text constructs certain qualities of the
product as highly valued, and in so doing assumes shared values – 'we' like
our products (or at least our cigars) to be 'fine', or high quality; 'we' also
see mildness, coolness and smoothness as desirable qualities in cigars.

Turning to *representing*, the text gives, as I suggested above, a rather
sanitized representation of the process of producing cigars, which excludes
the workers who do the various types of work referred to and the
conditions under which they do it. The only workers identified are
"blenders", and they are constructed as part of the company ("our"
blenders), and as artists. The focus on constructing the distinction of the
product gives a rather idyllic and pastoral representation of working in the
tobacco industry.

In terms of *relating*, I have already referred to social relations as
knowledge relations – the ones who know telling the ones who don't. But
the ones who know are also trying to sell something to the ones who don't.
But unlike much commodity advertising, the selling is not explicit (readers
are not urged 'Get Hamlet cigars!', indeed they are not directly addressed at
all). The restraint is another part of the claim to distinction.

With respect to *identifying*, the producers construct themselves as a
rather high-class company. This follows from the construction of the
product as superior to others ("the artistry of our blenders" presupposes
that 'we have blenders who are artists', which of course constructs 'us' as

high-class). But the visual semiotics of the package design also contribute. The Benson & Hedges company always uses gold lettering and this together with the typography in which the company name and address are printed here, connote an 'upmarket' company. Readers are not explicitly identified or constructed in the text, but implicitly they are constructed as sharing the values I referred to above and as being discriminating as consumers (under the 'bother to mention' principle – the advertiser would presumably only 'bother to mention' quality features of the cigars on the assumption that consumers attend to such matters). They are also, of course, constructed as cigar smokers.

The work of representing, relating, identifying and valuing is done in the course of the text, textually (or texturely) produced in space (from beginning to end, top to bottom). So, for instance, distinction is partly produced through the structuring of informational prominence in the text, the patterning from one sentence to the next of themes which produces the series "Finest grade cigar tobaccos" – "Choice leaves" – "The artistry of our blenders".

There is a paradoxical feature of this example which allows us to see schematically how the text analysis might lead into a full critical discourse analysis (though I shall not pursue that in detail). Hamlet cigars are, I imagine, displayed in practically every tobacco shop in the UK. They are a market leader. There is nothing high-class about them in this sense. So why are they constructed as high-class – why (to speak interdiscursively) is the indirect advertising genre used, why these discourses of quality and 'artistry'? Perhaps because of the nature of the product (smoking cigars is, after all, seen as somewhat elite). Yet this is not a sufficient explanation. De Beaugrande (1997: 5ff) noticed a similar construction of distinction in an advertisement for bottled beetroot. And, in fact, many advertisements construct products and companies in this way. The social practice here is that of economic exchange – buying and selling – and that is located within a network of practices which constitutes production, exchange and consumption; the particular form of capitalist economy which is sometimes referred to as 'consumer capitalism'. Without going into details, it is evident that one feature of consumer capitalism is a preoccupation with distinction which is constantly fed by advertisers.

3   The Green Paper on Welfare Reform

We shall now work through a longer example in terms of the analytical framework set out above. It is an extract from the Green Paper on Welfare Reform published by the British (New Labour) Government in March 1998. The Green Paper is a stage in the reform process at which the Government sets out its proposals for public consultation and discussion before introducing legislation. The following extract is taken from the third chapter of the Green Paper ('The importance of work') and consists of the first 19 of its 40 paragraphs.

Extract 2

Chapter Three

The importance of work

> **Principle One**
>
> **The new welfare state should help and encourage people of working age to work where they are capable of doing so.**

1   The Government's aim is to rebuild the welfare state around work. The skills and energies of the workforce are the UK's biggest economic asset. And for both individuals and families, paid work is the most secure means of averting poverty and dependence except, of course, for those who are retired or so sick or disabled, or so heavily engaged in caring activities, that they cannot realistically support themselves.

2   For many people the absence of paid work is a guarantee of a life on low income. One of the reasons children make up a higher proportion of those at the bottom of the income distribution is that a growing number of parents, especially lone parents, are out of work. Paid work also allows people to save for their retirement.

3   For too long, governments have abandoned people to a life on benefits. Far too many individuals and families are penalised, or gain too little, if they move from benefit to work.

4   **Chapter One** described how work has changed over the last 50 years. The rewards for skills have grown, widening the wage gap. Some people reap the rewards of fairly paid work, while others are either stuck on benefit or switching between benefit dependency and short-term, low-skilled jobs. There has also been a shift in balance from full-time manual jobs to part-time and service-sector posts. In households with two working adults, the loss of a job for one can mean that the other would be better off giving up work too.

5   The Government aims to promote work by:

- **helping people move from welfare to work through the New Deals and Employment Zones;**

- **developing flexible personalised services to help people into work;**

- **lowering the barriers to work for those who can and want to work;**

- **making work pay, by reforming the tax and benefit system, including a Working Families Tax Credit, reforming National Insurance and income tax, and introducing the national minimum wage; and**

- **ensuring that responsibilities and rights are fairly matched.**

■ POLICY DIRECTION

Welfare to Work – The New Deals

6   The Government's biggest investment since taking office has been in a large-scale **welfare to work** programme. Our ambition is nothing less than a change of culture among benefit claimants, employers and public servants – with rights and responsibilities on all sides. Those making the shift from welfare into work will be provided with positive assistance, not just a benefit payment.

7   Our comprehensive welfare to work programme aims to break the mould of the old, passive benefit system. It is centred on the five aspects of the New Deal for:

- **young unemployed people;**
- **long-term unemployed people;**
- **lone parents;**
- **people with a disability or long-term illness; and**
- **partners of the unemployed.**

8   Alongside these national programmes, we are also piloting targeted help for areas of high long-term unemployment through the new Employment Zones.

Young unemployed people

9   For young people, entering the labour market is a critical rite of passage to adulthood. One of the factors causing social exclusion is an unacceptably high level of youth unemployment. The **New Deal for Young People** is a radical step forward because it emphasises quality, choice and above all meeting the needs of individuals. It will address all the barriers to work that young people face, including homelessness and drug dependency. It aims to help young unemployed people, aged 18 to 24, to find jobs and remain in employment. In the Budget, the Chancellor also announced that partners of young unemployed people who have no children would be included in the New Deal, and given access to the same opportunities for work.

The New Deal for Young People

- **Is being piloted in 12 pathfinder areas.**
- **Will go nationwide in April 1998.**
- **Is an investment of £2.6 billion.**

The New Deal for Young People *continued*

- Will offer participants, aged 18 to 24, four opportunities:
  - work with an employer who will receive a job subsidy of up to £60 a week;
  - full-time education or training;
  - work with a voluntary sector organisation; or
  - work on the Environmental Taskforce.
  All these options involve training.

- Support will also be given to those young people who see self-employment as the best route out of benefit dependency.

- Includes a special £750 grant to employers to provide their New Deal employees with training towards a recognised qualification.

- For those who do not wish to take up offers of help there will be no 'fifth option' of simply remaining on benefit.

10 Every young person who receives Jobseeker's Allowance (JSA) for six months without securing work will enter the New Deal Gateway – an exercise in promoting job-readiness and providing a tailor-made package of help. People with particular disadvantages may enter earlier. For those with adequate skills and appropriate work experience – the 'job-ready' – the immediate focus will be on securing an unsubsidised job. For those young people less equipped to enter the job market, the Gateway will provide careers advice and guidance, assessment of training needs, work trials with employers and tasters of other options. This Gateway period may last for up to four months.

Long–term unemployed people

11 For those who lack skills and become unemployed, the risks of remaining out of work for a long period are high. So prevention is better than cure. The Government's plans for lifelong learning, described in **Chapter Five**, are designed to raise skills in the adult population and promote employability, so that people find it easier to get and keep jobs.

12 There is already a sizeable group of long-term unemployed people who may need additional help to overcome barriers to work. Employers are often sceptical of the job-readiness of a person who has been out of the labour market for long periods. And, over time, skills, confidence and health can deteriorate. The **New Deal for the Long-Term Unemployed** represents the first serious attack on the waste of talents and resources represented by long-term unemployment.

The New Deal for the Long-Term Unemployed

- Due to start in June 1998.

- Initial investment of £350 million.

- For those aged over 25 who have been out of work for more than two years.

- Substantial job subsidy of £75 a week for employers for six months.

- Changes to benefit rules to improve access to full-time education or training.

Additional pilots are due to start in November 1998:

- Pilots of an intensive approach for 70,000 people, providing individualised advice, counselling and help, which may include training and work experience, at a cost of £100 million.

- Special assistance tailored to the needs of those aged over 50.

Lone Parents

13   The twin challenges of raising children alone and holding down a job are considerable. The vast majority of single parents want to work, to gain a decent wage and a foothold on the ladder out of poverty. But the old welfare system did little to help, simply handing out benefits rather than offering active support in finding and securing work, training or childcare. The **New Deal for Lone Parents** will provide a more active service.

The New Deal for Lone Parents

- Piloted in eight areas since July 1997, offering help to 40,000 lone parent households.

- Available nationwide to lone parents making a new or repeat claim for Income Support from April 1998.

- Available to all lone parents on Income Support from October 1998.

- The service is aimed at lone parents whose youngest child is at school, but is also available to those with pre-school children.

14   There will be a full, independent evaluation of the first phase of the New Deal for Lone Parents, available in autumn 1999. Early indications are encouraging. Lone parent organisations, employers and lone parents themselves have all welcomed this New Deal, and the staff responsible for delivering the service have

been particularly enthusiastic. The staff have welcomed the opportunity to become involved in providing practical help and advice. The first phase of this New Deal has aroused considerable interest: lone parents in other parts of the country are asking if they can join in.

People with a disability or long-term illness

15   People with a disability or long-term illness are another group that often face difficulties in finding or remaining in work. Of course, many people with a disability or long-term illness are simply not in a position to undertake work. Our commitment to their welfare is unwavering. But there are others who may be able to work and who should get more help to do so. The **New Deal for Disabled People** has been introduced for this purpose. It is described in detail in **Chapter Six**.

Partners of the unemployed

16   The partner of an unemployed person can face additional disincentives to work: some people feel forced to give up their job once a partner becomes unemployed to avoid being made worse off. This is one cause of the deepening divide between *work-rich* and *work-poor* households. The partners of unemployed people are not offered the same assistance by the Government that is extended to the claimant unemployed. There are workless households in which the claimant (usually a man) is required to seek work actively, while the partner (usually a woman) is offered no help because of her assumed dependency.

17   We have therefore launched the **New Deal for Partners of the Unemployed.** As announced in the Budget, we have set aside £60 million of Windfall Tax receipts to provide partners with expert, personalised help to find work, through pilot projects in every region of the UK. Thousands of people – the vast majority of whom are women – will be helped by this expansion of the New Deal programme. In addition, we are expanding the New Deal for Young People to include partners of the young unemployed (see above).

Employment Zones

18   Alongside the New Deal, we are targeting intensive and innovative help on areas in particularly acute need. As our manifesto made clear, we are committed to finding ways of bringing together money currently spent separately on benefit, training and other programmes to be used more flexibly and innovatively in certain areas of the country, designated as **Employment Zones.** Local partnerships will draw up plans to give unemployed people opportunities to improve their employability and move back into and remain in employment.

19   Within existing legislation, we are already testing the approach in five prototype Employment Zones in Glasgow, South Teesside, Liverpool, North West Wales and Plymouth. £58 million has been provided to run these prototypes until the year 2000. We are considering how best to build fully-fledged Employment Zones on the experience of the prototypes from 2000.

3.1   Analysing the extract

The network of social practices within which the process of welfare reform and the Green Paper are located is immediately that of government (including the welfare system itself) and politics, though linked to practices in the economic domain (work) and in everyday life. Governmental and political practices are changing quite radically, and New Labour is, itself, contributing substantially to what it calls their 'modernization'. Part of what is at issue is the relationship between government, the management of social life by the state, and politics, as well as contestation between different interest groups over the distribution of social goods. If we think of this in terms of forms of 'communication', politics requires 'two-way', dialogical communication, whereas government tends towards 'one-way' communication, i.e. communication in the management and control of perception and action.

But the picture is more complex: one aspect of the current 'modernization' of government is a move towards 'partnerships' between government, business, the voluntary sector, and so forth, and towards 'devolution'. But there is a tension between the loosening of central control which these imply and the manifest tendency of New Labour to tighten central control, for instance in the central management of perception through what is called 'media spin'. It is not clear yet to what extent the discourse of 'partnership' and 'devolution' will lead to a real dispersal of power, nor does it seem that such 'partnership' opens up political space for real dialogue rather than incorporating certain interests (especially business interests) into the management and 'governance' of social life. The semiotic element of this shifting network of practices is important when analysing them: establishing what space there is for politics in processes like welfare reform is, to a large degree, establishing what sort of communicative interaction takes place. So I suggest that in this example we focus on a quite specific aspect of this larger question: how 'dialogical' is this important consultative document, i.e. how much space does it open up for dialogue?

Activity 2

I shall begin with my own analysis for the first part of the analytical framework – identifying a social problem in its semiotic aspect – so that we are focusing on the same issues. You should then work through the extract in terms of other parts of the analytical framework before reading the rest of my analysis.

3.2   Green Paper analysis, Stage 1: A social problem in its semiotic aspect

For this part of the analysis, we need to go outside the text, using academic and non-academic sources to get a sense of its social context. A **'needs-based' problem** which arises with the Green Paper is the problem of the 'public sphere' (Arendt, 1958; Fairclough, 1999; Habermas, 1989). A widely noted negative effect of neo-liberal globalization is that it tends to squeeze out democratic politics. Control over major aspects of social life, especially the economy, is increasingly outside the reach of governments, because political parties of both the Left and the Right tend to converge in policies and political ideologies around an acceptance of the neo-liberal order as inevitable, and look for ways of succeeding within it. Part of the squeezing out of democracy is a crisis of the 'public sphere' – the sphere of social life in which citizens can deliberate together on matters of social and political concern, outside the constraints of the state and the market. This can be seen in semiotic terms: there are neither adequate spaces in contemporary social life nor adequate forms of deliberative dialogue to sustain a vigorous public sphere. Documents such as the Green Paper on Welfare Reform can be seen as part of the problem. Although supposedly a consultative document which sets out to encourage public debate, it is, effectively, a promotional document designed to 'sell' the Government's proposals for welfare reform.

The Green Paper also raises various **problems of representation**. One is the representation of work. The Government's declared strategy is to deal with poverty and social exclusion by getting people off welfare and into work. The discourse of 'work' which dominates the document is a traditional one – 'work' is paid employment. Yet huge increases in productive capacity due to technological innovation mean that there is no longer the need for the mass labour forces of the past, and there are not enough full-time, secure, paid jobs for everyone. If the Government does succeed in increasing the number of people in paid employment, it must mean that many of them will be in insecure and poorly-paid jobs. A strategy of 'welfare to work' would seem to call for a radical rethinking of what 'work' is, that is, what is recognized and rewarded as useful social activity, perhaps to include many forms of voluntary work, or give more generous recognition to those who care for dependent relatives or friends. Yet there is no such rethinking in the document or in the welfare reform process.

Let us focus below on the needs-based problem, the problem of the public sphere and its semiotic aspect: the promotional nature of the document and its lack of real dialogue.

Activity 3

Work though the other stages of the analytical procedure. The following notes are provided only for guidance – you may want to go in different directions. Note that the focus on the needs-based problem entails a focus on genre and on relating.

Stage 2: Obstacles to tackling the problem

a) The network of practices. Think of the relationship between party politics, government, and the media. My comments following Activity 2 have already indicated some aspects of this relationship.

b) Relationship of semiosis to other elements in the network. Think of the relationship in government between changing social systems such as the welfare system, and winning consent for such changes through changing people's perceptions and beliefs.

c) The discourse (the semiosis itself):

i)   The order of discourse – think of the relationship between official documents, press releases, reports in the media, focus groups, and political speeches. You might try to construct a sort of 'flow chart' to show how these different types of discourse tend to be linked together in real cases.

ii)   The text – look for the presence of different genres in the text – party political manifesto, public information leaflet, as well as policy statement. How are they combined together? Compare, for instance, paragraph 1 with paragraph 5 – how do you think they differ in genre? And look closely at paragraph 6: to what extent is this the genre of policy statement, to what extent the genre of party political manifesto?

iii) How is the combination realized in the language in terms of whole-text language organization; the way clauses and sentences are linked together; the grammar and semantics of clauses; the words that are used?

      Without a background in linguistics, you will find it difficult to give detailed answers here – I will give more detail in my analysis. But look closely, for instance, at paragraphs 1, 5 and 6. Look at how the combination of policy statement and political manifesto is realized in the semantics (look at the shift between "the Government" and "our") and the words that are used. Look at the overall organization of paragraph 5, and at how its clauses are linked together. Compare that with the overall organization and clause/sentence linkage in paragraph 1.

Stage 3: Does the social order 'need' the problem?

Consider whether the problem could be tackled without fundamental change.

Stage 4: Ways past the obstacles

Are there tensions, contradictions or gaps which could provide leverage for change – in the networking of practices, in the relationship of semiosis to other elements, in the order of discourse, in the texts? In the text, look at the alternation between third person ("the Government") and first person ("we") – already referred to in paragraph 6; and at how "work" is represented.

Stage 5: Reflection

Reflect on the analysis you have done, and on whether and how such analysis might make a difference to the problem.

3.3   Green Paper analysis, Stage 2: Identify obstacles to the problem being tackled

Obstacles to the problem being tackled can be identified in the networks of practices it is located within at different levels of generality: the network constituted within the process of welfare reform; the network which constitutes government; or the wider network referred to above – the emergent neo-liberal global order. These levels are not mutually exclusive: limitations of the public dialogue around welfare reform can partly be attributed to practices of government under New Labour (including their attachment to 'media spin') though, as I have suggested above, there is a general pressure on democracy and the public sphere arising from the structure of the new global capitalism.

What about obstacles in the relationship between semiosis and other elements of practices? Part of what the practices of government produce is social and institutional change – in this case, change to the welfare system, change in the focus of welfare (from benefits to moving people off welfare into work), how welfare is 'delivered', etc. There is a pervasive emphasis on the importance of 'communication' in contemporary social life, and government is no exception. 'Communication' means various things, but one of them is a one-sided process of government 'communicating with' (or better, 'to') the public. This receives increasing attention in the management of policy and institutional change. Semiosis in the form of essentially promotional genres, such as that of the Green Paper, are a crucial element in producing change. And part of what such genres do is manage perception, shape the way people see (in this case) welfare and promote new discourses of (in this case) welfare. So one of the obstacles to dealing with the crisis of the public sphere is that 'communication' in the process of producing policy and institutional change increasingly has this one-sided, promotional, perception-management character – even when the process is ostensibly public 'consultation'. But it is also necessary to trace how such 'communication' is located in the procedural chains which turn a policy conception into institutional change – to see winning consent to new discourses as a stage in a process which leads the restructuring of the institutional system which constitutes social welfare, including, for instance, the physical and spatial instantiations of new discourses in the redesign of buildings (Iedema, 1997).

Next, I'll look at obstacles in the structuring of the order of discourse. Of course there are forms of the public sphere in contemporary social life – think, for instance, of the discussions and debates that go on about government policy (including welfare reform) in sections of the press, on radio or on the internet, as well as in more traditional forms such as public meetings. But what is at issue here is how such forms of semiosis are structured in relation to the promotional forms represented by the Green Paper, and in other areas of the press and broadcasting which are shaped by the Government's notorious reliance on 'media spin' (Franklin, 1998). What is at issue is the structuring of orders of discourse. We can think of this in terms of the structuring of relations between the semiotic forms of the public sphere and the semiotic forms of 'public relations'. We need to bring into the picture the Government's attempts to simulate the public sphere in ways they can keep under control, such as the use of focus groups and interactive web sites. It is the dominance of public relations over the public sphere in the order of discourse of government and politics that constitutes part of the obstacle.

Orders of discourse are also characterized by a sort of syntagmatic or 'syntactic' structuring which we can refer to as **generic chains**. That is, there are regular ordering relationships between different genres so that one is framed by others. If we trace the course of the campaign around welfare reform in semiotic terms (using government publications that are now freely available on the internet, as well as media sources), we find generic chains of the following general form in the welfare reform process:

> speech <press release> – (media reports) – document
> <press release> – (media reports) – speech <press release> ...

The Green Paper was preceded and followed up by important ministers giving speeches, each of which (like the document itself) came with its own press release (systematically incorporating a media 'spin'). Each subsequent move in such a chain is responsive to media reactions to earlier moves. Practices such as focus groups may be inserted into such chains through research reports, which also come with press releases attached. On occasion, press conferences will also figure in such chains.

The press release for the Green Paper on Welfare Reform is a 'boundary' genre which links the fields of government and media, and it is apparently a combination of two genres:

- a media genre – a press report, with the familiar beginning of headline + lead, i.e.:

Frank Field Launches New Contract for Welfare
Frank Field, Minister for Welfare Reform, today unveiled the Government's Green Paper on Welfare Reform "New Ambitions for Our Country – A New Contact for Welfare" ...

- a governmental (administrative) genre – a set of background notes.

The 'report' is also a resource for producing further reports, and the latter part of it consists of important elements of that resource – key principles of the Green Paper, and key quotes from Frank Field and Tony Blair. It is, in a sense, an official summary, but a summary which selects and orders what it summarizes with a partly promotional intent. The process of summarizing is crucially important not only in press releases but also throughout the practices of government. The Green Paper itself includes its own internal summaries – the first chapter is a summary of the whole document, there is a summary of the main points in the last chapter, the Prime Minister's Foreword incorporates his summary, the press release constitutes a summary oriented to media uptake, and the document is then summarized over and over again in speeches. It is through summarizing that media 'spin' is added.

Activity 4

Use the internet to find a sample of government press releases. To what extent do your examples indicate that press releases generally have the properties of a 'boundary genre' suggested above?

Interactional analysis

The Green Paper consists of a (signed) Preface by the Prime Minister, Tony Blair, followed by a summary of the whole document, Chapter One sets out the case for welfare reform, Chapter Two identifies four "ages" of welfare and eight "key principles" of welfare reform which constitute the topics of Chapters 3–10. Chapter Eleven is about the longer-term future of welfare, and there is an Appendix on the evolution of social security. Each of the central chapters (3–10) is structured as follows: a chapter title ("The importance of work" in the case of Chapter Three) below which there is coloured box containing one of the eight 'principles' of the proposed welfare reform. In this case "Principle One":

Principle One
The new welfare state should help and encourage people of working age to work where they are capable of doing so.

There is then an unheaded introductory section focusing on past and present welfare practices, and the case for reform (paragraphs 1–5); a section headed "Policy Direction" which takes up the bulk of the chapter (paragraphs 6–40; Extract 2 covers just paragraphs 1–19) and sets out proposed future welfare practices; and under the heading "Success Measures" a short list of criteria against which the success of the proposed reforms will be judged (end of paragraph 40, reproduced below in Extract 3). Each of the chapters tells readers what the case is for welfare reform but, above all, what the Government has done, is doing and intends or aims to do in the way of welfare reform.

Since the concern is with the question of the public sphere and therefore with the question of dialogue, I shall focus on the textual 'work' of *relating*, though I shall add brief comments on *representing, identifying* and *valuing* later. The focus on relating means that in the interdiscursive analysis I shall concentrate on genre (rather than discourse) in my comments, and in the linguistic analysis of the texts I shall focus on features (such as mood and modality) which are particularly relevant to genre.

Interdiscursive analysis

The genre is hybrid, but what is missing from it is a dialogical element – it is a promotional genre, not a dialogical genre. Although, in the words of the Prime Minister's Foreword, the document is supposed to be part of a process of "consultation" and "discussion", this is one-way communication rather than the two-way (dialogical) communication these words imply. This is in contrast, for example, to the Department of Education and

Employment's Green Paper 'The Learning Age', published at approximately the same time, which constantly moves between presenting policy and posing questions about the proposals for discussion.

The genre includes elements one might expect to find in government policy statements, party political manifestos, explanatory public information leaflets or policy summary documents used internally within government. That is, it includes descriptions of intended policies (e.g. paragraph 10), party political rhetoric (e.g. the first sentence of paragraph 7), and pedagogical devices for presenting information in an easily digestible form (the coloured boxes with bullet points in, for instance, paragraphs 5 and 7). The policy summary element is just the "Success Measures" in paragraph 40 (shown below in Extract 3).

How are these generic elements worked together in the text? Sections of the document generally move between the policy statement element which shifts occasionally into political propaganda, and the public information element. These two major elements are visually distinct – the latter are highlighted in colour, sometimes with headings, and with a distinctive layout using 'bullet points'. Examples of these sections are: paragraphs 1–5; paragraphs 6–8; paragraphs 9–10. An example of the shift into political propaganda within the policy statement element is in paragraph 6. I would say the second sentence is political propaganda (notice the shift between third-person and first-person plural "our"). The constant movement in sections between policy statement and public information elements constitutes a slippage between the process of forming policy (which is what is supposed to be going on), and the quite different process of presenting policy which is already established in a publicly accessible form. (This is facilitated by the fact that some of the policies are planned, whereas others have already been initiated.) It is a shift from argument and exposition to pedagogy. This is part of the promotional nature of the document – in these public information elements, it is written as if the argument is over and all that is at issue is that the public should understand the new system. The "Success Measures" at the end of the chapter have a similar effect.

Extract 3

Success Measures
1. A reduction in the proportion of working age people living in workless households.
2. A reduction in the proportion of working age people out of work for more than two years.
3. An increase in the number of working age people in work.
4. An increase in the proportion of lone parents, people with a long-term illness and disabled people of working age in touch with the labour market.

There is no discussion of the "Success Measures" – why they are a good idea or what they should measure. They are merely listed, as if this were an internal government document setting out a system which has already been agreed and established. The "Success Measures" are located at the end of each chapter, and give one the sense in coming to the end of a chapter that issues are closed.

Activity 5

Look at one or two public information leaflets (e.g. leaflets on welfare benefits). Compare them with the extract from the Green Paper in terms of genre.

Activity 6

Consider to what extent Extract 2 from the Green Paper is organized in terms of a problem-plus-solution structure. How much reported speech is there in the text? To what extent are voices other than the official and party voice of the Government included?

Linguistic analysis of the text

Whole-text language organization

As I said above, I focus on linguistic features which relate specifically to genre, beginning with whole-text language organization. The chapter basically has a problem–solution structure – more exactly, it is structured overall as: *objective* + *problem* (obstacles to achieving it) + *solution* + *evaluation of solution* (get people of working age into work, obstacles to people working, proposed Government steps to facilitate work, how they will be evaluated).

The objective is formulated in "Principle One" which heads the chapter after the chapter title. The title presupposes the proposition: work is important. Notice that it might have more dialogically been a question – 'How important is work?'. The introductory section (paragraphs 1–5) moves from arguing for the objective, to describing obstacles to achieving it, to summarizing the Government's solution. The "Policy Direction" section which takes up the bulk of the chapter (paragraphs 6–40) is primarily presenting solutions, but reiterates from time to time the objective and the obstacles. The evaluation is just a summary list at the end of the final paragraph of the chapter.

The problem–solution structure is one aspect of the promotional character of the document, particularly since only one set of solutions is presented and they are the Government's. As this is supposed to be a consultation document, alternative policy directions might have been set out. A notable feature of the document is the paucity of 'voices' represented, and this is evident linguistically in the absence of reported speech. There are many 'voices' in the domain of welfare (including claimants, claimants' organizations, welfare staff, and experts on welfare), but most of these are simply absent from the document. There is reported speech in paragraph 14: "lone parent organizations, employers and lone parents themselves have all welcomed this New Deal"; "the staff have welcomed the opportunity ..."; "lone parents in other parts of the country are asking ..." (notice also the 'reported thought' in paragraph 13 – "the vast majority of single parents want to work"). Presumably this is reporting statements that have been made by lone parents, employers and, perhaps, staff organizations. But what is being reported in the case of "lone parents themselves" and "the vast majority of single parents"? On what evidence do the authors of the document claim that lone parents "have welcomed", "are asking", and "want"? The only plausible answer is that these claims are based on opinion research (surveys, questionnaires, perhaps focus groups), which might be seen as a technology for legitimizing the Government speaking for people. So where other voices do appear, it is on a very restricted basis. This relative absence of voices is one way in which the document is non-dialogical. Why, in a consultative document, do we not hear what various interested parties have to say?

I have referred above in discussing intertextuality to another promotional aspect of whole-text organization – the oscillation between the policy statement element and the public information element, and the appearance within the former of political persuasion. The coloured 'boxes' in which the public information element is located also, in some cases, serve an organizing function for the chapter. The bullet points in paragraph 5, for instance, set out the structure of the chapter (each is one of the main sections). On one level this is 'reader-friendly', but it is also 'reader-directive', and therefore part of the promotional character of the document: it pre-structures reader expectations.

Activity 7

Look at your sample of public information leaflets in terms of what features make them 'reader-friendly' (and 'reader-directive').

Activity 8

Are the sentences in Extract 2 mainly simple, compound or complex? To what extent are logical and other connections between sentences explicitly marked, e.g. with words like *therefore* or *however*?

Clause combination

Most sentences are simple, consisting of a single clause, and there are few **compound** or **complex sentences**. Exceptions include the third sentence of paragraph 14, which is compound (two clauses linked with 'and', the second beginning "(and) the staff responsible", and the third sentence of paragraph 11 which is complex (a main clause + a subordinate clause "so that"). The latter is one of the few explicit cases of legitimization – giving reasons or purposes. The document is not written as a set of arguments, but, rather, as a set of assertions. Even when there is an argument going on as in paragraph 9, the argumentation is implicit rather than explicit – an explicitly argumentative version of the first three sentences might go something like: 'finding a job is critical to entering adulthood, *yet* there is a great deal of youth unemployment, *so* we are setting up the New Deal for Young People ...'. The italicized conjunctions mark explicitly the links in the argument. There is also an argument which is left implicit in paragraph 12. What we actually have in the document is a series of **declarative** sentences which are connected mainly through vocabulary, but with a lack of conjunctions or sentence adverbials (like 'however') to connect all these assertions into an argumentative thread. Even when co-ordinating conjunctions might have been used they tend not to be (e.g. the fourth sentence of paragraph 10 might have begun with 'but' – "[But] for those young people less equipped"). An exception is paragraph 11, where two connectors ("so", "so that") make the argument more explicit.

The syntax is thus mainly **'paratactic'** rather than **'hypotactic'** i.e. compound rather than complex. This is particularly obvious in the coloured boxes with bullet points – what bullet points do is turn a series of clauses (or phrases) into a list. Yet a 'listing' syntax is used throughout the document. Why is this so? Why is it that argumentative links are left implicit? This is another aspect of what makes this text non-dialogical. If a text is explicitly structured as an argument, it is dialogical, it is engaging with readers, trying to convince them, and also in so doing it opens itself to counter-argument. But the paratactic, listing syntax of the document sets up a non-dialogical divide between those who are making all these assertions, and those they are addressed at – those who tell and those who are told, those who know and those don't.

Activity 9

I am going to refer now to the following linguistic features:

Mood – whether clauses are declarative, interrogative or imperative

Modality – marking of degrees of commitment to truth

Transitivity – what types of processes (and verbs) are used in clauses.

Look at these features in Extract 2 before you read my comments below. Are sentences interrogative or imperative as well as declarative? Are statements modalized with expressions like 'in our view'? What types of process are there? Are verbs mainly transitive or intransitive? Do they relate mainly to action, or thought, or being, or having? (If you don't have a background in linguistics, this is probably the part of the analysis you will find most difficult. Don't worry – have a try.)

Clauses

The clauses, as I have already said, are *declarative* – the document is a series of assertions, which itself contributes to its non-dialogical character. It would be perfectly possible in a document of this sort to move between declaratives and interrogatives, making assertions and asking questions, thus drawing readers into dialogue. The Department of Education and Employment's Green Paper referred to above does precisely that.

But the *modality* of these declarative clauses is also striking. The document consists not just of a series of assertions, but a series of mainly categorical assertions. Take the opening paragraph as an example. The second and third sentences are judgements, opinions which might have been marked as such by modalizing expressions such as 'in our opinion' or 'we believe', but they are not. There is no sense of welfare being a difficult and controversial area where problems may be difficult to resolve. On the contrary, the effect of this absence of modalization, combined with the declarative mood, gives the sense of a Government in perfect and solitary control of a process where the issues are clear-cut.

The *transitivity* features of clauses also contribute to this. Many of the processes are actional and transitive – an agent acting upon a goal. The agent in actional processes is generally the Government – "the Government", "we" – or a Government initiative such as one of the 'New Deals'. Claimants generally figure as goals or beneficiaries (those for whose benefit an action is taken) in actional processes. The Government acts, claimants are acted upon. For instance in the bullet points in paragraph 9: "The New Deal for Young People ... will offer participants, aged 18 to 24, four opportunities" ("participants" is beneficiary), "support will also be given to those young people ..." ("those young people" is beneficiary, "The New Deal" is implicitly the agent). Welfare staff rarely act, welfare professionals never, and claimants generally only where their actions are initiated/managed by the Government (e.g. in paragraph 9: "It aims to help young unemployed people ... to find jobs" – "young unemployed people" is both the goal of "help" and the agent of "find jobs"). However, claimants and staff do act in the special sense of acting verbally ("welcoming", "asking") in paragraph 14, which I discussed earlier as a rather rare case of the voices of claimants and staff being reported. Overall, the Government is represented as the primary actor and mover in the represented world of welfare, which is another aspect of the promotional character of the document.

Words

Part of the non-dialogicality of the document is the vocabulary it uses, including the way in which it monologically promotes particular discourses, including particular vocabularies. An example is in the representation of welfare benefit, and the use of the words 'benefit' and 'dependence' as shown in the first four paragraphs.

In paragraph 1, 'dependence' is in collocation with 'poverty' in the phrase "averting poverty and dependence". The need to avert poverty is hardly controversial, so collocating 'dependence' with 'poverty' is a covert way of constructing 'welfare dependence' as being just as much an evil as poverty. In paragraph 3, welfare benefits are disparagingly constructed as something people are "abandoned to" by governments – similarly "stuck on" in paragraph 4. And in paragraph 4 there is the collocation "benefit dependency" – receiving welfare benefits is constructed as the evil of 'dependence/dependency'. This discourse of welfare benefit as 'dependence' comes from the 'New Right' ('Reaganism' in the US, 'Thatcherism' in the UK) and is highly controversial, yet it is simply used in this Green Paper without any acknowledgement of the controversy.

The shift between descriptions of policy and party political rhetoric is partly marked in the oscillation between third-person and first-person, between "the Government" and "we". An example is paragraph 6, which moves from third-person to first-person and then back to third-person. But there is also an accompanying shift in vocabulary. Notice, for instance, the contrast between the Government's "aims" in paragraph 1 and paragraph 5 and "our ambition" in the second sentence of paragraph 6 – a move from a policy vocabulary to a vocabulary of aspiration. Notice also the metaphor "break the mould" in the first sentence of paragraph 7. At the same time, the language becomes more explicitly evaluative: "nothing less than" in paragraph 6 highlights the fundamental nature of the change which the Government is undertaking, "comprehensive" in paragraph 7 is a positive evaluation whereas "old" and "passive" are negative evaluations.

Relating, Representing, Identifying, Valuing

In terms of the different facets of the 'work' of the text which I distinguished earlier, my focus here has been on *relating* (the social problem I am discussing is a problem in social relationships in politics and government). But let me briefly note how questions to do with representing, identifying and valuing nevertheless arise. Above I refer to the work of *valuing* – devaluing for instance 'dependency', 'living on benefits' and 'passivity'. I discussed earlier the *representing* of work as one aspect of the non-dialogical character of the document. And an aspect of the promotional work that is going on is the work of *identifying* the Government and the (New) Labour Party as having a political vision, knowing where they are going and being firmly in control of the process of change.

3.4   Green Paper analysis, Stage 3: Does the social order 'need' the problem?

As with the initial identification of social problems in their semiotic aspect, at this stage we need to draw upon sources (academic analysis, media, etc.) which take us away from the immediate example and the text. Does the social order in a sense 'need' the public sphere to be squeezed out? Or to put the question differently: does the nature of the new capitalism preclude an effective public sphere? An argument along these lines would consider whether the emergent neo-liberal order is inherently anti-democratic, and if it would be threatened by a vigorous public sphere. There are reasons for thinking that this is so. For instance, crucial economic decisions affecting nation-states are taken by multinational corporations and institutions such as the World Bank, the International Monetary Fund and the European Union Commission, which are not subject to real democratic control. A strengthening of democracy through an invigorated public sphere could threaten this system, especially if it developed on an international scale. This is already apparent in the capacity of international mobilization around events such as the 'Earth Summit' (the UN conference on protecting the environment) and meetings of the World Trade Organisation to shape and inflect agendas and outcomes. There are potentially radical implications if we see the new order as incompatible with vigorous public spheres: a successful struggle for democracy would demand fundamental changes to the new order.

3.5   Green Paper analysis, Stage 4: Possible ways past the obstacles

Is it possible to discern hitherto unrealized possibilities for progressive change in this network of practices, including its semiotic element? What are the gaps, what are the contradictions which might provide points of leverage in struggles to constitute an effective public sphere? One is the tension I referred to earlier between New Labour's commitment to the 'modernization' of government, to 'devolution' and 'partnership', and the tight control it exercises from the centre. There is an unresolved tension, a contradiction, in the restructuring of the network of practices of government. This is partly a matter of 'rhetoric and reality' – the gap between the Government's discourse of government and how it actually governs. The actuality of, in particular, a Scottish Parliament means that this tension is likely to be increasingly exposed and opened up, and this may produce a terrain offering possibilities for progressive advancement.

The tensions and gaps are present also in the *semiotic* aspect of the network of practices. At the level of the *order of discourse*, one might, for instance, focus on the positioning of focus groups within the generic chains of public relations. If focus groups are a link in the chain of the Government's semiotic strategy, how does this square with claims that they represent a new form of 'open government'? But there are also tensions and gaps in particular *texts*. One is the tension between discourse and genre – between, for instance, the semiotic representation of welfare reform in the Green Paper as a process of consultation and dialogue, and the promotional, non-dialogical nature of documents such as the genre – of the way in which the process of reform is semiotically enacted there. This is one aspect of the tension and contradiction between what is said and what is actually done. Another tension I referred to above within the semiotic enactment is the oscillation between third-person and first-person: "the Government" and "we". This provides a point of leverage within the text: by insistently asking why there is this oscillation, we can open up the question of whether this is the text of a government dispassionately setting out proposals which are open to change through consultation, or a partisan text seeking to manipulate public opinion. Of course, we can only pursue such questioning to some end if there is an opening up of the tensions within the network of practices to the point that there is an available terrain on which we can do that – that circumstances require the Government to listen and respond.

Another tension within the text is in the construction of 'work', which I noted as a problem earlier. For the most part, the word 'work' is used without modification to mean 'jobs' in the traditional sense – relatively stable and regular work providing enough to live on. This is the dominant discourse of work. However, it is sometimes used in the collocation "paid work", as in paragraphs 1 and 2. (By 'collocation' I mean a repeated co-occurrence between particular words in a text.) It is significant that it occurs here, at the beginning of the chapter dealing centrally with work. The shift from "work" in sentence 1 of the first paragraph to "paid work" in sentence 3 is informationally backgrounded – 'paid work' is the unmarked theme and is thus constructed as simply a repetition of 'work' in sentence 1. There is no explicit contrast between 'paid' and other sorts of work. Nevertheless, the shift does implicitly signal a contrast – the specification of 'work' as 'paid work' is an implicit acknowledgement that there are other discourses of work. There is also a trace of an alternative discourse of 'work' later in the chapter in paragraph 9 which is the only such case in the document. A list of 'opportunities' for young unemployed people includes: "work with an employer who will receive a job subsidy", "work with a voluntary sector organisation", and "work on the Environmental Taskforce". Only the first is a 'job' in the usual sense. On the other hand, when the document refers to what parents do in caring for children, it does not refer to that activity as 'work'.

Different discourses of work are hinted at but not attributed to particular voices, rather, they are assimilated into the monologue. Their presence in the document constitutes another point of leverage, and a potentially significant one given that the 'welfare-to-work' strategy is being pursued in a context where 'jobs', in the traditional sense, are disappearing in vast numbers, yet without any radical rethinking of 'work'. One might refer here to research on changing patterns of employment.

3.6 Green Paper analysis, Stage 5: Reflection on the analysis

How can analyses such as this contribute to democratic struggle? How can we connect academic papers or books (such as Fairclough, 2000a; 2000b) to, for instance, campaigns against genetically modified food or the rules of 'free trade' being introduced by the World Trade Organisation? Academic life is organized as a distinct network of practices, indeed as a distinct market, and critical research which stays within its confines is unlikely to have much effect. It may have some; people who spend some of their time in higher education can 'carry' ideas and approaches into other parts of their lives. But I think we have to keep rethinking how we research, how and where we publish, and how we write. How we research: what I have said above about the public sphere is cut off from struggles over the public sphere – why not work with activists in designing and carrying out research, tying it, for instance, to the campaigns of disabled people over welfare reform? How and where we publish: the publications I have referred to (as well as this book) are all firmly within academic life – why not seek to publish pamphlets, articles in newspapers and magazines, or on

the web? How we write: these publications are written in academic ways –
is it possible to develop ways of writing which are accessible to many
people without being superficial?

Further Reading

Chouliaraki, L. and Fairclough, N. (1999) *Discourse in Late Modernity:
Rethinking Critical Discourse Analysis*, Edinburgh, Edinburgh University Press:
the version of CDA used in this chapter is more fully explained.

Fairclough, N. (1995) *Critical Discourse Analysis*, Harlow, Longman: application
of CDA to a range of different types of discourse, but using an earlier version
of the framework.

Fairclough, N. (2000a) 'Discourse, social theory and social research: the case of
welfare reform', *Journal of Sociolinguistics*, vol.4: theoretical elaboration of the
same version of CDA, linked as in this chapter to the issue of welfare reform.

Fairclough, N. (2000b) *New Labour, New Language?* London, Routledge: CDA
applied to the language of New Labour in a book designed for a general
public.

Fairclough, N. and Wodak, R. (1997) 'Critical discourse analysis' in van Dijk, T.
(ed.) *Discourse as Social Interaction*, London, Sage: overview of work in CDA.

Wodak, R. (1996) *Disorders of Discourse*, Harlow, Longman: a different version
of CDA applied to a range of types of discourse.

References

Althusser, L. (1971) 'Ideology and ideological state apparatuses' in *Lenin and
Philosophy*, London, New Left Books.

Arendt, H. (1958) *The Human Condition*, Chicago, University of Chicago Press.

Bakhtin, M. (1986) *Speech Genres and Other Late Essays*, Austin, TX, Texas
University Press.

Bernstein, B. (1990) *The Structuring of Pedagogic Discourse*, London,
Routledge.

Bhaskar, R. (1986) *Scientific Realism and Human Emancipation,* London,
Verso.

Bourdieu, P. and Wacquant, L. (1992) *An Invitation to Reflexive Sociology*,
Cambridge, Polity Press.

Cameron, D. (2000) *Good to Talk?*, London, Sage.

Chouliaraki, L. and Fairclough, N. (1999) *Discourse in Late Modernity:
Rethinking Critical Discourse Analysis*, Edinburgh, Edinburgh University Press.

De Beaugrande, R. (1997) *New Foundations for a Science of Text and
Discourse,* Norwood: NJ, Ablex.

Fairclough, N. (1992) *Discourse and Social Change*, Cambridge, Polity Press.

Fairclough, N. (1993) 'Critical discourse analysis and the marketization of public
discourse', *Discourse and Society*, vol.4.

Fairclough, N. (1995) 'Ideology and identity in political television' in *Critical Discourse Analysis*, Harlow, Longman.

Fairclough, N. (1999) 'Democracy and the public sphere in critical research on discourse' in Wodak, R. (ed.) *Challenges in a Changing World: Issues in Critical Discourse Analysis*, Vienna, Passagen Verlag.

Fairclough, N. (2000a) 'Discourse, social theory and social research: the case of welfare reform', *Journal of Sociolinguistics*, vol.4.

Fairclough, N. (2000b) *New Labour, New Language?*, London, Routledge.

Forgacs, D. (ed.) (1988) *A Gramsci Reader*, London, Lawrence and Wishart.

Franklin, B. (1998) 'Tough on Soundbites, Tough on the Causes of Soundbites: New Labour and News Management', *Catalyst Paper 3*, London, Catalyst Trust.

Giddens, A. (1991) *Modernity and Self Identity*, Cambridge, Polity Press.

Habermas, J. (1971) *Knowledge and Human Interests*, Boston, MA, Beacon Press.

Habermas, J. (1984) *Theory of Communicative Action, Volume 1*, London, Heinemann.

Habermas, J. (1989) *The Structural Transformation of the Public Sphere*, Cambridge, Polity Press.

Harvey, D. (1996) *Justice, Nature and the Geography of Difference*, Oxford, Blackwell.

Iedema, R. (1997) 'The language of administration: Organizing human activity in formal institutions' in Christie, F. and Martin, J.R. (eds) *Genre and Institutions. Social Processes in the Workplace and School*, London, Cassell.

Kristeva, J. (1986) *The Kristeva Reader*, (ed. T. Moi), Oxford, Blackwell.

Laclau, E. and Mouffe, C. (1985) *Hegemony and Socialist Strategy*, London, Verso.

Lyotard, J.F. (1986–7) 'Rules and paradoxes and svelte appendix', *Cultural Critique*, vol.5, pp.209–19.

Pecheux, M. (1982) *Language, Semantics and Ideology*, London, Macmillan.

Robertson, R. (1992) *Globalization*, London, Sage.

Sarangi, S. and Slembrouck, S. (1996) *Language, Bureaucracy and Social Control*, Harlow, Longman.

Talbot, M. (1998) *Language and Gender*, Cambridge, Polity Press.

Volosinov, V. (1973) *Marxism and the Philosophy of Language*, New York, Seminar Press.

CHAPTER SEVEN

Unmarried Motherhood 1830–1990: A Genealogical Analysis

Jean Carabine

Introduction

This chapter uses the example of illegitimacy and unmarried motherhood in the early decades of the nineteenth century to demonstrate how to undertake a Foucauldian discourse analysis. The aim is to show how we can apply Foucault's genealogical approach – his concerns with power, knowledge and discourse – through the example of an analysis of historical social policy documents. The chapter draws primarily on an analysis of the 1834 New Poor Law Act and Commissioners' Reports and, in particular, the Bastardy Clauses within them, in order to trace the ways that sexuality – specifically unmarried motherhood – is spoken of and with what effects – through what I refer to as the discourse of bastardy.

My reason for choosing to undertake a discourse analysis of social policy documents written over 160 years ago arose out of my interest in trying to understand and explain the relationship between sexuality and social policy both as a discipline and as practice. Analyses of sexuality, such as this, are rarely, if at all, included as either an integral or even marginal part of social policy work on historical or contemporary work on poverty. In particular, one aspect not yet examined in social policy studies of discourse and poverty is the role played by sexuality discourses in poverty policies and debates in constituting welfare subjects and eligibility for benefits. This is not surprising given that the relationship between sexuality and social policy, as practice or discipline, is also largely ignored and under-researched (Carabine, 1996a and b). Within the field of social policy, the role of sexuality in social policies and analyses continues to be ignored despite its prominence in public debates about homosexuality, teenage pregnancy, unmarried motherhood, the decline of marriage, the age of sexual consent and sex education, to name just a few. My project has been to argue that ideas about sexuality, particularly heterosexuality, play a significant role in social policy whether as a discipline or as practice.

1   Foucauldian concepts

To answer the question 'what is a Foucauldian discourse analysis?' we need first to address what Foucault means by discourse, and second to consider two key concepts – **power** and **knowledge** – at the heart of his work. Indeed, as we shall see, **discourse/power/knowledge** are an interconnected triad. Next, the chapter will consider Foucault's methodology for examining this triad – **genealogy** – before going on to consider how it can be used to analyse social policy discourses. However, before doing this perhaps I should make it clear that there are no 'hard and fast' rules which set out, step by step, what a genealogical analysis is. What Foucault's genealogy offers us is a lens through which to undertake discourse analysis and with which we can read discourses. As we shall see this lens means that we read discourses as, on the one hand, being infused with power/knowledge and, on the other, as playing a role in producing power/knowledge networks. Because Foucault didn't provide us with a 'how to' guide to genealogy, the method adopted by individual researchers varies. What is common to all, however, is the application of Foucault's concepts of discourse/power/knowledge and therefore the lens through which they read their data. My particular approach takes what Foucault says about discourse/power/knowledge and combines it with what he has to say about a specific knowledge – sexuality – as a lens for interpreting the relationship between sexuality and social policy. How this works will become apparent later in Section 2 on applying genealogical discourse analysis. Let's look first at Foucault's notion of discourse.

1.1 Discourse

Foucault's interest in discourse has been on a number of levels. It is:

> sometimes ... the general domain of all statements, sometimes as an individualizable group of statements, and sometimes as a regulated practice that accounts for a number of statements.

> (Foucault, 1972: 8)

My interest in discourse is less with the way that discourse is structured and governed by internal rules, which are a feature of the discourse itself i.e. the linguistic analysis of the nature and processes of discourse (as described in the latter part of the above quotation), and more with the idea of discourse as defined in the first two parts of the quotation. That is, the idea of discourse as consisting of groups of related statements which cohere in some way to produce both meanings and effects in the real world, i.e. the idea of discourse as having force, as being productive. Let me explain further what I mean by 'cohere', 'effect', force', 'productive', etc.

Let's begin by thinking of discourse as the ways that an issue or topic is 'spoken of', through, for example, speech, texts, writing and practice. These various different and sometimes contradictory ways of speaking about a topic or issue come together – that is 'cohere' – to build up a picture or representation of the issue or topic. For Foucault, discourses are productive. They produce the objects of which they speak – sexuality, madness or, in the case of this research, unmarried mothers. In other words, they are constitutive; they construct a particular version of unmarried motherhood as real. Discourses are also productive in that they have power outcomes or effects. They define and establish what is 'truth' at particular moments. So in the case of my research, the discourse of bastardy operates to produce a particular 'truth' of unmarried motherhood which seeks to invalidate other accounts of bastardy and unmarried motherhood. As we shall see, the constitution of unmarried motherhood through the discourse of bastardy produces particular effects – it constitutes unmarried mothers as immoral and as undeserving of poor relief except through the workhouse, more widely, it contributes to a stigmatizing of unmarried mothers which extended into the twentieth century.

Discourses are also fluid and often opportunistic, at one and the same time, drawing upon existing discourses about an issue whilst utilizing, interacting with, and being mediated by, other dominant discourses (about, for example, family, femininity, morality, gender, race, ethnicity, sexuality, disability and class, etc.) to produce potent and new ways of conceptualizing the issue or topic. This is another sense in which discourse is productive. In so doing, discourses 'hook' into normative ideas and common-sense notions, say, about sexuality (that heterosexuality is natural and normal, that homosexuality is abnormal and deviant), morality or motherhood. This produces shortcut paths into ideas which convey messages about, for example, 'good' and 'bad' (mothering, sexualities, etc.), morality and immorality (behaviours and relationships), and acceptable and inappropriate behaviours. These representations or ways of speaking not only convey meanings about the topic, they also have material effects.

To illustrate this, take for example the way lone motherhood was 'spoken of' in Britain in the early 1990s.

Activity 1

Read through the following extracts. As you do so try to identify the ways in which lone/single mothers are 'spoken of', that is, what discourses of motherhood are evident in the examples? Think about what picture of lone/single motherhood is being created. What do the extracts tell us about lone/single motherhood?

It might help here to consider what the extracts say about the relationship of lone/single mothers to

- the family
- welfare
- communities, society, Britain
- their children
- crime.

Extract 1

the family is the foundation stone of a free society ... But today family life is breaking down ... growing illegitimacy and family breakdown, the reduction in the work ethic and rising crime are signs of a general malaise affecting British culture

(Green, 1992: vii)

Extract 2

... the disintegration of the nuclear family is the principal source of so much misery and unrest. The creation of an urban underclass, on the margins of society, but doing great damage to itself and the rest of us, is directly linked to the rapid rise of illegitimacy. The past two decades have witnessed the growth of whole communities in which the dominant family structure is the single-parent mother on welfare, whose male offspring are already immersed in criminal culture by the time they are teenagers and whose daughters are destined to follow the family tradition of unmarried mothers ...

(*Sunday Times*, 28 February 1993)

Extract 3

Does my hon. Friend agree that family stability comes best from children being born of a loving relationship between a man and a woman? The strong movement towards girls and very young women to have babies to get flats and houses is damaging to them and to the children, because those children do not have the proper background that they should have. Will my hon. Friend consider that point and do all that he can to encourage proper family stability, because it is the bedrock of the nation? (Mr. Harry Greenway)

...

... expenditure on benefits for all lone parents has increased from £2.4 billion in 1981–82 to £6 billion in 1991–92 at constant prices. (Mr. Burt)

...

Those are pretty incredible figures. Does my hon. Friend agree that, when the welfare system encourages young women to have babies out of wedlock so that they can qualify for council houses and benefits, perhaps the system has gone too far? Will he confirm that the Government will take action to extend and encourage parental responsibility, particularly paternal responsibility? (Mr. Riddick)

...

Will the Minister take this opportunity to condemn unreservedly not only the question put by the hon. Member for Colne Valley (Mr. Riddick) but the speech made by the Secretary of State for Wales over the weekend, which quite outrageously alleged that young women deliberately make themselves pregnant to benefit from housing and social security benefits, when the Minister knows, as do Conservative Members, that there is absolutely no evidence whatever to support those scurrilous allegations? (Ms Glenda Jackson)

(*Hansard* (Commons) 5 July 1993, Column 11)

Discussion

Discourses of 'lone' motherhood

Here are some of the ways that single/lone motherhood is spoken of that you might have identified:

- as a problem (because of their increasing number and their dependency on state benefits)

- as a threat to marriage and the traditional family (because they are unmarried and bringing children up outside marriage and the traditional family)

- as irresponsible – having children without adequate means of support

- as deliberately getting pregnant to obtain council housing and benefits

- as dependent on and/or undeserving of welfare

- as 'bad' mothers responsible for producing delinquent and disaffected youth, especially boys, and young girls who themselves become single mothers dependent on welfare

- homogeneously – implying that all single mothers are the same and become so for the same reasons; and that *all* single motherhood is problematic and a threat

- you might also have identified a '**counter-discourse**' (from MP Glenda Jackson) challenging the representation of single mothers as deliberately getting pregnant so as to obtain benefits.

In the discourse – which I refer to here as the 'discourse of "lone" motherhood' – unmarried mothers, lone mothers (through divorce, death or separation), and young single mothers tend to be grouped together and treated as homogeneous. In the extracts above we can see how a variety of discourses were called upon to produce a discourse of lone motherhood specific to the early 1990s period. These included discourses about family, marriage, morality, the underclass, desert, dependency, and parenting. All of which came together to constitute lone mothers as a problem and a threat with particular effects. Some commentators have described the media and mainly Right-wing political responses to increasing numbers of never-married mothers and lone parents in the early 1990s as a 'moral panic' (Roseneil and Mann, 1996: 92). In 1994 lone mothers constituted 21 percent of all families with dependent children compared to 7.5 percent in 1975 (Kiernan *et al.*, 1998: 23). During the early 1990s, these women were vilified as both a problem and a threat to the traditional nuclear family and to the nation. In part, they were seen as a problem because of their increasing numbers and the signal that this was thought to convey about marriage and the traditional family. Through not marrying and by having children outside marriage the increasing numbers of never-married mothers were presented as a threat to the stability of marriage and the traditional family, both of which were seen, by the then Conservative government and others, as the backbone and conduit of the nation's morals.

Through invoking a discourse of welfare dependency (a discourse that was particularly influential in the early 1990s and still is powerful today) it was also possible to present lone mothers as irresponsible and undeserving of welfare. After all, it was argued, they were irresponsibly having children without any adequate means of support (husband/marriage/work) and were a drain on the state's finances. They were also blamed for producing children who themselves were likely to be irresponsible and to become welfare dependent. In 1988, Margaret Thatcher, the then Prime Minister, spoke of the problem of young single girls who were deliberately getting pregnant in order to obtain benefits and jump council housing queues (*The Guardian*, 23 November 1988). And we can see from extracts 1–3 above that this still had potency almost five years later. In the early 1990s, debate in the media was also dominated by concerns about the cost of lone mothers to the state (Kiernan *et al.*, 1998: 1) and their role in producing an underclass (see Roseneil and Mann, 1996). These ideas were more forcibly endorsed in the run-up to the 1993 Conservative Party Conference. It was clear that welfare services and benefits should be available only to respectable married mothers.

Discourses about the underclass and 'good' and 'bad' mothers were also utilized in the 1990s discourse of lone mothers. Roseneil and Mann show how, for example, debates about lone parents/unmarried mothers drew upon discourses about the underclass which 'dichotomised women along age-old lines – good women who do the right thing, get married and then have children, versus bad women, who have children, don't get married and depend on state benefits' (1996: 192). In invoking the underclass discourse, unmarried mothers were blamed for all sorts of ills – teenage motherhood, delinquent children, juvenile crime, a crisis in masculinity, and social and educational failure in fatherless boys (see for example, Dennis and Erdos, 1992; Roseneil and Mann, 1996). Another aspect of the discourse (although not evident in the extracts above) was concerned with issues of morality. This focused on the increasing number of women who were failing to marry, and who were having sex and giving birth to children outside marriage. Many social commentators (such as Dennis and Erdos, 1992; Morgan, 1995) and politicians found these shifts in family and marriage practice indicative of: 'a crisis in traditional authority relations and moral codes which [need] to be addressed. From this standpoint lone mothers become both the cause and effect of this crisis in traditional morality and thus [were] constructed as a social problem' (Lentell, 1999: 252–3). We can see from the above discussion that several discourses cohere to constitute the 'truth' that was the discourse of lone motherhood in the early 1990s.

Effects

I have suggested above that discourses have effects. What can be identified as some of the effects of the discourse of lone motherhood? One effect arising out the idea that lone mothers were a drain on the state and that young single mothers, in particular, were deliberately getting pregnant in order to get benefits has been to make access to benefits more difficult or conditional. In the case of young single mothers, local authorities no longer have a legal responsibility to prioritize them when allocating council housing. Also, the Child Support Agency was introduced in 1993 in an attempt to get separated and absent fathers to pay child maintenance. Similarly, in another attempt to reduce the financial burden of lone motherhood on the state, the lone parent payment was abolished in April 1997. More recently, government policies have emphasized the need for lone mothers to work (also an example of a shift in the discourse on lone motherhood) – through the New Deal for Lone Parents – as a way of reducing their dependence on the state. Discourses can also influence the way that people understand or think about an issue. For example, when people were asked about their attitudes to unmarried mothers, 30 percent agreed that 'unmarried mothers who find it hard to cope have only themselves to blame' and only 26 percent agreed that 'unmarried mothers get too little sympathy from society' (1995 British Social Attitudes Survey quoted in Lentell, 1999: 250). A combined effect of these discourses is to convey messages about what is appropriate behaviour, not only for lone mothers but for all mothers. In suggesting that discourse influences how we think and behave, I want to stress that we should not think of discourses as 'all powerful' and individuals as submissive recipients of discourse. Instead, we should think of discourses as constantly being contested and challenged and therefore not necessarily always omnipotent.

What this example of the discourse of lone motherhood shows is that discourses are variable ways of 'speaking of' an issue which cohere or come together to produce the object of which they speak. The example also shows that discourse interacts with, and is mediated by, other discourses to produce new, different, and forceful ways of presenting the issue. Our example of lone motherhood shows that discourses also produce effects – discursively and through practice – which influences the way we understand, experience, and respond to the issue or topic.

Tracing a history of lone motherhood

If we were to trace the ways that lone motherhood has been 'spoken of' throughout history we would find that these ways varied at different historical moments and in different social and cultural contexts, that is, the idea of discourse as historically variable ways of speaking. Thus, if we were to take again the British example, we would see that, from the mid-1830s, such mothers, particularly poor working-class women, were constructed as immoral and undeserving of welfare. From the start of the twentieth century until about the 1940s, single mothers were likely to be seen in terms of mental deficiency – as being inherently mentally deficient/feeble-minded – and as producing feeble-minded offspring and as a threat to the purity of the British race. For their and society's good, many were still incarcerated in Poor Law institutions until the 1980s and 1990s. In the 1950s, women who had children outside marriage were often pathologized and their single motherhood explained in terms of some psychological lack or problem. (For more detailed information and discussion of constructions of unmarried/lone motherhood see Gill, 1977; Kiernan *et al.*, 1998; Phoenix, 1991; Smart, 1996.)

Looking back, the history of discourse of lone motherhood illustrates, first, that discourses are not continuous or unchanging over time. Indeed, it shows that discourses are historically variable ways of 'speaking of' lone motherhood. Second, each of these different constructions of lone motherhood is significant in conveying specific messages about lone motherhood at any given time and has certain effects and outcomes. Third, whilst this brief history or genealogy of lone motherhood reveals the different ways it has been constructed, it also shows how certain themes – the unacceptability of unmarried motherhood, lone motherhood as a moral, social, and/or economic issue, as a threat (to family, nation, society) – reappear, albeit in different forms at different times. This 'tracing' of the history of unmarried motherhood, through the examination of discourses about it, is central to Foucault's genealogical method which will be discussed in Section 1.3.

Discourses are historically variable ways of speaking, writing and talking about, as well as practices around, an issue. They have outcomes/ identifiable effects which specify what is morally, socially and legally un/acceptable at any given moment in a culture.

Implicit in the discussion about different constructions of lone motherhood is the idea of knowledge and its relationship to discourse.

Activity 2

Look back over the history or genealogy of lone motherhood presented in the discussion following Activity 1. Can you begin to identify, albeit on the basis of somewhat sketchy information, the knowledges which framed or informed the construction of lone motherhood in each period?

Discussion

You might have identified:

- 1830s: ideas about morality and desert

- 1900–1940s: ideas about mental deficiency/feeble-mindedness as inherent in certain groups, ideas about race purity (eugenics)

- 1950s: ideas about unmarried motherhood as a pathological state, interpreted in psychological terms

- 1980–90s: moral and economic issues, ideas about the underclass.

A more detailed and in-depth genealogy of lone motherhood might reveal other influences.

Discourses at one and the same time draw upon and sometimes transform existing knowledge to produce new knowledge and new power effects. The following comment from Kiernan *et al.* (1998: 123) sums up neatly this relationship between discourse and knowledge: 'It is striking that the problem of unmarried motherhood has, over what is a relatively short period of time, been so completely reconstructed time and again with touching faith that each successive construction constituted truth'.

1.2 Power/knowledge

As we have seen, discourses are historically variable ways of specifying knowledges and truths, whereby knowledges are socially constructed and produced by effects of power and spoken of in terms of 'truths'. Foucault (1990; 1991) argues that power is constituted through discourses. Thus, power is important in the construction of knowledge and what counts as knowledge. It may help to think of discourses as functioning as sets of socially and historically constructed rules designating 'what is' and 'what is not'. In his book *The History of Sexuality* (1990), Foucault investigates the ways in which sexuality has come to be seen and spoken of; the development of knowledges about sex, as a means of understanding the operations of power. His analysis in *The History of Sexuality* challenges the universality of sexuality, showing it, instead, to be socially and culturally constructed, thereby questioning the popular belief of sexuality as 'natural', fixed and/or biologically determined. In his unravelling of sexuality throughout history, Foucault reveals how sexuality has been produced differently at specific historical moments through the operation of discourse (see Hall, Reading Seven in Wetherell *et al.*, 2001).

Discourses can be powerful because they specify what is and what is not. Not all discourses have the same force. Some discourses are more powerful than others and have more authority or validity. In the case of sexuality, dominant discourses are the means by which what we know to be the 'truths' of sexuality are established. These knowledges or 'truths' about sexuality tell us what is 'normal' and 'natural' whilst establishing the boundaries of what is acceptable and appropriate. For example, the discourse of heterosexuality is awarded validity and authority as the only natural and normal sexuality. Although what we know to be heterosexuality at any given time is historically, culturally and socially specific and subject to redefinition and transformation, it is heterosexuality that persists as the benchmark of 'normal' and 'natural' sexuality. In this way, ideas about heterosexuality become naturalized in commonplace thinking with the effect that heterosexual relationships are taken for granted as the norm. Knowledge about sexuality permeates all aspects of society, at the level of the institutional, professional, expert and personal, and influences how sexuality is understood and experienced, as well as the boundaries of what is possible.

To understand discourse we have to see it as intermeshed with power/ knowledge where knowledge both constitutes and is constituted through discourse as an effect of power. If our study of discourse is to be more than a study of language, it must look also at the social context and social relations within which power and knowledge occur and are distributed.

1.3 Genealogy – a history of the present?

I have already indicated that Foucault's primary concern in *The History of Sexuality* (and also in *Discipline and Punish*) was with understanding the operations of power through examining the development of discourses and knowledges about sexuality. Genealogy was the name given to the methodological approach he used to study discourse to reveal power/ knowledge networks.

Foucault's genealogy is more about methodology than method. We can use it as a lens through which to read discourses. Although genealogy is very much a methodology for analysing history, it does not adopt a traditional historical methodology. It is not concerned with seeking the truth, or with finding the *real* sexuality or the *real* unmarried mother, nor is it concerned with unity or with presenting a correct and full picture of what went before. In the words of Bell, it does not:

> ... seek to record the progress and continuity of societies. It avoids the search for depth, avoids the search for what 'really happened' underneath historical events, and locates its analysis instead on the surface, on the details; it is 'meticulous and patiently documentary' ... Genealogy is opposed to the totalizing effects of 'superhistories' [such as Marxism] ... that see one great plan unfolding as time progresses.

(Bell, 1993: 46)

Rather, genealogy is concerned with describing the procedures, practices, apparatuses and institutions involved in the production of discourses and knowledges, and their power effects. For me this is not simply about exposing the processes through which discourses are produced, but also about establishing the ways that those discourses are practised, operationalized and supported institutionally, professionally, socially, legally and economically. In his examination of the past, Foucault sought to trace the development of knowledges and their power effects in order to reveal something about the nature of power/knowledge in modern society. Genealogy is concerned to map those strategies, relations and practices of power in which knowledges are embedded and connected.

Thus, we might use genealogy to interrogate present discourses about teenage or unmarried motherhood, say, with the aim of tracking their history and the regimes of power/knowledge involved in that history (see the example of constructions of unmarried motherhood discussed in Section 1.1). One way of understanding genealogy is to see it as a way of reading history through discourse to find out how power/knowledge circulates. In the box below, Dreyfuss and Rabinow (1986) explain how Foucault applied his genealogical approach to an examination of the confession.

A genealogy of the confession – an example

In *The History of Sexuality*, Foucault isolates the confession as an important ritual of power in which a specific technology of the body was forged. As this is genealogy one is not going to find a simple unity of meaning or function or changeless significance. The confession, as Foucault demonstrates, did not have the same meaning in the thirteenth century, the seventeenth, or the nineteenth century as it does in the present ... Foucault is not attempting to give a complete picture of, say seventeenth century society. He is not trying to give a traditional history and then pose the question: Given that history, what does the confession mean to us today? Rather, he is saying that the confession is a vital component of modern power ... Foucault writes the history of the con-

fession in the seventeenth century for the purposes of writing 'a history of
the present' ... he asks what it was in earlier periods and what it has
become today.

(Dreyfuss and Rabinow, 1986: 119)

Genealogy is about tracing the history of the development of
knowledges and their power effects so as to reveal something about the
nature of power/knowledge in modern society. It does this through
the examination of discourses and by mapping the strategies, relations
and practices of power in which knowledges were embedded and
connected.

Reconceptualizing power through genealogy

Through the application of his genealogical method (in *The History of
Sexuality* and *Discipline and Punish*) Foucault challenges traditional
conceptions of power.

He argues that many social theorists continue to base their understandings
of power solely on a model based on a notion of sovereign power that is
no longer appropriate (1979; 1990). Sovereign power is juridico-discursive,
final and ultimate. It operates through laws and rules which carry with
them the threat or practice of violence, torture or physical punishment,
even death. However, as Foucault demonstrates in both *Discipline and
Punish* and *The History of Sexuality*, not all power is exercised or enforced
through the threat of death or physical force. In *The History of Sexuality*,
Foucault outlines an alternative and contemporary mechanism of power.
He argued instead that power circulates and operates at all levels of society
(see Hall Reading Seven in Wetherell *et al.*, 2001). He identifies
normalization as one way that power is deployed.

1.4 Normalization

The relationship between normalization and discourse is that discourses
convey messages about what is the norm and what is not. In effect they
establish the norm.

In this section I will outline Foucault's concept of normalization and
explain how I have adapted it to understand the relationship between
social policy and sexuality.

Defining sexuality and social policy

I use social policy in this context to refer broadly to those policies (social,
economic, fiscal, legal) and practices (social work, medicine, law,
psychiatry, education, etc.) concerned with the formal and informal
provision of welfare by the state (local and national), markets, families,

groups and individuals. Of particular interest is the way that these social and legal policies implicitly and explicitly convey messages about appropriate and acceptable sexualities, that is, their role in constituting sexual norms.

My interpretation of sexuality is somewhat ambiguous as it embodies identity, behaviour, acts, desires, relations and relationships. I take it to refer to a category of person (heterosexual, homosexual, lesbian, queer, bi-sexual, etc.) the focus of their desire (same-sex, opposite sex, child) and as embracing all sexual behaviours, acts and relationships (cohabitation, partnering, marriage or otherwise) as well as the meanings attached to those acts and behaviours. It also refers to a system of knowledge that encompasses what we know as sexuality and what dominates as the 'truth' of sexuality at any moment in time, and power relations – heterosexuality. For me, sexuality is socially, historically and culturally constructed.

Foucault has shown that through normalization individuals are compared and differentiated according to a desired norm. In *Discipline and Punish*, through the application of his genealogical method, Foucault maps the various methods and procedures used to judge, measure and compare individuals. Therefore, normalization establishes the measure by which all are judged and deemed to conform or not. This normalization process produces homogeneity through processes of comparison and differentiation. However, we should not think of normalizing judgement as simply about comparing individuals in a binary way – as in good/bad, mad/sane or healthy/ill. It is also a 'norm' towards which all individuals should aim, work towards, seek to achieve, and against which all are measured – 'good' *and* 'bad', sick *and* healthy, 'mad' *and* 'sane', heterosexual *and* homosexual. In his notion of 'norm', Foucault did not conceive power as being imposed by one section, class or group of society on another.

I just want to sound a note of caution here in case I'm giving you the impression that the effect of normalization is overwhelming. As with discourse, we must not conceive of normalizing strategies as uncontested nor as leading to successful and complete regulation or outcomes. Instead, we need to envisage a continual, if uneven, and contradictory process, whereby we as individuals are in the constant process of reassessing, establishing and negotiating our position in relation to the norm. Normalization is a means through which power is deployed. It is a dynamic of knowledge, practised and learned, dispersed around various centres of practice and expertise. Both social policy and sexuality can be understood as such centres of expertise and practice.

Normalization, sexuality and social policy

I have adapted Foucault's notion of normalization and applied it to the social policy context where I suggest it operates in three main ways. First, in constituting appropriate and acceptable sexuality. Second, as operating

in a regulatory capacity through which not only is heterosexuality
established and secured but also bodies and sexuality are disciplined and
controlled. This regulatory function can be seen to operate explicitly
through legislation and statutes and implicitly through:

- normative assumptions about (hetero)sexuality as 'normal' and 'natural'
  underpinning and informing social policy

- linking of notions of eligibility for welfare to ideas about appropriate
  and acceptable sexuality.

We have to be careful here, because although discourses may have
regulatory intentions, this does not mean that they ultimately result in
regulatory outcomes. Individuals are active agents and discourses are
themselves in a state of constant reconstitution and contestation. Nor do
discourses exist in splendid isolation but, rather, are themselves also
mediated by other dominant, sometimes more powerful, discourses. Third,
the normalization process produces differentiating effects and fragmented
impacts being variously regulatory, penalizing or affirmative in respect to
different groups, of, for example, women.

   Perhaps an example of this would help. One way normalizing ideas
about appropriate sexuality inform and influence social policy and welfare
is through an explicit relationship between ideas about 'appropriate'
sexuality and access to, and eligibility for, welfare. Take the claims made
by the Conservative government (and others) in Britain in the late 1980s
and early 1990s that teenage mothers deliberately became pregnant in
order to obtain benefits and council housing. The implied message
contained in such attacks was that welfare benefits and housing should
be available only to 'respectable' married women. Similarly, it was
reported in 1993 (*Independent*, 7 October 1993) that in some states in the
US, Norplant, a contraceptive implant, was being targeted at teenage
women and poor women from racial minorities. In Baltimore, women in
receipt of benefits were offered cash payments and extra benefits as an
incentive to have the Norplant contraceptive implant. Those refusing to
have the implant were threatened with removal of benefits (*World in
Action*, ITV, October 1993), as were unmarried mothers considering
becoming pregnant again whilst in receipt of welfare. US politicians
supporting this approach made it clear that women should only
be able to have children that they were in a position to support. By
implication, sex and pregnancy outside marriage is only acceptable for
those who have sufficient means of support (husband/work/independent
income).

   We can use Foucault's genealogical methodology alongside his concept
of normalization to interrogate, first, sexuality as a discourse which is
constituted, amongst other things, through social policy, and second, social
policy as practice and discipline as one means by which sexuality itself is
constituted. This shows that not only are discourses of sexuality 'played'
through social policy as an effect of normalization but also that sexuality
discourses interact with and traverse other discourses central to welfare
and social policy and in so doing are mediated by those discourses.

Summary of Section 1

The following concepts are key to undertaking a Foucauldian genealogical discourse analysis.

- The idea of power as operating and circulating at every level of a society.
- Normalization as one method of deploying power.
- The notion that power/knowledge/discourse are intricately intermeshed: 'it is in discourse that power and knowledge are joined together' (Foucault, 1990: 100).
- The need to account for social context and relations so as to situate the power/knowledge realm.
- Discourses are constitutive.
- Discourses have a normalizing role and regulatory outcomes.
- The idea of discourse as uneven, contradictory and contested.
- The idea that knowledge, truth and discourse are all socially constructed and historically specific.

2   Applying genealogical discourse analysis

So far we have looked at Foucault's concepts of power/knowledge, discourse, normalization and genealogy, and how we might begin to apply these to social policy analyses. Having set genealogy up as a historical method for tracing discourses and their effects, I want to explain briefly the way I apply genealogy to the study of sexuality and social policy, and to suggest that we can use genealogy to provide a 'snapshot' of a particular moment without resorting to tracing its history, and that this will still tell us something about discourse/power/knowledge. Perhaps an example of how I apply genealogy to my work might help. I do this on two levels. The first is nearer to Foucault's original intentions for genealogy, that is, I use it to explore and trace the power/knowledge networks evident in social policy, specifically, the 'building up' of a picture of the ways that ideas and knowledges about sexuality have constituted social policy and welfare discourses and practices (and vice versa) throughout history, and ask 'with what effect?' My second approach looks at a specific sexuality issue and how it is dealt with at a particular moment. The aim is the same, however, that is, to identify how sexuality is constituted through social policy and with what effects. It's just that the concern is with looking at a specific moment – as with the 1834 New Poor Law or with constructions of teenage pregnancy in the Government's 1999 'Social Exclusion Report on Teenage Pregnancy' – rather than with tracing the history of a discourse. The usefulness of this second approach is two-fold. First, although it is a 'stand-alone' project, it can contribute to understandings of power and/or knowledge at any given moment. Second, it can also be used to contribute a genealogy of sexuality and social policy, that is, to the 'building up' of the different ways sexuality is constituted through social policy over time.

Guide to doing Foucauldian genealogical discourse analysis

1   *Select your topic* – Identify possible sources of data. If you were undertaking a social policy analysis then sources might include policy documents, discussion papers, parliamentary papers, speeches, cartoons, photographs, parliamentary debates, newspapers, other media sources, political tracts, and pamphlets from local and national government, quangos, and political parties. You might also wish to include an analysis of counter-discourses and resistances; here you might use material from campaigning and lobbying groups, activists and welfare rights organizations, etc.

2   *Know your data* – read and re-read. Familiarity aids analysis and interpretation.

3   *Identify themes,* categories and objects of the discourse.

4   Look for evidence of an *inter-relationship* between discourses.

5   Identify the discursive strategies and techniques that are employed.

6   Look for *absences* and *silences.*

7   Look for *resistances* and *counter-discourses.*

8   Identify the *effects* of the discourse.

9   *Context 1* – outline the background to the issue.

10 *Context 2* – contextualize the material in the power/knowledge networks of the period.

11 Be aware of the *limitations* of the research, your data and sources.

Select your topic

There is no one starting point for doing genealogical discourse analysis. It will depend upon your chosen topic or particular interest. When I first began doing my historical analysis I had no definite idea of the specific topics or policies that I would research except that these had to fit within what I saw as sexuality (very loosely defined) and social policy (widely defined).

I began the project with a visit to my local university and city libraries where I spent the next weeks, possibly even months, reading through

copies of parliamentary papers, reports and legal statutes on a range
of issues including nineteenth century reports from factory inspectors, and
reports on pauper lunatics and asylums. Next I read the *Reports of His
Majesty's Commissioners on the Administration and Practical Operation of
the Poor Laws and Assistant Commissioners' Reports 1834 with Appendices,
Parts I, II, & III Reports from the Assistant Commissioners (1834 (44)
vol. xxvii–xxxviii)*. The version of the documents used was the 1971
British Parliamentary Papers Series (vols. 8–18) published by the Irish
University Press. I could just as easily have selected a report on crime or
civil disturbance or transport. In a way it didn't matter because I was
interested in any representations of sexuality in any social policy materials.
The Commissioners' Reports on the Poor Law turned out to be something
of a goldmine. Other documents might also have been equally rewarding
but I haven't managed to get around to looking at those – yet!

The 1834 New Poor Law was chosen for a number of reasons. First, it is
considered to have been significant in its impact on the form of welfare
provision provided in this country for a period lasting over one hundred
years. Some would argue it influenced the foundations for welfare in the
UK through to the present day: 'Its organizing assumptions cast a continuing
shadow over the attitudes towards social obligation and dependency ...
[It] touched almost every aspect of life and labour in Victorian Britain.
Employment and wages, housing and rents, migration and settlement,
medicine, marriage, charity and education ...' (Englander, 1998: 1). This is
particularly so not just in terms of the organization and administration of
welfare, but also in terms of ideas, for example, about deserving and
undeserving welfare subjects, and about eligibility for welfare services and
benefits.

Know your data

The next months (I'm afraid to say years in case I put you off) were spent
immersing myself in a range of secondary and original sources on the Poor
Laws (Old and New) and eighteenth and nineteenth century sexuality,
gender relations, working class and family life, marriage, fatherhood,
illegitimacy, and other related topics. Initially, I read and re-read, and read
again (whilst taking photocopies and making detailed notes as
appropriate) the many volumes of the Commissioners' and Assistant
Commissioners' reports. I did this primarily to get a 'sense' of what the
documentation was about and secondly to establish where sexuality
entered the discussion, that is, to identify the instances, occurrences and
ways and means that sexuality was 'spoken of' in the reports, at which
points, and to identify the objects of the discourse.

Identify themes, categories and 'objects' of the discourse

A reading of the whole of the Poor Law Commissioners' and Assistant
Commissioners' Reports revealed that sexuality was 'spoken of' in a number
of ways, for example:

- fears about population growth

- marriage, especially early and improvident marriages

- the need for celibacy

- the irresponsibility of the labouring classes in having large families they could not support

- the relationship between population, marriage and the provision of poor relief

- proposed segregation of the sexes, including married couples, in the workhouses

- the immorality of men and women working together in the mines and factories

- sexual immorality of the labouring classes

- bastardy

- unmarried mothers and female immorality

- women's responsibility for sexuality

- disadvantages of being a single man (lower wages/levels of poor relief, less work).

In an annex to the Main Report known as the Bastardy Clauses, the focus is confined entirely to bastardy, female immorality and unmarried mothers. It is these three areas that are the focus of this case study. Once I had decided to focus on the issue of illegitimacy, that is, on the sections known as the Bastardy Clauses, I widened my search to include the *Hansard* records of the parliamentary debates on the amendment of the Poor Laws. I also reviewed working-class newspapers such as the *Owenite Pioneer* and *The Poor Man's Guardian* to see if they concerned themselves with bastardy and unmarried motherhood. This was to get a sense of how widespread the discourse was and to what extent it was supported or contested.

Having decided to focus on the Bastardy Clauses, the ways bastardy was spoken of was analysed. The approach adopted was not a content or micro-discursive analysis (though this is not to suggest that such an approach would not reveal valuable insights about social policy), rather, my aim here was to get an overall 'feel' for the data. (You can see why repeated reading is an important part of this process.) I also began to identify various themes, categories, representations in, and objects of, the discourse. This process of interpretation and analysis becomes more finely tuned and nuanced as the analysis developes. In practical terms this means that I noted down every instance where bastardy was discussed, identifying the different contexts, the way the problem was 'framed', how it was presented and discussed, and the solutions that were recommended. For example, initially, the Commissioners indicated that their concern was with:

- the support of illegitimate children

- the relief afforded to mothers

- attempts to obtain payment from fathers.

But, as we shall see, their concerns about these three became expressed through a discourse of bastardy, which focused on unmarried mothers and their lack of sexual morality. The existing bastardy laws were presented as disadvantaging men and the illegitimate child was almost absent.

Reading the Bastardy Clauses, themes and categories began to emerge, and I next did a general sweep of the material and gathered together everything said on the following (the sections in brackets indicate the different ways each category was 'spoken of'):

- **Women** (as unmarried mothers, widows, wives, their immorality/ sexuality, as seducers, as profiting from poor relief, bad mothers, men, marriage, as deceiving and lying, as deserving and undeserving, and so on)

- **Men** (as fathers, as victims, non-payment of maintenance, their sexuality/morality, as innocent, and so on)

- **Marriage** (good marriage, improvident and early marriage, as a premium, bundling, prenuptial pregnancy, etc.)

- **Bastardy**

- The **illegitimate child**

- **Population** (poor relief and bastardy as responsible for an increase in population

- **Class** (and morality, attitudes and values about the labouring classes, unmarried mothers, illegitimacy, etc.)

- **Morality** (different contexts including sexual, financial, perjury/ honesty, etc.)

- **Sexuality** (female immorality, illegitimacy, marriage, population, prostitution, bundling, etc.)

- **Poor Relief** (as responsible for bastardy, women's immorality and men's oppression, improvident marriages, women profiting from unmarried motherhood).

And so the list goes on. The formation of categories etc. developed mainly from a reading of the bastardy sections. However, these were later refined and added to in the process of context building and analysis. In an attempt to understand and map the power/knowledge networks existing and operating in the eighteenth and nineteenth centuries, I read:

- general texts on eighteenth and nineteenth century social, political, and economic history – this helped to identify specific areas to be focused on and specialist texts to be read

- texts on the Old and New Poor Laws covering the period 1500–1930s

- texts on eighteenth and nineteenth century sexuality and sexual morality, illegitimacy, family, fatherhood, medico-moral politics, gender and class relations and political activism, civil protests, etc.

- original nineteenth century pamphlets, newspapers, and parliamentary documents.

Absences and silences

I also looked for absences and silences, that is, what is not present or not spoken of that you might expect to be. For example, the concern of the Commissioners was with increased levels of illegitimacy, yet the bastard child was rarely mentioned, nor occurrences of illegitimacy amongst the middle or upper classes: female sexuality was discussed but male sexuality was not.

Inter-relationship between discourses

There was also a process of cross-referencing. Often categories/themes were interrelated. For example, what ideas about poverty, gender, class and marriage, family, rights and responsibilities informed the bastardy discourse? Another important thing for this research was to continually be looking at the data through the lens of sexuality. What ideas about sexuality informed the construction of the problem of illegitimacy in the report? What ideas about sexuality informed the constructions of men and women in the reports and with what effects? What was the role of sexuality in determining eligibility for poor relief? For example, one key influence in the Poor Law reports was Thomas Malthus' ideas about population.

Context

It is also important to know the context for the issue, topic or document that you are researching. So my concern was to establish the background to the policy or issue, and to ask, 'What are the key influences'? This was partly developed through a reading of relevant recent and historical text and analyses as outlined above in the sections on 'Know your data' and 'Identifying themes and categories'.

A final point

It is difficult to identify the different stages step by step as though following a recipe because, in practice, some processes occur simultaneously and at other times different bits of information get added to the picture later on. So analysis is often a dynamic process of interpretation and reinterpretation.

3 The 1834 New Poor Law and the discourse of bastardy

The bastardy sections of the Reports and the subsequent 1834 New Poor Law Amendment Act are particularly significant for what they say about sexuality (especially women's sexuality) and marriage, and for what they can tell us about the relationship between sexuality, poor relief and social policy. In these sections women are dealt with in a qualitatively different way to men. Unmarried mothers, not fathers, are constituted as sexualized subjects and a normative construction of them as morally corrupt welfare recipients is established. In contrast, men are portrayed as victims, aggrieved and oppressed by women and, significantly, with their morality intact.

To illustrate this, and by way of providing a context to the issue of illegitimacy in the 1830s, I will first look at the reasons for the establishment of the Royal Commission on the Poor Laws and 1834 Act. Then I will outline the evolution of the discourse of bastardy and of attitudes towards unmarried mothers in the decades leading up the 1834 New Poor Law. Third, I will illustrate the ways in which a discourse of bastardy was constituted which took women as its central focus. Fourth, I will argue that the discourse played a normalizing role in reasserting female virtue through constituting unmarried mothers as undeserving welfare subjects. The final section explores what this analysis tells us about discourses of poverty.

3.1 Context

The Old Poor Law

The Commissioners were appointed to look into the operation and administration of the Poor Laws which had been in existence since 1601 (herein referred to as the Old Poor Law). The system provided support for the destitute, sick, orphaned, disabled, unemployed, mentally ill and the aged, etc., paid from local rates. Dissatisfaction with the existing system centred upon a belief that it was too generous, too expensive and corrupt. The old system was criticized for encouraging men and women to believe that poor relief was theirs 'as a right' and for discouraging individuals from making provisions for their future needs. Those critics, influenced by the work of Thomas Malthus, argued that poor relief combined with the allowance system encouraged the poor to marry early and to have large families which they could not, or would not, support. Such criticisms, combined with fears about rapid population growth (especially amongst the labouring classes), industrialization, increased social mobility, the increasing cost of poor relief, the increasing numbers of poor claiming relief, along with a fear of social unrest, led to the establishment of the Royal Commission on the Poor Laws (1832–34).

Membership of the Royal Commission comprised a group of influential politicians, economists and clerics. According to Dunkley (1982: 179) the New Poor Law took 'its shape from the efforts and views of a relatively small group of individuals at the centre of power and events'.

1834 New Poor Law

The 1834 New Poor Law was fundamentally about reducing the costs of poor relief, the desire being to replace it with a more economical, more efficient and less generous system of relief. These objectives were to be achieved through centralization, the principle of reduced eligibility, a system of deterrence – the workhouse – and the restoration and reaffirmation of the work ethic. The main part of the Poor Law Commissioners' Report, which resulted in the 1834 New Poor Law, was entirely directed at the management, for relief purposes, of the adult able-bodied male labourer and with the family that was dependent on him. Women in their own right in terms of their poverty, failed to get anything but a passing mention either in the Reports or in the subsequent Act. However, where women came into their own and became the focus of the Commissioners' attention was as mothers of illegitimate children in the Bastardy Clauses.

Bastardy

The purpose here is to set the scene for what was happening prior to the appearance of the discourse of bastardy in the New Poor Law. In the 1830s, under the Old Poor Law, bastardy itself was not illegal but having an illegitimate child that was chargeable to the parish was. Bastardy was therefore seen as an offence against the Poor Laws (Marshall, 1926: 207). Under pre-1834 New Poor Law legislation, both unmarried mothers and putative fathers were legally financially responsible for their illegitimate children. This is not to suggest that both men and women were treated the same under the law. They were not. Indeed, the duties and circumstances under which they could be punished were different. If a woman was unable to provide support for an illegitimate child and requested poor relief, she could be imprisoned for a period of no less than six weeks and up to 12 months in a house of correction. Women were imprisoned for the crime of having being a lewd woman rather than for bad debt. For women, having an illegitimate child, when it was seen as a crime, was a sexual crime. Where the mother was unable to support the child and sought parish relief, men were held to be financially responsible for any offspring. Those unable or refusing to pay or marry could be imprisoned for up to three months. Men who were unable or unwilling to provide maintenance were imprisoned for bad debt.

In practice, men rarely paid maintenance and usually only as little as between a fifth and a third of maintenance was ever repaid. Some men were able to exert sufficient influence with the overseers and churchwardens to be able to avoid payment altogether (Marshall, 1926: 219). Women were seldom imprisoned because magistrates were reluctant to do so, thus supporting the Commissioners' view that single women were insufficiently punished for becoming pregnant.

In the decades prior to the Bastardy Clauses illegitimacy was generally tolerated and many people sympathized with the plight of unmarried mothers: 'Formally, a female having a bastard became an outcast of society; now such a circumstance adds little or no taint to her character.' (Mr Chapple, Devon, in Mr Villiers' Report, Appendix A in *British Parliamentary Papers, Poor Law*, vol.9, 1971: 9)

During this period, premarital pregnancy was common amongst the working-classes. Under the Old Poor Law an informal but strict moral code concerning premarital pregnancy and illegitimacy existed which was variously enforced and involved forms of public shaming (Weeks, 1981:

22). What mattered more to communities was the potential economic burden of illegitimate children rather than any immorality associated with premarital sex (see Gill, 1977: 204–10; MacFarlane, 1980; Weeks, 1981: 22). However, as a result of industrialization, urbanization, housing shortages, and labour market and economic insecurities, marriage did not always follow pregnancy.

The Commissioners were unhappy that illegitimacy was rising, leading to increased demands for parochial relief, and, further, that the existing bastardy legislation was ineffectual in either stopping illegitimacy or in ensuring that parents supported their illegitimate offspring. Worse still, they believed the bastardy laws and poor relief provision were significant in encouraging women to have illegitimate children. In focusing on bastardy, the Commissioners stated they were principally concerned with three aspects:

- the support of illegitimate children

- relief awarded to the mother by the parish

- attempts to obtain repayment for maintenance from fathers.

3.2 The discourse of bastardy

At the core of the Commissioners' concerns with illegitimacy was a triad – the single pregnant woman/unmarried mother, the father and the bastard child. Yet, significantly, of these three, the bastard child is absent in the discourse and the father is absolved of any moral, sexual or financial liability or responsibility for his actions. It is the woman who is its central concern, a concern articulated through the conduit of female sexuality as a set of anxieties about, first, female morality, particularly women's sexual immorality, and second, women's power over men. The following section illustrates how the discourse of bastardy constituted unmarried mothers in this way.

Discursive strategy

A **discursive strategy** refers to the ways that a discourse is deployed. It is the means by which a discourse is given meaning and force, and through which its object is defined. It a device through which knowledge about the object is developed and the subject constituted. So, in this example, it is a device through which unmarried motherhood is put into discourse.

Three discursive strategies can be detected operating through the discourse of bastardy.

The first discursive strategy, is the construction of women as immoral subjects through a process of negative depiction and through the representation of men as victims of women's immorality. The second strategy is achieved through the absence of male responsibility. The final discursive strategy is the attempt to distinguish unmarried mothers from other recipients of poor relief through notions of who is 'deserving' and who is 'undeserving'. These three interdependent discursive strategies, separated here for the purposes of clarity, are considered below.

3.3 Discursive strategy 1 – Constituting the immoral subject

Negative representations of unmarried mothers

The aim of this section is to demonstrate the role of discourse in constituting unmarried mothers as immoral subjects. Let's begin first with looking at how the Commissioners 'speak' of unmarried mothers.

Activity 3

Read through Extracts 4–7 below, which provide some examples of how the Commissioners refer to unmarried mothers. Consider how unmarried mothers are 'spoken of' or are constituted in the extracts.

It might help to consider:

- whether unmarried mothers are presented in a positive, neutral or negative way

- who is identified as being responsible for unmarried motherhood/ prenuptial pregnancy

- how premarital sex and prenuptial pregnancy is presented

- the language used to refer to unmarried mothers

- the tone of the Commissioners' comments.

Extract 4

... the female in the very many cases becomes the corruptor

    (*British Parliamentary Papers, Poor Law*, vol.8, Main Report, 1971: 94)

Extract 5

... continued illicit intercourse has, in almost all cases, originated with the females

    (Mr Richardson, *British Parliamentary Papers, Poor Law*, vol.8, Main
Report, 1971: 96)

Extract 6

... the women, ... feel no disgrace, either in their own eyes, or in the eyes of others, at becoming mothers of bastards, have still less reluctance in allowing the claims of a husband to anticipate the marriage ceremony, in fact they are almost always with child when they come to the church

    (Mr Richardson, *British Parliamentary Papers, Poor Law*, vol.8, Main
Report, 1971: 96)

Extract 7

I met with a striking instance, which proves that the female in these cases is generally the party most to blame; and that any remedy, to be effectual, must act chiefly with reference to her

> (Mr Walcott's evidence, *British Parliamentary Papers, Poor Law*, vol.8,
> Main Report, 1971: 97)

Discussion

Discursively the language and tone adopted by the Commissioners towards unmarried mothers is judgmental, moralistic and often damning. Unmarried mothers of illegitimate children are characterized, as the extracts illustrate, as deceiving, lying, promiscuous, and immoral – for example "the female in the very many cases becomes the corruptor" (Extract 4). And "continued illicit intercourse has, in almost all cases, originated with the females" (Extract 5). The women have no shame – they "feel no disgrace" (Extract 6). It is they who are blamed for illegitimacy (see Extracts 4 and 6). Indeed, throughout the sections of the Report dealing with bastardy, unmarried mothers of illegitimate children are presented and treated in a negative manner.

We begin to see a particular representation of unmarried mothers developing in the bastardy sections. These are all examples of the different ways the Commissioners 'speak' of unmarried motherhood. These come together – cohere – to constitute unmarried motherhood as immoral. The Commissioners strengthen their claims – their 'truth' of unmarried motherhood – about women as immoral and deceiving by including apposite accounts. An extract from the reports of the Assistant Commissioners is given below.

Extract 8

A woman of Swaffham was reproached by the magistrate, Mr Young, with the burdens she had brought upon the parish, upon the occasion of her appearing before him to present the parish with her seventh bastard. She replied, 'I am not going to be disappointed in my company of men to save the parish' ... The premium upon want of chastidy (sic), perjury and extortion, is here very obvious;

> (Mr Cowell, 'Report on Norfolk', *British Parliamentary Papers, Poor Law*,
> vol.8, Main Report, 1971: 95)

In this extract the Commissioners select a more 'extreme' example of unmarried motherhood – first a woman who is unmarried and unable to support herself (she is a burden on the parish) and she has seven illegitimate children. Worse still, the example presents her as being unconcerned that she is a burden to the parish and as being prepared to continue to pursue her liaisons with men. Thus, "I am not going to be disappointed in my company of men to save the parish". Reading the extract again we also note the absence of the father or fathers of the seven illegitimate children and the lack of reference to his/their failure to support the children or to a lack of chastity on his/their part.

The construction of unmarried mothers as immoral subjects was further supported through claims to 'mischievous and immoral consequences' as the extract below shows.

Extract 9

[t]he charge of bastardies is accompanied by a very large share of mischievous and immoral consequences. The disgrace, such as it is, is the only punishment which awaits the mother

(Mr Power's evidence, *British Parliamentary Papers, Poor Law*, vol.8,
Main Report, 1971: 96)

Unmarried mothers are also presented as bad mothers selfishly concerned with securing their own financial gain and as women who 'don't in reality keep the children; they let them run wild, and enjoy themselves with the money' (Mr Wilson, Sunderland, Appendix A in *British Parliamentary Papers, Poor Law*, vol.9, 1971: 136). When not being presented as bad mothers, unmarried mothers are portrayed as voluntarily, even deliberately, choosing to get pregnant, seeking to profit for personal gain either financially or to obtain a husband, as shown in the extracts below.

Extract 10

An unmarried mother has voluntarily put herself into the situation of a widow: she has voluntarily become a mother, without procuring for herself and her child the assistance of a husband and a father.

(*British Parliamentary Papers, Poor Law*, vol.8, Main Report, 1971: 196)

Extract 11

At present a bastard child, instead of being an incumbrance (sic), is a source of profit to the mother

(*British Parliamentary Papers, Poor Law*, vol.8, Main Report, 1971: 196)

All these different discourses, which present unmarried mothers as promiscuous, lying, selfish, greedy, irresponsible, as bad mothers and as deliberately getting pregnant, come together to present a negative picture of unmarried motherhood which confirms their immorality.

Women as predatory, men as victims

This process of characterization of women as immoral subjects is further developed through constructions of women as predators and men as victims, as can be seen in the extract overleaf.

Extract 12

The consequence is, that a woman of dissolute character may pitch upon any unfortunate young man whom she has inveigled into her net, and swear that child to him: and the effect of the law, as it now stands, will be to oblige the man to marry her.

(Mr Walcott's evidence cited in *British Parliamentary Papers, Poor Law*, vol.8, Main Report, 1971: 98)

The articulation of the Commissioners' anxieties about bastardy through a focus on women can be seen in the way that men were generally presented in the Bastardy Clauses as being at the mercy of women, susceptible to women's dishonesty and immorality. Wider research into the other nineteenth century materials about and dealing with the 1834 New Poor Law, such as the *Hansard* record of parliamentary debates, can be a useful means of cross-checking the accuracy of your interpretations of both the language and meaning of discourses. So for example, we find that a similar observation was also made by the Bishop of Exeter, Henry Philpotts, in a speech on the Poor Law to the House of Lords in 1834. He pointed out how, in the Reports, emotive language was used: 'in which the fathers of bastard children were uniformly spoken of as "unfortunate persons" while whenever the mother was mentioned allusion was made to "vice". The language of the report was "The female is most to blame"' (*Hansard* (Lords) 28 July 1834).

Activity 4

The aim of this activity is to identify how men and women are 'spoken of' – constituted – in Extract 13, 'Exeter Lad'. The text in the extract is part of a lengthy commentary on bastardy provided by the Commissioners in the Main Report in which a case is being made for the repeal of the existing bastardy laws.

Read carefully through the text – you may have to do this several times so as to get a 'sense of it'.

It might help you to:

- first identify the main arguments being made

- consider the main arguments being made in the text specifically about the bastardy issue

- look at how women are referred to in the text

- look at how men are referred to in the text

- consider the ways in which the Commissioners differentiate between men and women in their discussion of the problem of illegitimacy

- look at the tone and language used by the Commissioners in the text and the imagery they invoke

- consider the way that the bastardy issue is presented

- consider what case is made for the repeal of the existing bastardy laws.

Extract 13 'Exeter Lad'

If there were no other objection to these laws, than that they place at the mercy of any abandoned woman, every man who is not rich enough to give security or to give sureties, that they expose him to be dragged without previous summons, on a charge made in his absence, before a tribunal which has no power to examine into the merits of the case; if these were their only faults, we should still feel it our duty to urge their immediate abolition. What can be conceived more revolting than a law which not only authorizes but compels the oppression thus detailed by Captain Chapman.

> 'At Exeter, an apprentice under 18 years of age was recently committed to the house of correction for the want of security. It was admitted that there was no chance of his absconding, but the overseers said he had been brought for punishment. The woman stated that she was only three months gone with child; and thus the boy is taken from his work, is confined five or six months among persons of all classes, and probably ruined forever, on the oath of a person whom he has not confronted, with whom he denied having had any intercourse.'

The overseers, it seems, said, "that he had been brought for punishment." For what was he punished? for (sic) having committed the act with which he is charged? That act was an offence not punished by the English law. Whether punishable or not, he denied having committed it; and the tribunal which sentenced him, though competent to punish, was not competent to hear his defence; he was punished simply for his youth, poverty and friendlessness, for not being able to give security or find sureties, and his punishment was five or six months imprisonment, a punishment severe even to hardened criminals, but absolutely ruinous to a boy of eighteen.

But these are not the only, they are not even the principal, objections to the enactment of which we have stated the substance. The mode in which they oppress the innocent, revolting as it is, is far less mischievous to society than that by which they punish the guilty. Without recurring to the proceedings that may take place during the mother's pregnancy, we will consider those which follow the birth of the illegitimate child. The mother, as a matter of course, requires the parish to support her child. The overseers apply to the magistrates, who make an order that the woman, and the man whom she swears to be the father, shall each pay to the parish a weekly sum for the child's support. The sum charged on the woman is scarcely ever enacted as she is supposed to earn it by nursing the child. If the man on demand refuses to pay the sum charged on him, he may be imprisoned for three months, and so from time to time while the order remains in force. What ever is received from the man is paid over by the parish to the woman, and in almost every case the parish pays to the woman the sum, whatever it may be, that has been *charged* [original emphasis] on the man ... To the woman, therefore, a single illegitimate child is seldom any expense, and two or three a source of positive profit. To the man indeed it is a burthen, unless as is frequently, perhaps we might say most frequently, the case, he avoids it by flying to some part of the country where he is unknown, or so distant from the scene of his delinquency as to make the expense of endeavouring to enforce payment a sufficient motive to leave him unmolested.

(*British Parliamentary Papers, Poor Law*, vol.8,
Main Report, 1971: 93)

Discussion

You may have identified some of the following.

- 'Exeter Lad' is 'spoken of' in terms of his innocence, friendlessness, youth and poverty, as honest, as being harshly and unfairly punished, as corrupted by prison; illegitimacy is presented as a burden to men.

- It is implied that the mother is lying, guilty, profits from illegitimacy and is of bad character.

- The bastardy laws are criticized because they punish the innocent (men) and reward the guilty (women). They give women power over men. The laws place men at the mercy of women. The laws result in the parish having to support the child.

In the narrative above, the young man is positioned as both innocent (of any offence) and as victim (of the law and of the woman swearing him to be the father). The Commissioners frame the 'Exeter Lad' account so as to invoke our sympathy by describing him as young, friendless and poor. Similarly, prison is presented as "a punishment severe even to hardened criminals, but absolutely ruinous to a boy of eighteen". Also, he is the one imbued with the capacity of moral integrity; he is believed when he claims he did not have 'intercourse' with the woman (the implication of this is that the woman is therefore lying) and it is also he who risks his morality/ innocence being compromised, even corrupted, through imprisonment. As a consequence he is presented as the one who is 'duped', presumably made easier by his youth, rather than as the seducer. This is not to suggest that we should be unsympathetic to the imprisonment of a young man, particularly for six months, prior even to the birth of the child for lack of financial security. Indeed, one might also wish to agree with the Commissioners that it was foolhardy to take him away from his work – his one possible means of finance. However, when looked at within the

overall context of the treatment of women in the Report, it is evident that
the Commissioners applied different criteria to men from those they
applied to women.

The Commissioners use this section of the Report and the 'Exeter Lad'
example as a basis for a lengthy commentary on the operation of the
Bastardy Laws. In the text they develop their case for the abolition of
these laws which allow an unmarried pregnant woman to swear a man to
be the father of her child. Once sworn, the magistrates would place an
order of maintenance upon the putative father in respect of the child. Let
us look at the case they develop. First they argue that: "If there were no
other objection to these laws, than that they place at the mercy of any
abandoned woman, every man who is not rich enough to give security or
to give sureties, that they expose him to be dragged without previous
summons, on a charge made in his absence, before a tribunal which has
no power to examine into the merits of the case".

In this short extract is expressed a concern about a woman's power over
a man to swear him to be the father of her child. They criticize the
legislation for placing men, especially poorer men, at the 'mercy' of
women. The Commissioners then go on to present the unfairness of the
law to men who are "dragged ... before a tribunal which has no power to
examine into the merits of the case" – the latter referring to the absence of
a legal right to question the woman's claims. And they continue: "but these
are not the only, they are not even the principal, objections to the
enactment" – having two or more illegitimate children is a "source of
positive profit" for a woman.

Whilst some women may have resorted to the strategy of swearing an
'innocent' man as the father, it is significant that men – those who usually
instigated such false swearing – were not blamed. Indeed, 'it is a matter of
general notoriety that the persons receive money from those with whom
they may have had intercourse to induce them not to affiliate upon them,
but to swear some poor man who is frequently paid, and from whom
nothing can be recovered' (Captain Chapman quoted in *British
Parliamentary Papers, Poor Law*, vol.8, Main Report, 1971: 94). When a
'respectable' man regrets that he did not encourage his partner to falsely
swear another man this is neither commented upon nor is it condemned
by the Commissioners.

However, it is unlikely that all women behaved in this way.
Henriques (1967: 126) suggests such false accusations 'were probably
associated with the more sophisticated village or town prostitute' rather
than the majority of unmarried mothers. In close-knit communities, people
would usually know who was the father. Indeed, many overseers
opposed to the New Poor Law argued that their local knowledge
'enabled them to know the deserving from the undeserving poor', and
that on this basis they should be allowed to exercise their discretion in
determining poor relief (Rose, 1970: 84). Additionally, in evidence
provided to the 1844 Commission of Inquiry for South Wales, that was
established to investigate the Welsh Rebecca Riots against the 1834 New
Poor Law, claims that women falsely accused men to be fathers were

firmly denied – 'it is not so here; not one woman in ten thousand will take a false oath' (Evidence of Rev. Henry Davies and others, Narbeth: Minutes of Evidence, 1844: 203). Again we see here how the use of other material helps to construct a picture of the particular way that unmarried mothers were constituted at this time, as well as beginning to reveal the power/knowledge processes involved in this. Reference to the reports on the Rebecca Riots shows to what extent the discourse was contested and the way it operated to silence other accounts of unmarried motherhood.

Returning to the 'Exeter Lad' extract, as we have already seen, prison is presented as damaging to men. However, if we look to other parts of the Report we can see that for women imprisonment is presented as an 'easy number'. For example, '[a] very sensible overseer in Norfolk expressed to me a strong opinion of the absolute uselessness of punishing mothers by sending them to gaol, where they are well-fed and moderately wrought' (Henry Stuart, Norfolk & Suffolk, *British Parliamentary Papers, Poor Law*, vol.8, Main Report, 1971: 629). Also, '[i]f a woman *gets into trouble* she is probably taken into the workhouse, where she is better lodged and fed than at any period in her former life, and maintained perhaps for a year in perfect idleness; it is not wonderful then that she comes back under the same circumstances' (Mr Majendie quoted in *British Parliamentary Papers, Poor Law*, vol.8, Main Report, 1971: 94, emphasis in original). The 'Exeter Lad' example is not an isolated case and further references are made in the Reports to the 'victimisation' of men who are referred to as 'unfortunate persons' and 'innocent' victims (*British Parliamentary Papers, Poor Law*, vol.8, Main Report, 1971: 198).

What the above examples show is the different devices used to constitute unmarried mothers as immoral subjects solely responsible for illegitimacy. This is achieved by presented them as promiscuous, lying, shameless and greedy, etc., and through presenting men as innocent victims of female sexuality.

3.4 Discursive strategy 2 – The absence of male responsibility

At the beginning of this chapter I said that absences and silences can be as important as what is said. In this section we shall see how the representation of women as immoral is strengthened through the absence of a morality discourse in discussions of men in the reports. If we examine the way that men are represented in the Reports, what do we find? We find that men are treated differently from women. It is only women who were subject to a morality discourse in the bastardy sections and the tone and language dealing with men appears relatively neutral and descriptive by comparison.

Activity 5

Read through the extracts below which deal with provision of poor relief following the non-payment of maintenance. The aim of this activity is to:

- establish how men and women are constituted within the texts

- compare the different ways each is dealt with

- identify the relationship between poor relief and illegitimacy

- consider the effects of the way each is constituted

- identify any absences.

Extract 14

In some districts ... the custom prevails of overseers paying over to the mother of a bastard the sum directed by the order of maintenance whether it be recovered from the father or not, and this comes under the denomination of 'Pay' in pauper language. The sum allowed to the mother of a bastard is generally greater than that given to the mother of a legitimate child; indeed the whole treatment of the former is a direct encouragement to vice.

> (Mr Majendie, *British Parliamentary Papers, Poor Law*, vol.8, Main
> Report, 1971: 94)

Extract 15

The allowance made to the mother for the support of her child, *and secured to her by the parish in the case of the putative father failing to pay the amount awarded,* is an encouragement to the offence; it places such women in a better situation than many married women.

(Captain Pringle quoted in *British Parliamentary Papers, Poor Law*, vol.8, Main Report, 1971: 95, emphasis in original)

Extract 16

The certainty of women obtaining care and provision for themselves during pregnancy and birth of children born in bastardy, as well as parish allowance for the maintenance of their children so born, tends to remove those checks to irregular intercourse which might otherwise operate were they in such cases left more dependent upon the honour of the men to support them in such difficulties. No restraint is now imposed by necessity of circumstances to influence women to observe caution or forbearance, or even decent scruples in their choice.

> (Colonel A'Court, JP, Castleman's, near Maidenhead, June 1832
> cited in *British Parliamentary Papers, Poor Law*, vol.8,
> Main Report, 1971: 93).

Discussion

You might have identified the following:

- men and women were treated differently

- men are rarely criticized for non-payment of maintenance

- bastardy is a burden to men and a benefit to women

- poor relief paid in lieu of men's non-payment of maintenance is seen as encouraging women to be immoral

- an absence of either a sexuality or morality discourse in relation to men

- the idea that women are somehow responsible for illegitimacy and should be punished is strengthened and that this should be reflected in social policy and practice.

We can see in the extracts from the bastardy sections above that there is little moral condemnation of men's behaviour: men are rarely, if at all, criticized for non-payment of maintenance. When the men don't, can't or won't pay and the parish must, it is the women who carry the blame. In the extracts above, any criticism or condemnation of the men for non-payment of maintenance for their child is absent. In Extract 16 there is passing reference to men's honour, as in "tends to remove those checks to irregular intercourse which might otherwise operate were they in such cases left more dependent upon the honour of the men to support them in such difficulties". The implication here being that men are unlikely to support a woman whose child they have fathered outside marriage. The way that this is phrased suggests a certain 'taken for granted' acceptance of men's behaviour. Again, there is no criticism or comment about men's behaviour. Instead, the focus of the extract is upon the relationship between the payment of relief and its effect on women's morality. The payment of relief is presented as encouraging women to have intercourse before marriage. For example, neither the speaker nor the Commissioners criticize the possible role of poor relief in encouraging men to have sex outside marriage and in encouraging them to ignore their financial and legal obligations to maintain their illegitimate offspring. In the extracts, the mothers are not only presented as benefiting but also as being better off than a married mother with a legitimate child: "The sum allowed to the mother of a bastard is generally greater than that given to the mother of a legitimate child" (Extract 14) and "is an encouragement to the offence; it places such women in a better situation than many married women" (Extract 15).

The idea that men ought not be held responsible for their illegitimate offspring is strengthened through the presentation of bastardy as a burden to men. Thus, 'To the men indeed it is a burden (Main Report, 1834: 93) and [a] further evil lay in bastardy ... the result was often *grievously unfair* to men so accused, but they had no recourse' (Checkland and Checkland, 1974: 36, see also 261, emphasis added).

There is further evidence that men were not held responsible in the way that the role played by men in these sexual encounters/relationships was ignored in the Reports. In Extract 6 (p.289), it is the woman, not the husband/man, who is the responsible party, it is the woman who is criticized for feeling 'no disgrace' and she who is responsible for sex and pregnancy before marriage, not the husband. One exception is in the report from Stephen Walcott in North Wales who comments in a section devoted to bastardy, '[t]he man is never punished for the offence against morality' (*British Parliamentary Papers, Poor Law*, vol.9, Appendix A, 1971: 179). However, this is not referred to in the Main Report.

In the following extract from Mr Simeon, which was quoted by the Commissioners, there is a sense of men having an active sexuality but this is elided rather than explicit.

> I feel convinced that three-fourths of the women that now have bastard children would not be seduced, if it were not for the certainty that the law would oblige the men to marry
>
> (*British Parliamentary Papers, Poor Law*, vol.8, Main Report, 1971: 98)

The Commissioners go on to point out that '[t]he guidance of nature has been neglected, the task of resistance has been thrown upon the man instead of the woman' (*British Parliamentary Papers, Poor Law*, vol.8, Main Report, 1971: 98), articulating women's responsibility for male sexuality and sexual restraint. Similarly, there was no recognition that some men may have seduced and even raped the women swearing them to be the fathers of their child, despite the existence during this time of ideas about men sexually exploiting women. Indeed, according to Mr Villiers (*British Parliamentary Papers, Poor Law*, vol.9, 1971: 10): 'cases of seduction of which mention is made are less founded on fact than it is usual to suppose'.

One effect of this process of presenting men and women differently is the apportionment of blame. The Commissioners displayed a reluctance to accept that two parties, the man and the woman, were involved in producing an illegitimate child. Instead, the woman was repeatedly represented as the guilty party. Consequently:

> the female in these cases is generally the party to blame; and that any remedy, to be effectual, must act chiefly with reference to her.
>
> (Mr Walcott, Wales, *British Parliamentary Papers, Poor Law*, vol.8, Main Report, 1971: 97)

> We shall never be able to check the birth of bastard children by throwing the onus upon the man ... the getting of bastard children will never be checked ... I would throw the *onus* entirely upon the woman
>
> (Mr Simeon, House of Lords Committee on the Poor Laws 1831: 361–2, cited in *British Parliamentary Papers, Poor Law*, vol.8, Main Report, 1971: 97 and 98; emphasis in original)

3.5 Discursive strategy 3 – Deserving and undeserving recipients of relief

A third discursive strategy adopted by the Commissioners in the bastardy sections was to distinguish between deserving and undeserving recipients of relief. This can be understood as part of a process of normalization, in which individuals are contrasted, compared and differentiated according to a desired norm. What is happening here is that unmarried mothers are being constituted as falling outside the norm of married motherhood. An example of this can be seen in the way unmarried mothers are characterized as undeserving, taking relief from those with an unquestioned and earned right to it, such as the elderly and widows. As this comment shows, unmarried mothers were 'defrauding of the relief of the impotent and aged *true poor of the same parish*' (*British Parliamentary Papers, Poor Law*, vol.8, Main Report, 1971, vol.8: 92, emphasis in original). Another example of this can be seen in the way that unmarried mothers were presented as living in the lap of luxury in comparison to their neighbours, but particularly, in relation to widows who were husbandless and therefore dependent on poor relief through no fault of their own.

Extract 17

... so the sum the woman receives with the whole of her children, and what the mother can earn, enables them to live as comfortably, or indeed more so, than most families in the neighbourhood

(*British Parliamentary Papers, Poor Law*, vol.8, Main Report, 1971: 95)

Widows were seen as possessing an unquestionable right to relief simply by virtue of having been married unlike unmarried mothers who did not – this was 'one of the many premiums on marriage' (*British Parliamentary Papers, Poor Law*, vol.8, Main Report, 1971: 196). The Report went on:

Extract 18

[an] unmarried mother has voluntarily put herself into the situation of a widow: she has voluntarily become a mother, without procuring for herself and her child the assistance of a husband and father

(Eighteenth Recommendation, Remedial Measures, *British Parliamentary Papers, Poor Law*, vol.8, Main Report, 1971: 196)

The tenor of the language of the Report does not suggest that the Commissioners were seeking equity, as perhaps this comment might suggest. 'There can be no reason for giving to vice privileges which we deny to misfortune' (Eighteenth Recommendation, Remedial Measures,

British Parliamentary Papers, Poor Law, vol.8, Main Report, 1971: 196). The Commissioners wanted to see unmarried mothers being punished and such women's right to poor relief withdrawn.

The device of comparing unmarried mothers with others and singling them out as undeserving of relief on the basis of a) not having a husband and b) immoral behaviour and deception, was employed to stigmatize them as a group and to punish them by marking them out as less deserving, and therefore as not eligible for relief. Their eligibility for relief was thereby determined on the basis of their sexual behaviour. Consequently, through this discursive process, their right to relief was withdrawn and their sexual behaviour became the means by which they could be denied poor relief. In practice, post-1834, this meant that unmarried mothers were given poor relief but only through the workhouse where they were subjected to punitive practices and hard physical labour.

The Commissioners' employment of the deserving/undeserving device was not new. Indeed, the device was central to the principles informing the main part of the Report and subsequent Act. What was novel, however, was the way it functioned in relation to women. Women were deemed undeserving on the basis of their sexuality whereas men, if able-bodied, were considered undeserving on the basis of being idle or unwilling to work.

4   Acceptable sexualities, family and middle-class values

It is one thing to identify a discourse and its objects and to begin to identify its effects. But to fully appreciate its impact and the extent to which it draws upon existing power/knowledge networks and/or creates new ones, we need to embed it within the social, political, cultural and economic context of the time. We need also to consider what force the discourse had. How potent was it? Was it **resisted**? To what extent was it put into practice? We can only begin to answer these questions through undertaking the kind of context analysis I refer to in the 'Guide to doing Foucauldian genealogical discourse analysis' in Section 2 (p.281). We can understand this part of the research as part of the analysis process. So what does a wider reading reveal? To find out we return to two concepts, normalization and power/knowledge, first covered in Sections 1.2 and 1.4.

4.1 Normalization

As I have suggested above, the discourse of bastardy was not simply about illegitimacy, nor was it just a discourse of poverty or even simply a negative discourse about women. It can also be understood as part of a process whereby what we know as sexuality, or at least, acceptable and appropriate sexuality, was discursively produced; it was part of a process of normalization and constitution in relation to sexuality.

Through the identification of pregnant single women and unmarried mothers with illegitimate children as undeserving, predatory and immoral, a 'norm' of what was seen as appropriate and acceptable moral and sexual behaviour was being established and a process of '**othering**' introduced. In the Reports and the subsequent Poor Law Act, appropriate and acceptable sexuality was presented as either sexual relations within an economically viable marriage (although not discussed in the examples above) or celibacy until an economically viable marriage was possible. This became the 'norm' by which all women would be measured and judged to be moral or immoral, to be deserving (or not) of poor relief. Acceptable moral behaviour was rewarded through eligibility to relief as a *right*; unacceptable moral/sexual behaviour was to be punished, and eligibility to relief as a right denied. In this way, single pregnant women and unmarried mothers were measured against widows and the 'true poor' of the parish. The effect of the discourse went beyond those women claiming relief, impacting on all women with illegitimate offspring. The influence of this discourse can also be seen in later responses to unmarried motherhood right through to the early 1990s. Indeed, Carol Smart (1992: 23) identifies the nineteenth century as a highpoint in a continuum in the historic condemnation of unmarried mothers. The discourse of bastardy can, therefore, be read as part of a strategy for producing historically-specific acceptable and appropriate heterosexualities – i.e. appropriate and acceptable sexual behaviour and relations, and, as such, can be seen as an attempt to regulate sexuality.

4.2 Power/knowledge

Further, the discourse of bastardy reveals concerns about wider issues of power and sexuality in society. By the 1830s, the middle class ideal of the family had become firmly embedded in dominant English culture as the only proper and correct way to live (Hall, 1992: 91). The evangelicalism of the period demanded a new national moralism, aimed initially at the aristocracy, but after the French Revolution this was extended to 'putting the houses of the poor in order' (Hall, 1992: 79; Weeks, 1981: Chapter 2). Central to achieving this new morality was the home, marriage and the family, and women had an important role to play as 'moral regenerators of the nation' (Hall, 1992: 85). Hall identifies this as a part of an ideology of domesticity (see also Weeks, 1981) through which ideas about appropriate morality, social and sexual roles, marriage and family were played out. The middle-class model of the family and marriage, which the 'good' mother, wife and the widow encapsulated in the Bastardy Clauses, was used as a device to reinforce unmarried mothers' 'otherness' through emphasizing the absence of marriage. Consequently, unmarried mothers were compared to and judged against their married counterparts and were found to be 'living in the lap of luxury' and were criticized for benefiting from the parish in the same ways as widows who had 'earned' their right to poor relief through marriage. In this way, marriage, or rather its absence, is used to stigmatize unmarried mothers. Their 'lack' of a husband, together with their immoral sexual behaviour – as evidenced in the illegitimate child – was constituted as the means by which they could be denied poor relief, except through the workhouse.

Linked to this, Mitchell Dean has argued that the poverty discourse of 1834 constituted men as breadwinners where the 'able-bodied *man* [w]as economically responsible for themselves, their wives and children by depriving this group of assistance outside the deterrent institution of the workhouse' (Dean, 1991: 96, emphasis in the original). In this way, women's access to poor relief is possible only through their dependency on men through marriage, thereby reinforcing the middle class institution of marriage further. As a result, rights and respectability could only be successfully gained by women through a financially secure marriage or through celibacy. The Bishop of London (one of the Commissioners) strongly opposed irregular marriage and saw it as 'calculated to desecrate the holy estate of matrimony' (*Hansard* (Lords) 28 July 1834: 597). Within and through the discourse, we see the emergence of a process which marginalized and stigmatized unmarried mothers whilst at the same time creating a discursive hierarchy – in which marriage was central – and which privileged married mothers over married women, married women over widows, widows over separated and deserted wives, and all of these over single pregnant women and unmarried mothers.

4.3 Contesting the Bastardy Clauses

If we read outside of the Bastardy Clauses we find that there was widespread hostility and opposition to the 1834 New Poor Law which was 'rejected by working people as a thoroughly heartless attack on the comfort, dignity and customary rights of the poor' (Dinwiddy, 1986: 72). According to Henriques (1967) the Bastardy Clauses were the most unpopular part of the 1834 Act. Protests focusing specifically on the provisions contained in the clauses criticized them for dealing with women unfairly, operating a dual standard of morality and for allowing men to seduce women with impunity (see Henriques, 1967: 112; 1979: 52–8; Rendall, 1985: 197; Taylor, 1983: 201–4). Indeed, the Bastardy Clauses were hotly debated in the House of Lords (see *Hansard* (Lords) 28 July 1834: 586–94,) and they were only just approved by 93 to 82 votes (see *Hansard* (Lords) 8 August 1834: 1096–7).

Summary

In the case of the 1834 New Poor Law, the poverty discourse utilized other discourses concerned with immorality and sexuality through the discourse of bastardy with a number of effects. First, through constituting appropriate and acceptable sexuality as economically viable marriage – the acceptable context for reproduction to take place. It does this by categorizing/identifying sexual behaviours which are not acceptable. In the discourse of bastardy it is both sex and reproduction outside marriage and economically insecure marriage which are unacceptable. Second, the discourse differentiates between men and women and plays a role in the construction of **gendered welfare subjects**. The discourse takes women as its concern and as the focus for regulation. Third, the discourse reflects and monopolizes concerns of the time, that is, fears and anxieties about social change, class, increasing immorality as a result of industrialization, urbanization and population growth, and also women's developing economic and political independence. Finally, the discourse has regulatory implications for women with respect to their sexual behaviour and relations, and material implications with respect to their eligibility for poor relief.

4.4   What does the analysis tell us about sexuality and social policy?

At the beginning of this chapter I indicated that one of my aims was to examine the relationship between sexuality and social policy, specifically the role played by sexuality in poverty discourses. Analysing the 1834 New Poor Law and related Reports through the lens of sexuality reveals, first, that poverty discourses can be understood as a means of categorizing the poor into the deserving with rights (the elderly and widows) and the undeserving poor with duties and responsibilities, and that sexuality plays a role in this process. Second, the research illustrates that the constitution of welfare subjects are the outcome of the interaction of multiple discourses. Further, the constitution of welfare subjects, whilst clearly powerful and influential, often bears little resemblance to individual experiences and 'realities'. In and through the discourse, all unmarried mothers become constituted as a problem – sexually immoral and undeserving; as a group worthy of stigmatization.

This has left us with a legacy of single unmarried mothers as stigmatized, albeit in different ways. This research shows that social policy played a significant role in this process. It has also left us with a legacy of differentiated gendered rights and responsibilities. Men have not, until recently at least, tended to be the focus of social policy in this area (see Williams, 1998). This is in part due to the way that male and female sexuality have traditionally been perceived and the operation of the sexual double standard. This analysis also illustrates that poverty discourses are concerned with much more than simply poverty. Not only are other dominant discourses 'played through' poverty discourses but poverty discourses play a part in constituting those other dominant discourses. Thus, in this case, ideas and discourses about sexuality, morality, gender relations, the family and marriage are embedded in poverty discourses. Correspondingly, poverty discourses become a means by which appropriate sexuality, gender relations, morality, the family and marriage are spoken about. This process, albeit historically specific, is evident in contemporary analyses of social policy. In this example, it can be seen that 'sexuality' is produced through social policy. This is not a one-way process because what we know to be the 'truths' or knowledges of sexuality also constitute social policy in a specific way which reflects the existing power-knowledge relations centred on sexuality, as well as other discourses, such as class, 'race', gender, politics and welfare.

5   Limitations

Activity 5

Having been taken through the process of doing a Foucauldian discourse analysis of social policy in the 1830s, what do you consider to be the limitations of this approach?

It may help to think about the following.

- What are the drawbacks of using historical sources: are they easy to access? Is all the information available? What records exist? Which perspectives do they represent? How reliable are our sources?

- How reliable can our interpretations be of material that is over 150 years old?

- Do the words and language used then have the same meanings as today?

- Is it appropriate to assume that the concepts (poverty, the poor, bastardy, sexuality) and practices (marriage, poor relief) of the 1830s have the same meanings etc. today?

5.1 Sources

When undertaking historical research the only sources that you can use are those which exist. This may sound like an obvious statement to make, but it is an important one, because you are dependent upon those records that were made at the time or have survived. Such sources are likely to be partial, reflecting particular interests especially if they are official documents or the accounts of the rich and powerful. According to Checkland and Checkland (1974: 30):

> There can be little doubt that the Commissioners shared the new ethos of self-help, strongly biasing them against liberal provision for the poor. They expected to find certain evils rampant: they were fearful of the indigent and debauched working class.

Another difficulty when undertaking research such as this is obtaining the accounts of 'ordinary' people. So one limitation in this research is that there is an absence of accounts which reflect the experiences and views of the unmarried mothers themselves. This can make it difficult to assess the extent to which unmarried mothers accepted or challenged the construction of them contained in the New Poor Law. It may also be difficult to obtain accounts reflecting counter discourses or resistances.

5.2 Interpretation

Historical texts may be difficult to interpret or understand. There is the
problem of interpreting what was happening in the 1830s through the lens
of the twenty-first century. So, for example, ideas about sexuality or
marriage will not be the same as they are today. We have to be careful
therefore to contextualize the material in the beliefs, values and ideas of
the time in which it was created, taking care not to make judgements
based upon our own assumptions, about, for example, sexuality or
gender. Additionally, being written in a specific 'moment', the language
use may be distinct with different phrasing, sentence construction and
word usage. Some words may be archaic and no longer in common usage
or may now have a different meaning. Take for example, 'moral',
'morality' and 'immorality'. Mort, who has researched the same period,
explains:

> Morals ... condensed a plethora of meanings all jostling for attention. The
> term served as a synonym for culture, or cultural lack, to impute blame.
> Under its rubric were subsumed the terrifying catalogue of barbarous
> habits ... the collapse of family life, drunkenness, prostitution and political
> sedition. It was through this nexus of concerns that a specific domain of
> sexuality was produced.
>
> (Mort, 1987: 26)

> Not surprisingly, therefore, the loose and expansive use of the term 'moral'
> often makes it difficult to deconstruct its fields of reference ... leaving it
> subject to a wide number of connotative meanings.
>
> (Mort, 1987: 37)

However, within the context of the bastardy sections, we can be
reasonably sure that the use of morality and immorality refers in the main
to sexual im/morality. One clue to this is the context in which the words
are used. In the bastardy sections im/morality is used in the context of sex
and pregnancy outside marriage. Having said this there are indeed other
occasions where im/morality is used differently or more expansively to
include perjury, deceit and financial dishonesty but again the context in
which it is used helps in understanding the meaning. Another way of
checking the meaning of words at the time they were used or of finding
the meaning of archaic words is to check their meaning in the Oxford
English Dictionary.

5.3 Selectivity

A possible criticism of any work such as this is that the analysis is selective,
drawing upon apposite extracts to support the argument. This is a difficult
criticism to refute and in doing research such as this you have to be
careful not just to collect information on those aspects which support your
argument. Instead, look for discontinuities or examples that challenge
your claims. Similarly, the research could be criticized for being 'just one

person's account'. One way of dealing with this is to situate the interpretation within other historical accounts and analyses of the period in an attempt to immerse and contextualize the ideas, beliefs, values and practices of the time. So it's a way of checking that your interpretation is not totally 'off the wall'.

5.4 Current policy discourse analysis

Can we adopt the approach described above to doing a Foucauldian discourse analysis of more recent social policy documents? The approach to doing current policy discourse analysis is similar and in some respects it can sometimes be easier. For example, it is usually much easier to obtain data, documents, and materials from a range of sources – government and non-governmental, and to establish information about the background to the topic or policy and, therefore, to understand the context. Being a current policy issue/topic means that it is usually also easier to understand the language used and there is less risk of misinterpretation. There are, however, some drawbacks to doing current policy discourse analysis. The most significant is the difficulty of 'stepping outside' the data. It is sometimes difficult to identify discourses within which we ourselves are immersed, or that we agree with, or which we accept as 'taken for 'granted' or common sense.

Further Reading

The texts below all provide different examples of work which draws upon genealogical analysis, sometimes explicitly, sometimes implicitly. These texts, with the exception of Bell, also provide further contextual information about the 1830s – about culture, politics, sexuality and poverty. Bell's book uses Foucault to look at the ways different understandings of incest have informed legal policies and responses to incest.

Bell, V. (1993) *Interrogating Incest: Feminism, Foucault and the Law*, London, Routledge.

Dean, M. (1991) *The Constitution of Poverty: Toward a Genealogy of Liberal Governance*, London, Routledge.

Mort, F. (1987) *Dangerous Sexualities: Medico-Moral Politics in England Since 1830*, London, Routledge and Kegan Paul.

Poovey, M. (1995) *Making A Social Body: British Cultural Formation 1830–1864*, Chicago, University of Chicago Press.

References

Primary Sources

Parliamentary Papers

British Parliamentary Papers (1971) *Poor Law, Volume 8:* Reports of His Majesty's Commissioners on the Administration and Practical Operation of the Poor Laws with Appendix A, Part I, Reports from the Assistant Commissioners,1834, Shannon, Irish University Press.

British Parliamentary Papers (1971) *Poor Law, Volume 9*: Reports of His Majesty's Commissioners on the Administration and Practical Operation of the Poor Laws Appendix A, Parts II, & III, Assistant Commissioner's Reports with Evidence and Index, 1834, Shannon, Irish University Press.

Hansard Parliamentary Debates (Commons), 6th Series, volume 228, Twenty-second volume of session 1992–93, 5 July 1993, London, Hansard.

Hansard Parliamentary Debates (Lords), 3rd Series, vols.XXI–XXVI, London, Hansard.

Poor Law Commission Official Circulars of Public Documents and Information, 1840–1851, vols. VII–X, (Reprinted 1970) New York, Kelley.

Report of the Commissioners of Inquiry (South Wales) and Other Papers Relating to the Maintenance of Civil Order, 1839–44, vol.2, Shannon, Irish University Press.

Newspapers

The Independent Owenite Pioneer

Sunday Times

The Poor Man's Guardian 1831–1835, H. Hetherington, London, The Merlin Press (1969 Reprint), vol.3.

Secondary sources

Bell, V. (1993) *Interrogating Incest: Feminism, Foucault and the Law*, London, Routledge.

Carabine, J. (1996a) 'Heterosexuality and social policy' in Richardson, D. (ed.) *Theorizing Heterosexuality*, Buckingham, Open University Press.

Carabine, J. (1996b) 'A straight playing field or queering the pitch? Centring sexuality in social policy', *Feminist Review*, vol.54, pp.31–64.

Checkland, S.G. and Checkland E.O.A. (1974*) The Poor Law Report of 1834*, Harmondsworth, Penguin.

Dean, M. (1991) *The Constitution of Poverty: Toward a Genealogy of Liberal Governance*, London, Routledge.

Dennis, N. and Erdos, G. (1992) *Families Without Fatherhood,* London, IEA Health and Welfare Unit (second edn. 1993).

Dinwiddy, J.R. (1986) *From Luddism to the First Reform Bill, Reform in England 1810–1832*, Oxford, Blackwell.

Dreyfuss, H. and Rabinow, P. (1986) *Michel Foucault: Beyond Structuralism and Hermeneutics*, Brighton, Harvester.

Dunkley, P. (1982) *The Crisis of the Old Poor Law in England 1795–1834: An Interpretive Essay*, New York, Garland Publishing.

Englander, D. (1998) *Poverty and Poor Law Reform in Nineteenth Century Britain, 1834–1914*, Harlow, Longman.

Foucault, M. (1972) *The Archaeology of Knowledge* (Translated by Alan Sheridan), London, Tavistock (originally published 1969).

Foucault, M. (1990) *The History of Sexuality, Volume 1: An Introduction* (Translated by Robert Hurley), New York, Vintage Books (first published in French, 1976; this translation first published 1978, London, Random House).

Foucault, M. (1991) *Discipline and Punish: The Birth of the Prison.* (Translated by Alan Sheridan) London, Penguin (this translation originally published 1977, London, Allen Lane).

Gill. D. (1977) *Illegitimacy, Sexuality and the Status of Women*, Oxford, Blackwell.

Green, D. (1992) 'Introduction', in Dennis, N. and Erdos, G. *Families Without Fatherhood*, London, IEA Health and Welfare Unit (second edn. 1993).

Hall, C. (1992) *White, Male, and Middle Class: Explorations in Feminism and History*, Cambridge, Polity Press.

Hall, S. (2001) 'Foucault: power, knowledge and discourse' in Wetherell, M., Taylor, S. and Yates, S.J. (eds) *Discourse Theory and Practice: A Reader*, London, Sage in association with The Open University.

Henriques, U. (1967) 'Bastardy and the New Poor Law', *Past and Present*, vol.37, pp.103–29.

Henriques, U. (1979) *Before the Welfare State: Social Administration in Early Industrial Britain*, London, Longman.

Keirnan, K., Land, H. and Lewis, J. (1998) *Lone Motherhood in Twentieth Century Britain*, Oxford, Clarendon Press.

Lentell, H. (1999) 'Families of meaning: contemporary discourses of the family' in Lewis, G., *Forming Nation, Framing Welfare*, London, Routledge.

Marshall, D. (1926) *The English Poor Law in the Eighteenth Century: A Study of Social and Administrative History* (1969 edition), London, Routledge and Kegan Paul.

McFarlane, A. (1980) 'Illegitimacy and illegitimates in English history' in Laslett, P., Oosterveen, K. and Smith, R.M. (eds) *Bastardy and its Comparative History*, London, Edward Arnold.

Morgan, P. (1995) *Farewell to the Family: Public Policy and Family Breakdown in Britain and the USA*, London, IEA Health and Welfare Unit.

Mort, F. (1987) *Dangerous Sexualities: Medico-Moral Politics in England Since 1830*, London, Routledge and Kegan Paul.

Phoenix, A. (1991) *Young Mothers,* Cambridge, Polity Press.

Rendall, J. (1985) *The Origins of Modern Feminism, Women In Britain, France and the United States, 1780–1860*, Basingstoke, Macmillan.

Rose, M.E. (1970) 'The anti-Poor Law agitation' in Ward, J.T. (ed.) *Popular Movements, 1830–1850*, Basingstoke, Macmillan.

Roseneil, S. and Mann, K (1996) 'Unpalatable choices and inadequate families' in Silva, E. (ed.) *Good Enough Mothering? Feminist Perspectives on Lone Mothers*, London, Routledge.

Smart, C. (1996) 'Deconstructing motherhood' in Silva, E. (ed.) *Good Enough Mothering? Feminist Perspectives on Lone Motherhood*, London, Routledge.

Smart, C. (ed.) (1992) *Regulating Womanhood, Historical Essays on Marriage, Motherhood and Sexuality*, London, Routledge.

Sunday Times (1993) 'Return of the Family', 28 February.

Taylor, B. (1983) *Eve and the New Jerusalem: Socialism and Feminism in the Nineteenth Century*, London, Virago.

Weeks, J. (1981) *Sex, Politics and Society: The Regulation of Sexuality Since 1800*, London, Longman, (1989, second edition).

Williams, F. (1998) 'Troubled masculinities in social policy discourses: Fatherhood' in Popay, J., Hearn, J. and Edwards J., *Men, Gender Divisions and Welfare*, London, Routledge.

CHAPTER EIGHT

Evaluating and Applying Discourse Analytic Research

Stephanie Taylor

Introduction

The first chapter of this book presented a guide to conducting a research project and an overview of discourse analysis as one form of social research. In Chapters Two to Seven, six academics have offered detailed accounts of their own discourse analytic research, showing some of the possibilities which exist within this wide-ranging field. I will begin the final chapter of the book by summarizing the work that has been covered, reviewing Chapters Two to Seven briefly with reference to Chapter One. I will then discuss two additional and important aspects of discourse analytic research: the assessment or evaluation of the quality of the research, and its possible applications.

1 Six exemplary projects

In this section I compare the different examples of discourse analysis presented in Chapters Two to Seven, looking back to some of the aspects which were discussed in Chapter One. So for each project I describe the disciplinary area, topic and research questions which are being considered; the approach to analysis; the nature of the data which is being used and the patterns the analyst investigates; the analyst's role and other notable features.

In Chapter Two, Robin Wooffitt introduces the form of discourse analysis which is probably best established as a distinct field of theory and data analysis, conversation analysis (CA). Its most famous originator is the sociologist Harvey Sacks. Wooffitt introduces Sacks' main ideas and describes some of his research. Wooffitt then outlines his own research project on the language of mediums. His data are audio-recordings of talk between psychic practitioners and clients, transcribed in the detail usual for CA.

The focus of Wooffitt's analysis is the sequential interaction between speakers. He looks for patterns in the ways they talk *to each other*, in contrast to some other analyses (see below) which may find regularities across a body of talk (by one or more speakers) without regard to sequence. The patterns Wooffitt identifies are normative, meaning that the regularities in talk are not inevitable (they are not determined, say, by physiology or culture) but they are *expected*. This is shown, for example, in Extract 2 in Chapter Two where a child demonstrates her awareness that the pattern of a question-answer sequence is incomplete. The patterns occur as a consequence of the "culturally available tacit knowledge" shared by speakers.

CA places great emphasis on language use as practice, on what speakers *do* when they talk. (This is often indicated by the use of the word 'doing' in the title of a research text.) Wooffitt's research questions derive directly from CA's general concern with how communication is done or accomplished, that is, the 'nature of communication' in this type of interactive situation (between psychic practitioners and their clients), and a pattern specific to it "in which a claim about the sitter is proposed, accepted by the sitter, and ... then characterized as originating from a paranormal source" (p.76). We can see these research questions as part of a cumulative CA project to describe how people talk and communicate. Findings are not presented as the analyst's interpretation but as the identification of these 'real life' practices as they are revealed in the data. As Wooffitt says, "analysis is data driven, not theory led" (p.58). The role of the analyst is therefore that of a detached observer, as in the positivist/post-positivist tradition outlined in Chapter One. The findings are generalizable as examples of practices which are common to culturally competent speakers from the same 'natural language-speaking community'; that is, people who can communicate in the same language. The practices are presumably learnt as part of the acquisition of language. Conversation analysts emphasize the emic nature of their analyses, confirmed by how the participants themselves orient to the talk (this is discussed further in Section 2). The analyst concentrates on the talk itself; details of background and context are relatively unimportant.

Conversation analysis originated in sociology and is still strongly associated with that discipline, although it has been influential in other areas such as discursive psychology (Chapters Four and Five). Chapter Three, by Simeon Yates, presents a study based in a different disciplinary area, linguistics, specifically interactional or sociolinguistics. The topic is computer mediated communication (CMC). As in Chapter Two, the focus is on how people interact using language, although this is not a study of (conventional) talk. Unlike Wooffitt, Yates focuses on patterns within language as a system, looking at linguistic units such as pronouns.

This chapter presents a distinctive form of discourse analysis in that computer mediated communication is not only the topic of study but has also created new kinds of interaction, new data and new means of analysis. Yates' research questions derive from this innovative status. He is interested in how this form of communication resembles more conventional forms (speaking and writing), as these have been distinguished in linguistics, and in how users of this technology interact. Perhaps most importantly, he investigates the nature of identity 'on-line': the major issue here is whether new communication media have given rise to different *kinds* of identities, or whether the processes of constructing and expressing identity on-line operate in much the same way as in other contexts.

The data for the study of interaction in CMC do not require transcription: they can be printed out, which is, of course, a huge convenience for the researcher. However they must still be selected. This can be done with reference to contexts (themselves new, such as 'chat rooms'), topics (possibly as these are given by the headings of messages) and also, more conventionally, to particular categories of users (defined, for example, through membership of an on-line discussion list). In addition, the analyst must decide how much detail the data encompass, such as the layout on the screen and the heading which states, perhaps, the number of the message being responded to, how many previous responses there have been, and so on. As with talk, therefore, the data are not given but need to be selected according to the analyst's focus. And just as data are partly constructed through the transcription, so CMC data can be modified through the attachment of further information, known as 'metadata'.

Because computers enable the storage and manipulation of enormous quantities of data, the sample can be very large, which has implications for its representativeness. This applies both to CMC data and to more conventional data, like transcribed talk, which are stored and processed electronically. The term 'corpus' (plural: corpora) can be used to describe any body of discourse data but is particularly associated with the huge collections stored on computer. By manipulating the data electronically, the analyst can look for new patterns. Chapter Three shows both quantitative (type-token ratios, lexical density) and qualitative analyses. However, as Yates emphasizes, his analyses are driven by theory. He identifies patterns within the data and offers an interpretation based in existing theories of, first, different forms of communication and, second, the connection between identity, including gender identities, and language use. The generalizability of his findings must be related back to these theories. This study is therefore different from Chapter Two in that the form of data analysis does not derive directly from the theory of language in use on which the analyst is drawing. Rather, it is part of his task to argue a connection between the findings, existing theories (in the area of linguistics) and his research questions. The strength of the findings as evidence depends on the strength of these arguments.

Chapter Four, by Mary Horton-Salway, belongs in a different discipline, psychology. Discursive psychology has set up a particular debate within psychology, mostly as a challenge to the assumptions of cognitive psychology. Influenced by conversation analysis, discursive psychologists have proposed that many topics which psychologists had previously discussed in terms of relatively fixed phenomena and features of the individual (such as identities, memories and attitudes) should instead be conceptualized as fluid, negotiated and interactional, in terms of activities rather than entities. (For a fuller exploration of this complex distinction and its relation to discourse analysis, see Potter and Wetherell, 1987, reproduced as Reading Fourteen in Wetherell et al., 2001.) In Chapter Four, Horton-Salway analyses talk between speakers, following conversation analysis. However, she also looks for patterns in a different way, in the 'family' of meanings and terms (including category terms) associated with a particular topic, a controversial illness, M.E. Her project investigates the identities, minds and selves of M.E. sufferers, as these are constructed by patients and practitioners. Her research questions include how the illness is defined and categorized and the implications this has for the identities of sufferers.

Her data are the transcribed talk of sufferers and of doctors, collected from a range of interactions, including interviews, a TV talk-show, and speakers' formal presentations to groups. The form of transcription is similar to that used by conversation analysts. Most of the patterns she identifies in the data are derived from analytic concepts developed in previous writings in discursive psychology (dilemmas of stake and interest, fact construction, accountability and variability) and brought together in Edwards and Potter's (1992) discursive action model. In addition, she identifies patterns of terms and meanings associated with M.E. and with illness in general, such as mind-body categories.

The study subtly combines several epistemological positions. First, in contrast to conventional medical accounts of illness, Horton-Salway's analysis treats differing descriptions of the illness and sufferers as alternative and equally valid versions of reality, carefully avoiding judging these as true or false. This is a relativist position; we have no independent means of assessing what the reality of M.E. is, only different people's versions. A second and different position is taken, however, with respect to the findings of the study. These are presented more definitely as a description of the possible constructions and categorizations of illness, particularly M.E., which speakers use. Without predicting that future speakers *will* draw on these, the study seems to be making a claim for its findings as representing the range of ways M.E. can be talked about in our society. In other words, the findings are generalizable as shared knowledge which other speakers are likely to use. Society is not precisely defined but the historical context setting (which Horton-Salway acknowledges as one possible version) suggests it refers to Britain. Thirdly, Horton-Salway's identification of people's actions, to manage the dilemma of stake and interest, to deal with accountability, and so on, is again descriptive, in the CA tradition, and seems to present these as general practices in talk which are also a form of shared knowledge, but one common to a wider society (English language speakers? people in general?).

The role of the analyst is similarly complex. As Horton-Salway discusses, her use of dialogue boxes within the main text is a device to acknowledge reflexivity and introduce the presence of the analyst as interpreter. However, concepts like the dilemma of stake and fact construction are presented less equivocally (again, more in the CA tradition) as descriptions of features which exist in talk. The analyst as interpreter seems here to give way to an objective observer, in the positivist/post-positivist tradition. It should be noticed, however, that although there are similarities with CA, there are also differences. In particular, the analysis often focuses on one speaker's talk, rather than on an interactive sequence as in CA, reflecting this analyst's interest in the content as well as the processes of interaction. This focus on content is taken further in the rather different discursive psychological study which is presented in the next chapter.

In Chapter Five Nigel Edley presents another study in the disciplinary area of discursive psychology. He, too, is interested in identity but although his study has similarities with Chapter Four, there are also significant differences. Like Horton-Salway, Edley is arguing against other traditions in psychology which would treat talk as evidence of something else. Edley is specifically challenging understandings of gender identities as innate. He places his research within discursive psychology but his theorizing of the topic also has connections to sociology and cultural studies. (He makes reference to the work of Michel Foucault, the major theoretical source for Carabine's study in Chapter Seven.) He is interested in 'masculinity', a term which itself must be unpacked to show its theoretical grounding and history. (It would not be the same to refer to, say, 'maleness' or 'manhood' even though these have similar dictionary definitions.) Specifically, he is interested in masculinity as "a way of being" that is constructed and negotiated, especially in talk. The study is to some extent culturally specific, making particular reference to Britain.

Edley's data are talk which are transcribed following a simplified version of the set of symbols used in conversation analysis. As the transcription and selection of extracts reveals, he is less interested in the fine details of sequence which are important to conversation analysts than in the words and ideas used by speakers. (Consequently, as with most analyses outside the CA tradition, conversation analysts might criticize this as etic, since the way speakers themselves orient to topics is not confirmed through a detailed examination of sequences.) The talk was collected in small-group interviews and Edley gives quite detailed background or contextual information on the data sources and process of collection. His research question is, broadly: what is the nature of masculinity as it is constructed and negotiated in these men's talk?

Like Horton-Salway, Edley seeks out patterns which have been identified by previous writers in discursive psychology: interpretative repertoires (a family or set of terms around a topic), subject positions and ideological dilemmas. He is interested in the interrelatedness of language and activity. In particular, as the term 'ideological' suggests, the analysis is concerned with power and the potential problematic or conflictual aspects of identities, addressing these points more explicitly than Horton-Salway does in Chapter Four.

The reflexive nature of the study is acknowledged to some extent, for example, in the foregrounding of the identity of the researcher as both data collector and analyst. However, as in the other chapters (possibly because of the constraints of space) we are not given much detail about the researcher and his relation to the chosen topic. The process of analysis is discussed as one of interpretation rather than discovery. As in Chapter Four, there is a disjunction between the status of the analytic concepts, as apparently universal features of talk, and the culturally specific examples within these categories which are identified in the data. The findings about masculinity, like Horton-Salway's findings about M.E., are specific to a loosely British culture, with a historical basis.

In Chapter Six, Norman Fairclough presents another form of discourse analysis which, like CA, is a well-established and distinct tradition. This is critical discourse analysis (CDA). Like conversation analysis, CDA has been influential beyond its original disciplinary area and Fairclough makes a plea for "transdisciplinary" work which will connect "disciplines concerned with linguistic and semiotic analysis" with "disciplines concerned with theorizing, and researching social processes and social change" (p.230). However the unique emphasis of CDA derives from its origins in linguistics, particularly sociolinguistics. It challenges a conventional linguistic position which would assume the neutrality and reflectiveness of language (discussed in Chapter One). As this chapter shows, CDA analyses language within larger structures, exploring the implications of the particular words and grammatical forms which have been used in a specific context. It could be described as a study of the refractive aspects of language (returning to the image of the distorting glass introduced in Section 1.2 of Chapter One). The data are often, though not inevitably, written texts with an obvious social or institutional significance, such as newspapers or official documents.

Like the form of analysis used in Chapter Five, CDA is 'critical' in that it is concerned with power and inequalities within society. Fairclough describes an appropriate research problem for CDA as "a social problem which has a semiotic aspect" (p.236). In the main example given here, the topic is the nature of welfare reform as this is presented in a government policy document (a Green Paper). The data are the language of the official text. The process of analysis is set out as a series of steps. The patterns are found within the elements of language as a conventional linguistic system: words, clauses, etc. However, as I have said, these are considered for their significance within this context. The aim is not, therefore, to generalize about language but to understand and make explicit the potential social implications which follow from the way it has been used here.

There is some discussion of reflexivity but the researcher is not really present in this account. The findings are presented as description rather than interpretation, as a detailed exposition of the work done by the chosen text within the larger social order outlined. Fairclough's ultimate interest is in how power operates within society. In this respect, his study is similar to those of Edley in Chapter Five and Carabine in Chapter Seven. Where he differs from both of these authors is in his conception of society as an ordered structure. In Chapter Seven, as (less explicitly) in Chapter Five, the focus is less on structures than on more fluid practices. (The difference is, very roughly, that between the images of a hierarchical diagram and the uncontrolled flows of a river in flood.)

Carabine's study, in Chapter Seven, is the final of the six data analyses. It belongs in the disciplinary area of social policy (and also, as Carabine says, in social policy as practice), although again there is considerable overlap with other disciplines, particularly sociology. The main theorist, Foucault, would most commonly be associated with work in sociology. This study shares with Chapters Five and Six a concern with larger social issues and with power, but there are significant differences, as I have already described. In this study, language is understood as inseparable from wider social practices.

The conception of power being used is taken from Foucault and is contrasted with a conception of power as sovereign (which is closer to that used in Chapter Six). Power and knowledge are approached not as separate but as "intricately intermeshed". Carabine also draws on Foucault's concepts of normalization and, of course, discourse. She defines discourses in Section 1.1 as "historically variable ways of specifying knowledges and truths, whereby knowledges are socially constructed and produced by effects of power and spoken of in terms of 'truths'" (p.274). Discourses function as rules, specifically as "sets of socially and historically constructed rules designating 'what is' and 'what is not'" (p.275). This is a historical study but of a particular type also developed by Foucault, a genealogy. Carabine describes how the research was set up and the research questions formulated, pointing out some of the problems in obtaining data for a study of this kind.

The topic of the study is sexuality (not gender, as in Chapter Five: again, the theoretical background to the topic is an important part of the study). In particular, Carabine examines the relationship between sexuality, poor relief and social policy as these are presented in early nineteenth century English documents. The data are these documents, the patterns are discourses, as these are described above, and also the related patterns of discursive devices, strategies and techniques. Carabine does not aim to generalize but to study aspects of a particular society, namely, those connected with discourses, knowledge and power, which had wide effects and still persist in a particular society.

This is an example of research which would acknowledge the partial, contingent and, above all, situated nature of its findings, and their status as the analyst's interpretation. However, as in all the studies, simply by presenting such findings, the analyst may implicitly suggest that they describe real world entities. This is probably inescapable, and demonstrates again the importance of the writing process in social research. The particular aim of a genealogical study is to explore how meanings and practices *have* operated in the past, without making predictions for the future. (In line with the disorderly nature of the 'flow' image outlined above, such predictions would logically be impossible.) However, it is also clear that discourses do not just disappear or stop functioning, so ultimately the interest of such an analysis is in its recognizable relevance to present-day situations and material, like contemporary policy texts. As Carabine puts it, "genealogy is about tracing the history of the development of knowledges and their power effects so as to reveal something about the nature of power/knowledge in modern society" (p.276).

The final point to note in this section is that, inevitably, no research is perfect in that all can be criticized, as this review shows. A researcher cannot logically forestall all criticism. However, what *is* possible is to locate a particular piece of research with reference to wider debates and understand its strengths and relative weaknesses. A vital part of this, therefore, is the evaluation of research, the topic of the next section.

2   Evaluation

One aim of the previous chapters has been to show that discourse analysis is a process of exploration and interpretation, and simultaneously, one of evaluation. While analysing the data, the researcher is referring back to the aims of the particular project in hand and the premises which underlie it, evaluating her or his findings with reference to the research questions. As I noted in Chapter One, these questions may be developed and refined through the process of analysis. However, even when they are not fully formulated at the start of the project, the researcher will still begin with a certain theoretical position and assumptions. Analysis does not mean a naive or untheorized investigation in which the researcher looks directly to material to see what is 'there'. The purpose of this section is to present and discuss criteria for evaluation and their implications for the discourse analytic researcher. These criteria are themselves an integral part of the project. They will guide the researcher, be presented to others in written accounts of the project and will, hopefully, be the basis for *their* evaluation of it.

Most people reading this chapter will be aware of the three famous criteria by which academic research has conventionally been evaluated: reliability, validity and replicability. To define these very briefly, **reliability** is a criterion applied to measurement and means that the tools or instruments being used can be relied upon to measure consistently. From this arises the principle that, in a study with several researchers, there should be tests of inter-rater reliability to make sure that similar standards are being used and one researcher's measurements or assessments are not, say, excessively generous. The second criterion, **validity**, refers to the truth or accuracy of the generalizations being made by the researcher. Relatedly, in quantitative studies it means that the research measures what it purports to measure, and not something else. Many different types of validity can be specified. For example, internal validity refers to how far claims about cause are 'true' in the situation being studied; external validity to how true they are generally for other situations. Both reliability and validity come together in the third criterion, **replicability**, which is a means of evaluating the research project as a whole. The test here is whether a future researcher could replicate the project and produce the same or similar results. This will require, of course, that the original research is not only well-designed but also fully described in the report of the research.

You have probably already noticed that these criteria refer to a particular set of assumptions, which I summarized in Chapter One (Section 1.2) as belonging to the positivist and postpositivist tradition. In general, a researcher working in that tradition conducts research as a form of investigation of an external world. Good research is assumed to contribute to the sum of knowledge about the world, and its findings are directly or potentially applicable because they reveal enduring features and predictable causal relationships.

In contrast, other researchers make far more limited claims. The knowledge produced by research is assumed to be **situated**, meaning that claims which are made can refer only to the specific circumstances of place, time and participants in which the research was conducted. It is **contingent**, in that these claims therefore do not have the status of stable and enduring truth. The researcher acknowledges the **reflexivity** of the research process and the non-neutrality of research texts. These are not neutral but reflect a particular world-view and set of interests. Furthermore, as Atkinson (1990: 6) puts it "the notion of reflexivity recognises that texts do not simply and transparently report an independent order of reality. Rather, the texts themselves are implicated in the work of reality-construction". For all of these reasons, the knowledge produced by research is, inevitably, partial. These limitations are not simply a consequence of weaknesses in the research process: the issue is not that better research would produce more enduring and reliable findings. Rather, *all* knowledge is considered to be situated, contingent and partial. Truth is unattainable because reality itself is not single or static, and reality is also inevitably influenced and altered by any processes through which a researcher attempts to investigate and represent it.

Clearly, this latter set of assumptions challenges all three of the conventional criteria for evaluation. As Seale (1999) summarizes the problems: "conceptions of reliability and replicability ... are rooted in a realist view of a single external reality knowable through language" (p.41) and "[v]alidity in this tradition refers to nothing less than truth, known through language referring to a stable social reality" (p.34). However, perhaps the key words in the quotation are "in this tradition". For many purposes, clearly, it is both reasonable and necessary to return to assumptions of a relatively static world which is governed by predictable processes that operate unaffected by the point of view of the observer. This is the common-sense view which is itself probably derived from the positivist and postpositivist tradition. However, this is not the tradition in which many discourse analysts are working, making it necessary to look for different criteria for evaluation.

Writers on qualitative research, in particular, have discussed the problem of evaluation at length. Denzin and Lincoln (1998) refer to the "crisis" of legitimation (see Chapter One, Section 1.2). It is necessary to have some means of agreeing on the value of work, but unfortunately no specific alternative criteria for evaluation have gained widespread acceptance, although many have been proposed. Some have become better known than others but all are, inevitably, open to criticism. It therefore becomes necessary for the researcher to present an argument for the value of the analysis, which may include explaining and justifying the criteria for evaluation (see Chapter One on writing up the project). There is not space here to discuss all the possible criteria, but I will give a brief overview. In most cases, which ones are used in any particular project will follow from the published theories and research on which the current project draws.

2.1 Criteria for evaluation

As a starting point, the criteria for evaluation can be loosely divided into two categories: general principles for good practice in academic research, and specific criteria for evaluating discourse analysis. Certain general points can be made about academic research, especially in the social sciences. (As you read this, you may want to look back to Chapters Two to Seven, or the summary of these in the previous section, to see what criteria those researchers employed, implicitly or explicitly.) The research should be located in relation to **previously published work**, whether of theory or analysis, building on or challenging the claims of other academics. It should be **coherent**, depending for its persuasiveness on argument rather than, say, emotional impact. This point is worth stating because much qualitative research investigates 'sensitive' topics. (To take just two examples of such sensitive topics out of a wide range, Croghan and Miell, 1999, investigate discourse around childhood abuse; Harper, 1999, analyses interviews about psychiatric medication.) For a novice researcher immersed in a project on such a topic, especially if the research involves contact with participants, the material which is collected may seem so powerful that it can be left alone to speak for itself. However, this would *not* constitute academic analysis (although it may, of course, meet different purposes, such as raising popular awareness, which is relevant to the next section of this chapter). Analysis must involve more systematic investigation. This criterion is sometimes referred to as **rigour**.

There are different views on how rigour is to be attained. For example Seale (1999) suggests that a qualitative researcher may use some **quantitative techniques** as a form of rigour and good practice. He suggests, for example, using a representative sample, if at all possible, such as counting the number of times a feature occurs in a body of data (p.132, following Silverman), and testing or checking for inter-rater reliability (this may be facilitated through the use of computers: pp.154–5). All of these techniques would be feasible and relevant in some discourse analytic projects. Seale also recommends, with specific reference to discourse analysis (see discussion of Gill, 1993), that discourse analysts should seek out negative instances or **deviant cases** in their data as part of a fallibilistic approach (as in Chapter Six). Similarly, Potter and Wetherell (1987) recommend that analyses attend to **inconsistency** and **diversity**. They suggest that such inconsistency is a more general feature of natural talk (see their discussion of 'variation': p.39) and that an analyst should note where participants orient to it. This follows from the emphasis in conversation analysis on speakers' own orientations (see Chapter Two). In an analysis of interpretative repertoires (see Chapter Five), inconsistencies can signal the 'boundaries' of different repertoires and so serve as another form of validation of the analysis by the participants themselves. In addition, in discourse analyses, rigour can be linked on the one hand to the richness of **detail** present both in the data and in the analysis presented to the reader, and on the other to the **explication** of the process of analysis. These points draw attention, once again, to the importance of the way that the research is written up.

'Good' discourse analytic research will conform to the broad requirements for other research and will also include its own justification referring to one or more criteria for evaluation. One possibility is to retain a modified form of the criteria associated with quantitative research. For example, validity may be redefined in terms of **good practice**: this is similar to Seale's suggestions. Potter and Wetherell (1987: 169–72) argue for validation through reference to the coherence and **fruitfulness** of the findings, as well as with reference to participants' orientation and to new research problems which are raised. Rather similarly, Riessman (1993: 65–8), discussing the analysis of narratives in talk, suggests that validation be redefined in terms of persuasiveness, correspondence (discussed in more detail below), coherence and pragmatic use. Pragmatic use resembles Potter and Wetherell's concept of fruitfulness, referring to the extent that one study provides a basis for further work by other researchers. Riessman emphasizes, however, that validation cannot be reduced to neat rules or technical procedures. Other researchers, whether writing specifically about discourse analysis, or more generally about qualitative research, also redefine conventional criteria in different terms, such as those which are discussed below, or present these as criteria in their own right.

Another approach to evaluating or justifying discourse analytic research is to argue for the quality of the **interpretation**. One way to do this is to point to the researcher's special qualifications to interpret the data. This is usual in a participant study such as an interview study or ethnography. The researcher describes what she or he has in common with the participants, often making a claim to an **insider status**. For example, Back (1996) describes his connections, through work, residence and upbringing, with the people and the area in which he conducted his ethnographic study. However, importantly, he also discusses what he does not hold in common with them, making clear that gender and racial *difference* became an issue during the data collection and are also relevant to the analysis. Similarly, Wetherell and Potter (1992) refer to the shared nationality of participants and one of the researchers but, again, acknowledge the limits to 'sameness'. In summary, then, insider status can be an attractive claim but has several pitfalls. It can downplay inevitable differences which may be as important as similarities of situation. Also, importantly, it can obscure the power differences between academic researcher and voluntary participants by implying that they are equals (see Chapter One). Finally, there is the major danger that this can approach a truth claim, with the researcher suggesting that the insider status enables her or him to really 'know'. Similar problems arise with the common claim of authenticity, discussed below.

A second way of establishing the quality of the interpretation is through **member checking**, also called 'member validation' (Seale, 1999: 61) or 'respondent validation' (Mason, 1996: 151). Riessman refers to this method as 'correspondence' (1993: 67, see above). Whatever the term used, it involves the researcher seeking feedback on the research from participants. They might be asked to comment on a completed research document, or on a specially written report of its findings and claims. More narrowly, they might be given material related to their own contributions, such as interview transcripts. Although it may seem reasonable to 'return' the research to the participants, this method is problematic as a form of evaluation because it involves an implicit return to truth claims. If the interpretation is not being presented as truth but as an analysis underpinned by theory, there is no reason why non-academic participants should be especially qualified to validate it. Even at the level of a transcript, the participant is being asked to comment on a construction rather than a transparent record (see Chapter One). If the concern is simply to confirm what was said at the most superficial level, that could be better checked against a recording: the speaker is unlikely to recall the exact wording. But in any case, the speaker's approval of the transcript cannot 'prove' or 'disprove' the interpretation. This is not to say that there may not be other reasons for returning research material to participants. Riessman suggests that this may be politically important. If sensitive material is involved, there may be ethical grounds for asking for consent at this stage as well as at the beginning of the project. However, as a form of evaluation this is not convincing.

A third means by which the interpretation may be justified is through **triangulation**. This refers to the use of more than one (although not necessarily three) methods or forms of data to investigate the same phenomenon or problem. Once again, it is important not to blur this justification with a tacit truth claim. However, if this pitfall is avoided, this can be a convincing form of evaluation.

These arguments for the value of the research based on the special quality of the interpretation can also be presented as arguments based on the special quality of the data. The researcher/interviewer as insider can claim to have had privileged access to appropriate participants and to have encouraged freer discussion. Once again, this justification can come close to a truth claim, a suggestion that participants revealed or disclosed more than they would have done with a different interviewer. There is an obvious but unacceptable overlap here with journalistic celebrity interviews. These arguments for the value of the research often refer to **authenticity**. Atkinson and Silverman (1997) suggest that this claim about research interviews is not only inappropriately 'Romantic' but can also involve unexplored assumptions about the nature of the person (specifically about self and subjectivity as interior to the individual) which may conflict with other premises of the research. This could be particularly problematic for analyses located within the field of discursive psychology (see Chapters Four and Five).

A special claim for quality which is particularly relevant to discourse analysis is that of the quality or detail of **transcription**. This was discussed in Chapter One. One of the example transcripts given (Extract 4) was from an article by Seale and Silverman (1997). In the article, they present two transcripts of the same piece of talk and suggest that the first, incomplete transcription obscures events within an interaction which the second, fuller transcription is able to reveal. The transcript is of talk between a doctor and a patient. The point under contention is whether the patient has understood something the doctor has told him, about the severity of his illness. The fuller transcript reveals that the telling is acknowledged, minimally but definitely. The patient confirms that he heard what was said. The fuller transcript therefore validates a certain interpretation of events, namely, that the doctor gives information and the patient receives it. The argument is not just that the second transcript is better because it is more detailed, although that is important. The special point to note is that this interpretation is supported by the patient himself: we can accept that the information is received because the patient confirms he receives it. The transcript works as a form of validation because it is detailed *enough* and is able to capture what happened. This is an example of the validation claimed by conversation analysts (see Chapter Two). They argue that through the sufficiently close transcription of talk they can detect how speakers orient to each other. In other words, as noted in Section 1, the analysis is not given the status of an interpretation but of a discovery, with a claim to the status of truth, because it has been specially validated by the participants themselves, in their orientations.

A different claim which can be made for the data and one which is related to authenticity is that the data or the project as a whole have **relevance**. This usually means that there is some connection between the topic of research and a widely publicized social issue or political event. The claim is also often made in introductions and conclusions to academic publications of analyses and, as such, is a feature of an accepted and persuasive style. However, it is important to recognize that it is not, in itself, an adequate argument for the value of an analysis.

Finally, various arguments may be presented for the value of an analysis in terms of its **usefulness.** One of these (as was intimated in the discussion of fruitfulness and pragmatic use) is the usefulness in academic terms: data analysis may generate new theory and hypotheses (Seale and Silverman, 1997: 380). It may provide original, novel explanations, including explanations relevant to previous analyses (Potter and Wetherell, 1987: 171) and to situations other than the one being studied. This latter use is described as 'transferability' and comes close to the concept of generalization (see Seale, 1999: 45). Another more problematic argument is that the research is useful in terms of the 'real world'. These arguments relate to the **application** of the research and will be discussed in the next section.

This section has reviewed some of the forms of evaluation that have been used in qualitative analysis and particularly discourse analysis. It has suggested that, in the absence of agreed criteria, the onus is on the researcher to present arguments for the value of each particular study. This will usually require provision of detailed accounts of the processes of data collection and analysis as well as the more theoretical underpinning which has been discussed in previous sections. Ultimately, evaluation operates through persuading the academic community. It was noted in Chapter One Section 1 that the "methodological anarchy" warned of by Seale and Silverman (1997: 380) does not, in practice, prevail in academia. The processes of conference feedback and peer reviewing in academic journals are imperfect and sometimes emotional, yet they continue to operate fairly efficiently, suggesting that there is consensus on the evaluation of research. Requirements vary, particularly according to the social science discipline, but researchers can, and do, persuade their peers of the value of their work. These processes could ultimately be explained as part of on-going contests to reinforce or challenge values which, in other areas, are often the focus of discourse analytic research.

3   Applications

The final section of the chapter considers the potential applications of the discourse analytic research conducted by academics. This section is concerned with how the knowledge obtained through such research can be put to use outside academia. This is, of course, a concern for all social scientists. In addition, there are particular issues around the application of discourse analytic research.

Bloor (1997) discusses how the findings of research (in particular, sociological research) can be best fed back into society. Should academics aim to influence **policy** makers, for example? One alternative, he suggests, is for researchers to attempt to influence **practitioners** more directly, both those who are involved in the research, as research subjects or participants, and those who are an audience for its findings. He describes how this was done on two projects he was involved in. The first was a study of male prostitutes in Glasgow. The researchers combined conducting research with health promotion by distributing condoms, leaflets on HIV and phone numbers for counselling services to the participants. The project also had policy implications, of course, including that, in effect, it had operated as a pilot outreach project, identifying a group in need of services and showing how they could be contacted. But the more novel aspect was the attempt to influence practitioners directly. His second project was a comparative study of therapeutic communities of several kinds. In this case, the researchers addressed practitioners by presenting their findings to the staff in the different communities they had studied, recommending several practices which they had observed to be particularly effective.

Both of the studies which Bloor describes were ethnographies, not discourse analyses. They are particularly interesting, however, because they are qualitative studies, as are most discourse analytic projects. On a practical level, it has been suggested that policy makers are less likely to be influenced by qualitative than quantitative research. On a theoretical level, it can be argued that the double crisis of legitimation and representation (Section 1.2 of Chapter One) also has implications for the application of research. You will remember from Chapter One that this crisis is linked to the rejection of several key assumptions, associated with the positivist and postpositivist tradition. That tradition assumes, first, that through the use of appropriate methods a researcher can identify causal relationships, making it possible to apply this knowledge to real-world problems through accurate predictions and interventions. Another assumption is that knowledge is neutral, uninfluenced by the particular researcher who gathered it, and generalizable to a wide range of contexts. If these assumptions are rejected, it can seem contradictory for researchers to recommend interventions and practices to produce desired consequences and outcomes. And if they reject the status of description as a neutral representation of a static and enduring reality, it can be problematic to apply it to different contexts. How, then, can researchers outside the positivist and postpositivist tradition argue for the application of their findings?

These quandaries have led some writers to conclude that application is not possible. They suggest that qualitative researchers in the social sciences have the relatively modest aim of understanding and exploring meanings, rather than changing society. It has also been said that qualitative research is most useful as a preliminary, like a pilot study, to be followed by a different kind of project, which would presumably use 'hard' quantitative methods. However this latter position seems rather contradictory. As I have tried to show, research practices develop out of, and are constrained by, the researcher's theorizing of the project. In this case, the change from qualitative to quantitative methods seems to involve a corresponding change of assumptions, which seems illogical.

Other researchers would argue that research can still have applications, but of different kinds. A third position, which is probably closest to the one taken explicitly or implicitly by many discourse analysts, is described by Martyn Hammersley (1992) as "subtle realism". This accepts that we cannot have neutral certain knowledge of the reality of the world but suggests that we can have knowledge with the status of "beliefs about whose validity we are reasonably confident" (p.50). So researchers may accept that their findings are situated, partial and contingent but still suggest that they have implications for future practice and other contexts.

What, then, are the possible applications of discourse analysis? The suggestions of different writers and researchers can be divided into two broad areas, which tend to overlap. First, some discourse analytic studies do produce recommendations for different **practices** and for **interventions** to produce change. Second, there are the applications which result from the critical status of discourse analysis: in other words, it is argued that **critique** is not an abstract activity but has practical and significant consequences.

I will begin by discussing some of the recommendations for more direct interventions. Discourse analysts working in the conversation analytic tradition (see Chapter Two) have conducted a number of studies which have clear applications. Both Anssi Perakyla and David Silverman make recommendations on the basis of their analyses of HIV counselling sessions. For example, Silverman (1997) assesses the efficacy of a standard counselling technique (repetition) and shows its different functions within the counselling interaction. Perakyla (1995) studied sessions with HIV-positive patients where counsellors were using techniques based on a particular theory (family systems theory). His findings enabled him to assess the effectiveness of these techniques (within the counselling setting rather than therapeutically) and make recommendations for their further development. These findings are therefore applicable to the training of future counsellors.

Other analysts in the same tradition extend their analyses to the multiple interactions and practices occurring within a workplace context in order to make recommendations for training and also for the design of work environments and equipment. For instance, Suchman and others have studied the operations room of an airport (Suchman *et al.*, 1999) and Harper and Hughes (1993) have analysed interactions in air traffic control.

With less reference to conversation analysis, Willig (1999: 16) suggests that discourse analytic research has five types of application, three of which are closely connected to critique. These are the uses of discourse analytic research, first, to provide a space for alternative constructions or versions which are not usually heard; second, in campaigning, to inform strategies; and third, in lobbying, as research has conventionally been used, to support a position or argument.

A fourth, rather different application suggested by Willig is through therapeutic interventions, both to resist established forms of therapy and to develop alternatives. I have already mentioned Silverman's and Perakyla's work in this area. Following analyses which focus less on practice than on content, Gergen (1994) has criticized the "deficit discourse" and the associated negative positionings of conventional psychotherapies. Social constructionist therapies aim to avoid this discourse and to use discursive techniques positively (see McNamee and Gergen, 1992). Similarly, Brown (1999) suggests that the findings of his analysis of self-help books about stress could be used to resist certain established explanations and attributions of responsibility, for example in the workplace, and also to inform the writing of new and different popular texts on stress.

Willig's fifth application, education, is an elaboration of the aim of resisting certain discourses and discursive positionings. She suggests, for example, that sex education could challenge "disempowering constructions of sexual activity" (p.118) and of women's sexuality in order to lead, ultimately, to new behaviours. Outside the context of official education, Auburn *et al.* (1999) suggest that their analyses of police interviews could inform training materials for "groups such as gays, civil liberties organizations, mental health organizations, animal rights organizations and trade unionists" (p.62).

I have said that some writers see the application of discourse analytic research not in terms of direct interventions but as relating to its critical status. One major, and intended, effect of critique is to discredit the *status quo*, especially by challenging established authorities and debunking accepted wisdoms. It has been suggested, for example, that a primary concern of those working in the area known as critical discourse analysis, or CDA, is to question and expose how dominance is established discursively (van Dijk, 1993: 249). Fairclough, in Chapter Six, discusses practical ways in which this might be done. The same concern is reflected in the topics and data of many CDA studies, including the media (Fairclough, 1995); parliamentary talk (van Dijk, 1993) and nationalism (de Cillia *et al.*, 1999). Similar concerns operate in other areas of discourse analysis. A few out of many examples are analyses to investigate racism in Australia (Augoustinos *et al.*, 1999), New Zealand (Wetherell and Potter, 1992) and South Africa (Dixon *et al.*, 1997); and political ideologies (Lynch and Bogen, 1996). Often the critique contains an implicit recommendation for change: this is the case in Rose's (1985) genealogical studies of how schools categorize students, including the development of the IQ test and also Mehan's very different analysis of talk in a school context to expose the authority of a psychologist in a process to assess 'problem' pupils (Mehan, 1996, reproduced as Reading Twenty-five in Wetherell *et al.*, 2001).

A different, although related, way in which critique can operate for change is as a form of empowerment. A critical analysis can aim to raise awareness and legitimize what was previously denied or negatively valued (see Weeks, 1981, on homosexuality, for example). It may do this by unravelling negative associations, including through genealogical studies which show how a conjunction of ideas was set up by haphazard or relatively trivial circumstances. A famous example would be Foucault's study of madness (1971) which suggests that the negative associations of madness can be partly traced back to the stigma of leprosy, because certain buildings had been used to house both kinds of sufferers. Empowerment may also be brought about through offering a voice to those who were previously unheard, as noted in Chapter One. However, as I pointed out there, the analyst must always be cautious about claiming to speak for others.

It has also been claimed, less convincingly, that discourse analyses which are intended to empower may ultimately have the opposite effect. The suggestion is that studies of oppressed groups may "end up locking them within different restrictive discourses" (Willig, 1999: 9). In fact, discourse analytic studies can also expose how such 'locking' occurs. For example, Taylor and Wetherell (1999) and Wetherell and Potter (1992) show how the apparently positive (re-)construction of indigeneity, which draws on discourses of culture, can be negative because it can work to position indigenous people as belonging in the past, and therefore exclude them politically and economically. However, this is not an argument against critique and change, including the challenges to discourses of race which promoted culture as a more positive alternative. Rather, it is a reminder of the dynamic and on-going nature of the processes of construction, critique and counter-construction. It emphasizes that the findings of discourse analytic research, and any other kind of research, are inevitably situated and contingent. Yesterday's critique may no longer be relevant, and liberatory discourses can always be subverted. For example, critiques of institutional mental hospitals were drawn on in political arguments for cost-cutting decisions which contributed to the discredited policy of Care in the Community (Rogers and Pilgrim, 1996). 'Political correctness' was intended to be liberatory but is now criticized as pedantically restrictive. These consequences cannot be foreseen. In general, though, critique aims to produce acknowledgement of a problem, encourage demystification (Taylor, 1994: 112) and create possibilities for new spaces, positions and positive identities. It is intended to open new opportunities, while acknowledging that struggles continue.

References

Atkinson, P. (1990) *The Ethnographic Imagination*, London, Routledge.

Atkinson, P. and Silverman, D. (1997) 'Kundera's *Immortality*: the interview society and the invention of the self', *Qualitative Inquiry*, vol.3, pp.304–25.

Auburn, T., Lea, S. and Drake, S. (1999) '"It's your opportunity to be truthful"': disbelief, mundane reasoning and the investigation of crime' in Willig, C. (ed.) *Applied Discourse Analysis: Social and Psychological Interventions*, Buckingham, Open University Press.

Augoustinos, M., Tuffin, K. and Rapley, M. (1999) 'Genocide or failure to gel? Racism, history and nationalism in Australian talk', *Discourse and Society*, vol.10, pp.351–78.

Back, L. (1996) *New Ethnicities and Urban Cultures*, London, UCL Press.

Bloor, M. (1997) 'Addressing social problems through qualitative research' in Silverman, D. (ed.) *Qualitative Research: Theory, Method and Practice*, London, Sage.

Brown, S. (1999) 'Stress as regimen' in Willig, C.(ed.), *Applied Discourse Analysis: Social and Psychological Interventions*, Buckingham, Open University Press.

Croghan, R. and Miell, D. (1999) 'Born to abuse? Negotiating identity within an interpretative repertoire of impairment', *British Journal of Social Psychology*, vol.38, pp.315–35.

de Cillia, R., Reisigl, M. and Wodak, R. (1999) 'The discursive construction of national identities', *Discourse and Society*, vol.10, pp.149–73.

de la Rey, C. (1997) 'On political activism and discourse analysis in South Africa' in Levett, A., Kottler, A., Burman, E. and Parker, I. (eds) *Culture, Power and Difference: Discourse Analysis in South Africa*, London, Zed Books.

Denzin, N. and Lincoln, Y. (1998) 'Introduction: entering the field of qualitative research' in Denzin, N. and Lincoln, Y. (eds) *The Landscape of Qualitative Research*, Thousand Oaks, Sage.

Dixon, J., Reicher, S. and Foster, D. (1997) 'Ideology, geography, racial exclusion: the squatter camp as "blot on the landscape"', *Text*, vol.17, pp.317–48.

Fairclough, N. (1995) *Critical Discourse Analysis*, London, Longman.

Foucault, M. (1971) *Madness and Civilisation: A History of Insanity in the Age of Reason*, Tavistock, Routledge.

Gergen, K. (1994) *Realities and Relationships: Soundings in Social Construction*, Cambridge: MA, Harvard University Press.

Gill, R. (1993) 'Justifying injustice: broadcasters' accounts of inequality in radio' in Burman, E. and Parker, I. (eds) *Discourse Analytic Research*, London, Routledge.

Hammersley, M. (1992) *What's Wrong with Ethnography? Methodological Explorations*, London and New York, Routledge.

Harper, D. (1999) 'Tablet talk and depot discourse: discourse analysis and psychiatric medication' in Willig, C. (ed.) *Applied Discourse Analysis: Social and Psychological Interventions*, Buckingham, Open University Press.

Harper, R.H.R. and Hughes, J.A. (1993) '"What a f-ing system! send 'em all to the same place and then expect us to stop 'em hitting": making technology work in air traffic control' in Button, G. (ed.) *Technology in Working Order: Studies of Work, Interaction and Technology*, London and New York, Routledge.

Lynch, M. and Bogen, D. (1996) *The Spectacle of History: Speech, Text and Memory at the Iran-Contra Hearings*, Durham: NC and London, Duke University Press.

Mason, J. (1996) *Qualitative Researching*, London, Sage.

McNamee, S. and Gergen, K. (eds) (1992) *Therapy as Social Construction*, London, Sage.

Mehan, H. (1996) 'The construction of an LD student: a case study in the politics of representation' in Silverstein, M. and Urban, G. (eds) *National Histories Discourse*, Chicago, University of Chicago Press.

Perakyla, A. (1995) *AIDS Counselling: Institutional Interaction and Clinical Practice*, Cambridge, Cambridge University Press.

Potter, J. and Wetherell, M. (1987) *Discourse and Social Psychology: Beyond Attitudes and Behaviour*, London, Sage.

Rogers, A. and Pilgrim, D. (1996) *Mental Health Policy in Britain: A Critical Introduction*, Basingstoke, Macmillan.

Riessman, C. (1993) *Narrative Analysis*, Newbury Park: CA, Sage.

Seale, C. (1999) *The Quality of Qualitative Research*, London, Sage.

Seale, C. and Silverman, D. (1997) 'Ensuring rigour in qualitative research', *European Journal of Public Health*, vol.7, pp.379–84.

Silverman, D. (1997) *Discourses of Counselling: HIV Counselling as Social Interaction*, London, Sage.

Suchman, L., Blomberg, J. and Trigg, R. (1999) 'Reconstructing technologies as social practice', *American Behavioural Scientist*, vol.43, pp.392–408.

Taylor, M. (1994) 'Action research' in Banister, P., Burman, E., Parker, I., Taylor, M. and Tindall, C. (eds.), *Qualitative Methods in Psychology: A Research Guide*, Buckingham, Open University Press.

Taylor, S. and Wetherell, M. (1999) 'A suitable time and place: speakers' use of 'time' to do discursive work in narratives of nation and personal life', *Time and Society*, vol.8, pp.39–58.

van Dijk, T. (1993) 'Principles of critical discourse analysis', *Discourse and Society*, vol.4, pp.249–83.

Weeks, J. (1981) *Sex, Politics and Society: The Regulation of Sexuality Since 1800*, London, Longman.

Wetherell, M. and Potter, J. (1992) *Mapping the Language of Racism*, Hemel Hempstead, Harvester Wheatsheaf.

Wetherell, M., Taylor, S. and Yates, S.J. (eds) (2001) *Discourse Theory and Practice: A Reader*, London, Sage in association with The Open University.

Willig, C. (1999) 'Introduction: making a difference' in Willig, C. (ed.) *Applied Discourse Analysis: Social and Psychological Interventions*, Buckingham, Open University Press.

Index

Acknowledgements

Grateful acknowledgement is made to the following sources for permission to reproduce material in this book:

Text

Chapter Six: *Green Paper Command 3805. New Ambitions for Our Country: A New Contract for Welfare, p.23-27.* Crown copyright, reproduced with the permission of the Controller of Her Majesty's Stationery Office. © Crown Copyright 1998; Chapter Seven: British Parliamentary Papers (1971) *Poor Law,* Volume 8, Shannon, Irish University Press.

Photographs

p.193: 'National Guard bayonets block Beale Street, as protest marchers pass', Memphis, Tennessee March 29, 1968, © Corbis-Bettman/UPI; p.209: Illustration by Alfred Leete, 1882–1933, for cover of *London Opinion Magazine,* 1914, later adapted and used as a recruiting poster. ©The Imperial War Museum; p.242: Hamlet Brand cigar packet (back) ©Gallaher Ltd.